Seeking Truth
AND
Speaking Truth

Seeking Truth
AND
Speaking Truth

LAW AND MORALITY IN
OUR CULTURAL MOMENT

Robert P. George

New York • London

© 2025 by Robert P. George

All rights reserved. No part of this publication may be reproduced, stored in a retrieval system, or transmitted, in any form or by any means, electronic, mechanical, photocopying, recording, or otherwise, without the prior written permission of Encounter Books, 900 Broadway, Suite 601, New York, New York, 10003.

First American edition published in 2025 by Encounter Books, an activity of Encounter for Culture and Education, Inc., a nonprofit, tax-exempt corporation. Encounter Books website address: www.encounterbooks.com

Manufactured in the United States and printed on acid-free paper. The paper used in this publication meets the minimum requirements of ANSI/NISO Z39.48-1992 (R 1997) (*Permanence of Paper*).

FIRST AMERICAN EDITION

LIBRARY OF CONGRESS CATALOGING-IN-PUBLICATION DATA IS AVAILABLE

Library of Congress CIP data is available online under the following ISBN 978-1-64177-421-5 and LCCN 2025009675.

To my beloved grandchildren.

May you always be determined truth seekers
and courageous truth speakers.

CONTENTS

Preface / XI

PART ONE
The Human Person:
Ethical and Metaphysical Questions

CHAPTER ONE
The Nature and Basis of Human Dignity / 3
with Patrick Lee

CHAPTER TWO
The Soul: Not Dead Yet / 25
with Patrick Lee

CHAPTER THREE
Dualistic Delusions / 31
with Patrick Lee

CHAPTER FOUR
Natural Law / 39

CHAPTER FIVE
The Natural-Law Foundations of Medical Law / 57
with Christopher O. Tollefsen

CHAPTER SIX
Human Embryos Are Human Beings / 87

CHAPTER SEVEN
Death with Dignity: A Dangerous Euphemism / 95
with Christopher Kaczor

PART TWO
Constitutional Law and Political Philosophy

CHAPTER EIGHT
What *Obergefell* Should Have Said: / 115
Girgis and George, Dissenting
with Sherif Girgis

CHAPTER NINE
Equal Protection and the Unborn Child: / 129
A *Dobbs* Brief
with John Finnis

CHAPTER TEN
Constitutional Structures and Civic Virtues / 197

CHAPTER ELEVEN
Catholicism and the American Civic Order / 217

CHAPTER TWELVE
The Baby and the Bathwater / 231
with Ryan T. Anderson

PART THREE
Culture and Education

CHAPTER THIRTEEN
Markets, Morality, and Civil Society / 249

CHAPTER FOURTEEN
Is There a Cure for Campus Illiberalism? / 261

CHAPTER FIFTEEN
Universities Shouldn't Be Ideological Churches / 273

CHAPTER SIXTEEN
Christianity and Paganism: Then and Now / 281

CHAPTER SEVENTEEN
Catholic Teaching on Jews and Judaism / 293

CHAPTER EIGHTEEN
Gnostic Liberalism / 299

PART FOUR
Seekers of Truth and Bearers of Witness

CHAPTER NINETEEN
Aleksandr Solzhenitsyn's Plea to the West / 313

CHAPTER TWENTY
Heinrich Heine's Prophecy of Nazism / 323

CHAPTER TWENTY-ONE
Joseph Raz: Philosopher of Freedom / 327

CHAPTER TWENTY-TWO
Rabbi Jonathan Sacks: A Moral Voice / 335

CHAPTER TWENTY-THREE
Ralph Stanley: Traditionalist / 343

Acknowledgments / 349
Notes / 351
Index / 399

PREFACE

Some historians divide epochs into "the age of this" and the "age of that." And so we are sometimes told that the medieval period, at least in Europe, was the "Age of Faith." The general idea is that in that era the touchstone of truth was conformity to religious doctrines. Now this is certainly an oversimplification, at least to the extent that it suggests that the medievals—especially the great Jewish, Christian, and Muslim thinkers of that period—did not hold natural reason and the power of human intellect in high esteem. They certainly did. Still, it is not flatly false.

Faith mattered to the people of the Middle Ages. The great thinkers of the era—Thomas Aquinas, Ibn Sina, Anselm of Canterbury, Maimonides, just to name a few particularly influential ones—were people of faith. They believed (as I myself believe) that there is harmony, rather than conflict or even "tension" between faith and reason, and that faith can and should be reasoned and reasonable. What's more, they regarded the apparent incompatibility of a proposition with the doctrines of their faith as indicating a problem with the proposition, just as they regarded a proposition's apparent incompatibility with a principle of logic or other norm of rationality as indicating a problem with the proposition.

Then we are sometimes told that the Enlightenment period was the "Age of Reason" (or the "Age of Science"). The idea here is that in that era the touchstone of truth was conformity to what reason establishes or confirms. Of course this, too, is an oversimplification, at least insofar as it suggests that people in the period of the Enlightenment (or, better, the period of the various European and British Enlightenments) were all strict rationalists who saw no legitimate role for faith in the quest for truth. Still, the idea of the period of the Enlightenments as an "Age of Reason" is not flatly false. Even the religiously observant among the great thinkers of the era placed an extremely high premium on rational inquiry, deliberation, and judgment in every domain of knowledge, including the theological.

Well, if the medieval period was, at least in some meaningful sense, the "Age of Faith" and the Enlightenment era was the "Age of Reason," what should be said of our own time? How might we label our "age"? My answer, as I will propose in the pages that follow, is that we are living in the "Age of Feeling" or of "Feelings." A great many people today have come to believe that the touchstone of truth is not faith or reason (or, as I myself believe, faith and reason) but rather feeling or feelings.

Because feelings are subjective, what this development has produced is a widespread subjectivism or relativism. But to say that is to oversimplify and potentially mislead. Things are more complicated. Most people today do not believe that their personal values and convictions, though the products of feeling, are subjective or relative. They believe, or at least are prepared to act on the belief, that those values and convictions are, in some sense, objectively true. And not only that, in practice many people treat their beliefs as *infallibly* true and thus treat their feelings as if they are infallible sources of truth. And so we witness the spectacle of many people embracing a fierce moral absolutism based on beliefs that are the products of nothing more than subjective feelings. It is this aggressive—and, let me add, rationally indefensible and dangerous—absolutism that undergirds people's willingness to throw basic civil liberties, such as freedom of speech, under the bus, and to join "cancellation" mobs determined to ruin the reputations and destroy the careers and lives of people whose ideas they regard, often quite absurdly, as "hateful" and "harmful."

The chapters of this book, drawn from essays and other writings that I've published over the past several years, often with co-authors, are presented as a challenge to the dominant ideology and sensibility of the Age of Feeling. They represent my best effort to seek the truth and speak the truth about many of what I believe to be the most important and urgent moral, political, and legal issues facing us as a culture. Drawing on, and in some essays recounting and celebrating, the work of people I regard as inspiring seekers and speakers of truth, I proceed in the full knowledge that as a frail, fallen, fallible human being I am bound to be making some mistakes—perhaps even some big mistakes. I trust my critics to identify and correct them.

This book is arranged in four parts, which address issues that I have thought about and taught about throughout my career as a scholar and teacher. In the final part, I pay special tribute to some great thinkers whose teaching and witness have deeply influenced my life and work. Throughout the book, I defend a robust understanding of human dignity, grounded in a natural-law account of the human person, human goods, and human flourishing. Along the way, I address some central arguments, claims, and ideas proposed by the secular progressive thinkers and activists who, beginning with the Sexual Revolution of the 1960s, ushered in the Age of Feeling. My writings in this book mount a renewed defense of the inherent and equal worth and inviolability of every member of the human family—every human being, without exception—from the womb to the tomb. I challenge the dogmas and doctrines of the marriage-revisionist movement, arguing that contemporary efforts to normalize and glamorize so-called "polyamorous" lifestyles represent a logical progression of the ideology of the movement that has advocated—successfully in the West—the destruction of marriage's unchanging reality as the conjugal union of husband and wife.

The book's contents address hotly contested questions in philosophy of law, constitutional interpretation, and the nature of civil liberties—all subjects on which I regularly teach at Princeton University. I also reflect on subjects that touch on the intersection between faith and reason: the spiritual bond between Catholic Christianity—my own faith—and the faith of our Jewish brothers and sisters; how Catholics should view America and the American civic order; paganism and the neo-paganism of our day; and the relationship between body and soul. Other essays present my thoughts on the state of our nation's universities, the morality of free markets, and trends toward illiberalism on the political Left—as well as, at least in some cases, on the political Right.

I address a diversity of subjects, controversies, and thinkers, but this book is unified by my unwavering commitment to getting at the truth of those things that divide and vex our fractured society. *The* truth, not "my truth" or "your truth"—because, contrary to what many influential voices in our culture, politics, and even our institutions of higher education would have you believe, the truth about even the most controversial matters can be objectively known, and cannot be altered by one's subjective feelings or "lived experiences." Indeed, one's acknowledgment of truth's objectivity is essential to being a committed truth seeker and a courageous truth speaker. From the morality of intentional killing and the meaning of marriage to more abstract philosophical and theological propositions, there are right and wrong answers. It is incumbent upon all of us to resist the temptation—and the social pressure—to say that there is only "my" truth and "your" truth and no such thing as "the" truth. Moral subjectivism is not something that people reason or argue their way to these days; rather it functions as an unspoken, and ordinarily unnoticed, premise of the Age of Feeling. In my view, that subjectivism is a direct impediment to earnest and honest truth-seeking, whether by persons or institutions. My own academic home, Princeton University, despite being a non-sectarian institution, rightly recognizes the objectivity of truth in its acknowledgment, within its principles of general conduct and regulations, that the central purpose of the university—its *telos*—is "the pursuit of truth."

Now, none of this takes away from the fact that truth-seeking is a collaborative enterprise. That's in no small part because all of us are indeed frail, fallen, fallible human beings. Any of us can be wrong, and all of us are wrong sometimes. And we can be, and sometimes are, wrong not only about the comparatively minor, trivial, superficial things of life, but also about the big, important things: human nature, the human good, human rights, human dignity, human destiny.

By challenging others—something I do quite a bit of in this book—and allowing others to challenge us, especially on the big issues, errors can be corrected, and we can deepen our understanding and get nearer to the fullness of truth. Of course, progress is not inevitable. Decline can happen. Securely held truths can be abandoned or displaced. But the proper response to the possibility of decline is not to insulate one's ideas and beliefs, or the dominant ideas and beliefs of some group or of some time and place, from challenge and criticism. That is the high road to obscurantism, dogmatism, tribalism, and groupthink. Don't go there—we must not become the evil we deplore.

The "free exchange" or "marketplace" of ideas, supported by principles of freedom of thought, inquiry, and discussion, cannot guarantee the attainment of truth or the avoidance of error. In this vale of tears, nothing can give us such a guarantee. Intellectual freedom, open inquiry, robust civil discourse, and openness to genuine dialogue with people who see things very differently from the way we ourselves see them provide our best shot at getting to the truth. We should tolerate—and in a truth-seeking spirit, we should engage—ideas we think are wrong, even badly, indeed tragically, wrong. We should do that not because there is no truth, but precisely because the free exchange of ideas is the best way available to us for getting at the truth, deepening our knowledge and understanding, and achieving that rarest and most precious of all categories of truth, namely, *wisdom*.

PART ONE

The Human Person: Ethical and Metaphysical Questions

CHAPTER ONE

The Nature and Basis of Human Dignity

with Patrick Lee

Some people hold that all human beings have a special type of *dignity* that is the basis for (1) the obligation all of us have not to kill them, (2) the obligation to take their well-being into account when we act, and even (3) the obligation to treat them as we would have them treat us. Those who hold that all human beings possess a special type of dignity almost always also hold that human beings are *equal* in fundamental dignity. They maintain that there is no class of human beings to which other human beings should be subordinated in considering their interests or their well-being, and in devising laws and social policies.

Other thinkers deny that all human beings have a special type of dignity. They maintain that only some human beings, because of their possession of certain characteristics in addition to their humanity (for example, an immediately exercisable capacity for self-consciousness or for rational deliberation), have full moral worth. In this paper we defend the first of these two positions. We argue that all human beings, regardless of age, size, stage of development, or immediately exercisable capacities, have equal fundamental dignity.

Let us begin by offering a few preliminary thoughts on the general concept of *dignity*. Dignity is not a distinct property or quality, like a body's color or an organ's function. It is not a quality grasped by a direct intuition. Although there are different types of dignity, in each case the word refers to a property or properties—different ones in different circumstances—that cause one to *excel*, and thus elicit or merit respect from others. Our focus will be on the dignity of a person, or personal dignity. The dignity of a *person* is that whereby a person excels other beings, especially other animals, and merits respect or consideration from other persons. We will argue that what distinguishes human beings from other animals, what makes human beings *persons* rather than *things*, is their rational nature. Human beings are rational creatures by virtue of possessing natural capacities for conceptual thought, deliberation, and free choice, that is, the natural capacity to shape their own lives.

These basic, natural capacities to reason and make free choices are possessed by every human being, even those who cannot immediately exercise them. Being a person derives from the kind of substantial entity one is, a substantial entity with a rational nature—and this is the ground for dignity in the most important sense. Because personhood is based on the *kind* of being one is—a substantial entity whose nature is a *rational* nature—one cannot lose one's fundamental personal dignity as long as one exists as a human being.

There are other senses of the word "dignity." First, there is a type of dignity which varies in degrees, which is the *manifestation* or *actualization* of those capacities that distinguish humans from other animals. Thus, slipping on a banana peel (being reduced for a moment to a passive object), or losing our independence and privacy (especially as regards our basic bodily functions), detract from our dignity in this sense. However, while this dignity seems to be compromised in certain situations, it is never completely lost. Moreover, this dignity, which varies in degree, is distinct from the more basic dignity that derives from simply being a person.

Second, it is important also to distinguish one's dignity from one's *sense of* dignity. Something may harm one's *sense of* dignity without damaging or compromising one's real dignity. People who become dependent on others often *feel* a certain loss of dignity. Yet their personal dignity, and even their manifestation of that dignity, may not have been harmed at all. Often one's sense of dignity can be at variance with one's real dignity. Those who are sick and who bear their suffering in a courageous or dignified manner often inspire others even though they themselves may *feel* a loss of dignity.

Third, a human person may be treated in a way at odds with his or her personal dignity. Human beings may be enslaved, they may be killed unjustly, raped, scorned, coerced, or wrongly imprisoned. Such treatment is undignified, yet it too, like a person's low sense of dignity, does not cause a victim to lose personal dignity; the slave and the murder victim are wronged precisely because they are treated in a way at odds with their genuine personal dignity.

In truth, all human beings have real dignity simply because they are persons—entities with natural capacities for thought and free choice. *All* human beings have this capacity, so all human beings are persons. Each human being therefore deserves to be treated by all other human beings with respect and consideration. It is precisely this truth that is at stake in the debates about killing human embryos, fetuses, and severely retarded, demented, or debilitated human beings, and many other debates in bioethics.

To demonstrate how human beings inherently possess dignity, we will first explain more precisely the problem concerning the basis of human dignity; then we will examine proposals that deny that every human being has an intrinsic dignity which grounds full moral worth; then we will present and defend our position; finally, we will show how the feature (nature) that grounds full moral worth is possessed by human beings in all developmental stages, including the embryonic, fetal, and infant stages, and in all conditions, including severely cognitively impaired conditions (sometimes called "marginal cases").

THE PROBLEM OF MORAL STATUS

The general problem regarding the ground of moral status can be expressed as follows. It seems that it is morally permissible to use *some* living things, to consume them, experiment on them for our own benefit (without their consent, or perhaps when they are unable to give or withhold consent), but that it is not morally permissible to treat *other* beings in this way. The question is: Where do we draw the line between those two sorts of beings? By reference to what criterion do we draw that line? Or perhaps there just is no such line, and we should always seek to preserve *all* beings, of whatever sort.

But we must eat, we must use some entities for food and shelter, and in doing so we inevitably destroy them. When we eat, we convert entities of one nature into another and thus destroy them. Moreover, no one claims that we should not try to eradicate harmful bacteria, which are forms of life. In fact, we should kill harmful bacteria in order to protect ourselves and our children. And it seems clear that we must harvest wheat and rice for food, and trees for shelter. So, plainly it is permissible to kill and use some living things. Given that it is not morally permissible to kill just any type of being, it follows that a line must be drawn, a line between those entities it is morally permissible to use, consume, and destroy, and those it is not permissible to use, consume, and destroy. How can the line be drawn in a non-arbitrary way?

Various criteria for where the line should be drawn have been proposed: sentience, consciousness, self-awareness, rationality, or being a moral agent (the last two come to the same thing). We will argue that the criterion is: having a rational nature, that is, having the natural capacity to reason and make free choices, a capacity it ordinarily takes months, or even years, to actualize, and which various impediments might prevent from being brought to full actualization. (Severely retarded human beings have the same nature and thus the same basic rights as other humans: Were a therapy or surgery developed to correct whatever defect causes their mental disability, this would not change their nature. It would not change them into a different kind of being; rather, it would enable them to flourish more fully precisely as the kind of beings they are—human beings.) Thus, every human being has full moral worth or dignity, for every human being possesses such a rational nature.

While membership in the species *Homo sapiens* is sufficient for full moral worth, it is not in any direct sense the criterion for moral worth. If we discovered extra-terrestrial beings of a rational nature, or learned that some other terrestrial species have a rational nature, then we would owe such beings full moral respect. Still, all members of the human species do have full moral worth because all of them do have a rational nature, though many of them are not able immediately to exercise basic capacities. One could also say that the criterion for full moral worth is *being a person*, since a person is a rational subject.[1]

The other suggestions listed above, we believe, are not tenable as criteria of full moral worth, and when they are taken as such, they often have the practical effect of leading to the denial that human beings have full moral worth, rather than adding other beings to the set of beings deserving full moral respect.[2] Hence it is vital to explain how being a person, that is, being a distinct substance with the basic natural capacities for conceptual thought and free choice, is a basis for the possession of dignity and basic rights.

THE CAPACITY FOR ENJOYMENT OR SUFFERING AS A CRITERION

Animal welfarists argue that the criterion of moral worth is simply the ability to experience enjoyment and suffering. Peter Singer, for example, quotes Jeremy Bentham: "The question is not, Can they *reason*? nor Can they *talk*? but, Can they *suffer*?"[3] Singer then presents the following argument for this position: "The capacity for suffering and enjoyment is *a prerequisite for having interests at all*, a condition that must be satisfied before we can speak of interests in a meaningful way.... A stone does not have interests because it cannot suffer. Nothing that we can do to it could possibly make any difference to its welfare. The capacity for suffering and enjoyment is, however, not only necessary, but also sufficient for us to say that a being has interests—at an absolute minimum, an interest in not suffering."[4]

In short, Singer's argument is: All and only beings that have interests have moral status; but all and only beings that can (now) experience suffering or enjoyment have interests; therefore, all and only beings that can (now) experience suffering or enjoyment have moral status.

The major difficulties with Singer's position all follow from the fact that his proposed criterion for moral status involves the possession of an accidental attribute that varies in degree. Both the capacity for suffering and the possession of interests are properties which different beings have in different degrees, and the interests themselves are possessed in varying degrees. As we shall show, this feature of Singer's theory leads to untenable conclusions. We will mention four.

First, although Singer has made the slogan, "All animals are equal" famous, this premise actually leads to *denying* that all animals, including all humans, have equal moral worth or basic rights. Singer means that "All animals are equal" in the sense that all animals are due "equal consideration." Where the interests of two animals *are* similar in quality and magnitude, then those interests should be counted as equal when we decide what to do, both as individuals and in social policies and actions. However, as Singer himself points out, (on this view) some animals can perform actions which others cannot, and thus have interests which those others do not. So the moral status of all animals is not, in fact, equal. One would not be required to extend the right to vote, or to education in reading and arithmetic, to pigs, since they are unable to perform such actions. This point leads to several problems when we attempt to compare interests. According to Singer's view it is the *interests* that matter, not *the kind of being* that is affected by one's actions. So, on this view, it would logically follow that if a human child had a toothache and a juvenile rat had a slightly more severe toothache, then we would be morally required to devote our resources to alleviating the rat's toothache rather than the child's.

Second, a newborn human infant who will die shortly (and so does not appear to have long-term future interests), or a severely cognitively impaired human, will be due *less* consideration than a more mature horse or pig, on the ground that a mature horse or pig will have richer and more developed interests. Since the horse and the pig have higher cognitive and emotional capacities (in the sense of immediately or nearly immediately exercisable capacities) than those newborn infants that will die shortly and severely cognitively impaired humans—and it is the interests that directly count morally, not the beings that have those interests—then the interests of the horse and the pig should (on this account) be preferred to the interests of the newborn or cognitively impaired human.[5]

Third, let us consider the differences between types of interests. Singer's position actually implies an indirect *moral elitism*. It is true that according to this position no animal has greater moral status than another solely on the ground of its species (that is, according to its substantial nature). Still, one animal will be due more consideration—indirectly—if it has capacities for higher or more complex mental functions. As Singer puts it, "Within these limits we could still hold that, for instance, it is worse to kill a *normal* adult human, with a capacity for self-awareness, and the ability to plan for the future and have meaningful relations with others, than it is to kill a mouse, which presumably does not share all of these characteristics...." (emphasis added).[6] But this difference between degrees of capacity for suffering and enjoyment will also apply to individuals within each species. And so, on this view, while humans will normally have a greater capacity for suffering and enjoyment than other animals, and so will have a higher moral status (indirectly), so too, a more intelligent and sophisticated human individual will have a greater capacity for suffering and enjoyment than a less intelligent and less sophisticated human individual, and so the former will have a higher moral status than the latter. As Richard Arneson expressed this point, "For after all it is just as true that a creative genius has richer and more complex interests than those of an ordinary average Joe as it is true that a human has richer and more complex interests than a baboon."[7]

Finally, there is a fourth difficulty for the animal welfarist position, a difficulty that also clarifies the principal difference between that position and traditional morality. Singer's argument was that moral worth is based on interests, and interests are based on the ability to experience suffering or enjoyment. In other words, a key premise in his argument is that only beings with feelings or some level of consciousness can be reasonably considered to have interests. However, this is simply not true. Rather, all living beings, not just those with consciousness, have interests. It is clear that living beings are fulfilled by certain conditions and damaged by others. As Paul Taylor, who defends a biocentrist view (*all* living beings have moral worth), explains, "We can think of the good of an individual nonhuman organism as consisting in the full development of its biological powers. Its good is realized to the extent that it is strong and healthy."[8]

One can then say that what promotes the organism's survival and flourishing is *in its interest* and what diminishes its chances of survival or flourishing is *against its interests*. Further, while it may be initially plausible to think that all animals have rights because they have interests, it is considerably less plausible to think that all living beings (which include wheat, corn, and rice, not to mention weeds and bacteria) have rights. But the interest argument would lead to that position.

And this point, we think, clarifies the issue. The arguments advanced by Singer and Taylor do not actually attempt to establish that nonhuman animals and other living things have moral rights in the full sense of the term. We think it is true of *every* living being, in some way, that we should not *wantonly* destroy or damage it.[9] With sentient beings, whether their lives go well or badly for them will significantly include their pleasure, comfort, or lack of suffering. And so their flourishing includes pleasure and lack of pain (though it also includes other things such as their life and their activities). Yet it does not follow from these points that they have full basic and inherent dignity (moral worth) or rights.[10] There simply is no conceptual connection between pleasure and pain (enjoyment and suffering), on the one hand, and full moral worth (including genuine rights), on the other hand.[11]

However, almost no one actually argues that these beings have basic dignity or full moral rights. Rather, biocentrists argue that all living things merit *some* consideration, but also hold that human beings are due *more* consideration (though not, apparently, a different *kind* of consideration).[12] In effect, instead of actually holding that all living beings (in the case of biocentrists), or all animals (in the case of animal welfarists) have *rights*, they have simply denied the existence of rights in the full sense of the term.[13] Rather, they hold only that all living beings (or animals, or higher mammals) deserve some (varying) degree of respect or consideration. We agree with this point, but we also maintain that every human being is a subject of rights, that is, every human being should be treated according to the Golden Rule.[14] In other words, we grant that we should take account of the flourishing of living beings and the pleasures and pains of nonhuman animals. But we are not morally related to them in the same way that we are related to other beings who, like ourselves, have a rational nature—beings whom (out of fairness) we should treat as we would have them treat us.

But one might argue for animal rights starting from our natural empathy or affection for them (though most people's natural empathy or affection, notably, does *not* extend to all animals, for example, to spiders or snakes). If one identifies what is to be protected and pursued with what can be felt, that is, enjoyed or suffered in some way, then one might conclude that every entity that can have pleasure or pain deserves (equal?) consideration. If the only intrinsic good were what can be enjoyed, and the only intrinsic bad were suffering, then it would not be incoherent to hold that sentience is the criterion of moral standing, that is, that every entity with sentience has (some degree of) moral standing. In other words, it seems that one can present an *argument* for animal rights that begins from natural feelings of empathy only by way of a hedonistic value theory. We can think of no other arguments that begin from that natural empathy with, or affection for, other animals.

But hedonism as a general theory of value is mistaken. The central tenet of hedonism—that the good consists in the experiential—is false. Real understanding of the way things are, for example, is pleasurable because it is fulfilling or perfective of us, not vice versa. The same is true of life, health, or skillful performance (one enjoys running a good race because it is a genuine accomplishment, a skillful performance, rather than vice versa). So, as Plato and Aristotle pointed out, hedonism places the cart before the horse. We are capable of desiring certain things while other things leave us unmoved, uninterested. Clearly, some desires are bad and some are merely whimsical, but some desires are neither. So, in many cases, prior to being desired, the object desired has something about it that makes it *fitting*, or *suitable*, to be desired. What makes it fitting is that it is *fulfilling* or *perfective* to us in some way or other. Thus, what makes a thing good cannot consist in its being enjoyed, or in its satisfying desires or preferences. Rather, desires and preferences are rational only if they are in line with what is genuinely good, that is, genuinely fulfilling.[15] So hedonism is mistaken. It cannot provide support for the view that sentience (or the capacity for suffering and enjoyment) is the criterion of full moral worth. While we are prepared to grant, at least for the sake of argument, that it is wrong to kill a plant, insect, or other non-rational creature wantonly, still it can be morally right to do so for a good reason.[16]

These difficulties in Singer's position are all due to the selection of a criterion of moral worth that varies in degrees. If the moral status-conferring attribute varies in degrees—whether it be the capacity for enjoyment or suffering, or another attribute that comes in degrees—it will follow that some humans will possess that attribute to a lesser extent than some non-human animals, and so inevitably some interests of some non-human animals will trump the interests of some humans. Also, it will follow that some humans will possess the attribute in question in a higher degree than other humans, with the result that not all humans will be equal in fundamental moral worth, that is, *dignity*. True, some philosophers bite the bullet on these results. But in our judgment this is too high a price to pay. A sound view of worth and dignity will not entail such difficulties.

Rather, our position is that a rights-bearing subject has rights in virtue of the kind of substantial entity he or she is, not in virtue of accidental attributes such as race, sex, ethnicity, age, size, stage of development, or condition of dependency. There are many things to be said in defense of this position, but let us make here just a few brief points. First, this view will explain why it seems to at least most people that our moral concern should be for *persons*, rather than only for their properties or accidental attributes. After all, when dealing with other persons we at least tend to think that the locus of value is the persons themselves. We do not normally view persons as mere vehicles for what is intrinsically valuable: One's child, one's neighbor, or even a stranger, is not valuable only because of the valuable attributes he or she possesses. If persons were valuable as mere vehicles for something else—some other quality that is regarded as what is *really* of value—then it would follow that the basic moral rule would be simply to maximize those valuable attributes. It would not be morally wrong to kill a child, no matter what age, if doing so enabled one to have two children in the future, and thus to bring it about that there were two vehicles for intrinsic value rather than one. So persons themselves are valuable, rather than mere vehicles for what is really intrinsically valuable.

But if that is so, then it would make sense that what distinguishes those entities that have full moral status (inherent dignity) from those that do not should be the type of substantial entity they are, rather than any accidental attributes they possess. True, it is not self-contradictory to hold that the person himself is valuable, but only in virtue of some accidental attributes he or she possesses. Still, it is more natural, and more theoretically economical, to suppose that *what* has full moral status, and *that in virtue of which* he or she has full moral status, are the same.

Second, this position more closely tracks the characteristics we tend to think are found in genuine care or love. Our genuine love for a person remains, or should remain, for as long as that person continues to exist, and is not dependent on his or her possessing further attributes. That is, it seems to be the nature of care or love that, at least ideally, it should be unconditional, that we should continue to desire the well-being or fulfillment of someone we love for as long as he or she exists. Of course, this still leaves open the question whether continuing to live is always part of a person's well-being or fulfillment; we also maintain that a person's life always *is* in itself a good, but that is a distinct question from the one being considered just now.[17] The point is that caring for someone is a three-term relation. It consists in actively willing that a good or benefit be instantiated *in* a person, viewed as a subject of existence, in other words, as a substance. And this structure is more consonant with the idea that the basis of dignity or moral worth is being a certain sort of substance, rather than possessing certain attributes or accidental characteristics.

THE DIFFERENCE IN KIND BETWEEN HUMAN BEINGS AND OTHER ANIMALS

Human beings are fundamentally different in kind from other animals, not just genetically but in having a rational nature (that is, a nature characterized by basic natural capacities for conceptual thought, deliberation, and free choice). Human beings perform *acts of understanding*, or conceptual thought, and such acts are fundamentally different kinds of acts from acts of sensing, perceiving, or imaging. An act of understanding is the grasping of, or awareness of, a nature shared in common by many things. In Aristotle's memorable phrase, to understand is not just to know water (by sensing or perceiving this water), but to know what it is to be water.[18] By our senses and perceptual abilities we know the individual qualities and quantities modifying our sense organs—this color or this shape, for example. But by understanding (conceptual thought), we apprehend a nature held in common by many entities—not this or that instance of water, but what it is to be water. By contrast, the object of the sensory powers, including imagination, is always an individual, a *this* at a particular place and a particular time, a characteristic, such as this red, this shape, this tone, an object that is thoroughly conditioned by space and time.

The contrast is evident upon examination of language. Proper names refer to individuals, or groups of individuals that can be designated in a determinate time and place. Thus, "Winston Churchill" is a name that refers to a determinate individual, whereas the nouns "human," "horse," "atom," and "organism" are common names. Common names do not designate determinate individuals or determinate groups of individuals (such as "those five people in the corner"). Rather, they designate *classes*. Thus, if we say, "Organisms are composed of cells," the word "organisms" designates the whole class of organisms, a class that extends indefinitely into the past and indefinitely into the future. All syntactical languages distinguish between proper names and common names.

But a class is not an arbitrary collection of individuals. It is a collection of individuals all of whom have something in common. There is always some feature (or set of features), some intelligible nature or accidental attribute, that is the criterion of membership for the class. Thus, the class of organisms is all, and only those, that have the nature of *living bodily substance*. To understand the class as such, and not just be able to pick out individuals belonging to that class, one must understand the nature held in common. And to understand the class as a class (as we clearly do in reasoning) one must mentally apprehend the nature or features (or set of features) held in common by the members of the class, and compare them to those individual members. Thus, to understand a proposition such as, "All organisms require nutrition for survival," one must understand a nature or universal content designated by the term "organism": The term designates the nature or feature which entities must have in them in order to belong to the class.

Human beings quite obviously are aware of classes as classes. That is, they do more than assign individuals to a class based on a perceived similarity; they are aware of pluralities as holding natures or properties in common.[19] For example, one can perceive, without a concept, the similarity between two square shapes or two triangular shapes, something which other animals do as well as human beings. But human beings also grasp the criterion, the universal property or nature, by which the similars are grouped together.[20]

There are several considerations tending to confirm this fact. First, many universal judgments require an understanding of the nature of the things belonging to a class. If I understand, for example, that every organism is mortal, because every composite living thing is mortal, this is possible only because I mentally compare the nature, *organism*, with the nature, *composite living thing*, and see that the former entails the latter. That is, my judgment that every composite living thing can be decomposed and thus die, is based on my insight into the nature of a composite living thing. I have understood that the one nature, *subject to death*, is entailed by the other nature, *composite living being*, and *from* that knowledge I then advert to the thought of the individuals which possess those natures. I judge that individual composite living beings must be included within the class of individuals that are subject to death, but I judge *that* only in virtue of my seeing that the nature, *being subject to death*, is necessitated by the nature, *composite living being*. This point is also evident from the fact that I judge that a composite living being is *necessarily* capable of dying.[21] By the senses, one can grasp only an individual datum. Only by a distinct capacity, an intellect, only by apprehending *the nature* of a thing, can one grasp that a thing is *necessarily* thus or so.[22]

The capacity for conceptual thought in human beings radically distinguishes them from other animals known to us. This capacity is at the root of most of the other distinguishing features of human beings. Thus, syntactical language, art, architecture, variety in social groupings and in other customs,[23] burying the dead, making tools, religion, fear of death (and elaborate defense mechanisms to ease living with that fear), wearing clothes, true courting of the opposite sex,[24] free choice, and morality—all of these and more, stem from the ability to reason and understand. Conceptual thought makes all of these specific acts possible by enabling human beings to escape fundamental limitations of two sorts. First, because of the capacity for conceptual thought, human beings' actions and consciousness are not restricted to the spatio-temporal present. Their awareness and their concern go beyond what can be perceived or imagined as connected immediately with the present.[25] Second, because of the capacity for conceptual thought, human beings can reflect back upon themselves and their place in reality, that is, they can attain an objective view, and they can attempt to be objective in their assessments and choices. Other animals give no evidence at all of being able to do either of these things; on the contrary, they seem thoroughly tied to the here and now, and unable to take an objective view of things as they are in themselves, or to attempt to do so.[26]

The capacity for conceptual thought is a capacity that human beings have in virtue of the kind of entity they are. That is, from the time they come to be they are developing themselves toward the mature stage at which they will (unless prevented from doing so by disability or circumstances) perform such acts. Moreover, they are structured—genetically, and in the non-material aspect of themselves—in such a way that they are oriented to maturing to this stage.[27] So, every human being, including human infants and unborn human beings, has this basic natural capacity for conceptual thought.[28]

Human beings also have the basic natural capacity or potentiality to deliberate among options and make free choices, choices that are not determined by the events that preceded them, but are determined by the person making the choice in the very act of choosing. That is, for some choices, the antecedent events are not sufficient to bring it about that these choices be made in this way rather than another way. In such choices, a person could have chosen the other option, or not chosen at all, under the very same conditions. If a choice is free, then, given everything that happened to the person up to the point just prior to his choice—including everything in his environment, everything in his heredity, everything in his understanding and in his character—it was still possible for him to choose the other option, or not to choose at all. Expressed positively: He himself in the very act of choosing determines the content of his willing. Human beings are ultimate authors of their own acts of will and partial authors (together with nature and nurture) of their own character.[29]

How, then, does a person finally choose one course of action rather than another? The person by his own act of choosing directs his will toward this option rather than that one, and in such a way that he could, in those very same circumstances, have chosen otherwise.[30]

A good case can be made to support the position that human beings do make free choices.[31] First, objectively, when someone deliberates about which possible action to perform, each option (very often, in any case) has in it what it takes to be a possible object of choice. When persons deliberate, and find some distinctive good in different, incompatible, possible actions, they are free, for (a) they have the capacity to understand the distinct types of good or fulfillment found (directly or indirectly) in the different possible courses of action, and (b) they are capable of willing whatever they understand to be good (fulfilling) in some way or other.[32] That is, each alternative offers a distinct type of good or benefit, and it is up to the person deliberating which type of good he will choose.

For example, suppose a student chooses to go to law school rather than to medical school. When he deliberates, both options have a distinctive sort of goodness or attractiveness. Each offers some benefit the other one does not offer. So, since each alternative has some intelligible value in it (some goodness that is understood), then each alternative *can* be willed. And second, while each is good, to a certain extent, neither alternative (at least in many situations) is good, or better, in *every respect*. Here the role of conceptual thought, or intellect, becomes clear. The person deliberating is able to see, that is, to *understand*, that each alternative is good, but that none is best absolutely speaking, that is, according to every consideration, or in every respect. And so neither the content of the option nor the strength of one or another desire determines the choice. Hence there are acts of will in which one directs one's will toward this or that option without one's choosing being determined by antecedent events or causes. Human persons, then, are fundamentally distinct from other animals in that they have a nature entailing the potentialities for conceptual thought and free choice.

HAVING A RATIONAL NATURE, OR BEING A PERSON, IS THE CRITERION FOR FULL MORAL WORTH

Neither sentience nor life itself entails that those who possess it must be respected as ends in themselves or as creatures having full moral worth. Rather, having a rational nature is the ground of full moral worth.

The basis of this point can be explained, at least in part, in the following way. When one chooses an action, one chooses it for a reason, that is, for the sake of some good one thinks this action will help to realize. That good may itself be a way of realizing some further good, and that good a means to another, and so on. But the chain of instrumental goods cannot be infinite. So there must be some ultimate reasons for one's choices, some goods which one recognizes as reasons for choosing which need no further support, which are not mere means to some further good.

Such ultimate reasons for choice are not arbitrarily selected. Intrinsic goods—that is, human goods that as basic aspects of human well-being and fulfillment provide more-than-merely-instrumental reasons for choices and actions—are not just what we happen to desire, perhaps different objects for different people.[33] Rather, the intellectual apprehension that a condition or activity is *really fulfilling* or *perfective* (of me and/or of others like me) is at the same time the apprehension that this condition or activity is a fitting object of pursuit, that is, that it would be worth pursuing.[34] These fundamental human goods are the actualizations of our basic potentialities, the conditions to which we are naturally oriented and which objectively fulfill us, the various aspects of our fulfillment as human persons.[35] They include such fulfillments as human life and health, speculative knowledge or understanding, aesthetic experience, friendship or personal community, harmony among the different aspects of the self.[36]

The conditions or activities understood to be fulfilling and worth pursuing are not individual or particularized objects. I do not apprehend merely that *my* life or knowledge is intrinsically good and to be pursued. I apprehend that life and knowledge, whether instantiated in me or in others, are good and worth pursuing. For example, seeing an infant drowning in a shallow pool of water, I apprehend, without an inference, that a good worth preserving is in danger and so I reach out to save the child. The feature, *fulfilling for me or for someone like me*, is the feature in a condition or activity that makes it an ultimate reason for action. The question is: In what respect must someone be like me for his or her fulfillment to be correctly viewed as worth pursuing for its own sake in the same way that my good is worth pursuing?

The answer is not immediately obvious to spontaneous, or first-order, practical reasoning, or to first-order moral reasoning. That is, the question of the extension of the fundamental goods genuinely worthy of pursuit and respect needs moral reflection to be answered. By such reflection, we can see that the relevant likeness (to me) is that others too rationally shape their lives, or have the potentiality of doing so. Other likenesses—age, gender, race, appearance, place of origin, and so forth—are not relevant to making an entity's fulfillment fundamentally worth pursuing and respecting. But being a rational agent *is* relevant to this issue, for it is an object's being worthy of *rational* pursuit that I apprehend and that makes it an ultimate reason for action, and an intrinsic good.[37] So I ought primarily to pursue and respect not just life in general, for example, but the life of rational agents—a rational agent being one who either immediately or potentially (with a *radical* potentiality, as part of his or her nature) shapes his or her own life.[38]

Moreover, I understand that the basic human goods are not just good for me as an individual, but for me acting in communion—rational cooperation and real friendship—with others. Indeed, communion with others, which includes mutual understanding and self-giving, is itself an irreducible aspect of human well-being and fulfillment—a basic human good. But I can act in communion—real communion—only with beings with a rational nature. So the basic goods are not just goods for me, but goods for me and all those with whom it is possible (in principle, at least) rationally to cooperate. All of the basic goods should be pursued and respected, not just as they are instantiable in me, but as they are instantiable in any being with a rational nature.

In addition, by reflection we see that it would be inconsistent to respect my fulfillment, or my fulfillment plus that of others whom I just happen to like, and *not* respect the fulfillment of other, immediately or potentially, rational agents. For entailed by rational pursuit of my good (and of the good of others I happen to like) is a demand on my part that others respect my good (and the good of those I like). That is, in pursuing my fulfillment I am led to appeal to the reason and freedom of others to respect that pursuit, and my real fulfillment. But in doing so, consistency, that is reasonableness, demands that I also respect the rational pursuits and real fulfillment of other rational agents—that is, any entity that, immediately or potentially (that is, by self-directed development of innate or inherent natural capacities), rationally directs his or her own actions. In other words, the thought of the Golden Rule, basic fairness, occurs early on in moral reflection. One can *hope* that the weather, and other natural forces, including any non-rational agent, will not harm one. But one has a moral *claim* or *right* (one spontaneously makes a moral *demand*) that other mature rational agents respect one's reasonable pursuits and real fulfillment. Consistency, then, demands that one respect reasonable pursuits and real fulfillment of others as well. Thus, having a rational nature, or being a person, as traditionally defined (a distinct subject or substance with a rational nature) is the criterion for full moral worth.

MARGINAL CASES

On this position every human being, of whatever age, size, or stage of development, has inherent and equal fundamental dignity and basic rights. If one holds, on the contrary, that full moral worth or dignity is based on some accidental attribute, then, since the attributes that could be considered to ground basic moral worth (developed consciousness, and so forth) vary in degree, one will be led to the conclusion that moral worth also varies in degrees.

It might be objected, against this argument, that the basic natural capacity for rationality also comes in degrees, and so this position (that full moral worth is based on the possession of the basic natural capacity for rationality), if correct, would also lead to the denial of fundamental personal equality.[39] However, the criterion for full moral worth is having a nature that entails the capacity (whether existing in root form or developed to the point at which it is immediately exercisable) for conceptual thought and free choice—not *the development* of that basic natural capacity to some degree or other. The criterion for full moral worth and possession of basic rights is not the possession of a capacity for conscious thought and choice considered as an accidental attribute that inheres in an entity, but being a certain kind of thing, that is, having a specific type of substantial nature. Thus, possession of full moral worth follows upon being a certain type of entity or substance, namely, a substance with a rational nature, despite the fact that some persons (substances with a rational nature) have a greater intelligence, or are morally superior (exercise their power for free choice in an ethically more excellent way) than others. Since basic rights are grounded in being a certain type of substance, it follows that having such a substantial nature qualifies one as having full moral worth, basic rights, and equal personal dignity.

An analogy may clarify our point. Certain properties follow upon being an animal, and so are possessed by every animal, even though in other respects not all animals are equal. For example, every animal has some parts which move other parts, and every animal is subject to death (mortal). Since various animals are equally animals—and since being an animal is a type of substance rather than an accidental attribute—then every animal will equally have *those* properties, even though (for example) not every animal equally possesses the property of being able to blend in well to the wooded background. Similarly, possession of full moral worth follows upon being a person (a distinct substance with a rational nature) even though persons are unequal in many respects (intellectually, morally, and so forth).

These points have real and specific implications for the great controversial issues in contemporary ethics and politics. Since human beings are intrinsically valuable as subjects of rights at all times that they exist—that is, they do not come to be at one point, and acquire moral worth or value as a subject of rights only at some later time—it follows that human embryos and fetuses are subjects of rights, deserving full moral respect from individuals and from the political community. It also follows that a human being remains a person, and a being with intrinsic dignity and a subject of rights, for as long as he or she lives: There are no subpersonal human beings. Embryo-destructive research, abortion, and euthanasia involve killing innocent human beings in violation of their moral right to life and to the protection of the laws.

In sum, human beings are animals of a special kind. They differ in kind from other animals because they have a rational nature, a nature characterized by having the basic natural capacities for conceptual thought and deliberation and free choice. In virtue of having such a nature, all human beings are persons; and all persons possess profound, inherent, and equal dignity. Thus, every human being deserves full moral respect.

CHAPTER TWO

The Soul: Not Dead Yet
with Patrick Lee

In a 2017 essay for the *New York Times*, the late eminent English philosopher Sir Roger Scruton rightly argued that human persons are not reducible to material forces, correctly insisting that we are aware of ourselves and others as subjects of moral responsibility, of free choice, and of rationality.[1] However, he also argued that "philosophers and theologians in the Christian tradition have regarded human beings as distinguished from the other animals by the presence within them of a divine spark," which they call the soul, and that "recent advances in genetics, neuroscience and evolutionary psychology have all but killed off that idea."

We agree that human beings are both animals and persons, but it is important that the Christian (and Jewish, and Muslim, and classical) description of the soul not be reduced to a caricature. Indeed, properly understood, the traditional philosophical and theological concept of the soul is indispensable in integrating what the empirical sciences reveal about the world and ourselves with what we know about ourselves as rational and moral beings.

The claim that genetics has helped "kill off" the idea of the soul usually rests on the notion that the actions of DNA molecules are sufficient to explain the events occurring in the larger-level entities of which they are parts—namely, the organisms, human beings included. The idea is that the characteristics of organisms are sufficiently explained by the properties of and the spatial relations among their microphysical components. And so (on this view) there is no need to appeal to the causal powers of the organism as a whole to account for what occurs in it. Therefore, genetics can assist in a general program to explain away higher-level properties such as nutrition, growth, perception, and thought, by reference to the properties of the microphysical components.

However, while bold promissory notes to provide such explanations have been given, actual payment—in the form of adequate explanations—has never been provided. Moreover, if such a reduction could succeed, animals would not then actually be single entities—"composite substances," to borrow Aristotelian language—but mere aggregates of microphysical entities. This reduction would negate not just the idea of the soul but also the idea that we are both animals and persons.

Of course, many complex objects *are* mere aggregates. Many of the things we might view as unitary objects actually only produce effects that can be fully explained by the properties and interrelations of their constituents. For example, as Trenton Merricks points out in his *Objects and Persons,* what a baseball does can be fully explained by the concerted actions of its constituents.[2] A baseball shatters a window, not in virtue of any property of the baseball as a whole, but in virtue of the properties and spatial relations of microphysical entities it contains. However, other composite objects, particularly organisms, have causal powers belonging to the complex substance as a whole. When a human being walks to the refrigerator to retrieve food for a meal, this is a behavior performed by the organism in virtue of conscious properties—properties that belong to the complex substance as a whole. She walks to the kitchen and not to the living room because of her memory and belief that that's where the food is. Such a conscious belief can scarcely be conceived of as inhering in this or that particle, or as a structural relation of the particles to each other. Rather, it inheres in the organism as a whole and guides the behavior of that organism as a whole. Thus, the unity and causal properties of the organism as a whole are irreducible to the powers and relations of the microphysical entities it contains as parts.

Nor has neuroscience helped "all but kill off" the concept of a soul. It could do so only if it showed how thought could be reduced to neuro-processes. But many have pointed out the insuperable difficulties for such a reduction. Any argument advanced to support such a feat would logically undermine itself. For the point of the reduction would be to show that one's thoughts are fully explained by the interactions of electrochemical processes operating according to physical, not necessarily logical, laws. But if one's thought—including the reductionist's argument itself—rests on such non-rational causes, it is undermined, since beliefs that are determined by non-rational causes, rather than reasons, are thereby made suspect. If my thoughts are merely the result of the electrochemical processes in my brain, then they are non-rational.

Of course, a proponent of the reduction might object that there can be more than one explanation for an event, and so the thought's explanation on one level (neurons firing) does not preclude its simultaneous explanation on another level as well (logic). And thus, he might say, thoughts are identical with or fully determined by brain processes, but these processes can be explained in both physical and logical terms. Just as the same material event can be explained both by biology and by physics, and the two explanations are compatible, so here (it might be argued), one can give both an explanation by reference to logical laws and an explanation by reference to brain processes and their wholly materially determined interactions.

The proposed reduction of thought to neurochemical processes could succeed, however, only if the actions of the neural components, *operating according to physical laws,* determine the reasoning processes—that is, determine which conclusions one draws in an argument. On a reductive view of mental events, the premises (or the acts of accepting the premises) have the causal powers they do only in virtue of their *physical* properties, and so the *logical* laws—the relations among contents of thought just as such—will be utterly irrelevant. Thus, if thoughts are just neuro-processes, governed by physical laws, then the laws of logic are dispensable, and the physical antecedents of a thought (such as a conclusion) determine it regardless of the *contents* of those antecedents. But this renders the argument by which one defends the attempted reduction unworthy of acceptance. Thus, thought cannot be adequately explained by neuroscience alone.

Thus, some properties and causal powers of organisms belong to them as wholes rather than merely as a result of the sum of the properties and causal powers of their components, and so organisms *are* substantial entities rather than mere aggregates. But as complex substances, each organism must have a principle of unity making its components a single whole. This principle cannot itself be a concrete component, or else the resulting unity would not be a single substantial entity composed of parts, but one entity acting on others—an accidental whole, a mere aggregate. Nor can the source of unity be merely a relation accruing to those components, which remain what they are but acquire ordered relations to others. What is required is a factor that unifies the materials in order to make them one being, one substance, and makes the parts be what they are because of their place within that whole. It must be a principle of organization that is logically prior to and not merely the result of the causal properties of the parts. Such a principle is precisely what the Aristotelian tradition called a "substantial form." In a living being, such a form is a *soul*.

The role of such a principle can also be understood as follows. Animal organisms die, and some are consumed by other animals. It is obvious that some of the matter-energy that once went into the make-up of one animal ends up in the make-up of another. In fact, *all* of the materials, or matter-energy, within an animal *could* end up in the make-up of another. And so within the animal now there must be a formal principle, a principle of unity, determining the matter-energy in its make-up to be of this kind rather than of another kind. This is the substantial form that in a living being is called a soul.

One can of course rightly affirm many things without affirming the existence of a soul, but some of these affirmations cannot be *made sense of* without affirming a soul. One could agree that human beings are both animals and persons without first appealing to the notion of the soul—and one could even be derisive of that concept at the same time. But one can give no intelligible account of those affirmations of our nature as personal animals without the concept of a soul—as that term has traditionally been used and understood.

Moreover, while organisms are irreducible to the laws and properties of the chemicals and particles composing them, likewise the human person (as Sir Roger rightly suggests) is irreducible to the laws and properties of organisms. Human thoughts and choices cannot be fully explained by biological laws and properties: The dimensions of logic and morality are distinct and irreducible types of reality.

Still, the source of thought and choice in a human person cannot be a distinct agent or a substance distinct from the human organism. It must be the same agent that believes the food is in the kitchen (a person or thinker) and that walks there (an organism). So, on the one hand, the human thinker and the human body are not two different things, but one complex substance with different powers. On the other hand, the human person engages in operations—thought and choices, for example—that are not reducible without remainder to the laws and properties of natural, material entities.

If one denies the first point, one will view the bodily aspect of the human person as a mere extrinsic instrument, without inherent meaning and importance. If one denies the second point, one fails to acknowledge the human being precisely as a person, as a source of uniqueness and originality and the bearer of rights. But to make sense of the compatibility of both points one needs the concept of a substantial form—*soul*. Without that, the organic aspect of the person will lack substantial unity and either the distinctiveness of the person will be denied (reverting to materialism), or the person will be viewed as separate from the organism ("ghost in a machine").

We are directly aware that we persist through time and that our plans, deliberations, and choices extend through time. Such activities cannot be attributed to this or that material component, or to a group of components in a mere accidental whole. So if the organism is viewed as a mere aggregate, a mere mass of particles, the personal subject will inevitably be viewed as a separate agent making use of that mass of particles as a mere extrinsic tool. Without the idea of a human substantial form or soul one cannot intelligibly relate the organic to the personal—the world of the "life-form" to the world of the empirical sciences.

CHAPTER THREE

Dualistic Delusions
with Patrick Lee

Disputes about metaphysical issues rarely make the newspapers. The ancient argument about the nature and identity of the human person, however, turns out to be highly relevant to issues that contemporary Americans read about, and argue about, every day. As Yale psychology professor Paul Bloom once observed in a 2004 op-ed piece in the *New York Times*, "What people think about...gay marriage, stem-cell research, and the role of religion in public life...is intimately related to their views on human nature."

Consider, for example, the abortion issue. Many defenders of abortion implicitly suppose that a human person is a consciousness or series of conscious acts that has or inhabits a body, and so they hold that your human organism came to be at one time but that *you* came to be at another time (say, with the emergence of your self-consciousness). But if they are wrong, if instead a human person is a human physical organism, then the person came to be whenever this physical organism came to be. Similarly, if the human person is a bodily entity, then it makes no sense to regard the body as a mere extrinsic tool which we may legitimately use simply for the sake of obtaining desirable effects in our consciousness (which is regarded by people who accept dualism as the "person that inhabits," or is somehow "associated with," the body)—a view widely held by defenders of sexual liberalism and same-sex "marriage" in particular.

And yet it is often the proponents of traditional morality who are accused of holding a body-self dualism. For example, advocates of abortion often assume that defenders of prenatal human life maintain their position on purely religious grounds, believing on faith that the soul is present from conception onward. Abortion advocates then say that "souls" cannot be shown to exist, assert that this view is backed up by science, and smugly conclude that science is on their side against religious zealots who believe in an unprovable and mysterious soul.

In fact, intelligent pro-lifers do not first inquire whether the soul is present and from that inquiry conclude that there is or is not a human being present. Rather, they understand that it makes more sense to begin by asking whether there are characteristics—physical characteristics— which indicate the presence of a human being, however small and developmentally immature he or she is; it is on the basis of the answer to that question that one can conclude that the human soul must be present. It is actually defenders of abortion who often implicitly assume body-self dualism, even though at other times in the debate they deny or disparage the idea of a soul and embrace or postulate materialism. We will show below that neither body-self dualism nor materialism is sound, that a third possibility represents an intellectually superior view of what a human person is, and that this view is key for understanding many of the great ethical controversies of the day.

An almost pure case of the oscillation between dualism and materialism occurs in Paul Bloom's op-ed piece titled "The Duel Between Body and Soul." Professor Bloom begins his article by rightly noting that dualism is both widespread and mistaken. He then further states correctly that the question of when human life begins is colored by one's view of what a human being is. This, he says, is why people often appeal to science to answer the question, "When does human life begin?" But this question, Bloom contends, is not really about life in the biological sense, but about "the magical moment at which a cluster of cells becomes more than a mere physical thing. It is a question about the soul." Bloom then says that science cannot answer that question because science has in fact demonstrated that qualities of mental life we associate with souls are purely corporeal; "they emerge from biochemical processes in the brain." According to Bloom, "This is starkly demonstrated in cases in which damage to the brain wipes out capacities as central to our humanity as memory, self-control, and decision-making."

But here Bloom is gravely mistaken. First, his "stark demonstration" is no demonstration at all; it rests on what is manifestly a non sequitur. Shutting off action X prevents action Y: this shows either that X is identical with Y, or that, though X and Y are distinct, Y depends on X to occur. Severe brain damage prevents conceptual thought and decision-making—this much the medieval Christian philosopher and theologian Thomas Aquinas recognized centuries ago, and Aristotle centuries before that. Their view was that conceptual thought and decision-making in human beings depends on brain operations (to provide sense experience), but (for different reasons) they also held that conceptual thought and free choice are distinct and nonbodily operations. Thus, Bloom has presented no compelling argument at all for his materialism or for the "great conflict between science and religion" that he claims exists on the question of human nature.

Second, *pace* Bloom, if science did show that all human acts, including conceptual thought and free choice, are just brain processes, then science would provide answers to important moral questions. It would just provide answers different from those we have traditionally accepted. In particular, it would mean that the difference between human beings and other animals is only superficial—a difference of degree rather than a difference in kind; it would mean that human beings lack any special dignity worthy of special respect. Thus, it would undermine the norms that forbid killing and eating human beings as we kill and eat chickens, or enslaving them and treating them as beasts of burden as we do horses or oxen.

In fact, however, the empirical sciences themselves have nothing to say one way or the other about whether there is an aspect of human beings—such as the source of conceptual thought and free choice—that is not simply a material process or a by-product of material processes. And given the limitations of their methods, the empirical sciences have nothing directly to say about an intrinsic human dignity and what the basis of that intrinsic dignity might be. So there is no "great conflict" between religion and science with respect to psychology; this "conflict" is a fiction invented by scientists unwarily wandering into the domain of philosophy. Of course, there are philosophers who defend materialism and who argue intelligently with their fellow philosophers who reject it, but the argument by which Bloom purports to demonstrate materialism is worthless.

Bloom's reasoning here exemplifies a common confusion. Defenders of abortion and euthanasia often oscillate between body-self dualism and unscientific materialism, depending on which one will further a given line of argument. For example, faced with evidence that the life of a human individual begins at conception, they deny that embryonic humans are persons or selves, implicitly identifying "persons" with consciousnesses. But then, later in the debate, accused of drawing the line between persons and nonpersons in an arbitrary way, they claim that such line-drawing must be arbitrary since we are all just aggregates or concatenations of material particles. One moment they claim that we are consciousnesses that use our bodies; the next moment they say we are purely material, different only in degree from other material entities.

Bloom contends that because science has established materialism, it is therefore unable to answer the question, "When does human life begin?" But the premise is untrue and the argument invalid. Science does not establish materialism, and even if it did, this would not preclude it from answering the question of when human life begins. Actually, the opposite of this argument is closer to the truth: If body-self dualism were true, then science could not answer that question. Bloom's mistake here is the common one of supposing that the idea that life begins at conception (in a way that can settle debates over abortion and embryo-destructive experimentation) is somehow tied to the idea that there must be a "magical moment" when a soulless body becomes ensouled: "There is no moment at which a soulless body becomes an ensouled one and so scientific research cannot provide objective answers to the questions that matter most to us" (emphasis added). This is confused. It is true that (empirical) science cannot by itself settle the whole ethical issue concerning the moral worth of embryonic and fetal human life. But if it is true that every distinct, human individual has intrinsic dignity (a proposition that most Americans hold, and one for which we have offered philosophical arguments in chapter 1), then science, and in particular embryology, can answer an important question—namely, when does a distinct human individual come to be?

And the answer provided unanimously by the leading texts in embryology is quite clear. As one text puts it, "Human development begins at fertilization when a male gamete or sperm (spermatozoon) unites with a female gamete or oocyte (ovum) to form a single cell—a zygote. This highly specialized, totipotent cell marked the beginning of each of us as a unique individual."[1]

Ironically, Bloom (like many others) seems to be misled on this question by an implicit consciousness-body dualism. He evidently holds that nothing is intrinsically valuable (as a subject of rights) without a functioning mind. And because he supposes that science has shown that the mind is material and develops gradually, he concludes that it cannot be determined with certainty and precision when this intrinsically valuable entity is present and when it isn't.

However, contrary to this view, what is intrinsically valuable is not the mental functions or qualities we have, but the being, the substantial entity, that you and I are. (By "substantial entity" we mean the thing that one is rather than the characteristics or properties one possesses.) You and I are intrinsically valuable and equal in fundamental worth and dignity because of what we are, not because of qualities we may (if all goes well) acquire at some point during our lives—qualities that come and go, and which some human beings possess in greater degree than others. And so we are intrinsically valuable in a way that makes us possessors of dignity and bearers of rights from the point at which we come to be, and we remain possessors of dignity and bearers of rights until we die.

Since dualism is mistaken—since we are not consciousnesses inhabiting bodies but are physical organisms possessing from the beginning a human (that is, rational) nature—it follows that we came to be when these physical organisms came to be. And the science of embryology does determine when that occurs—namely, conception. Bloom uses materialism to rule out the possibility that one can draw the line in an objective and nonarbitrary way between persons (beings with full moral worth) and mere things, but he implicitly adopts the very body-self dualism he criticizes when he assumes that there is something intrinsically valuable in human beings only when actual mental functions or states are present.

Like many others, Bloom seems to have rushed to an acceptance of materialism because he erroneously supposes that if dualism is false then materialism must be true. It is widely assumed that dualism and materialism exhaust the alternatives: Either we are souls which possess or inhabit our bodies, or everything in us is completely explainable by matter and material processes. But there is a third possibility, one that avoids the problems associated with both dualism and materialism.

On the one hand, a human being is essentially a physical organism, an animal. This point is shown (though the full argument would require more space than we have here) by the fact that you and I—not any entities which we merely possess or inhabit—perform and undergo bodily actions. Sensation and perception are clearly bodily activities: They are performed with bodily organs such as the senses and parts of the brain. So the subject that does the sensing and perceiving is a bodily entity, an animal organism. But it must be the same subject, the same "I," that senses or perceives and that engages in conceptual thought (though conceptual thought is not itself a bodily action—more on this in a moment). For it must be the same subject that perceives the ink marks on a page, for example, and that understands the intelligible message signified by them.

On the other hand, conceptual thought and free choice cannot be material actions; they must be spiritual or nonmaterial actions. Conceptual thought inevitably refers to a universal feature or aspect of the object of thought (for example, what an animal is, as opposed to this or that particular animal), a feature or aspect not of itself restricted to a particular place or time. But every material action has as its object an entity that is restricted to a particular place and time. Hence there is an aspect of us, a capacity or power, which is nonmaterial. It is nonmaterial in the sense that the actions in it and its existence do not depend on matter—whereas the material aspect of a thing is intrinsically circumscribed by a particular space and a particular time.

But this immaterial aspect is not the whole self, only an aspect or part of the self. On the one hand, then, one can hold that the human being is not a soul alone, but the whole living bodily entity, a composite of body (or matter) and soul (the "form" or organizing principle of the living thing). On the other hand, there is an aspect of the human being that is nonmaterial, and could not have emerged from matter and material forces. So neither body-self dualism nor materialism is correct. We are essentially physical organisms, and so we come to be when these organisms come to be—at conception. Yet we are more than just the latest product of blind evolution, since there is an immaterial aspect of us that could not have emerged from lower material forces.

The third alternative we have outlined here is hardly an invention of ours. In one variant or another, it has been held by many of the most distinguished philosophers in history, and many hold it today. Moreover, it has been accepted by some religious traditions, including the world's largest religious body, the Catholic Church. The Church rejects both materialism and body-self dualism. The human being is not just a set of material processes, nor is it a consciousness possessing or inhabiting a body. As Aristotle recognized even in antiquity, and as many others have understood since, the human being is a rational animal—an integrated unity of body and soul.

CHAPTER FOUR

Natural Law

Theories of natural law are reflective critical accounts of the constitutive aspects of the well-being and fulfillment of human persons and the communities they form. The propositions that pick out fundamental aspects of human flourishing are directive (that is, prescriptive) in our thinking about what to do and refrain from doing (our practical reason). In other words, they are, or provide, more than merely instrumental reasons for action and self-restraint. When these foundational principles of practical reflection are taken together (that is, integrally), they entail norms that may exclude certain options and require others in situations of morally significant choosing. So natural-law theories propose to identify principles of right action—moral principles—specifying the first and most general principle of morality, namely, that one should choose and act in ways that are compatible with a will towards integral human fulfillment.[1] Among these principles are respect for rights people possess simply by virtue of their humanity—rights which, as a matter of justice, others are bound to respect, and governments are bound not only to respect but, to the extent possible, also to protect. Theorists of natural law understand human fulfillment—the human good—as variegated. There are many irreducible dimensions of human well-being. This is not to deny that human nature is determinate. It is to affirm that our nature, though determinate, is complex. We are animals, but rational. Our integral good includes our bodily well-being, but also our intellectual, moral, and spiritual well-being. We are individuals, but friendship and sociability are constitutive aspects of our flourishing. We form bonds with others not only for instrumental purposes, but because of our grasp of the inherent fulfillments available in joining together in a wide variety of formal and informal types of association and community. In ways that are highly relevant to moral reflection and judgment, man truly is a social animal.

Natural-law theorists propose to arrive at a sound understanding of principles of justice, including those principles we call human rights, by reflecting on the basic goods of human nature, especially those most immediately pertaining to social and political life. In light of what I've already said about how natural-law theorists understand human nature and the human good, it should be no surprise to learn that natural-law theorists typically reject both strict individualism and collectivism. Individualism overlooks the intrinsic value of human sociability and tends to view human beings atomistically. It reduces all forms of human association to the instrumental value they possess, which is not to deny that some forms of association are indeed purely instrumentally valuable, or that virtually all forms of human association have instrumental value in addition to whatever intrinsic value they may have. Collectivism compromises the dignity of human beings by tending to instrumentalize and subordinate their well-being to the interests of larger social units. It reduces the individual to the status of a cog in the wheel whose flourishing is merely a means rather than an end to other things—including governments, systems of public and private law, and other institutions created by members of human communities for the sake of their common good—which, however noble and important, (or, to use Aristotle's description "great and god-like")[2] are in the end merely means. Individualists and collectivists both have theories of justice and human rights, but they are, as I see it, highly unsatisfactory. They are both rooted in important misunderstandings of human nature and the human good.

Neither can do justice to the concept of a human person, that is, a rational animal who is a locus of intrinsic value (and, as such, an end-in-himself who may never legitimately be treated as a mere means to others' ends), but whose well-being *intrinsically* includes relationships with others and membership in formal and informal communities in which he or she has, as a matter of justice, both rights and responsibilities.

I am sometimes asked whether natural-law theorists suppose that rights are "hard-wired into our nature." I fear that this metaphor is more likely to mislead than to illuminate. There are human rights if there are principles of practical reason directing us to act or abstain from acting in certain ways out of respect for the well-being and the dignity of persons whose legitimate interests may be affected by what we do. I certainly believe that there are such principles. They cannot be overridden by considerations of utility. (So a complete defense of any account of natural law and natural rights must include a telling critique of utilitarian and other consequentialist or aggregative accounts of moral reasoning.)[3] At a very general level, they direct us, in Kant's phrase, to treat human beings always as ends and never as means only. When we begin to specify this general norm, we identify important negative duties, such as the duty to refrain from enslaving people.

Although we *need* not put the matter in terms of "rights," it is perfectly reasonable, and I believe helpful, to speak of a *right* against being enslaved, and to speak of slavery as a violation of human *rights*. It is a moral right that people have—one that every community is morally obliged to do its best to protect by law—not by virtue of being members of a certain race, sex, class, or ethnic group, but simply by virtue of our humanity.[4] In that sense, it is a *human* right. But there are, in addition to negative duties and their corresponding rights, certain positive duties. And these, too, can be articulated and discussed in the language of rights, though here it is especially important that we be clear about by whom and how a given right is to be honored. Sometimes it is said, for example, that education or health care is a human right. It is not unreasonable to speak this way, but much more needs to be said if it is to be a meaningful statement. Who is supposed to provide education or health care to whom? Why should those persons or institutions be the providers? What place should the provision of education or health care occupy on the list of social and political priorities? Is it better for education and health care to be provided by governments under socialized systems, or by private providers in markets? These questions go beyond the application of moral principles. They require technical (for example, economic) and prudential judgments—including judgments of the sort that can vary depending on contingent circumstances people face in a given society at a given point in time. Often, there is not a single, uniquely correct answer. The answer to each question can lead to further questions; and the problems can be extremely complex, far more complex than the issue of slavery, where once a right has been identified its universality and the basic terms of its application are fairly clear. Everybody has a moral right not to be enslaved, and everybody an obligation as a matter of strict justice to refrain from enslaving others; governments have a moral obligation to respect and protect that right and to enforce the corresponding obligation.[5]

What I have said so far will provide a pretty good idea of how I think we ought to go about identifying what are (and aren't) human rights—natural rights. But in each case the argument must be made, and in many cases there are complexities to the argument. I should further note that the natural-law understanding of human rights I'm here sketching is connected with a particular account of human dignity. Under that account, the natural human capacities for reason and freedom are fundamental to the dignity of human beings—the dignity that is protected by human rights. The basic goods of human nature are the goods of a rational creature—a creature who, unless impaired or prevented from doing so, naturally develops and exercises capacities for deliberation, judgment, and choice.

Now, what about the authority for this view of human nature, the human good, human dignity, and human rights? Natural-law theorists are interested in the intelligible *reasons* people have for their choices and actions. We are particularly interested in reasons that can be identified without appeal to any authority apart from the authority of reason itself. This is not to deny that it is often reasonable to recognize and submit to religious or secular (for example, legal) authority in deciding what to do and not do. Indeed, natural-law theorists such as Yves Simon have made important contributions to understanding why and how people can sometimes be morally bound to submit to, and be guided in their actions by, authority of various types.[6] But even here, the special concern of natural-law theorists is with the *reasons* people have for recognizing and honoring claims to authority. We do not simply appeal to authority to justify authority.

Now, if I am correct in affirming that human reason can identify human rights as genuine grounds of obligation to others—rights which people possess as a matter of natural law (what have been termed "natural rights")—how can we explain or understand widespread failures to recognize and respect human rights and other moral principles? As human beings, we are rational animals; but we are imperfectly rational. We are prone to making intellectual and moral mistakes and capable of behaving grossly unreasonably—especially when deflected by powerful emotions that run contrary to the demands of reasonableness. Even when following our consciences, as we are morally bound to do, we can go wrong. A conscientious judgment may nevertheless be erroneous. Some of the greatest thinkers who ever lived failed to recognize the human right to religious liberty. Their failure, I believe, was rooted in a set of intellectual errors about what such a right presupposes and entails. The people who made these errors were neither fools nor knaves. The errors were not obvious, and it was only with a great deal of reflection and debate that the matter was clarified. Of course, sometimes people fail to recognize and respect human rights because they have self-interested motives for doing so. In most cases of exploitation, for example, the fundamental failing is moral, not intellectual. In some cases, though, intellectual and moral failures are closely connected. Selfishness, prejudice, partisanship, vanity, avarice, lust, ill-will, and other moral delinquencies can, in ways that are sometimes quite subtle, impede sound ethical judgments, including judgments pertaining to human rights. Whole cultures or subcultures can be infected with moral failings that blind large numbers of people to truths about justice and human rights, and ideologies hostile to these truths will almost always be both causes and effects of these failings. Consider, for example, the case of slavery in the antebellum American South. The ideology of white supremacy was both a cause of many people's blindness to the wickedness slavery, and an effect of the exploitation and degradation of its victims.

Let me now turn to the ways in which natural-law theories are both like and unlike utilitarian (and other consequentialist) approaches to morality, on the one hand, and Kantian (or deontological) approaches on the other. Like utilitarian approaches, and unlike Kantian ones, natural-law theories are fundamentally concerned with human well-being and fulfillment and, indeed, take basic human goods as the starting points of ethical reflection. Unlike utilitarian approaches, however, they understand the basic forms of human good (as they figure in options for morally significant choosing) as so incommensurable with the utilitarian strategy of choosing the option that overall and in the long run promises to conduce to the net best proportion of benefit to harm (however "benefit" and "harm" may be understood and defined) as to render that strategy senseless. Natural-law theorists share the Kantian rejection of aggregative accounts of morality that regard the achievement of sufficiently good consequences or the avoidance of sufficiently bad ones as justifying choices that would be excluded by application of moral principles in ordinary circumstances. Unlike Kantians, however, they do not believe that moral norms can be identified and justified apart from a consideration of the integral directiveness of the principles of practical reason directing human choice and action towards what is humanly fulfilling and away from what is contrary to human well-being. Natural-law theorists do not believe in purely "deontological" moral norms. Practical reasoning is reasoning about *both* the "right" and the "good," and the two are connected. The content of the human good shapes the moral norms which are applied in judgments about right (and wrong) choices and actions, and moral norms themselves are entailments of the primary practical principles which direct us to basic aspects of human well-being or fulfillment and whose integral directiveness is articulated in the master principle of morality and its specifications in morality's norms.

Philosophers in the natural-law tradition, going all the way back to Aristotle, have placed particular emphasis on the fact (or in any event what we believe to be the fact) that by our choices and actions we not only alter states of affairs in the world external to us, but also at the same time determine and constitute ourselves—for better or worse—as persons with a certain character.[7] Recognition of this self-shaping or "intransitive" quality of morally significant choosing leads to a focus on *virtues* as habits born of upright choosing that orient and dispose us to further upright choosing—especially in the face of temptations to behave immorally. People sometimes ask: Is natural law about rules or virtues? The answer is that it is about *both*. A complete theory of natural law identifies norms for distinguishing right from wrong as well as habits or traits of character whose cultivation disposes people to choose in conformity with the norms and thus compatibly with what we might call, borrowing a phrase from Kant, a good will—a will towards integral human fulfillment.

Now, human beings live not as isolated individuals, but in families, kinship groups, clans, and various forms of political association. And, as I've mentioned, natural-law theorists hold that among the irreducible aspects of human flourishing are various forms of harmony or unity with others. And so we propose accounts of the *common good* of communities, including political communities. The political common good is understood not as some additional human good alongside the others, but, rather, as the securing of conditions in which people can flourish by cooperating with each other as fellow citizens. There is a common good because (a) the basic human goods are aspects of the flourishing of each and every member of the human family; (b) many of these goods can be enjoyed, or enjoyed more fully, by common action to secure them;

and (c) common action itself can be intrinsically fulfilling inasmuch as humans are indeed "political animals" whose integral good includes intrinsically social dimensions.[8]

The common good of any human society demands that governments be established and maintained to make and enforce laws. Law and government are necessary not merely because human beings may treat one another unjustly and even behave in a predatory manner towards each other, but more fundamentally because human activity must often be coordinated by authoritative stipulations and other exercises of authority to secure common goals. Consider the simple case of regulating highway traffic. Even in a society of perfect saints, law and government would be necessary to establish and maintain a system of traffic regulation for the sake of the common good of motorists, cyclists, pedestrians, and everyone who benefits from the safe and efficient transportation of goods and persons on the highways. Since it is often the case that there is no uniquely reasonable or desirable scheme of regulation—only different possible schemes with different benefits and costs—governmental authority must be employed to choose—by stipulating—one from among the possible schemes. Authority in such a case is necessary because unanimity is impossible. Authority serves the common good by making a stipulation and enforcing its terms. Assuming that there is no corruption or other injustice involved in the choice of a certain scheme of traffic regulation or the enforcement of its terms, we can regard this as a focal case of legal authority under a natural-law account of the matter. Of course, the complete account would begin by identifying the human goods that schemes of traffic regulation are meant to advance and protect—including (but not limited to) the protection of human life and health—and the evils that they seek to allay. It would observe that in the absence of a legally stipulated and enforced scheme of regulation these goods would be in constant jeopardy as motorists—even motorists of goodwill who were doing their best to exercise caution—crashed into each other or created traffic gridlock of the sort that often could easily be avoided by the prudent stipulation of coordinated schemes of driving norms. It would then defend the legitimacy of governmental authority to make the required stipulations not by reference to the unique desirability of the scheme it happens to choose, but rather by appeal to the need for a scheme to be given the standing of law.

Law-making and law enforcement are central functions and responsibilities of legitimate political authority. The justifying point of law is to serve the common good by protecting the goods of persons and the communities of which they are members. Where the laws are just and effective, political authorities fulfill their obligations to the communities they exist to serve. To the extent that the laws are unjust or ineffective, they fail in their mission to serve the common good. As Aquinas says, the very point of the law is the common good.[9] In that sense, law is, as he defined it, "An ordinance of reason for the common good given by whoever who has the responsibility to care for the community."[10] Inasmuch as the moral point of law is to serve the integral good of human beings—people as they are—laws against many of the sorts of wrongdoing common, alas, in human societies are necessary and proper. Aquinas's definition of law also requires that there be some individual, group, or institution exercising authority in political communities and fulfilling this authority's moral function by translating certain principles of natural law into positive law and reinforcing these principles with legal sanctions, that is, the threat of punishment for law-breaking. In this sense, we can say that justified authorities derive the law they make (positive law) from the natural law (or equivalently, translate natural-law principles of justice and political morality into the rules of positive law).

Following Aquinas, who was himself picking up a lead from Aristotle, natural-law theorists hold that all just positive law, from schemes of traffic regulation to complex sets of rules governing, say, bankruptcy, is "derived" from natural law, though there are two different types of derivation corresponding to different types of law.[11] In certain cases, the legislator, for the sake of justice and the common good, simply and directly forbids or requires what morality itself forbids or requires. So, for example, in making murder a criminal offense the legislator puts the force and sanctions of positive law behind a principle by which people are bound as a matter of natural law even in the absence of positive law on the subject, namely, the principle forbidding the direct or otherwise unjust killing of one's fellow human beings. Aquinas noted that in acting in this way, the legislator derives the positive law from the natural law in a manner akin to the deduction of conclusions from premises in mathematics or the natural sciences. For other types of positive law, however, such a "deductive" approach is not possible. Here again the case of traffic regulation is illustrative. In choosing a scheme from among a possible range of reasonable schemes, each with its own costs and benefits, the legislator moves not by a process akin to deduction, but rather by an activity of the practical intellect that Aquinas called "*determinatio*." Although, unfortunately, no single word in English captures all that the Latin term denotes and connotes, the concept is not difficult to understand. Aquinas explained it by analogy with the activity of a craftsman commissioned to build a house—what we would probably call an architect. There is, of course, no uniquely correct way to design a house. Many different designs are reasonable. Certain design features will be determined by the needs of the person or family that will occupy the dwelling, others are simply matters of style and taste and others again of optional compromises between expense and risk. So, in most cases the architect will exercise a significant measure of creative freedom within a wide set of boundaries. Consider the question of ceiling height. While some possibilities are excluded by practical considerations—for example, ceilings only four feet in height would make living in the house impossible for most people; and ceilings of forty feet in height would ordinarily be impractically expensive—no principle of architecture fixes ceiling heights at seven feet four inches or nine feet or anything in between or a bit higher or lower. In executing his commission, the architect will endeavor to choose a height for the ceilings that harmonizes with other features of his design, including features (such as door heights) that are themselves the fruit of *determinationes*.

Like the architect, the lawmaker or lawmaking body will in many domains exercise a considerable measure of creative freedom in working from a grasp of basic practical principles directing actions towards the advancement and protection of basic human goods and away from their privations to concrete schemes of regulation aimed at coordinating conduct for the sake of the all-round well-being of the community, the common good. Among the considerations that a good legislator will always bear in mind is the fairness of the distribution of burdens and benefits attending any scheme of regulation. Because on the natural-law account all persons have a profound, inherent, and equal dignity, the interests (that is, the well-being) of each and every person must be taken into account, and no one's interests may be unfairly or otherwise unreasonably favored or disfavored. The common good is not the utilitarian's "greatest net good" or "greatest good of the greatest number";[12] rather, it is the shared good of all, including the good of living in a community where the dignity and rights of all—including the right to have one's equal basic dignity respected—is honored in the exercise of public authority.

Although the natural law sets the translation/derivation of laws as the task of the legislator (and it is only through his efforts that the natural law can become effective for the common good), it is important to note that the body of law created by the legislator is not itself the natural law. While the natural law is in no sense a human creation, the positive law is indeed created (posited, put in place)—and not just implemented—by humans. This point is telling about the metaphysical status of the positive law. Following Aristotle, we might say that the positive law belongs to the order of "making" rather than the order of "doing." It is thus fitting that the positive law is subject to technical application and is analyzed by a sort of technical reasoning. Hence, law schools do not (or do not just) teach their students moral philosophy, but focus the attention of students on distinctive techniques of legal analysis, for example, how to identify and understand legal sources, how to work with statutes, precedents, and with the (often necessarily) artificial definitions that characterize any complex system of law. At the same time, we must be careful to distinguish a different metaphysical order that attaches to the moral purpose of the law. It is in the order of "doing" (the order of free choice, practical reasoning, and morality) that we identify the need to create law for the sake of the common good. The legislator creates a cultural object, the law—which is deliberately and reasonably subject to technical analysis—for a purpose that is moral and not merely technical.[13]

The fact that the law is a cultural object that is created for a moral purpose engenders much confusion about the role of moral philosophy in legal reasoning. For instance, a much-debated question in American Constitutional interpretation is about the scope and limits of the power of judges to invalidate legislation under certain allegedly vague or abstract Constitutional provisions. Some Constitutional theorists, such as the late Ronald Dworkin, defend an expansive role for the judge, arguing that the conscientious judge must bring judgments of moral and political philosophy to bear in deciding hard cases.[14] Others fear such a role for the judge and hold that a sound constitution—at any rate, the Constitution of the United States—does not give the judge any such role.[15] They maintain that moral philosophy has little or no place in judging, at least within the American legal system. Where should natural-law theorists stand on this complex issue?

Natural-law theory treats the role of judge as itself fundamentally a matter for *determinatio* and not for direct translation from the natural law. Accordingly, it does not presuppose that the judge enjoys (or should enjoy) as a matter of natural law a plenary authority to substitute his own understanding of the requirements of the natural law for the contrary understanding of the lawmaker in deciding cases at law. On the contrary, the Rule of Law (ordinarily understood as a necessary but insufficient condition for a just system of government) morally requires—that is, obligates as a matter of natural law—the judge to respect the limits of his own authority as it has been allocated to him by way of an authoritative *determinatio*. This entails a hypothetical solution to the puzzle that confronts us: If the law of the judge's system constrains his law-creating power in the way that many believe American fundamental law does, then he is obliged—legally and, presumptively, morally—to respect these constraints, even where his own understanding of natural justice deviates from that of the legislators (or constitution makers and ratifiers) whose laws he must interpret and apply. Hence, we see that the question of what degree of law-creating power a judge enjoys is itself a matter of the positive law of the Constitution and is not determinable by natural law alone.

I will conclude by briefly treating an issue—which I believe is actually a non-issue—that has exercised some influential modern critics of natural-law theory, such as Hans Kelsen.[16] They have seized upon the slogan, found in St Augustine and echoed by Aquinas, that "an unjust law is not (or seems not to be) a law."[17] They claim that the proposition expressed in this slogan, which they regard as being at the heart of natural-law thinking, is utterly implausible. Either it sanctifies injustice by entailing that any law possessing validity by reference to the criteria of a positive system of law is morally good and therefore creates an obligation to obey, or it contradicts plain fact by suggesting that what everyone takes to be laws (that is, rules possessing validity by reference to the criteria of a positive system of law) are in fact not laws if they are unjust. But this line of criticism is misguided. Natural-law theorists through the ages have taken note of the distinction between the systemic validity of a proposition of law—the property of belonging to a legal system—and the law's moral validity and bindingness as a matter of conscience. They have had no difficulty accepting the central thesis of what we today call legal positivism, that the existence and content of the positive law depends on social facts and not on its moral merits. (Indeed, it is hard to see how one would otherwise make sense of the locution "an unjust law.") Note, however, that accepting this thesis is independent of denying other modal connections between morality and the law. In particular, it is unlikely that we would be able to understand significant aspects of the law if we were unable to grasp moral reasons. This is so because the reasons that people have for establishing and maintaining legal systems are often moral reasons that issue from normative practical deliberation that is aimed at the common good. Far from threatening the thesis of positivity, such explanatory connections are necessary to provide any fine-grained descriptive account of the law.[18] How else would we home in on the focal cases of the law or appreciate the standards by which laws are judged to be defective qua laws (as we surely do, for example, in the case of laws that show unjustified partiality to certain groups)? A particularly fundamental connection in this vein is the way in which the normativity of practical reasoning and its directiveness towards human well-being and fulfillment explain the normativity and the action-guiding character of law's authority. (Thus we see that while natural-law theory preserves a descriptive characterization of the law, it does not commit the fallacy of explaining prescriptive features by reference to nothing but descriptive features.)

Natural-law theorists join with many self-described legal positivists, such as Herbert Hart and his great student (and my teacher) Joseph Raz in deploying the concept of "law" in a way sufficiently flexible to take into account the differences between the demands of (a) intrasystemic legal analysis or argumentation (for example, in the context of professional legal advocacy or judging); (b) what, following Hart, we might call "descriptive" social theory (for example, "sociology of law"); and (c) fully critical (that is, "normative," "moral," conscience-informing) discourse. Aquinas, for example, made central to his reflections the question whether, and, if so, how and to what extent, do unjust laws bind in conscience those subject to them to obey.[19] It is clear enough that Aquinas believed that human positive law creates a moral duty of obedience even where the conduct it commands (or prohibits) would, in the absence of the law, that is, morally, as a matter of natural law, be optional. This critical-moral belief in the power of positive law to create (or, where moral obligation already exists, reinforce) moral obligation naturally suggests the question whether this power (and the duties that are imposed by its exercise on those subject to it) is absolute or defeasible. If defeasible, under what conditions is it defeated?

To answer this question, it is necessary to press the critical-moral analysis. What is the source of the power in the first place? Plainly it is the capacity of law to serve the cause of justice and the common good by, for example, coordinating behavior to make possible the fuller and/or fairer realization of human goods by the community as a whole. But then, from *the critical-moral viewpoint*, laws that, on account of their injustice, damage, rather than serve, the common good, lack the central justifying quality of law. Their law-creating power—and the duties they purport to impose—are therefore weakened or defeated. Unjust laws are, Aquinas says, "not so much laws as acts of violence."[20] As violations of justice and the common good, they lack the moral force of law; they bind in conscience, if at all, only to the extent that one is under an obligation not to bring about bad side effects that would, in the particular circumstances, likely result from one's defiance of the law (for example, causing "demoralization or disorder,"[21] as by undermining respect for law in a basically just legal system, or unfairly shifting the burdens of a certain unjust law onto the shoulders of innocent fellow citizens).[22] That is to say, unjust laws bind in conscience, if at all, not "*per se*," but only "*per accidens*." They are laws, not "*simpliciter*," or, as we might say, "straightforwardly" or in the "focal" or "paradigmatic" sense, but only in a derivative or secondary sense ("*secundum quid*," that is, in a certain respect but not in all respects).

Nothing in Aquinas's legal theory or in the thought of modern natural-law theorists, such as myself, suggests that the injustice of a law renders it something other than a law (or "legally binding") for purposes of intrasystemic juristic analysis and argumentation. It is true that Aquinas counseled judges, where possible, to interpret and apply laws in such a way as to avoid unjust results where, as best they can tell, the lawmakers did not foresee circumstances in which a strict application of the rule they laid down would result in injustice, and where they would, had they foreseen such circumstances, have crafted the rule differently.[23] But even there he does not appeal to the proposition that the injustice likely to result from an application of the rule strictly according to its terms nullifies those terms from the legal point of view.

Nor does Aquinas say or imply anything that would suggest treating Augustine's comment that "an unjust law seems not to be a law" as relevant to social-theoretical (or historical) investigations of what is (or was) treated as law and legally binding in the legal system of any given culture (however admirable or otherwise from the critical-moral viewpoint). Now Professor Hart was careful never to promote the sort of caricature of natural law one finds in the writings of Kelsen and Holmes. He had a real if qualified respect for the tradition of natural-law theorizing and was, in fact, the person who commissioned for Oxford's Clarendon Law Series the book by John Finnis—*Natural Law and Natural Rights*—that revived interest in natural law among analytic legal philosophers in our time. Still, Hart was among those who misunderstood Aquinas and his stream of the natural-law tradition on precisely this point. He seemed to think that there was something antithetical to the principles of natural-law theory in the "descriptive sociology" of law he proposed in his masterwork *The Concept of Law*.[24] But this is the reverse of the truth. Natural-law theorists need not suppose that Hart erred by treating as laws (and legal systems) various social norms (and social norm-generating institutions) that fulfill the criteria or conditions for legality or legal validity of Hart's concept of law, despite the fact that his social-theoretical enterprise (reasonably!) prescinds to a considerable extent (indeed, it seeks to prescind as far as possible) from critical moral evaluation of laws and legal systems. The criticism Hart's work invites from a natural-law perspective has nothing to do with his willingness to treat unjust laws as laws; it has rather to do with his unwillingness to follow through on the logic of his own method and his insight into the necessity of adopting or reproducing what he calls the *internal* point of view—a viewpoint from which (*pace* Hobbes, Bentham, and Austin) law is understood not as causing human behavior, but as providing people with certain types of reasons for action, what Hart described in chapter 10 of his *Essays on Bentham* as "content-independent peremptory reasons."[25]

Finnis and others have argued that a rigorous following through of Hart's method will extricate legal philosophy from Benthamism altogether by identifying the focal or paradigmatic case of law as just law—law that serves the common good—and the focal or paradigmatic case of the internal (or what Raz calls the "legal") point of view as the viewpoint of someone who understands law and legal systems as valuable to establish and maintain (and legal rules as ordinarily binding in conscience) insofar as they are just—and, qua just, fulfill what natural-law theorists contend is the justifying moral-critical point of law and legal systems, namely, to serve the common good.[26]

CHAPTER FIVE

The Natural-Law Foundations of Medical Law
with Christopher O. Tollefsen

Natural-law theorists hold that the foundations of morality are in the well-being and fulfilment of human persons, individually and in the communities they form. When natural-law theorists turn, therefore, to questions of medical practice and medical law, they seek to reveal the foundations of that practice and law precisely in prescriptions about well-being and human fulfilment, for both individuals and their communities. The effort is normative: No practice, and no body of law, is entirely as it should be. But the effort is also explanatory, demonstrating that certain features of law and practice are as they are, or were as they were, because of the insights into human well-being and fulfilment that explicitly or implicitly guided the development of medicine and medical law, and the moral principles specifying its integral directiveness.

This chapter seeks to identify: first, the basic human goods that are the foundational principles of the natural law; second, a derived set of moral norms that emerge from consideration of the integral directiveness or prescriptivity of those foundational principles; and third, the implications of these norms for medical practice and medical law, specifically as regards four questions. First, how should medical practice and medical law be structured with respect to the intentional taking of human life by members of the medical profession? As we will see, a sound answer to this question requires consideration of the so-called Principle of Double Effect. Second, who, in the clinical setting, has authority for medical decision-making, and what standards should guide their decisions? Third, what standards should govern the distribution of health-care resources in society, and do those standards give reasons for thinking, from the natural-law standpoint, that there is a "right to health care"? Fourth, what concern should be shown in medical practice and medical law for the rights of "physician conscience"?

FOUNDATIONS OF THE NATURAL LAW

To reiterate: The foundations of the natural law are basic goods that are constitutive aspects of the well-being and fulfilment of human persons, individually and in community, and specifically the principles that direct human persons to realize or participate in those goods—goods that are intrinsically as well as instrumentally constitutive of the well-being of human persons. In being constitutive of our fulfilment as human persons, those principles provide more-than-merely-instrumental reasons for actions:[1] They are indeed principles of human reason. It is because reason is "natural" to human persons—human beings are beings whose nature is a rational nature—that the principles of human reason may be called principles or precepts of "natural" law. (It is not, as is often wrongly supposed, because of any presumed "derivation" of the moral "ought" from the "is" of nature.) Moreover, these principles of human reason are prescriptive: They emerge from reason when it is functioning practically, namely, in a mode that is directive towards human action; they are principles of practical reason.[2] Thus, the most basic principles of natural law direct us (by appealing to our intellects and not merely to sentient aspects of our selves) towards basic human goods, the variegated aspects of human well-being that provide our most fundamental reasons for action.

Basic human goods include human life and health, which are, of course, the most important of human goods for our topic. Threats to, or compromises of, these goods bring medical professionals and patients together in an effort to stave off disease, disability, and death. Few would deny that human life and health are good in some sense, but most natural-law theorists agree further that this complex and multifaceted good is basic and intrinsic, rather than merely instrumental. Theories that deny this are committed to some form of self-body dualism, a separation of the human "person" (considered as the psyche, mind, or spirit) from the human animal (the biological organism). According to natural-law theorists, however, that animal organism is the person (though it is not all that there is to the person) and not merely a vehicle in which the person rides or an extrinsic instrument of the person considered as the conscious and desiring aspect of the self.[3]

Life and health are not the only basic human goods, and this claim too will be shown to be important in the context of medicine and medical practice. The other constitutive aspects of human fulfilment include knowledge, aesthetic experience, work and play (as skillful performances), friendship, marriage, integrity, and religion (understood as the quest for harmony with the ultimate source or sources of meaning and value). Each such good provides its own distinct category of opportunity for human fulfilment, distinct from and incommensurable with the others. There is no natural hierarchy of goods of a sort that would require one kind of good always to give way before another.

Similarly, the options for morally significant choosing provided by the basic human goods are also incommensurable. Thus options may not be measured by a common standard of goodness so as to find the "greatest good" (or "greatest good of the greatest number", or "net best proportion of benefit to harm overall and in the long run"). Options may be generated by different basic goods, such as the choice to become a doctor or a philosopher or professional athlete or rabbi or insurance salesman, or by the same good, such as the choice between pursuing a medical intervention promising greater mobility, but with an increased risk of mortality, or an increased life expectancy, but with diminished mobility.

Were such options fully commensurable in terms of their goodness, as the utilitarian claims, no choice would be needed, or even possible: the agent would select what offered the greatest good. Any other selection would be irrational, unthinkable. So where there is full commensurability, there are not, in fact, genuine options. But when the options are genuine, each option offers benefits, and typically burdens, different from the competing options; thus a choice is necessary, and something will be lost or forgone in the option passed over; the option chosen will not have in it everything of value available in the alternative option plus some more.

How can a choice between incommensurable options be guided if not by a consideration of which option promises the greatest good? A key claim of the tradition of natural-law thought is that the standard for upright choice in natural law is provided by right reason. And reason, faced with a multiplicity of incommensurable goods, directs rightly when it directs integrally, that is, in a way that is open to the fullness of all the goods for all the persons for whom they are good, and is not deflected by sub-rational factors, such as emotions or other preferences that are not themselves guided by reason.[4] The first (in the sense of most abstract) principle of morality may thus be articulated as, "Always will and choose in ways that are compatible with a will to integral human fulfillment." The immediate implications of this principle will be the subject of the next section of this chapter; we then turn to the further implications for medical practice and law.

INTERMEDIATE PRINCIPLES OF MORALITY

In this section, we identify three norms that are implications of the first principle of morality and that, as we will show below, are of central importance to medical morality and law.[5] These norms concern the intentional destruction of basic goods, the need for fairness between persons, and the necessity of accepting one's personal vocation. These norms are essential for addressing the morality of abortion, physician-assisted suicide, and euthanasia; the location of the decision-making authority in the clinical setting; the right to health care; and, ultimately, the role of physician conscience in medicine.

No Intentional Damage or Destruction of Basic Goods

The first norm bears upon unreasonable damage or destruction of basic human goods. This occurs when we act directly against one good for the sake of another: for example, we deliberately inflict harm on one person for the sake of benefiting another, or damage one instance of a basic good for the sake of another. Such action could only be fully reasonable, and compatible with a will to integral human fulfilment, if goods and good options were in fact commensurable and therefore "weighable" for purposes of comparing value. It would make sense to harm or destroy this instance of a basic good—this person's life, say—for the sake of some other good only if that other good were a greater good.

Yet, as we have seen, the notion of "greater good" is out of place in speaking of basic goods. And so a norm that emerges from consideration of the rational requirement of openness to (in the sense of having a will favorably disposed to) all the basic aspects of human well-being and fulfilment (the human good integrally conceived) is this: Never directly damage or destroy one instance of a basic good for the sake of some other or putatively "greater" good; such choices can never be fully reasonable, or in line with full openness to basic goods and persons. Of course, one would also be unreasonable in choosing directly to damage or destroy an instance of a basic good out of hostility. So the norm can be expanded: Never directly damage or destroy an instance of a basic good.

This norm clearly has implications for questions of killing, since killing clearly damages, and indeed destroys, an instance of the basic good of human life. Thus, the norm rules out direct killing. What is the sense of "direct" in this norm? The natural-law tradition converges on the claim that the form of damage that is never permissible is intended damage: damage pursued as a means or as an end. It is thus not the case that every form of damage to a basic good that would be impermissible if intended would be impermissible if brought about as a side effect (though, similarly, not every form of damage that is not intended is therefore permissible). We will return to this point in our discussion of Double Effect. Distinguishing between intended killing and death accepted as a side effect will be important for the discussion of abortion, assisted suicide and euthanasia, and the refusal of medical interventions.

Fairness and the Golden Rule

A second norm that is implied by the first principle of morality relates to fairness and the so-called Golden Rule. Consider the way our lives are shaped by particular attachments to those near to us, like us, or in some other way specially connected to us. This can be entirely reasonable: We are attached to our children or spouse, or parents; we have neighborhood, religious, cultural, or national attachments as well. These are important, and can play a significant role in our moral deliberations. But sometimes we privilege such persons (or ourselves) in ways that are arbitrary and unfair. We are deflected from full practical reasonableness by emotions that are not guided by reason. We allow our child to take a greater share of some common stock than the other children simply because she is ours, for example. How can we test for this kind of arbitrary privileging of what is near and dear to us? One traditional test for such arbitrary privileging of persons is the Golden Rule, which in a negative formulation says: Do not do to others as you would not have them do to you.

Thus, when our privileging of some comes at the expense of others in such a way that we would reasonably object to such privileging were we on the receiving end, then we have reason to think that our privileging is unreasonable, arbitrary, unfair. So a norm of fairness emerges from the requirements of reason integrally considering all the goods for all persons: We should never let mere emotion blind us to the goodness of the goods for others in ways that unfairly benefit some and harm others.

Parents who help their children cheat to get ahead in school, for example, act unfairly as regards other people's children.

There are times when our commitments do require that we give some people special treatment: Physicians' commitments to their patients, for example, entitle them to carve out a special space in their lives for those patients and their needs. But this is clearly fair: Everyone has reason to accept special commitments like this, for without them, there could be no medical profession, no doctor-patient relationships, none of the benefits that come from a doctor's special knowledge and even friendship with his or her patients. So, while the doctor gives privileged treatment to her patients, that treatment is not for that reason unfair.

Although not the whole of justice, which involves what is owed to others, fairness is a necessary condition for ensuring justice within any community. A community, for our purposes, involves persons engaged in cooperative and shared action for the sake of some common good or goods.[6] In natural-law thought, the concept of "common good" is far ranging; in its most generic use, it simply refers to any good which is the object of a shared pursuit among multiple persons. But in different communities, the common good is specified in more determinate ways. For doctors and patients, the common good is the patient's health; for families, it is the overall welfare of the family members individually and as a unit; for a political society, it is the totality of conditions necessary for citizens to pursue upright and flourishing lives, individually and in community (communities) with one another. Fairness ought normatively to structure all of these cooperative pursuits so that the distribution of benefits and burdens, understood ultimately by reference to the basic human goods, does not arbitrarily favor some at the expense of others. Failures in this respect will result in injustices in the relevant communities; success will protect opportunities for genuine human flourishing. The norm of fairness will be essential to the discussion of beginning- and end-of-life ethics below (much, though not all, killing is unfair) and to the discussion of the right to health care in a political community.

Vocation

The third norm implied by the first principle of morality relates to the idea of vocation. It is clear that a person's life must be ordered in his or her pursuit of human goods. A life in which goods are pursued in a merely serial or unreflective manner, without prudent discernment and organization or structure, would inevitably be both shallow and chaotic in ways detrimental to human flourishing. Consider, for example, the following sorts of difficulties.

First, such a life would and could involve no true achievement of excellence at anything: no excellence of scholarship, medicine, or virtue. Second, such a life could involve no commitments to other persons; life in community, even the simplest community of friendship, is impossible if it is not deliberately ordered towards the goods of others and towards cooperation with those others. And third, such a life would be chaotic; life without an overarching ordering structure would easily lead to conflict when the demands of one desired good conflicted with the demands of another.

Accordingly, human persons require something like a rational life plan if our actions and lives are to be reasonably oriented to goods and persons. This line of thought, congenial to many outside the natural-law tradition, such as John Rawls, is enhanced within the natural-law tradition by reflection on the relationship between the natural law and God's eternal law, which, inter alia, directs human persons to their good for their own sake, while orienting and ordering their actions for the service of others and God. God is the source of all order, not just in general, but for each particular person. Thus, human beings naturally and reasonably seek to identify the upright, virtuous, and flourishing lives to which they have been called by God. This calling is their personal vocation, and natural-law reflection encourages each person to consider his or her life vocationally. Persons must ask to what they are being called, and how they may respond to that call in such a way as to cooperate with the Divine One who is calling. Responding to this invitation to cooperate in one's vocation is understood by many people as a central feature of their pursuit of the good of religion, and likewise as essential to the good of personal integrity. We will see later the implications of this for questions of physician conscience. The idea of personal vocation is also important for understanding the nature and limits of patient decision-making authority, which we will discuss below.[7]

MEDICAL PRACTICE AND LAW: KILLING AT THE BEGINNING AND END OF LIFE

We now turn to four disputed areas of medical practice and medical law. For a considerable period in the history of the West, natural-law reflections such as those we will provide guided both medical practice and law, even if at times only implicitly or inchoately and imperfectly. Of late, by contrast, there is strong and often explicit opposition to the principles, norms, and conclusions we will discuss. This is especially evident where questions at the beginning and end of human life are concerned.

Should physicians ever be engaged in the intentional taking of life, whether at its beginning or at its end? Widespread toleration of the practice of abortion suggests an affirmative answer as regards the beginning of life; rapidly increasing toleration of the practice of assisted suicide and voluntary euthanasia suggests a similarly affirmative answer at the end of life. The natural-law tradition, by contrast, offers negative answers in both cases.

Abortion

Natural-law thought approaches the question of abortion from a moral, a medical-professional, and a political-legal standpoint. The three-fold approach is necessary: For example, to demonstrate that a practice ought to be prohibited by law, it is not sufficient (though it is usually necessary) to show that the practice is morally impermissible. It is additionally necessary to show that the wrong in question is, or threatens, a serious wrong against persons, and is thus unjust, and that a restrictive, rather than a permissive, legal regime is a more reasonable way to prevent and educate about the wrong. Professional practice also might be more or less concordant with the demands of law and morality. Here it is necessary to show that the human goods served by the practice will be best served by considerations that are essentially moral, and not merely legal. Thus, that abortion or euthanasia (or capital punishment) is permitted at law may not be sufficient to show that these practices are compatible with medicine's vocational commitments.

As regards the moral question of abortion, natural-law theory offers the following considerations in defense of the inviolability of human life—that is, for the clam that it is not to be violated, damaged, or destroyed intentionally (whether as an end-in-itself or as a means to some other end).[8]

What is the nature of the being whose life is ended in abortion? Is it a living human being, or is it some living thing which is not (or not yet) a human being, something perhaps merely in transit towards being human?[9] Natural-law thinkers urge that the question must be addressed by the most up-to-date science, notably embryology and developmental biology. That science does indicate the nature of the being whose life is ended in abortion: The entity destroyed in abortion is a human being, a living member of the species *Homo sapiens*, genetically and functionally distinct from his or her biological parents, and possessed of the genetic and epigenetic primordia necessary to be the agent of his or her own growth and development to the next stage(s) of human life. Apart from disagreements about the very earliest stages of human life, when the human embryo is capable of twinning, most philosophers and virtually all human embryologists recognize that the early embryo is an identifiable human being.[10]

Moreover, even objections concerning the earliest stages of human life are weak; that the very early embryo is capable of dividing into twins (or perhaps budding to generate a second embryo) hardly shows that the embryo which does not twin, or even the embryo that will twin, is not a single unified whole organism. Individual organisms such as single-celled amoebae or multi-celled flatworms can be capable of division without this in any way jeopardizing their organic unity and determinateness. Thus, the possibility of twinning gives us no reason to doubt the unity and determinateness of the embryo.[11]

The answer to the question on the nature of the being whose life is ended in abortion is this: The unborn entities destroyed in abortion are human beings. Should the norm against intentional damage to a basic good—human life—be considered applicable where unborn human beings are concerned? Unborn human beings are human beings, precisely the class of beings for whom basic human goods are good. There are compelling reasons to protect the goods of life and health in and for all human beings, including unborn human beings. So the norm against intentional damage to a human life is applicable to unborn human beings, too.

Moreover, every attempt to deny basic moral protections to all human beings inevitably relies upon a contingently (and ultimately arbitrarily) drawn boundary between some human beings and others: that these human beings have achieved consciousness, or can now reason, or engage in self-conscious thought, for example, while those cannot. None of these boundaries divides one essential kind of thing from another, but the boundaries dividing what are human beings from what are not do divide entities in a morally non-arbitrary way. What is the source of the inviolability of human persons? Human beings are thought to be worthy of respect, and thus entitled to immunity from intentional killing, enslavement, torture, and the like, because of their intrinsic dignity: because they are persons, possessed of the capacities for freedom and reason. But those capacities are possessed in root, or radical form, by every member of the species, including human beings at the zygotic and fetal stages. Thus, those very young members of the species *Homo sapiens* are also possessed of human dignity, and are persons from the moment of fertilization, and they share with all other members of the species the grounds for said inviolability.

Is abortion intentional killing? The answer requires some nuance. Most abortion is surely intentional killing: whenever motivated by the desire "not to be a mother", for example, a desire that is satisfied only by the destruction of the entity whose existence makes one a mother. Judith Jarvis Thomson has argued, in effect, that some abortions might only include an intention to expel, which she believes is justified in the absence of a special duty to provide aid.[12] Natural-law thinkers have argued extensively against Thomson that there are natural obligations, some based in biological-familial relatedness, which mothers owe to their unborn children, and that the choice to expel in the absence of very serious reasons, such as the need to save the mother's life, is inevitably unfair and thus unjust.[13] A reasonable natural-law position on abortion would first identify abortion as the intentional or unjust expelling—namely, killing—of an unborn human being, and then conclude that abortion as so defined is always morally impermissible.[14]

Should medical practice allow the killing of unborn human beings, in spite of the moral impermissibility of such killing? It should not. Any upright practice, and thus any profession established on the basis of an upright practice, is constituted by its orientation to some basic good or goods. Practices are professionalized when there are good reasons to ensure widespread distribution of the benefits of the practice, to ensure that appropriate standards of education and behavior are transmitted to all practitioners, and to provide the external goods necessary for the practice to flourish. Medical practice is fundamentally guided by a vocational commitment to human life and health; as such, it would be contradictory and disastrous for the profession were its practitioners to include the privation of this good as among their purposes. Abortion as defined above (that is, as the intentional or unjust killing of an unborn human being) seems entirely contrary to the appropriate professional ethos of physicians, who are committed to healing, rather than killing. This recognition was crucial to the physicians' movement of the nineteenth century to eradicate abortion.[15]

Should medical law also hew closely to the moral judgment that abortion is always an offence against an innocent human life? It should;

abortion is not only contrary to the good of life, but an offence against that good in particular persons, without—ever—their consent. Abortion is thus always unjust, and is concerned with a grave violation of a basic good (that is, human life); it is precisely the sort of matter over which legal guidance is necessary. For the law even to remain "neutral" on this matter is for the law to permit attacks on innocent human life. This does not mean that natural lawyers favor criminal sanctions against women who seek or obtain abortions. Recognizing in some cases diminished responsibility, and other mitigating factors, natural lawyers generally recommend that it be illegal for doctors or others to perform abortions; criminal or regulatory penalties should thus fall on those who carry out, rather than those who undergo, abortions.[16]

Physician-Assisted Suicide and Euthanasia

When we turn to the question of so-called "medical assistance in dying," the situation is somewhat more complicated. Here, the most plausible proposals to allow, or perhaps require, physicians to aid their patients in ending their lives require that those patients give their informed consent in the form of a request; these proposals also argue that patients be assisted in ending their lives as a way to forestall or end human suffering. So there are significant differences from the abortion case: Unlike in abortion, the one killed, or helped to kill him- or herself, consents; and the killing is done for the benefit of the one killed.

Natural law's assessment of assistance in self-killing starts from a moral standpoint, and here the judgment is straightforward. If every intentional killing of an innocent life is morally impermissible, then so is self-killing, assisting in self-killing, and killing at the request of another.[17] It is true that the natural-law tradition has held, going back to Aristotle, that it is impossible for a man to do injustice to himself, or to suffer injustice willingly.[18] So self-killing, or assistance in self-killing, might not be unjust towards the one killed. But not every moral wrong is an injustice, and the moral demands of the natural-law prescription against intentional killing go beyond the demands of justice.

Should the medical profession take this moral standard as its own? Where abortion was concerned, the answer seemed straightforward: Killing is contrary to the medical profession's ethos of healing. That judgment may seem complicated in the case of euthanasia and assisted suicide by the presence of consent and suffering; doctors are to honor patient consent; and they are thought by many to have the relief of suffering as among their primary purposes. But proposals for a "right" to physician assistance in dying do not ask physicians to honor consent, but go beyond that in requiring physicians to acquiesce in all patient demands. And suffering, unlike disease or impairment, is in part a function of a patient's awareness of and response to the deficiencies in her own life and health. While the physician's task is surely to respond to some of those deficiencies, when possible, it is not clear that the good physician is charged with ending patient suffering at all costs, including where the means of achieving that goal is killing the patient or helping the patient to kill himself.

There are additional reasons for resisting the turn to physician assistance in dying, and some of these considerations will carry over to the discussion of medical law as well. Medical professionals—especially, but not only, those who care for patients at the end of life—are charged with caring for persons who are in a radically dependent and vulnerable state. The vulnerability of the patient requires a professional ethos that cultivates trustworthy physicians, and makes possible reasonable trust by patients. It is difficult to see how the necessary trust can be maintained, however, when doctors constitute an exception to the general and indefeasible norm against intentional killing of innocent human beings. Rather than knowing and trusting that a physician will never abandon the patient in her vulnerability, the patient will know that killing (that is, the taking of her life in her vulnerability) is always an option. The nature of the doctor-patient relationship will fundamentally change, and medical professionals are right to worry about this.[19]

The revision to the exception against the intentional killing of an innocent will require great care on the part of the medical profession to produce and enforce protocols to ensure that persons will not be killed against their will, or coerced, even subtly, to end their lives; moreover, these same protocols must ensure that the will of the patient requesting death should not be compromised by depression or other psychological impairment. These are all issues of justice, of what is owed to others, and the introduction of a practice of assisted death into the medical profession threatens pervasive injustice to those who are poor, depressed, or at the mercy of uncharitable (or greedy, or impatient) family members or others if exacting protocols are not developed and then rigorously enforced.[20]

Even many medical professionals not committed to the inviolability of human life as are natural-law theorists nonetheless have recognized the undesirability and perhaps impossibility of the medical profession developing protocols of this sort. They are further concerned that the availability of assisted death will detract from the efforts and resources necessary to care for dying patients. Thus, Ezekiel Emanuel writes, "Instead of attempting to legalize physician-assisted suicide, we should focus our energies on what really matters: improving care for the dying—ensuring that all patients can openly talk with their physicians and families about their wishes and have access to high-quality palliative or hospice care before they suffer needless medical procedures. The appeal of physician-assisted suicide is based on a fantasy."[21]

There is an additional difficulty. Two main justifications are typically given, as noted above, for a right to assistance in dying: that consent has been given autonomously, and that the patient is suffering. Both justifications, if followed to their logical conclusions, justify far more, however, than a right to assistance in dying for those who are dying. Rather, both autonomy and suffering seem capable of justifying a right to die, and to receive assistance in dying, for many non-terminal patients, who might nevertheless be suffering greatly, and autonomously desire death. Such patients might include those whose suffering is existential or moral (for example, an alcoholic who cannot quit the bottle), or whose "life narratives" lead them to desire an entirely controlled resolution to their story at the time of their choosing.[22]

For all these reasons, medicine should not admit the practice of assisted dying into its practice. But for the same reasons, neither should the law contemplate such. Recall that the common good of political society is the totality of conditions necessary for citizens to pursue upright and flourishing lives, individually, and in community (or communities) with one another. Those conditions include, preeminently—and thus a central task of the law is establishing and maintaining—just social conditions between citizens. But justice for the most vulnerable is threatened by a regime of assisted death. Moreover, the practice of assisted death threatens to erode the possibilities for upright self-constitution for members of the medical community, by encouraging them to abandon their commitment to heal and never to harm. The general and stringent legal restriction against intentional killing of the innocent should thus not be loosened for doctors treating patients at the end of life.[23]

Double Effect

An objection raised to those who oppose assistance in dying, however, leads to important further issues. How is it possible to refuse a permission on self-killing and assistance in self-killing, yet countenance current medical practice and law as regards refusal or withdrawal of forms of life-sustaining or life-saving treatment? Patients who refuse consent are not treated against their will, and some die as a result of their refusal. Similarly, life-sustaining technologies are withdrawn from some patients at the end of life, with death as the consequence. What principled line can be drawn between these practices and the practice of assisted death?

In this section of the chapter, we address the question of the principled distinction, which hinges on the notion of intention; in the next section, we address the related question of patient autonomy and patient authority.

The natural-law tradition is distinguished from a variety of approaches to ethics by its claim that there are some acts that are never to be done. Norms concerned with such acts may be called "moral absolutes": they do not mandate a single course of action for all agents in all circumstances; rather, they identify an action type which is never to be engaged in by an agent.[24] Such absolutes most typically flow from the general norm identified above: that basic goods are never to be directly (that is, intentionally—as an end or means) damaged or destroyed, whether out of hostility, or for the sake of some further good. Recall how that norm makes sense, given the incommensurability of the basic goods and the options for morally significant choosing generated by those goods.

That norm is clearly violated in suicide or euthanasia, for in both death is brought about as a means to a further benefit, such as the relief of suffering. Consider, by contrast, a case in which treatment options are framed as packages in which one set of health benefits is linked to a set of health burdens and compared to a different set of health benefits linked to another set of health burdens. The options are exclusive. So, for example, if one chooses the chemotherapy course in response to one's cancer, one may experience an increase in life expectancy, but accompanied by significant health burdens. Those burdens—nausea, hair loss, fatigue, sores, blood disorders, and others—are side effects: They are not, obviously, pursued as an end of the medical treatment; but neither are they chosen as a means to the desired health outcome—increased life expectancy. They are thus not intended. But similarly, if one refuses the chemotherapy because one desires to avoid the health burdens associated with that treatment, and thus to live one's fewer remaining days in a less health-compromised state, then one likewise does not intend the shortening of one's life. It too is a side effect of the choice to avoid burdens.

But it is thus clear that whatever choice one makes (for the chemotherapy or to refuse it) will have negative consequences for the goods of life and health: Such negative consequences are unavoidable and foreseeable. So the absolute norm against intentional damage or destruction to a basic good cannot be extended to include damage or destruction that occurs as a side effect (that is, an unavoidable, yet foreseeable, negative consequence). That is, there can be no norm of the form "You ought never to cause harm as a side effect," for ought implies can, and it is impossible always to avoid causing harm as a side effect.[25]

Thus there has emerged, in the course of the natural-law tradition, the Principle of Double Effect.[26] Put simply, an effect that would always be wrong to intend (for example, harming the basic goods of life and health) can sometimes (though not always; more on that in a moment) be permissible if brought about as a side effect and if there is a proportionate reason for permitting it. More traditional formulations articulate four parts to the rule: that the act be permissible in itself; that the evil effect not be intended; that the good effect not come about through the evil effect; and that there be a proportionate reason for accepting the bad effect in pursuit of the good.[27]

What is a proportionate reason? One answer can be given by returning to the case of abortion. In cases of vital conflict, where both the mother's and the child's life are at stake, natural-law theorists have considered it permissible to remove the child (for example, in a hysterectomy of a cancerous uterus) to save the mother. The child's death is not intended: It is neither an end nor a means. It is rather an accepted side effect. That side effect is considered proportionate because it is fair: It passes the test of the Golden Rule. By contrast, even if we assume, with Judith Jarvis Thomson, that there exist abortions that are merely expellings, with death as a side effect, that side effect will typically be disproportionate—unfair—if done for reasons less grave than preservation of the mother's life.

An account must likewise be given in end-of-life cases of the norms governing proportionate acceptance of bad, including lethal, side effects when life-sustaining or saving treatment is refused; we will provide that account in the next section of this chapter. Here, it is important to note that the distinction between what is intended and what is a side effect is one with important legal weight. U.S. Supreme Court Chief Justice William Rehnquist in *Vacco v Quill*, a case in which a right to assistance in death was claimed, detailed the importance that the distinction between intending death and permitting death as a side effect has had in a long line of precedents, and concluded that while a right to refuse treatment was constitutionally well-grounded, no such claim could be made for a right to hasten or bring about death.

Of course, some patients do refuse treatment in order to die; their refusals are, strictly speaking, suicidal. But, in general, the law correctly grants the right to refuse treatment to patients in order to protect them from unwanted interventions, with the side effect that this right might be abused; and the law straightforwardly prohibits the always impermissible act of intentionally taking life. The erosion of the distinction between intending and hastening death, on the one hand, and accepting death as a side effect, on the other, in recent law governing assistance in dying, as in Canada, some jurisdictions in the United States, and several European countries, obscures what the Rehnquist court, in its unanimous decision in *Quill*, saw clearly: While a right to refuse treatment is constitutionally well-grounded, no such claim could be made for a right to hasten or bring about death; this is a key moral distinction.[28]

Authority in Health Care

We can say something more about the justification for the patient's right to refuse treatment, and indeed this is necessary in order to stave off a line of argument for assisted death that begins from false claims about the patient's autonomy. Patients are granted, in law, a broad right of refusal of medical treatment, even when the consequences for the patient are lethal, and even when the motivations of the patient are obscure to many. Thus, Jehovah's Witnesses are not to be given blood transfusions against their will, even when the transfusion is necessary to save their life, and when it seems obvious to all non-Witnesses that the transfusion is reasonable and right.

Typically, bioethicists see the importance of consent as rooted in the value of autonomy: To act contrary to a patient's wishes is to violate that autonomy, and to fail to respect the patient as a person.[29] And many bioethicists track the rise of their discipline to the rise of awareness of the importance of autonomy by contrast to an era in which physicians are thought to have exercised an overly paternalistic approach to patients, failing to provide them with adequate information and treating them for their own good without seeking consent.[30] The extent to which this description accurately characterizes medicine prior to the second half of the twentieth century need not concern us here; what is important is that "respect for autonomy" has increasingly become the source not just of negative side constraints—do not treat without informed consent—but also of positive obligations: Do what the patient autonomously requests, provided that it is legal. We will return to this in our discussion of physician conscience in the final section of this chapter. For now, we will provide an alternative account of the side constraint on treating patients without consent.

The alternative account focuses less on patient autonomy than on patient authority. Medical decisions, like many other decisions, are made in a social space; in the case of medical decisions social space includes the patient, the patient's family and friends, the medical professionals involved, and often others (for example, institutional decision-makers, insurance providers, clergy). But all decisions involving more than one party face a similar problem: Given that the various persons involved will have different reasons for acting, and different conceptions of the reasons available to be acted on, how is a final decision to be reached?

There are, as John Finnis has argued, only two possible ways when it comes to the decision-making process: Either there must be unanimity, or authority.[31] There are no further options, for every way of making a decision short of unanimity involves some form of authority. Even a vote in which the majority wins substitutes the authority of the majority for the decision of all. It is not a third way. So, who is to have authority in the context of medical decision-making?

With rare exceptions, the authority is to be exercised by the patient. The reason for this can be seen by recalling that the goods of human life are variegated, whereas the goods of medicine are, for the most part, singular (though complex). Medicine is concerned for human life and health, and physicians have expertise precisely with regard to techniques, medicines, and other interventions that offer health-related benefits. But life and health are not the only goods for patients. Rather, the chief good for patients in some particular decision is usually a function of their commitments, obligations, and circumstances as regards a number of goods, and how those goods are ordered in the patients' lives with their families, communities, and neighbors. That ordering with regard to goods and persons, brought about by the agent's commitments, is itself the patient's life plan, or personal vocation. And this provides the rational standard by which the variety of options presented by the physician, in light of the physician's health-care expertise, are to be evaluated: which option fits best (and is otherwise morally reasonable) with the patient's overall vocation, with the ordering of his or her life as regards goods and persons.

A competent patient is clearly the person best placed to make that assessment. The idea of personal vocation thus plays two roles here: (a) it provides the justification for patient authority, an authority that is to be honored by the medical profession and protected legally; and (b) it provides the standard for patients themselves to bring to bear on their health-care choices. In those choices, each option will bring about competing sets of benefits and burdens that are incommensurable with one another; there can, therefore, be no "weighing up" to see which option is "the best." Yet the natural-law tradition has embraced the idea that burdens may be rejected, and benefits foregone, if those burdens are not "proportionate" to the promised benefits. The idea of patient vocation provides an interpretation for this claim: If it is unreasonable, in light of one's vocation, to accept some burden in the pursuit of the promised benefit, then that burden is not proportionate. If it is reasonable, in light of one's vocation, to accept some burden, then that burden is proportionate.[32] Thus, for example, a treatment option might be judged to be not proportionate if it offered some chance of extended life at the cost of rendering a patient unable to fulfil his or her familial responsibilities. It is important to note, of course, that when such a patient refuses a life-extending intervention, the shortening of life is not intended, but a reasonably accepted side effect.

This conception of patient authority overlaps considerably, but not entirely, with the notion of patient autonomy. The overlap extends to converging claims on both accounts that competent patients have a nearly absolute veto on proposed medical interventions. But it differs in at least the following two ways. First, it is commonplace that authority is always limited, and a patient's decision-making authority is likewise limited: It is primarily an authority to accept some offers made by physicians and to reject others. It is not of itself an authority to demand some particular intervention independently of the physician's best medical judgment. The idea of patient authority thus does not bring with it an internal nisus towards the idea of a patient entitlement to, for example, assistance in ending her life.

A second difference is this: Autonomous acts increasingly are thought to be self-ratifying; if the decision is autonomously made, then it is correct. But a decision may be legitimately authoritative, while also being wrong. Authority can be exercised legitimately, but foolishly, and even immorally, without eroding the reasons those under authority have for obedience. Thus, patients can and sometimes will make imprudent and even immoral choices to refuse care; that the decisions are their own does not render these decisions correct. But that the patient has authority does create a strong, though sometimes defeasible, obligation on the part of physicians and others to honor the patient's exercise of authority. The law, again, rightly recognizes this, and does not require physicians or others to subject a patient's refusals to a judgment of overall moral propriety in order to comply.

ALLOCATION OF RESOURCES AND THE RIGHT TO HEALTH CARE

We turn now to a rather different domain of medical law and public policy—that concerned with the allocation of health-care resources—and to the question of whether persons may be said to have a right to health care. Whereas questions concerning the refusal or withdrawal of medical care, particularly, though not exclusively, at the end of life, are questions that require essentially personal considerations, such as considerations of personal vocation, questions of the political distribution of resources and establishment of political or legal entitlements require more impersonal considerations, and are governed especially by norms of fairness.

The questions of this section are complicated and controversial, even among natural-law thinkers, to a much greater extent than any of the other issues addressed in this chapter. Nevertheless, natural-law thinkers in general start from a shared set of claims, which we will articulate here; working out the implications of these claims is beyond the scope of this chapter.

The foundational claims concern the natural-law justification for private property; the nature of interpersonal obligations of charity;[33] and the nature and role of political authority. As regards the natural-law approach to private property, theorists recognize a "natural" but not original right to private property. The goods of the world do not come with particular persons' names affixed to them, nor are they collectively owned. But ownership of the world's goods is a reasonable way of dividing up and caring for those resources which by their nature exist, all of them, for the benefit of all human persons. Private ownership is thought to foster the common good for a number of pragmatic reasons, such as facilitating the development and use of resources in ways that advance the common good, and avoiding quarrels; and because it promises greater personal discretion in the discerning and carrying out of individuals' personal vocations.[34]

Nevertheless, most natural-law thinkers hold with St. Thomas, and contrary to, for example, certain libertarians, that the "universal destination of the world's goods" remains a limiting principle on the authority that individuals have over their property. That which is not used for grave needs, of the person and those to whom he or she owes duties of care, and for the carrying out of personal vocation, is considered superflua, and is owed to those in need.[35] Of course, making decisions as to how to meet those needs with one's superflua is itself a self-constituting act and part of many persons' personal vocations, so there is value in persons making those decisions for themselves.

Under certain conditions, however, thinkers in the natural-law tradition have held that political authority may be permitted or required to ensure that the grave needs of some are met, and that the significant obligations of charity of those with superflua are not left unfulfilled.[36] The role of the state is, again, to ensure that the totality of conditions necessary for citizens to pursue upright and flourishing lives, individually and in community (or communities) with one another, is satisfied; this set of conditions is the political common good. It is also the source of political authority, for that authority is necessary and hence justified to ensure the successful realization of those conditions for flourishing that individuals and the many forms of civil society are incapable of providing for themselves.

Thus, where grave individual needs will go unmet despite individual and societal initiatives, and resources exist to meet those needs, then the state can, and sometimes ought to, ensure that those needs are in fact met. Indeed, even where needs can be met without the exercise of political authority, if those needs can be met more successfully or efficiently with the aid of political authority, then again, the exercise of that authority is called for. (By the same token, when those needs may be more efficiently met without the use of that authority, they should be.) So certain welfare rights or entitlements will be justified if (a) there are grave unmet needs; (b) there are adequate resources for meeting those needs; (c) the state can more efficiently help ensure those needs are met than can other agents; and (d) it can do so without seriously eroding the capacity of those with resources from being self-constituting agents, and without doing other harms.

One important feature of health care suggests that political authority in developed nations can and will need to be exercised with regard to its distribution.[37] This is the already deeply social nature of health care. Health-care services in developed nations are distributed across many agents, including patients, physicians, nurses, administrators, and others, and across many institutions, such as physician practices and networks, hospitals, drug companies, insurance companies, and others. This situation marks a significant change from health care in times past. Is it the case that such a widely distributed set of agents, practices, technologies, and institutions, with their competing interests, problems, and challenges, will be adequately efficient, upright, and cooperative to ensure that health care is fairly provided, paid for, and consumed? It seems unlikely.

Accordingly, at a minimum, political authority seems needed for regulatory and coordination purposes. Without such regulation and coordination, or with only poor regulation and coordination, access to health care is likely to be impaired for some persons, and this is an injustice.[38]

A second feature of health care is also relevant: All persons have an abiding and significant need for health care, yet not all will be adequately cared for in the absence of political authority, and not merely because some agents default on their responsibilities. Rather, as the cost of health care and health technology rises, it is increasingly difficult or impossible for the health-care needs of the poor to be met using their own resources, or to be met by charitable individuals or organizations, without assistance by the state (though it is desirable, to the extent possible, to rely on institutions of civil society rather than on the state). So not only must the state engage in some regulation of health care to ensure fairness, it must also create and maintain some political entitlements to health care for those unable to provide it for themselves.

It is in light of these considerations that a "right to health care" must be understood: That right will pertain in the minimum case to individuals who are unable to provide adequate health care for themselves, living in societies and states sufficiently developed that they can effectively provide, or coordinate the provision of, health care to those individuals. In any given society, however, this right must then be much more concretely specified than we have done here: Who precisely has that right; what precisely are they entitled to; how precisely are those entitlements to be funded and delivered; and so on.[39]

How far beyond this minimum does natural law carry us? That is a matter of controversy. Some, sensitive to natural law's demand that citizens not be taxed beyond their power to exercise their own self-determination and fulfil their obligations of charity themselves, advocate lesser state involvement, and perhaps more market-based solutions to meeting the broader health-care needs of citizens. Others, impressed with the difficulties of achieving transparent market conditions, and with the pervasive injustices found in much health-care provision and funding, argue for a more extensive use of political authority in addressing these issues. These disagreements do not admit of resolution here.[40]

There is also, inevitably, a natural degree of indeterminacy in how a particular political society can or should work out the details of its scheme of health-care entitlements and regulations. This indeterminacy results from different answers that can be given that arise from within the domain of health care: Different societies, for example, will make different judgments about what resources to direct to preventative, basic, or intensive care, as a result of differences in need, resources, and priorities. Other indeterminacies will result from the fact that resources spent on health care could also be spent elsewhere, for the sake of other equally important basic goods. What amount of resources should be directed to health care instead of education is a question that has no determinate answer, and that will be reasonably answered in different ways by different societies.[41]

For these reasons, natural-law theorists have not provided, and to some extent cannot provide, determinate answers to all questions about health-care distribution and rights. Settling such questions requires prudence and in many cases determinations of the law: decisions that things will be thus and so, even though they could reasonably have been determined to be otherwise.

CONSCIENCE

We turn now to the final area in which natural-law reflection generates sound norms for medical practice and law, the questions surrounding "physician rights of conscience." Such questions arise as a result of an erosion of agreement on the norms that should govern critical areas of health care, prominent among them being the areas we have discussed above, such as abortion and euthanasia. Western societies almost universally enforce, legally, extensive rights to abortion, and they increasingly enforce considerable rights to assistance in ending one's life. At the same time, a significant part of the population, and many members of the health-care profession, continue to recognize the truth of the norms we have articulated here concerning, especially, the protection of innocent human life, the difference between intention and side effect, and the limited authority of patients. They recognize, as well, other norms that we have not addressed but that follow from the principles we have identified, in particular the principle that the organic functioning and unity of a human person are not to be damaged save for the sake of the overall organic functioning and unity of that same person. Human health is to be considered integrally, and the removal of a diseased limb, for example, is not seen by natural-law theorists as intentional damage to health for the sake of health, but rather action for the patient's health, integrally understood. By contrast, surgeries meant to reassign the biological sex of a human being are characteristically seen by natural-law theorists as a form of mutilation, as are surgeries to eliminate an agent's reproductive capacity for non-medical reasons; they are thus ruled out by the natural-law prescription against intentional damage to the basic good of health.

Many physicians who adhere to these norms of the natural law are conflicted because the requirements of natural law and of the positive law (and increasingly the norms of their profession) point to different directions. This creates a situation of conflict among physicians and their patients, their profession, and the broader society. When physicians refuse to provide certain services (for example, abortion, euthanasia, gender reassignment surgery, or sterilization), patient expectations are thwarted; increasingly rigid professional norms are violated; and there is a default on a perceived social contract, ratified by the laws that give physicians a monopoly on certain rights (such as the right to perform surgery) in exchange for their willing provision of services.[42]

Natural-law thought raises two considerations in response to this situation that provide guidance for law and professional policy. First, it is to be stressed that the gap in current law and professional practice between physicians who adhere to norms against intentional killing and mutilation, and to consistently health-and-life-oriented practices, on the one hand, and laws and practices permissive of intentional killing, mutilation, and non-health-related expectations of medical professionals, on the other, is a failure on the part of the law and the medical profession, and not of those physicians with both good moral judgment and practical integrity. The first form of advice to be given in such circumstances is that better laws and professional standards need to be (re)developed that consistently respect the vocational commitment of medicine to heal and never to harm.

The second form of advice is that, in the current deficient state of affairs in which law and the medical ethos remain permissive of practices that are at odds with the goods of life and health, natural lawyers point to two important goods that will be served by accommodating physicians who accept the more traditional health-and-life-oriented norms—namely, integrity and religion. Integrity is the good of having an integrated practical character, in which judgment, choice, action, and emotion are all coherently unified. To some extent, that unity can be achieved in an evil person whose character is entirely oriented to what is bad. Nevertheless, like all basic goods, the good of integrity is realized more fully when it is realized in morally upright ways. But integrity is a basic good that is to be protected not just in oneself, but in others.

Thus, laws and practices that require acts of persons that are contrary to their integrity do a wrong to those persons if there is not adequate reason for requiring those acts.[43] Of course, persons may be thwarted from pursuing wicked plans even if they pursue them with integrity; but when possible human persons are to be given the practical possibility of living out their lives without significant threats to the integrity of their practical character.

The same is true of the good of religion. Agents who see their lives and character as shaped by religious commitments and concerns are, when possible, to be given the practical space necessary for them to be able to do so: This fosters a basic good. Of course, human sacrificers and suicide bombers are to be thwarted, even when they act for religious reasons, in order to safeguard the lives and health of innocent persons. And many other circumstances can be envisaged when the stakes are not so high that agents must be stopped from acting on the basis of religious convictions.[44] Thus, for example, many states have exemptions allowing certain drugs, such as peyote, to be used in religious ceremonies, but other states allow no such exemptions.

Both the good of integrity and the good of religion are obviously implicated in the decisions of many "dissenting" physicians and other health-care professionals who refuse to participate in abortions or a patient's suicide; or who refuse to aid in the mutilation of healthy bodies; or decline to prescribe medications whose purposes are, they believe, contrary to good health and morality. The integrity and religious commitments of such health-care practitioners ought to be protected to the extent possible, barring serious reasons not to. Can opponents of accommodating physician conscience in these situations offer such reasons?

In these cases, they cannot. The question is not to be settled simply by identifying what the law permits or what patients expect, since the question is primarily normative. Nor can doctors who refuse to perform these services be convicted of acting unfairly or in a discriminatory manner: They are acting from sincere and intelligently formed conscience in refusing to perform or cooperate with certain kinds of acts that harm the goods of life and health. Their refusals are thus unlike the refusals of racist doctors in times past to serve classes of persons. Are, then, the medical profession and its values put at risk by such dissenting physicians' actions? If they were, this too would be a good reason to refuse them accommodation. But they are not: Such physicians in fact act from considered convictions about the importance of the very goods on which the medical profession is based and towards which, in principle, its existence is ordered: the goods of life and health (this again differentiates them from racist physicians). There is no real medical profession absent this conviction, merely a set of technical skills that can be put at the service of whatever desires they are legally permitted to satisfy. Accordingly, we suggest, the medical profession is itself best served by accommodating those professionals whose conscientious refusals are governed by the considerations that reflect the authentic ethos of the profession, the authentic concerns of law, and the true and practically reasonable deliverances of the natural law.

CONCLUSION

Natural-law theorists approach the task of moral theory by enquiring into the foundational reasons for human action. Such reasons are found in basic human goods that are constitutive of human flourishing. Natural-law theorists then ask what norms are prescribed by practical reason as protecting those goods and what forms of authority, including legal authority, are likewise needed to protect those goods. Such an approach bears fruit in the domain of medical ethics and law, where especially vulnerable goods, life and health, are at stake. The natural-law approach to medicine, both in ethics and in law, thus serves to protect and promote human flourishing in this important domain.

CHAPTER SIX

Human Embryos Are Human Beings

Among the constants in human history is this: When people want to justify killing, enslaving, or otherwise abusing a class of their fellow human beings, they first dehumanize them. I suspect that the dehumanization of the victims is typically meant not only to persuade others to go along or look the other way; it is also to convince the dehumanizers themselves.

As a matter of scientifically demonstrable fact, human embryos, no less than human fetuses, infants, toddlers, children, adolescents, and adults, are human beings—living members of the species *Homo sapiens*. Those words—"embryo," "infant," "adolescent," and so forth—do not name different *kinds* of entities. They name the *same kind* of entity (a living member of the human species, a human being, like you or me) at different stages of development.

But some today, for various reasons, want to justify the deliberate killing of human beings at early stages of their development—the embryonic, fetal, even infant stages. And some want to justify the deliberate killing of people in certain conditions—such as people suffering from cognitive disabilities or severe dementias. So, as usual, they are at pains to deny that the victims are human. They insist that those whose killing they want to license are "non-human," or "sub-human," or "pre-human," or "not fully human," or whatever.

And so *Washington Post* columnist and editor Ruth Marcus, someone I like and respect despite our deep differences on moral and political issues, set out in a recent column to show that I am wrong to say that human beings in the embryonic stage of development are in fact human beings.[1] She invites her readers to reason backward: If human embryos were human beings, then things we (liberal readers of the *Washington Post*) believe, things we want to be true, things that are really important to us, would be false. But we—somehow—just know that they're not false. Elective abortion is a woman's right, and a regime of legal and widely available abortion is an enlightened and humane policy, so... embryos must not be human beings.

It's that constant in human history again: *Those whom others would kill or license the killing of, they first dehumanize.*

My friend Ruth's denial that human embryos and fetuses are human beings is a flat denial of science. It's true that gametes—sperm and egg—are not human beings. They are both genetically and functionally *parts* of other organisms—a man and a woman. But when they join, the resulting embryo has a new and complete genome of its own. More important, the embryo does not function as a mere part of anyone. He or she (in humans, sex is established from the start) functions as a whole organism. Like infants, toddlers, or teens, embryos and fetuses will—unless prevented by disease, violence, lack of nutrition or warmth—develop by an internally directed and gapless process into later stages of the life cycle of a human being. They will do so with their unity, determinateness, and identity intact.

What is the alternative? Since embryos are not inanimate, like minerals, but alive, each must be either a whole organism or part of one. If they were merely *part* of an organism, which organism would that be? The only candidates would be the man and woman who produced the gametes, but again, embryos are genetically and functionally distinct from both—as distinct as any children from their parents. So embryos must be whole organisms. But any whole organism belongs to some species—and which could it be in this case, if not *Homo sapiens*? Embryos have the same forty-six chromosomes as newborn humans, embodying the same program, unfolding along the same trajectory: infant, child, adolescent, adult, geriatric. So embryos can only be whole organisms of the human kind. Every textbook of developmental biology confirms this fact. There is no scientific controversy—none whatsoever—about it.

Thus, Ruth Marcus, for example, is the same whole, distinct, self-integrating human organism who was, at earlier stages, the adolescent Ruth, the child Ruth, the infant Ruth, the fetal Ruth, and, at the very beginning, the embryonic Ruth Marcus. Things happened—some of lasting significance—to the individual who is now the adult Ruth Marcus when she was an embryo and a fetus, just as some life-shaping things happened to her in adolescence, childhood, and infancy. The adult Ruth Marcus is *biologically continuous* with the embryonic Ruth Marcus. She is *numerically identical* to the embryonic Ruth Marcus. That is why IVF pioneer Dr. Robert Edwards, producer of the first "test-tube baby," recalling Louise Brown as an embryo in a petri dish, was not talking gibberish when he said at her birth, "She was beautiful then and she is beautiful now."

Edwards went on to speak with perfect scientific accuracy of the embryonic Louise Brown as "a microscopic human being—one in its very earliest stages of development." As he and a co-author put it, the embryonic human being is "passing through a critical period in its life of great exploration: it becomes magnificently organized, switching on its own biochemistry, increasing in size, and preparing itself quickly for implantation in the womb." What they describe is the self-integration and internally directed process of development that I mentioned a moment ago.

The bottom line is a *fact* that my friend Ruth is desperate to resist: Embryos and fetuses do not "gradually" *become* human beings. That *is* unscientific gibberish. Our *development to adulthood* is gradual, to be sure, but we come into existence *as* human beings—whole living members of the species *Homo sapiens*—and develop *as* (not *into*) human beings. Embryonic and fetal human beings differ from infant human beings in many ways. But then infants differ dramatically from adults. None differ in kind, as between humans and non-humans.

Now, one might ask: Since Ruth is so desperate for abortion to be right—and *a* right—why does she not just say that embryos and fetuses are human beings but not yet "persons"—that is, beings with moral rights equal to yours and mine? That is exactly what sophisticated pro-choice philosophers and bioethicists say, including my famously candid and consistent Princeton colleague, Peter Singer. I suspect that there are two reasons.

First, the logic of this view leaves too many human beings out. As Singer makes clear, if embryos and fetuses are not persons, it must be because they cannot, *here and now*, exercise certain mental powers such as self-awareness. But then neither can infants. So infants wouldn't be persons either, and infanticide, no less than abortion, would be morally acceptable—a conclusion Singer embraces. So a couple could legitimately conceive a child and give birth to it for the purpose of, say, harvesting vital organs to save the life of an older child.

Second, to adopt Singer's position is to give up the ideas of human equality and human rights (rights that people have in virtue of their humanity). After all, if the thing that gives us moral status comes in degrees—the degree of development of some mental capacity—our moral worth must come in degrees, too. *Even among persons*, some would have to count for more than others, having more of the trait that confers moral worth. Yet Ruth, I'm sure, wants to hang on to the idea that all humans have equal moral worth and basic human rights (and for that, I salute her). So to justify abortion she needs to posit a difference in *kind*, not degree, between unborn human beings and newborns. She needs the unborn to be non-human. Professor Singer's advantage is that he doesn't need to resort to science denial.

To her credit, Ruth does gesture at one *argument* for the notion that human embryos are non-human. She borrows it from another friend of mine, the Harvard political theorist Michael Sandel. It's superficially plausible but falls apart on inspection.

To show that embryos differ *in kind*, not just in *degree* of development, from human beings at later developmental stages, Professor Sandel offers an analogy:

> Although every oak tree was once an acorn, it does not follow that acorns are oak trees, or that I should treat the loss of an acorn eaten by a squirrel in my front yard as the same kind of loss as the death of an oak tree felled by a storm. Despite their developmental continuity, acorns and oak trees are different kinds of things.[2]

The fact that we mourn the loss of mature oaks but not acorns does not, however, prove that they differ in *kind*. After all, we don't mourn the loss of oak *saplings*, either, yet it's clear that saplings and mature oaks are the same *kind* of thing. Our reactions only show that we don't value oaks because of the *kind* of thing they are at all. We value them for their magnificence—a matter of *degree*. And in the case of oak trees, that is perfectly reasonable.

But the basis for valuing human beings is profoundly different, which is why the analogy fails. As Sandel acknowledges, human beings count because of the *kind* of entities they are. That is why all human beings are equal in basic dignity and human rights. Though we value mature oaks more than saplings, we do not value mature humans—adults—more than infants. And while we prize oaks for their magnificence, we do not think that the most developed humans—say, a wonderful athlete like Jim Thorpe or a brilliant physicist like Albert Einstein—are of greater moral worth than, say, the physically frail or mentally impaired. We would not tolerate the harvesting of organs from an ill or cognitively disabled person to save a Jim Thorpe or Albert Einstein. And we do not tolerate the killing of infants, which on the proposed analogy would be analogous to the oak saplings whose destruction (for example, in forest management) we don't mourn.

I began by mentioning a constant in human history. I will conclude by noting a constant in the rhetorical stratagems of abortion advocates: the ubiquitous suggestion that the pro-life view is really just a religious one, and that pro-life advocates would impose their religious ideas on those who don't share their faith. Thus, says Ruth, "however much anti-abortion advocates insist that their view is rooted in science, they also tend to be guided by a religious philosophy with which other Americans simply disagree."

Of course, many of the world's religious traditions rightly affirm the inherent dignity of every human person. And many decry the violence of abortion, infanticide, and euthanasia—just as they affirm the dignity of young women, and so decry sex trafficking. Some, it is true, do not condemn elective abortion (although Ruth's suggestion that Judaism is one such religion would be fiercely contested by such eminent scholars of Jewish law and ethics as the late Chief Rabbi of Britain Immanuel Jakobovits, Rabbi David Novak, Rabbi J. David Bleich, and many more). And certainly there is nothing wrong with people bringing religious arguments to the public square. It was not wrong when Martin Luther King Jr. unabashedly did so in the struggle to end segregation and Jim Crow. And it is not wrong when faithful Catholics, Protestants, Jews, or Muslims do the same in their fight against the lethal violence of abortion.

But all this business about "imposing religion" is a sideshow. Whether human embryos are human beings—living members of the species *Homo sapiens*—is a question resolved by human embryology and developmental biology. It isn't any more distinctly theological than the age of the earth is. And matters of justice and human rights—what is morally owed to human beings and whether all human beings are bearers of dignity and rights—are not the exclusive province of theology either. Otherwise, we couldn't protect *any* human beings and their rights without "imposing religion."

True, the principle that all human beings have moral worth is a contested philosophical claim. But so is the idea that some human beings—those in the embryonic, fetal, and infant stages, those who are physically severely disabled or cognitively impaired—*lack* moral worth. There is no morally neutral position.

The real difference between the pro-life and the pro-abortion positions is this: The pro-life view depends on an undisputed scientific fact plus a moral principle that explains and vindicates the worth of infants and the cognitively impaired, and affirms the profound, inherent, and equal dignity of every member of the human family. The defense of elective abortion depends on a moral view that must deny this principle, a biological view that contradicts science, or both.

CHAPTER SEVEN

Death with Dignity: A Dangerous Euphemism
with Christopher Kaczor

Advocates of physician-assisted suicide and euthanasia sometimes speak of "death with dignity" and the "right to die with dignity." In a certain sense, no one's right to die can ever be jeopardized because everyone's death is a certainty that no law, no political institution, and no culture can prevent. The "right" to die, in that sense, has no greater need of legal and ethical defense than the right to be subject to gravity. What is at issue is not a right to die but, rather, a right to kill—the legal or moral right to intentionally end someone's life. Not dying (considered as something that inevitably happens), but euthanasia (considered as killing someone putatively for their own good) is the issue. We mean by "euthanasia" or "mercy killing" the intentional killing of a human being, either as a means to an end other than making the person in question dead or as an end in itself, undertaken with the motivation of benefiting the one who is killed. The choice to kill may be carried out as either active euthanasia, which is an intentional act such as injecting someone with poison, or passive euthanasia, which is an intentional omission aimed at producing death by, for example, withholding the nutrition and hydration necessary for survival. Some forms of intentionally killing the sick, disabled, or suffering are not undertaken for the sake of the sick, disabled, or suffering. These killings are undertaken to help other people, such those who are tired of caring for the needy, those who wish to save money that would otherwise be spent on their care, or those who look to obtain organs for transplantation. Properly speaking, these are not cases of euthanasia, for in these cases one person is killed for the sake of benefiting another person or other people. We confine our discussion to euthanasia in the sense of intentional killing undertaken for the sake of the one killed rather than intentional killing of one person in hopes of aiding others.

FOUR KINDS OF DIGNITY

The right to intentionally kill an individual is sometimes justified by invoking "dignity." Like other words and concepts central to ethical discourse, such as "rights" and "autonomy," "dignity" is used in a variety of senses. In its root etymology, "dignity" is connected to worth and value. In its contemporary usage, we can distinguish four senses of the term, namely dignity as flourishing, dignity as attributed, dignity as intrinsic worth, and dignity as equivalent to or at least expressing autonomy.[1] We argue that none of these four senses of dignity justifies intentional killing.

Dignity as flourishing is a life lived enjoying basic human goods. A flourishing human life includes acting in ways that are upright, virtuous, and reasonable. So the person who habitually acts with personal integrity has dignity as flourishing in that respect. Daniel Sulmasy puts it as follows:

> Thus, dignity is sometimes used to refer to a state of virtue—a state of affairs in which a human being habitually acts in ways that express the intrinsic value of the human. We say, for instance, that so-and-so faced a particularly trying situation with dignity. This use of the word is not purely attributed, since it depends upon some objective

conception of human excellence. Nonetheless, the value to which this use of the word refers is not intrinsic, since it depends upon a prior understanding of the intrinsic value of the human.[2]

Dignity as flourishing need not be limited simply to flourishing brought about by reasonable choices. Any human being enjoying basic human goods such as knowledge, friendship, life, and health may be said to enjoy dignity as flourishing with respect to those goods. Thus, a human being suffering from cancer may lack dignity as flourishing inasmuch as her health is failing but enjoy dignity as flourishing in another respect inasmuch as she faces her declining health with equanimity and courageous resolve.

Dignity as attributed can be defined as worth, honor, and respect bestowed upon an individual by the community or by individual choice. As Sulmasy states,

> By attributed dignity, I mean that worth or value that human beings confer upon others by acts of attribution. The act of conferring this worth or value may be accomplished individually or communally, but it always involves a choice. Attributed dignity is, in a sense, created. It constitutes a conventional form of value. Thus, we attribute worth or value to those we consider to be dignitaries, those we admire, those who carry themselves in a particular way, or those who have certain talents, skills, or powers. We can even attribute worth or value to ourselves using this word.[3]

The President of the United States getting a twenty-one gun salute, the scholar getting hooded honoris causa, and the Olympic champion receiving the gold medal enjoy attributed dignity. The contrary of dignity as attributed is dishonoring, shaming, and even torturing particular people because they are viewed as deserving such treatment.

By contrast, intrinsic dignity does not depend on human choice, but rather on the inherent nature of the individual in question. Intrinsic dignity follows from the nature of the individual and remains as long as the individual continues to exist. Sulmasy describes it as follows:

> By intrinsic dignity, I mean that worth or value that people have simply because they are human, not by virtue of any social standing, ability to evoke admiration, or any particular set of talents, skills, or powers. Intrinsic dignity is the value that human beings have simply by virtue of the fact that they are human beings. Thus we say that racism is an offense against human dignity. Used this way, dignity designates a value not conferred or created by human choices, individual or collective, but is prior to human attribution.[4]

We might also call this endowment dignity because it is linked to the nature of the individual and is not achieved by the individual or given to the individual by others. We have endowment dignity or intrinsic dignity in virtue of our humanity, in virtue of our rational nature.

Finally, dignity may be understood as reducible to autonomy. Individuals have dignity if and only if they have the capacity to choose autonomously. To respect someone's dignity is nothing more than respecting someone's autonomy. As Ruth Macklin argues,

> "Dignity" seems to have no meaning beyond what is implied by the principle of medical ethics, respect for persons: the need to obtain voluntary, informed consent; the requirement to protect confidentiality; and the need to avoid discrimination and abusive practices. Why, then, do so many articles and reports appeal to human dignity, as if it means something over and above respect for persons or for their autonomy? Although the etiology may remain a mystery, the diagnosis is clear. Dignity is a useless concept in medical ethics and can be eliminated without any loss of content.[5]

On Macklin's view, dignity does not do any important work in medical ethics beyond respect for persons. This claim that dignity is a useless concept has been criticized and defended elsewhere,[6] but we do not need to adjudicate that dispute for our purposes. One way, although arguably not the only way, to understand dignity is as a respect for the autonomy of persons. How, then, do these four senses of dignity relate to forms of mercy killing?

EUTHANASIA AND DIGNITY AS FLOURISHING

Dignity as flourishing involves both moral well-being and non-moral well-being. To flourish is to enjoy the basic human goods. Human flourishing in its various dimensions presupposes and necessarily involves the human being's continued existence. No individual can have a flourishing life unless that individual is alive. To flourish or fail to flourish qualifies the life. One cannot have a low or a high quality of life without being alive.

But perhaps dignity as flourishing can be used as a justification for euthanasia in the following way. Once flourishing falls beneath a certain threshold, a human being benefits from being killed. We might debate about what exactly that threshold is and whether crossing that threshold is sufficient for justifying euthanasia or whether autonomous consent is also necessary to justify it. The intuition is that once dignity as flourishing has been irrevocably lost, it is better for the one in question no longer to exist at all.

Does illness, provided it is intense enough, make death beneficial? Imagine a sliding scale of human physical well-being. On one extreme, you find Olympic athletes in the flower of youth and the peak of strength, endurance, speed, and every dimension of healthy functioning. As you slide down the scale, this health functioning diminishes to increasingly lower levels until reaching the other extreme of the scale of human beings just on the verge of complete and irreversible loss of integrated organic functioning in all respects, namely death. The justification of euthanasia in terms of quality of life depends on the idea that intentional killing, even if authorized by the one killed, is ethically wrong and legally should be prohibited for the Olympic athlete, but not for the person on the verge of death. But it is difficult to understand why somewhere along the scale of physical well-being intentionally killing human beings becomes not a harm inflicted upon them but, rather, a benefit to them. How can moving an individual further down the "scale" of physical dysfunction be a benefit to the individual? The further down the scale the individual goes, the worse off the individual is in terms of physical well-being. To kill an individual is to completely destroy the physical well-being of the individual. Killing an individual can never be a benefit to an individual. Benefits make an individual in some respect better off than the individual was prior to receiving the benefit. Intentional killing, by contrast, does not make the individual killed better off but, rather, makes the individual nonexistent.

EUTHANASIA AND DIGNITY AS ATTRIBUTED

At first glance, dignity as attributed has little to do with euthanasia. No one views mercy killing as an honor bestowed because of outstanding achievement in service of the public good. Nor is the justification for mercy killing the imposition of a kind of dishonor upon those at the end of life that they deserve to die because of some bad action that they have done. Euthanasia is not capital punishment.

Dignity as attributed can be used to justify euthanasia in that those who are intentionally killed either no longer have or soon will no longer have any value. If human worth is understood simply as attributed, then it depends on the judgment and choice of human beings. Just as we can celebrate and honor certain kinds of people, we can denigrate and dishonor other kinds of people. We may, therefore, judge that a certain class of people—for instance, those in the last six months of life or those who are enduring grave physical or mental suffering—do not have lives worth living. If certain kinds of human beings, such as those suffering or unconscious at the end of life, have no value, there is no disvalue in killing them, aside perhaps from circumstantial considerations.

Is it true that such human beings have no value? Consider a woman in a hospital in a persistent vegetative state who will soon be dying. Just after midnight, a janitor enters her room and has sexual intercourse with her. Everyone recognizes that this woman would be wronged and her basic rights violated because it is always wrong to have sexual intercourse with someone without that person's consent (that is, to rape someone). But this intuition presupposes that the woman still has basic rights—that she is still someone who can be morally wronged. In other words, she still has value as a moral subject, despite her grave disability and imminent death.

Dignity as attributed can justify euthanasia only if we assume that human beings do not have intrinsic dignity. We might fail to value something that is in fact quite valuable, such as in mistakenly thinking a painting is a knock-off when it is an actual work by Rembrandt. So, too, if we classify the gravely disabled as not having value and worth, if we deny them dignity of attribution in a basic sense, we may be making a serious mistake. Thus, the case for euthanasia based on dignity of attribution depends on a denial of intrinsic dignity to some class of human individuals. For if human beings have intrinsic dignity, there is no human condition for which a basic dignity of attribution is not the proper response. Not every professor deserves an honorary doctorate; however, if dignity is intrinsic, every person deserves to be respected, even if the individual in question is suffering, at the end of life, or seriously disabled mentally and physically.

Of course, the suffering person may view herself as lacking any dignity. She may think that she currently is or will soon be worthless, and therefore that death is preferable to continuing to exist in her worthless condition. But it is certainly possible that an individual's self-evaluation is mistaken. The anorexic believes she is too fat and may seek help in losing weight. The severely depressed person may think that not only his life but also the lives of all human beings lack any meaning, purpose, or significance. If human beings have intrinsic value, then an individual human being may be mistaken in denying his or her own worth.

Another way dignity as attributed may be used to justify euthanasia is by appeal to respect for choices. We acknowledge and realize the dignity of another as attributed by various means, such as by providing honors to them, by giving them words of praise, and by granting them social status. Dignity is also attributed when we recognize, accept, and respect the choices of others. In so doing, we treat the other person, specifically that person as the source of free and autonomous choice, as having value. So, in cases of voluntary euthanasia as well as physician-assisted suicide, when choices to die are made autonomously, dignity as attributed leads to an acceptance of such decisions as a way of recognizing and reaffirming the worth of the agent as freely choosing his or her own way of dying. To respect other people, we must also respect their own autonomous choices, including their choice to die in the way that they choose.

Although dignity as attributed might be invoked to justify euthanasia or physician-assisted suicide, this justification is problematic. We should recognize and attribute dignity to others in ways that are fitting and responsible. But attributed dignity does not require accepting and respecting all the choices of others no matter what these choices may be. An autonomous choice can also be selfish, stupid, self-contradictory, irrational, or immoral. We can and should always respect the person who is choosing, but we cannot and should not respect every choice that is made. The choice of the segregationist to exclude African Americans from full legal protection and the choice of the advocate of equality to include all human beings in full legal protection cannot consistently both be respected.

In the case of euthanasia, the full legal protection of all human beings is at stake. Laws allowing euthanasia carve out an exception to the equal protection of the lives of all members of the community, legalizing some cases of intentional killing. Legally permitting euthanasia implies that the vast majority of people's lives are worth fully protecting, but a small minority of people's lives (those who are suffering or nearing death) do not merit the same protection, and so they may be intentionally killed.

Even advocates of euthanasia do not hold that respect for the decisions of others alone requires acceptance of euthanasia. Its legalization and/or ethical permissibility is characteristically said to depend not just on an individual's choice but also on other conditions, such as intense suffering, mental illness, or an incurable disease. These qualifications limiting euthanasia may arise from a recognition that political conditions would not allow euthanasia at any time or for any reason. But part of the reason such a policy is so politically unpalatable is that important goods, such as protecting the vulnerable, would be jeopardized by such a law.

Another way in which dignity of attribution could be used to justify intentional mercy killing might be seen by way of analogy. A customary way of honoring a tattered U.S. flag is to burn it. The rationale behind this practice is that it somehow dishonors what the flag represents to allow it to continue to fly when its condition has significantly deteriorated. In like manner, we intentionally kill an individual who is significantly deteriorating as a way of attributing dignity to the individual. We show dignity as attributed to deteriorating human beings at the end of life by no longer allowing them to continue in their deteriorated condition.

But we honor people by giving them something that is good. It is not honoring but, rather, dishonoring people to intentionally inflict evil upon them. To "honor" people by intentionally destroying their knowledge, their capacity to play, their friendships, or their appreciation of the beautiful is not to honor them at all but, rather, to harm them.

So the question about whether we can honor people by killing them depends in part on whether death is something good or evil for a human being. Like knowledge and friendship, life is intrinsically good for a human being. Indeed, to be a human person necessarily involves being alive, for without life only a corpse remains. We are human beings, living organisms of a particular species. If we have intrinsic value, then these living organisms have intrinsic value. If we are intrinsically valuable, our lives have intrinsic value. Death destroys the human being and so does not benefit a human being in any way. Yes, death may also lead to an end of suffering, but that does not mean that death itself is good. Good can come from evil and evil can rise from good without good being evil or evil being good. If someone is kidnapped and escapes, such a person may experience what positive psychologists call post-traumatic growth. The victim of the kidnapping may emerge more altruistic, patient, and virtuous. But this growth does not mean that kidnapping was not really evil.

Critics may respond that body-self dualism provides an alternative to the view that "we are human beings." According to body-self dualism, "we" are not properly speaking rational animals, organisms of a particular species; rather, "we" are our thoughts, beliefs, desires, and self-awareness. On this view, "we" may be intrinsically valuable, but our bodies are just akin to vehicles in which what is truly "us" (our thoughts, beliefs, desires, and so forth) is located. "We" are intrinsically valuable persons, but our bodies are merely animal organisms that "we" inhabit (or are in some mysterious way associated with).

For reasons to reject body-self dualism, see chapter 3 above, co-authored with Patrick Lee. That case is presented in greater detail in our *Body-Self Dualism in Contemporary Ethics and Politics*.[7] One consideration against body-self dualism arises from cases of multiple personality disorder. Suppose an individual human being has two independent sets of beliefs, desires, goals, and memories. This one human being is Dr. Jekyll and also Mr. Hyde. Now suppose a psychiatrist cures the multiple personality disorder, eliminating the Mr. Hyde set of memories, beliefs, and desires. Has the psychiatrist done an act of compassionate healing for which she deserves praise? Or should the psychiatrist be blamed for "destroying a person" and be subject to criminal prosecution for murder? If curing multiple personality disorder is praiseworthy rather than deserving of punishment, then "we" as valuable beings are not really constituted by our thoughts, beliefs, and desires rather than by a bodily human being.

EUTHANASIA AND DIGNITY AS INTRINSIC WORTH

Sulmasy holds that dignity as intrinsic worth undergirds the other senses of dignity. Immanuel Kant provided the classic case against euthanasia and suicide in the *Grounding for the Metaphysics of Morals*. Kant writes, "[If a person] destroys himself in order to escape from a difficult situation, then he is making use of his person merely as a means so as to maintain a tolerable condition till the end of his life. Man, however, is not a thing and hence is not something to be used merely as a means. He must in all his actions always be regarded as an end in himself. Therefore, I cannot dispose of man in my own person by mutilating, damaging, or killing him."[8]

Human persons have intrinsic dignity, unlike things, which have a price. Mere things may be used, abused, or even destroyed for the sake of some other end. But human beings must always be respected as ends in themselves and may never be used simply as a means, killed, or maimed for some other end.

On this view, the value of a human being does not depend on whether the individual is experiencing pleasure, pain, or nothing at all. Human beings do not have value because of what they are experiencing but because of who they are. Indeed, we care about what human beings experience precisely because we care about human beings. If human beings themselves lack value, then why should we care about what human beings experience? The slave holder does not care about the slave and therefore is indifferent to the suffering of the slave.

Kant's insight might be reformulated. The basic human goods provide the ultimate reasons for action. These basic goods—such as knowledge, health, life, and friendship—are intrinsic goods rather than merely instrumental goods, such as money, prestige, and power. But to kill a human being in order to attain some other end is to reduce an intrinsic good to the status of a merely instrumental good. To act in this way is to confuse what is merely a means with what is an end in itself. It is to act unreasonably and immorally.

Euthanasia may be undertaken with various goals in mind: to end suffering, to respect a decision, to save money, or to escape from a hopeless situation. But whatever motivates the choice to intentionally kill, the person (in his or her bodily existence) is destroyed—is used up, as it were, in order to attain this other state of affairs.

The view that euthanasia is impermissible does not entail that all treatments that extend life must always be used regardless of circumstances. To say that every human person has intrinsic worth is not to claim that every treatment offered to a human person has intrinsic worth. In fact, some treatments are more burdensome than beneficial. If a particular treatment is painful, costly, and difficult to administer, this treatment may not be worthwhile for a particular patient. If the burdens of a particular treatment are substantial and the benefits of the treatment not as significant, then the treatment may be refused or discontinued. The proper judgment is not about whether the person is worthwhile but, rather, whether the treatment is worthwhile.[9]

Is there a gap between affirming the value of all persons and affirming that the lives of all persons are valuable? Could we not claim that all persons are valuable but that the biological lives of persons have value if and only if each person himself or herself values his or her life?

Such questions presuppose a body-self dualism in which the person is one thing but the person's bodily existence is another: Each individual person is intrinsically valuable, but the biological life of a person has only instrumental value.

But human persons are not souls trapped in bodies or functioning cerebral cortexes riding around in bodies as in a vehicle. We are human beings, and a human being is a biological organism. So if we have value intrinsically, then human beings have value intrinsically, and these biological organisms have value intrinsically.

EUTHANASIA AND DIGNITY AS AUTONOMY

Let us assume for the sake of argument that the moral import of "dignity" can be reduced to autonomy. Autonomy can be understood in a variety of ways.

For Kant, autonomy is the self-given law of practical reason, which is the same for all rational beings and binds all rational beings in having a duty to act only in accordance with the categorical imperative. Kant views every human being, indeed every rational being, as something "whose existence has in itself an absolute worth, something which is an end in itself."[10] This insight grounds the categorical imperative, which in one formulation obliges all rational beings to "act in such a way that you treat humanity, whether in your own person or in the person of another, always at the same time as an end and never simply as a means."[11] The duty imposed by the categorical imperative binds all rational agents "as the supreme limiting condition of every man's freedom of action."[12] To destroy an individual having absolute, unconditional worth for the sake of some (indeed, any) further end, even an otherwise legitimate end such as elimination of suffering, is not to act autonomously but, rather, in Kant's terms, to act heteronomously, to act against duty, to act unethically.

In a different sense, autonomy is understood to be exercised in any decision made by an individual who gives informed consent. So if a patient understands the reality of his or her medical condition, appreciates the certain and/or likely ramifications of a potential choice, and after due reflection decides to execute a choice, then this choice is autonomous. Thus, if dignity is reduced to autonomy, and someone gives properly informed consent to physician-assisted suicide or voluntary euthanasia, then the value of human dignity supports physician-assisted suicide and voluntary euthanasia. In "The Philosopher's Brief," several authors including Ronald Dworkin offer perhaps the most famous argument for euthanasia based on autonomy: "Most of us see death—whatever we think will follow it—as the final act of life's drama, and we want that last act to reflect our own convictions, those we have tried to live by, not the convictions of others forced on us in our most vulnerable moment."[13]

Our choices determine the value of our lives and the circumstances of our deaths. So respect for our human dignity entails a respect for our autonomy, and this leads to respect for the choices of assisted suicide and voluntary euthanasia. On this view, the value of autonomy trumps the value of human life.

A challenge to this view can be raised by considering the ground for ascribing value to autonomous choices. As Colin Bird notes, "Every human agent must attribute worth to his purposes... [because an agent] regards his purposes as good according to whatever criteria enter into his purposes."[14] If an agent views his or her goals as worthwhile, implicitly that agent is also affirming some sense of personal worth. The agent is the source of the action. If the action is valuable, the agent must also be valuable. Alan Gewirth puts the point as follows: "They are his purposes, and they are worth attaining because he is worth sustaining and fulfilling, so that he has what for him is a justified sense of his own worth."[15] The conclusion is that the "generic purposiveness" of rational action, just as such, "underlies the ascription of inherent dignity to all agents" (including oneself).[16] If this reasoning is correct, then intrinsic dignity undergirds dignity as autonomy. Why should we respect autonomy? The autonomy of a person matters only if the person matters. But if the person matters as an end in itself, as oriented to the goods that are the ultimate reason for action, then autonomy does not justify euthanasia.

Appeals to autonomy to justify euthanasia are often at cross-purposes with appeals to eliminating suffering to justify euthanasia. If it benefits a person at the end of life to be killed, why should this benefit be withheld from patients because the patients cannot consent to receive the benefit? Imagine two patients at the end of life. Both experience intolerable pain. One patient has the competence to give informed consent for euthanasia. The other patient not only suffers physical pain but also suffers from mental illness to such a degree that he cannot give informed consent to any medical treatment. If autonomy is necessary to justify euthanasia, the second patient—the worse-off patient—is not eligible for euthanasia. On the other hand, if consent is not necessary for euthanasia, then the argument from dignity as autonomy is superfluous in the justification for intentional killing at the end of life. Indeed, justifications of euthanasia are often inconsistent in their appeals to autonomy. If there is no ethical difference between intentional killing and removing life support, because removing life support is permitted for the mentally ill and for minors lacking autonomy, then intentional killing of the mentally ill and minors should also be permitted. Of course, critics of euthanasia characteristically argue that there is an ethical difference between intentional killing and removing life support in cases in which the burdens of the treatment are not worth enduring or bearing in view of its comparatively meager benefits. But this difference is characteristically denied by advocates of the choice to kill. So if removing life support and intentional killing are not ethically different, then consistency demands that whoever accepts removing life support for minor children and the mentally ill also accepts intentional killing of incompetent individuals. Thus, autonomy does no real work justifying euthanasia.

Perhaps dignity as autonomy is not a necessary condition for justifying mercy killing, but it is a sufficient condition. If a competent individual deems his or her life no longer worth living, then he or she may licitly receive voluntary euthanasia or a physician's (or other health care worker's) assistance in committing suicide. What makes a human being valuable is that the human being values continuing to exist, and if a human being no longer desires to continue to exist, then this human life no longer has value. It is wrong to kill an individual because that individual values his or her life. So if the individual does not value his or her life, then it is not wrong to kill the individual.

As John Keown notes, the claim that "a person's life has value only if the person values it" is vague, arbitrary, discriminatory, and dualistic.[17] The claim is vague because our desires are by nature vague, shifting, difficult to define, and sometimes growing in intensity and then shrinking in intensity. How can we all have fundamental equality as persons if our value as persons depends on the vagaries and shifting foundation of human desires? The claim that we have value because we value our own lives is arbitrary. As John Finnis asks, "Why not pick out other features which characterize human nature in its flourishing—say linguistic articulacy, sense of humor, and/or friendship more deep, transparent, and supple than friendship between man and dog? Why not then call one or other or some set of these the capacity which, while it is enjoyed, makes us people and 'entitles an individual to be considered a person'?"[18]

The claim is discriminatory, for if an individual in his or her bodily existence is only valuable if he or she as a matter of subjective psychological fact happens to desire to continue to live, then some people who are so depressed, mentally handicapped, severely intoxicated, or brainwashed as to not value their own lives are excluded from equality in value with others in the human community. Finally, the claim that our value as human beings depends on our desires is implicitly dualistic, supposing that "we" (beings who can value) exist only when our desires begin to exist, as if our bodies were mere transporters of the reality of merely mental selves.

If autonomy is a sufficient justification for mercy killing, we have no reasoned justification for excluding non-suffering competent adults (or mature minors) from euthanasia. If competent people consider their own lives not worth living, on what basis should we exclude them from having a "right to die" just because they lack physical suffering or are not in the last stages of a terminal illness? People may consider their lives not worth living for a wide variety of reasons, such as the loss of a significant romantic relationship or frustrated life plans. You or I may not agree with such reasoning, but that fact is completely irrelevant, at least according to a purely subjective justification of euthanasia based on autonomy.

CONCLUSION

None of the four senses of dignity explored in this chapter—namely dignity as flourishing, dignity as attributed, dignity as intrinsic worth, and dignity as autonomy—provide a sound justification of euthanasia. "Death with dignity" and the "right to die with dignity" are dangerous euphemisms masking the reality of what is at issue in these cases, which is not precisely death or dying but, rather, intentional killing. Such euphemisms obscure the reality that all human persons are equal in fundamental dignity and that this basic value remains undiminished even at the end of life, even in the midst of suffering. The proper ethical response to human problems such as suffering is, if possible, to eliminate the problem, not to eliminate the human. The ethically proper legal response is to accord to every person fully and equally the law's fundamental protection against intentional killing.

PART TWO

Constitutional Law and Political Philosophy

CHAPTER EIGHT

What *Obergefell* Should Have Said: Girgis and George, Dissenting
with Sherif Girgis

In 2020, Professor Sherif Girgis and I contributed the following essay to a compilation put together by Yale Law School Professor Jack Balkin. Professor Balkin's book, called What Obergefell v. Hodges Should Have Said, *mimics a series of judicial opinions, with each author playing the role of a Supreme Court Justice. Professor Girgis and I make many references in this mock opinion to other opinions in Professor Balkin's collection. I encourage the reader to seek those opinions out for himself; thoughtful as they are, there is something to learn from each of them.*

We can dispose of the case in two sentences: The States' marriage laws closely reflect normative and policy judgments about marriage that are reasonable in themselves and cannot have had their origins in bigotry. A ruling for petitioners requires replacing those judgments with alternatives of which our Constitution and legal tradition and two centuries of cases are all wholly innocent.

These points alone block every path to the majority's destination. The laws it deems unconstitutional reflect no animus. They create no caste. They deny nothing so rooted in our legal traditions as to support even a half-baked claim under our less-than-half-baked substantive due process law. They flout no other constitutional provision or principle, whether real or even merely invented by our most enterprising predecessors on this Court.

All that remain are policy judgments—those of our colleagues and those of millions of voters across the nation. But in the majority's calculus, five lawless votes from this bench are worth more than forty million lawful ones at the ballot box.[1] From that judicial self-aggrandizement, so heedless of our constitutional limits, we dissent.

I. The Equal Protection Challenge

A. Appropriate Level of Scrutiny

Our colleagues would variously hold that the laws at stake today (the "States' laws") deserve heightened scrutiny for classifying by sexual orientation or by sex. Yet they make nothing hinge on sexual orientation, assumed or avowed—a point that one scholarly defender of the majority's ultimate ruling considers a "simple" and "devastat[ing]" objection to its view that the States' laws discriminate based on orientation.[2] They do have widely disparate impact, but that triggers no heightened scrutiny.[3] What does trigger it, as even opponents of the States' laws have observed,[4] is a law requiring officials to rely on suspect traits in distributing legal benefits or burdens. These laws don't require—they don't *allow*—doing that with sexual orientation.

The Court demurs: Seen in their "social context," it holds, the States' laws "pretend that [sexual orientation minorities] do not exist" or require them to "disguise their real selves." The first thing to note about this charge is that it puts the cart before the horse, effectively ruling on the laws' constitutionality in the course of deciding which level of scrutiny to apply.

The second thing to note is that it is outlandish. The States' marriage laws cast no one into outer darkness and require no dissembling about desires. All marriage laws work precisely by privileging some close bonds over all others; they will *always* leave out romantic relationships that some citizens prize the most. If that is enough to erase those citizens' social existence, then all marriage law is *ultra vires*; then all fifty states shove into the closet polyamorists. Then all require asexuals to form sexual relationships, as the Court says that the States' laws "require[] or expect[]" all men to have desire for women. The Court purports to leave these questions for another day; its opinion answers them now—in holding that the States' laws trigger heightened scrutiny because they discriminate by sexual orientation.[5]

Though Justice Koppelman agrees on the first point, he thinks the States' laws classify by sex. But even if this justified heightened scrutiny of the States' laws, it would provide no argument for a constitutional right *to same-sex marriage*. That requires the further premise that what traditional laws conditioned on sex was legal recognition of a category of relationships general enough to have included same-sex partnerships in the first place (for example, that of *intimate consensual bonds, period*). That is precisely what's in dispute.

Besides, a closer look at the *kind* of sex classification at issue here shows that it needn't and shouldn't trigger heightened scrutiny. For unlike every sex-based classification to which we have ever applied heightened scrutiny, the States' laws classify based *ultimately* on a couple's *sexual composition*. And the reasons to apply heightened scrutiny to other classifications—sex-based or otherwise—apply *not at all* to classifications by opposite-sex composition. Indeed, applying it here would undermine principles of our sex-discrimination law articulated most recently in the VMI case. So we needn't and shouldn't apply heightened scrutiny to the States' laws.

As the Chief Justice admits, tiers of scrutiny are not constitutional guarantees but judicially invented tools for implementing them. In equal protection cases, we first ask about the law's *form or structure*. If it classifies based on traits that we have prior reason to think may be relied on invidiously, we go on to examine the law's *substance* with special scrutiny. Suspect form calls for scrutiny of a law's rationale.

But here we can see at the first stage—looking at structure—that no suspicion is warranted. With these laws alone, you can't fully *describe* their criterion of classification without mentioning a social good. Their justification seeps into their form. After all, opposite-sex composition is *conceptually* related to a legitimate public end. So its connection to that end doesn't depend on further, questionable social conventions or empirical assumptions; we needn't go on to scour its rationale.

Male and female are not just any two sexes, as black and white are just two races. They are *necessarily interdefined*: You cannot fully explain either without reference to the other and a social good. What defines them—at a deeper level of explanation than anatomy or genes—is their biological organization (and, thus, their basic physical potency) for reproducing together. And reproduction, its social value, and its link to opposite-sex composition are not mere constructs. So a relation to an important public end appears on the face of this classification, without resting on any stereotypes.

Yes, same-sex couples can adopt or use reproductive technology. But our point is that male-female pairing is inherently linked to reproduction, so that a social good appears on the face of the marriage laws' classification, fully spelled out. It makes no difference to this point to say that other couplings might *also* be related (in other ways) to child rearing.

Nor is it relevant that some opposite-sex couples lack some physiological conditions for having children. The *tightness* of the link between the States' criterion and a social good would be an issue only at the second stage of heightened scrutiny analysis: precisely what we think the Court need not reach here.

Again, our point is about the appropriate level of scrutiny, still a question of presumptions. It is that any particular racial (or ethnic or religious) grouping is prima facie arbitrary—and its political relevance presumptively in need of justification—as the male-female sexual grouping is not. In none of the suspect groupings (racial, ethnic, and so forth)—whether individual or couple-based (as in *Loving v. Virginia*)—are the classification criteria inherently linked to a legitimate public goal. They seem to be linked to a social goal only where society has created or invented—or inferred by generalization—the goal or link or both. Those generalizations and goals have often been malign (like empirical claims about African Americans or the socially constructed goal of racial "purity"), so it makes sense not to presume their legitimacy.[6]

The same goes for perceived links between either sex and, say, particular professions. If a policy assumed a special link between women and teaching, empirical data would be needed to establish the link, to say nothing of showing that States may shape policy around it. That's why we heighten scrutiny of run-of-the-mill sex classifications. By contrast, opposite-sex composition is necessarily linked, by the concepts involved, to a social purpose we didn't just invent and can scarcely do without: society's reproduction. Here alone, the law's criterion on its face—fully spelled out—already refers to a public end. So our framework supports keeping heightened scrutiny for classifications by sex or race or racial composition, while applying the rational-basis test to classifications by opposite-sex composition.

This standard leaves intact every sex-discrimination case to date. But unlike Justice Koppelman's approach, it would make good on Justice Ginsburg's assurances in the most recent sex-discrimination case, *United States v. Virginia*, that "inherent" and "physical" sex differences—unlike alleged racial ones—are a cause for "celebration" but not for oppression or limitation.[7] What scheme could possibly hug this standard more tightly than one that heightened scrutiny for all sex classifications *except* one focused on a *necessarily* "celebrat[ed]"[8] social end, to which men and women's "physical" differences are *"inherent[ly]"* linked?[9] Rejecting the present approach, by contrast, would belie the contrasts this Court has drawn between sex and race.

Does our proposal rely on "outmoded"[10] notions about gender, like the "pervasive sex-role stereotype," repudiated by this Court, that "caring for family members is women's work"?[11] Would it subjugate women by "defin[ing] masculinity and femininity in terms of complementary traits and attraction to the opposite sex," as the Chief Justice suggests?[12]

Gender stereotypes can of course be excuses to subjugate. On the other hand, some people also fear the effects of rejecting *all* generalizations about sex or gender. According to some feminists,[13] ignoring even the most physically grounded sex differences would itself demean women, by holding up the "unencumbered, wombless male" body as ideal.[14] In fact, some generalizations about *behavioral* differences must also be acceptable, or else *affirmative action policies based on the value of gender diversity would be unconstitutional*—a point that devastates the majority's blithe and breezy denunciations of even the subtlest appreciation of sex differences.

But we needn't resolve these matters. The premise of our proposed deference is *not* that men are by definition those who are attracted to women or fatherhood, so that childless men or those who are attracted to other men are aberrations—nor, mutatis mutandis, women. It is that the sexes are conceptually specified by their biological organization and consequent *basic physical potency* (*not* moral obligation or proper desire)[15]—to advance together an obvious social interest. This is the sort of "undeniable difference" that Justice Ginsburg affirmed can inform our law without imposing a stereotype.[16]

And it is the difference on which respondent States rely.

B. Rational Basis

In *United States v. Windsor*, Justice Alito summarized the policy judgments and empirical conjectures behind laws enshrining the traditional view of marriage and those enshrining the "'consent-based' vision." *United States v. Windsor*, 133 S. Ct. 2675, 2718 (2013) (Alito, J., dissenting). Here, too, it is worth synthesizing arguments for the States' laws as gleaned from their and some amici's representations and the common-law tradition on which they rely—and juxtaposing these to policy defenses of same-sex marriage reflected in the petitioners' and other amici's arguments and desired relief.

As judges, our job is not to say which of these sets of normative ideals, policy choices, and empirical judgments is true. Neither is required by any aspect of constitutional text, structure, history, or precedent or by any underlying constitutional value or principle, however broadly construed. Since we should apply the rational-basis test, the only question is whether the States' defense is *reasonable*. It is.

To reach today's decision, therefore, the Court has had to take sides on normative and empirical disputes and policy choices in the face of (a) reasonable and legitimate alternatives, on which (b) the Constitution is silent. That makes its decision a usurpation of authority vested constitutionally in the people and their representatives—and not just by originalist logic. However loosely read, constitutional law does not make the normative and policy decisions on marriage that are needed to complete the petitioners' equal protection argument.[17]

Today's decision therefore does what Justice Holmes accused *Lochner* of having done (rightly or wrongly—recent scholarship rehabilitating *Lochner*'s reputation matters not here). It is "decided upon" a moral and political theory of marriage "which a large part of the country does not entertain."[18] For "the Fourteenth Amendment does not enact,"[19] we might say, Mr. Evan Wolfson's book on marriage.[20] "A constitution is not intended to embody a particular [marriage] theory, whether" traditional or consent-based.[21] "It is made for people of fundamentally differing views," and "the word liberty"—or equality—is misapplied if used "to prevent the natural outcome of a dominant opinion," unless any reasonable person would "admit" that the statute was invidious.[22] But studying the States' laws, "a reasonable man might think it a proper measure on the score of" public norms and the general welfare.[23]

In short, the Court has imposed an eminently debatable ideology—a "comprehensive doctrine"[24]—under the guise of enforcing the Fourteenth Amendment with all the blindfolded impartiality of Lady Justice. But whatever the merits of our colleagues' *Weltanschauung*, their fellow citizens are free to enact another. It is no constitutional objection to your worldview that the Progressivism that has dominated the professional and social worlds from which five justices are drawn happens (only lately, we might add) to reject it.

1. Reasonable and Legitimate

Petitioners cite *Loving v. Virginia*, which struck down Virginia's bans on interracial marriage. But while history provided grounds for ruling Virginia's defenses pretextual or illegitimate,[25] it *disproves* the idea that the sorts of judgments behind the States' defense originated in animus. Indeed, many of them find support among same-sex-marriage supporters.

a. The States' Normative Vision of Marriage

The nearly perfect global consensus on sexual complementarity in marriage,[26] together with certain intellectual traditions, supports two conclusions about the traditional vision of marriage (even the normative judgment that sexual complementarity makes possible a distinctly valuable form of union): It wasn't conceived in bigotry, and it isn't inherently theological.

It has prevailed in societies spanning the spectrum of attitudes toward homosexuality, including ones favorable toward same-sex intimacies and others lacking concepts of sexual orientation and gay identity. (Whatever proves discriminatory purpose against a class, ignorance of the class as such surely disproves it.) And some philosophical and legal traditions have even excluded certain opposite-sex bonds (because of unchosen impediments to conjugal union), belying the idea that they were targeting same-sex partners.

Thus, great ancient thinkers—including Xenophanes and Socrates, Plato[27] and Aristotle,[28] Musonius Rufus[29] and Plutarch[30]—found special public value in bonds embodied in sexual intercourse and uniquely apt for family life.[31] They were not influenced by Judaism or Christianity or ignorant of same-sex sexual attractions or relations (common in, for example, ancient Greece). That is, ignorance, theology, and hostility didn't motivate their conclusions about the meaning of marriage.

b. The States' Empirical Judgments and Choices
    of Policy Purposes

The majority and Justice Eskridge's concurrence reject the respondent States' claims that excluding same-sex bonds might advance the child-focused purposes that the States would use marriage law to serve. How a State treats one relationship, they suggest, cannot affect the decisions or behavior of any other.

This betrays a remarkably flat-footed view of social institutions. It is a truism that the law reflects culture; it would be astonishing if it didn't also *shape* culture, which in turn shapes individual choices. Thus, legally recognizing same-sex bonds will contribute to the beliefs that what sets marriage apart from other forms of common life is a certain emotional intensity and that biological parenting is not specially valuable.[32]

To begin with the former, some scholars have argued that basing civil marriage on romance-and-consent-alone might further entrench what the Johns Hopkins sociologist and same-sex-marriage supporter Andrew Cherlin, among others, calls the "expressive individualist" model of marriage,[33] on which a relationship that no longer fulfills you personally is "inauthentic and hollow," so that you "will, and *must*, move on."[34] It is no surprise that another study suggests that "conflict and divorce" tend to be higher where spouses internalize this view of marriage as defined by emotional fulfillment.[35]

The spread of this view might thus diminish social pressures and incentives for husbands and wives to remain together for their children or for men and women having children to commit to marriage first. Indeed, several scholars corroborate the social power of legal change by noting that another policy—no-fault divorce—yielded "new norms and expectations for marriage and family commitments,"[36] thus "open[ing] the door for some couples who would not have" sought divorce "without the new liberalization."[37] Though supported by a review of two dozen empirical studies,[38] this claim might of course be wrong. But it makes it *reasonable* for States to worry about undermining the stabilizing norms that they have chosen marriage laws to serve—or undercutting efforts to restore those cultural norms.

The reasonableness of such concerns is only reinforced by leading same-sex-marriage supporters' own arguments. Thus, some three hundred LGBT and allied activists and scholars have advocated legally recognizing multiple-partner, sexually open, and term-limited bonds.[39]

Some have *expressly embraced* the goal of weakening the institution of marriage by the recognition of same-sex partnerships.[40] A prominent marriage scholar has argued—in the most prestigious academic journal of moral philosophy—that justice requires a "minimal marriage" policy allowing any number and mix of partners to determine their own rights and duties.[41] These steady trends in scholars' efforts to work out the implications of their own support for same-sex marriage make it impossible to brand as irrational the States' concern that changing marriage law would undermine, in principle and practice, other stabilizing norms of marriage. But this is a real public harm, if there is distinctive value in growing up with one's committed biological parents (even if studies showed no difference between *same- and opposite-sex adoptive parenting*—empirical debates from which this point prescinds).

And it is reasonable for the States to think so. The value of biological parenting is encoded in the presumption of our law, and that of nearly every culture, that parents are responsible for their biological children.[42] It is supported by scholarly reflection on how biological ties facilitate "identity formation,"[43] by studies confirming that reflection,[44] and by studies suggesting other benefits of married biological parenting.[45] It's implausible to dismiss these points, right or wrong, as cover for bigotry.

Justice Eskridge suggests that this "deinstitutionalization" rationale for the States' laws fails "most fundamentally" because no-fault divorce laws show that respondents have already given up on promoting the stabilizing norms of marriage. The problem for his argument is that our Constitution contains no Ratchet Clause. Nothing forbids a State, having turned a few notches in one policy direction, from stopping to move back the other way. Nor does anything forbid it from serving certain policy goals imperfectly in the meantime; "no legislation pursues its purposes at all costs." *Rodriguez v. United States*, 480 U.S. 522, 525–26 (1987) (per curiam).

Even so, Justice Eskridge asks, "are [we] supposed to draw the line with LGBT couples and their families" in particular? No, and no one does. The States' laws leave out the most prized companionate bonds not only of those who identify as LGBT but also of those who are most inclined to polyamorous unions or legally presumptively nonsexual ones (the platonically intimate bond of cohabiting sisters, for example).

To think that there is a difference in principle between stopping at opposite-sex couples (as the States would) and stopping at pair bonds generally (as Justice Eskridge would) is tendentious. It takes as a neutral and unquestionable axiom what would be rejected by every thinker and culture before yesterday, by all but a narrow band of Western nations today, and even by many of Justice Eksridge's fellow same-sex-marriage supporters: that is, that there is something special about the bond of two adults—any two, but only two—so long as they also happen to be unrelated and romantically involved and pledged indefinitely. The cultural Left would be forgiven for thinking this an oppressively bourgeois grab bag of norms. The States think it harmful to their policy purposes for marriage law. Both may be wrong; for that matter, both may be right. Neither side's views are illegitimate bases for policy under our Constitution.

2. Caste?

The majority notes that the Fourteenth Amendment prohibits class legislation, which "singles out a group for special burdens or benefits without adequate" justification. A policy clearly stratifies in this unjust sense if it is based on the idea (behind Jim Crow laws, for example)[46] that some people should not interact with the rest on a plane of social equality.

But we have already seen, on historical grounds, that this cannot possibly explain the genesis of traditional-marriage laws, which preceded the modern concepts of gay and lesbian identity (as Jim Crow could not have preceded awareness of race) and which have prevailed in every civilization. Indeed, while marriage law has always been with us, "[w]idespread discrimination against a class of people on the basis of their homosexual status developed only in the twentieth century...and peaked from the 1930s to the 1960s." Brief of Professors of History

George Chauncey, Nancy F. Cott, et al., Lawrence v. Texas, 539 U.S. 558 (2003). Yet the only remaining way to find a caste here (as Chief Justice Balkin elsewhere concedes)[47] is to take sides between the rival visions of marriage sketched earlier, to hold that the States' laws thus impose *unjustified* burdens. That we cannot do. Even the view that marriage laws are unjust for perpetuating patriarchy simply assumes—incorrectly, as we have seen—that they have no possible alternative, legitimate basis.

3. Actual Motives?

To be sure, traditional-marriage laws' unobjectionable origins do not prove that benign motives actually inspired the respondents' recent constitutional amendments. On the other hand, a law cannot be struck down simply for its ratifiers' actual motives, if an identical law could have been passed on legitimate grounds. Then lawmakers could reenact the same law the next day, following only a change of heart. Constitutionality should not hinge on acts of contrition, as this Court has held.[48] Nor should the motives of millions of honorable citizens of many different faiths and shades of belief be so cavalierly impugned.

But petitioners argue that the *objective* purpose of the States' laws was to demean and that this can be gleaned from the rhetoric of campaigns to enact them. In this vein, Justice Koppelman has noted that malign purposes can be gleaned from "the text [of a traditional-marriage law] itself, consistently with other aspects of its context."[49] Thus, the *Loving* Court relied on context to find illegitimate purposes in Virginia's marriage ban, without having to search the hearts of Virginia's lawmakers.

Yet it would prove too much to say that a policy is unconstitutional if its enactment disadvantaged a group then facing popular hostility. An act repealing scholarships meant to enable students from low-income backgrounds to attend private schools[50] harms poor—and disproportionately minority—students, who remain targets of prejudice and injustice. Is it unconstitutional? Of course not. There is no uniquely tight fit between the repeal and the concurrent cultural prejudice; support for public schools is a perfectly good explanation.

Likewise, to rule against the States' laws on the basis of hostile purposes, we must find not only concurrent (or even historically pervasive) hostility toward same-sex partnerships but a tight fit between such hostility and objective features of the States' laws—the sort of fit that the Court rightly found in *Loving* between Virginia's marriage ban and white supremacy.

But as we have seen, there are legitimate alternative bases. They are not just abstract possibilities but *had* to be purposes of marriage laws historically. They are consistent with the cultural and legal context of the passage of the States' laws and were reflected in some prefatory and campaign materials. Nothing of the sort could be said in defense of the marriage ban in *Loving*.

Petitioners nonetheless argue that under *Windsor*, a law has malign objective purposes (the "intent" to "injure") if it imposes "a disadvantage, a separate status, and so a stigma" on same-sex partnerships. See *Windsor*, 133 S. Ct. at 2693. But if creating a separate status suffices to render a marriage regime unconstitutional, then again, none can stand. The function of marriage law is *precisely* to create a separate status for a narrow range of companionate bonds: marital status.

II. Due Process Clause

A final question is whether we have already rejected the States' normative and policy vision of marriage as a matter of constitutional law, in the course of enforcing the fundamental right to marry. The most frequently cited (and by far the most useful) case for this claim is *Turner v. Safley*, 482 U.S. 78 (1987), where we held that "important attributes of marriage" remain available to inmates. We said that the following features were sufficient, "taken together," to "form a constitutionally protected marital relationship": (i) expressions of commitment; (ii) exercise of religious faith; (iii) the expectation of consummation upon release; and (iv) legal and social benefits (such as Social Security benefits and the legitimation of children). Could these show that same-sex bonds come within the fundamental right to marry? No.

First, (i) and (iv) show that we were taking for granted the view of marriage long enshrined at common law: Consummation was satisfied only by male-female sexual intercourse, and the legitimation of children born to a relationship is relevant only to opposite-sex couples. Second, if we *did* bracket those hints that the traditional view was being assumed and tried to infer all the contours of the right to marry from the other attributes listed in *Turner*, there would be no end of it. Any consensual adult bond—including a group sexual bond or a nonromantic one—can involve commitment, religious significance, and (if the government chooses) legal benefits. *Turner* was not implying that all these bonds came under the fundamental right to marry.

So this case—about whether certain prison regulations were reasonably related to sound penological purposes—didn't commit our legal system to rejecting the traditional view. It took for granted that vision of the content of the right to marry. It simply added that the same right was not forfeited by convicts and that severely restricting it didn't serve (well enough) the goals of rehabilitation and security. Likewise, *Zablocki v. Redhail*, 434 U.S. 374 (1978), held that Wisconsin's restriction of marriage for those who were charged with failing to pay child support was not appropriately tailored to its asserted (child-centered) goals. There again, we did not commit our legal tradition to a purely companionate vision of marriage. We simply read off our history the basic contours of the fundamental right and then asked whether a state had curbed access to marriage *so understood* or imposed restrictions that were hard to justify on the same vision of its purposes. So a due process ruling for petitioners today—maybe even more clearly than an equal protection ruling—would require us to adopt a new vision of what makes a marriage.

Finally, to dispatch the privacy argument, our privacy cases are exclusively concerned with freedom from criminal bans.[51] From that, you cannot extrapolate to a right to legal *recognition*.

CHAPTER NINE

Equal Protection and the Unborn Child: A *Dobbs* Brief

with John Finnis

This chapter brings together the authors' Amicus Brief filed in Dobbs *on July 29, 2021, our subsequent Enhanced Amicus Brief in* Dobbs*, and our Supplement to an Enhanced Amicus Brief in* Dobbs*. It retains the broad outline and (with minor corrections) the whole content of the filed Brief, while expanding it fourfold with historical material and analysis.*

INTRODUCTION

Roe conceded that if, as Texas there argued, "the fetus is a 'person' within the language and meaning of the Fourteenth Amendment," the case for a constitutional right to abortion "collapses."[1]

But then the Court hurtled over text and history to an error-strewn denial that unborn human beings are persons under the Amendment.

Scholarship exposing those errors has cleared the ground for a reexamination of Texas's position in *Roe*. While recalling that scholarship, this Brief sheds fresh light on the Amendment's original public meaning, focusing on common-law and pre–Civil War history (including primary material) that previous scholarship has not adequately noted or explored. That history proves that prohibitions of elective abortions are constitutionally obligatory because unborn children are persons within the original public meaning of the Fourteenth Amendment's Due Process and Equal Protection Clauses.

SUMMARY OF ARGUMENT

The originalist case for holding that unborn children are persons is *at least* as richly substantiated as the case for the Court's recent landmark originalist rulings.[2] The sources marshalled in such decisions—text, treatises, common-law and statutory backdrop, and early judicial interpretations—here point in a single direction.

First, the Fourteenth Amendment, sustaining and going beyond the Civil Rights Act of 1866, guaranteed equality in the fundamental rights of persons—including life and personal security—as these were expounded in Blackstone's *Commentaries* and leading American treatises. The *Commentaries'* exposition began with a discussion (citing jurists like Coke and Bracton) of unborn children's rights as persons across many bodies of law. Based on these authorities and on landmark English cases, state high courts in the years before 1868 declared that the unborn human being throughout pregnancy "is a person" and hence, under "civil and common law, ... to all intents and purposes a child, as much as if born."[3]

From the earliest centuries at common law, (1) elective abortion at any stage was to "no lawful purpose" and functioned as an inchoate felony for not just one but two felony-murder purposes, and (2) elective abortion was an *indictable* offense at least when the woman was "quick with child"—a phrase with shifting meanings identified below.[4] (And contrary to *Roe*'s potted history, the sources show that the common law's concern was to protect the child's life, not simply to outlaw procedures dangerous to the mother.)[5] By 1860, the "quick-with-child" prerequisite for indictments had been abandoned in a majority of states, because science had shown that a distinct human being begins at conception. Such obsolete limits to the common law's criminal-law protection of the unborn had been swept away in a cascade of statutes, in almost three-quarters of the states, leading up to the Amendment's ratification.

In the 1880s, the Supreme Court held that corporations are "person[s]" under the Equal Protection and Due Process Clauses.[6] The rationale—combining the Blackstonian understanding of persons (as natural or artificial) with a canon of interpretation first expounded by Chief Justice Marshall and central to originalism today—itself blocks any analytic path to excluding the unborn. Indeed, the originalist case for including the unborn is much stronger than for corporations.

These textual and historical points show that among the legally informed public of the time, the meaning of "any person"—in a provision constitutionalizing the equal basic rights of persons—plainly encompassed unborn human beings.

Second, the only counterarguments by any Justice—and by the sole, widely discredited legal-historical writer cited in *Roe*—rest on groundless extrapolations and plain historical falsehoods subsequently exposed in scholarship that has never been answered, to which this Brief adds some new evidence.

Finally, acknowledging unborn personhood would be consistent with preserving the nation's long tradition of deference toward state policies treating feticide less severely than other homicides and guarding women's rights to pressing medical interventions that may cause fetal death. Nor would recognizing the unborn require unusual judicial remedies. It would restore protections deeply planted in law until their uprooting in *Roe*.

ARGUMENT

I. Unborn Children are Constitutional Persons Entitled to Equal Protection of the Laws

The Fourteenth Amendment bars states from depriving "any person of life...without due process of law" or denying "to any person...the equal protection of the laws."[7] It was adopted against a backdrop of established common-law principles, legal treatises, and statutes recognizing unborn children as persons possessing fundamental rights.[8]

A. The Common Law Considered Unborn Children to Be Persons
Authoritative treatises—including those deployed specifically to support the Civil Rights Act of 1866, which the Fourteenth Amendment aimed to sustain and enhance[9]—prominently acknowledged the unborn as persons. Leading eighteenth-century English cases, later embraced in authoritative American precedents decades before ratification, declared the general principle that unborn humans are rights-bearing persons from conception. And even before a nationwide wave of statutory prohibitions of abortion in the mid-nineteenth century, the common law firmly regarded abortion as gravely unlawful from the moment—supposed to have been established by science—when there emerged a new individual member of the human species, a human being. The treatises, cases, and statutes are identified and analyzed below, but it is not too early to state the three common-law criminal prohibitions that protected the unborn child's life, prohibitory rules that recur constantly in the exposition below. For at common law, century after century, any elective abortion engaged three indictable offences, three types of homicide:

[I] [*pre-natal* quasi-*felony-murder of the woman*] all attempts at elective abortion are so gravely unlawful when done that if they result in the death of the mother within a year and a day, they are murder;

[II] [*pre-natal* quasi-*felony-murder of the child*] all attempts at elective abortion are so gravely unlawful when done that if they demonstrably result in the child's death after being born alive, they are murder;

[III] every elective abortion is a serious misprision (near-felony) or very grave misdemeanor, *at least* when it results in the aborting of the pregnancy of a woman "quick with child."

Protections [I] (quasi-felony murder of the mother) and [II] (murder by abortifacient of the child born alive) were generally left in place by the reforming statutes of the Ratification Era—the two decades before and after ratification of the Fourteenth Amendment. Those statutes focused on rule [III] (the crime of elective abortion as such). More or less unanimously, though with many differences of detail, they retained the position settled at common law by 1601: Elective abortion as such, though a very serious crime, is not punished as murder or manslaughter, and the drawing of this distinction among kinds of unlawful killings is judged fully compatible with protecting the child in the womb as a person.

The distinction thus drawn between persons in the womb and persons partly or wholly outside the womb is in all our jurisdictions judged to be a distinction rationally and justly recognizing the unique situation of these two interdependent persons, the mother and her unborn child.

The common law and those reforming statutes agree that if the pregnant mother's life is threatened either by the presence of the unborn child or by a medical condition that cannot be relieved without termination of the pregnancy, such termination is fully lawful even though it foreseeably results in the death of the unborn child (just as, analogously, necessary measures of self-defense are fully lawful, and compatible with equal protection of the law, even when lethal). This Brief uses the term "elective abortion" to distinguish the cases covered by each of the three common-law rules, and their statutory successors, from such medical emergency cases.

Another relevant category of non-elective abortion—destruction of the child in the womb without the mother's consent—is given adequately distinct but also adequately balanced legal treatment only later than the Ratification Era. For although almost all the reforming statutes of that Era amend the common law by implicitly exempting the mother who consents to or requests abortion, it is, broadly speaking, only in the twentieth century that closer reflection on just (equal) protection of the unborn impels many state legislatures to treat this other type of non-elective abortion as murder.

A final introductory note. Both the common-law cases and treatises, and then the countless statutes of the Ratification Era, speak almost without exception of "the (unborn) child," and almost never of "the fetus." This Brief accordingly speaks likewise. To follow the "fetus/fetal" usage common in legal circles today would to some extent, even if only subliminally, impede getting a clear view of the original public meaning of "deny to any person the equal protection of the laws" in the Equal Protection Clause ratified in 1868.

1. The Foundational Treatise

Blackstone's *Commentaries*, expressly teaching that unborn human beings are rights-bearing "persons," contributed enormously to the term's shared legal meaning in 1776–91 and 1865–68. Little wonder that when House Judiciary Committee Chairman James F. Wilson introduced the Civil Rights Act of 1866, he said:

> [T]hese rights... [c]ertainly... must be as comprehensive as those which belong to Englishmen.... Blackstone classifies them... as follows: 1. The right of personal security... great fundamental rights... the inalienable possession of both Englishmen and Americans.[10]

Wilson was quoting Blackstone's *Commentaries*' first Book, "Of the Rights of Persons," and its first Chapter, "Of the Absolute Rights of Individuals." Wilson observed approvingly that the leading American treatise on common law—Kent's *Commentaries*—explicitly adopted Blackstone's categorization of these rights and description of them as "absolute"—natural to human beings.[11]

Blackstone's analysis, presented as uncontroverted and familiar to Wilson's listeners in Congress, begins with the "right of personal security"—"a *person's* legal and uninterrupted enjoyment of his life, his limbs, his body, his health...." And Blackstone's unfolding of this right of persons opens, *immediately* after Wilson's quotation, with two paragraphs about the rights of the unborn:

> 1. Life is the immediate gift of God, a right inherent by nature in every individual; and it begins in contemplation of law as soon as an infant is able to stir in the mother's womb.[12] For if a woman is quick with child, and by a potion, or otherwise, killeth it in her womb; or if any one beat her, whereby the child dieth in her body, and she is

delivered of a dead child; this, though not murder, was by the ancient law homicide or manslaughter.(*o*)[13] But at present it is not looked upon in quite so atrocious a light, though it remains a very heinous misdemeanor.(*p*)

The penultimate sentence's footnote "(*o*)" quotes a line from Bracton in Latin about abortion as homicide; the final sentence's footnote (*p*) cites a passage in Coke's *Institutes* that ends by quoting the same line from Bracton.[14] (These two sentences about one element—type [III]—in the criminal law's protection of unborn children's right to life are closely analyzed below, along with the fuller, contextualized treatment that students using 1 *Commentaries* knew they would find in Blackstone's treatise on criminal law, 4 *Commentaries*.)[15] The second of Blackstone's two paragraphs on unborn children's rights follows immediately, on a canvas much wider than criminal-law protections:

> An infant in *ventre sa mere*, or in the mother's womb, is supposed in law to be born for many purposes. It[16] is capable of having a legacy, or a surrender of a copyhold estate, made to it. It may have a guardian assigned to it; and it is enabled to have an estate limited to its use, and to take afterwards by such limitation, as if it were then actually born. And in this point the civil law agrees with ours.[17]

These two paragraphs received intense and merited attention from American courts and lawyers. The *first* paragraph's first sentence concerns the natural right of a living individual possessing human nature.[18] Blackstone here points to *natural realities* calling for legal embodiment, and to a *doctrine of common-law* criminal law that constitutes such an embodiment. The doctrine he mentions here is not the only or even the most important doctrine recalled in these paragraphs to illustrate the rights of the unborn, but it is mentioned immediately, in view both of the section's topic (the right to life) and of what may be inferred from the treatment of natural realities "in contemplation of law."

This last phrase, in Blackstone, signals legal fictions:[19] here, a legal doctrine's treatment of the infant's ability "to stir in the womb"[20] as the start of life for some purpose. Blackstone follows this first paragraph—about the criminal law's narrow, defendant-protective conception of homicide (requiring a "stir[ring]," perhaps partly for evidentiary reasons)—with a paragraph sketching laws that, *free* from artificial constraints, benefit all unborn humans. Thus he hints that the law bearing on rights of persons accommodates more than one "contemplation of law," more than one conception of the person, and may be refined.

For, quite generally and in all eras of our civilization, "person" can mean (1) a natural reality signified in our civilization by Boethius's definition ("an individual substance of a rational nature"), closely corresponding to the sense used in this foundational *Commentaries* text,[21] or (2) a social role signified by the term's root meaning *mask* or *assumed identity*—in which sense the law can deem anything a person (rights-bearing unit).

The Fourteenth Amendment uses "any person" (without qualifiers) paradigmatically in the first sense. Yet the Court, since the 1880s,[22] has also included corporations within "any person" because the meaning of "person"—in the then-prevailing linguistic-conceptual framework of a legally educated public brought up on Blackstone's *Commentaries*—linked under "the Law of Persons" (*the* topic of the whole of 1 *Commentaries*) both natural and artificial persons.[23]

Blackstone's *second* paragraph on unborn persons' rights states an even more pervasive common-law doctrine (construing common law broadly to include established equitable principles). Also essential to the legal context and meaning of "any person" in the 1868 Clauses, this doctrine treats the unborn as rights-bearing persons *from conception*, in many fields besides criminal law. It was developed and expounded in notable English cases adopted by leading state courts in the antebellum generation.

2. Status of Children *in Utero* in American Civil Law

The leading case of *Hall v. Hancock*,[24] which cited many English cases, formulated this doctrine thirty-two years before the debates on the Civil Rights Act of 1866. The Massachusetts Supreme Judicial Court ruled unanimously, per Chief Justice Shaw:

> [A] child is to be considered *in esse* [in being] at a period commencing nine months previously to its birth.... [T]he distinction between a woman being pregnant, and being quick with child, is applicable mainly if not exclusively to criminal cases [and] does not apply to cases of descents, devises and other gifts; and a child will be considered in being, from conception to the time of its birth in all cases where it will be for the benefit of such child to be so considered....
>
> Lord *Hardwicke* says, in *Wallis v. Hodson*,[25] that a child *en ventre sa mere* is a person *in rerum naturâ*, so that, both by the civil and common law, he is to all intents and purposes a child, as much as if born in the [testator's] lifetime....
>
> *Doe v. Clarke*[26] is directly in point[,] ... stat[ing] as a fixed principle, that wherever [it] would be for his benefit, a child *en ventre sa mere* shall be considered as absolutely born.[27]

This doctrine about the real and legal personhood of the unborn from conception was enunciated by an esteemed state chief justice not as a technical rule for one purpose but as a "fixed principle" "to all intents and purposes": the unborn is "a child, as much as if born" and "is a person *in rerum naturâ*."[28] The Georgia Supreme Court, too, in 1849, expressly applied that principle, paraphrasing Hardwicke and Shaw.[29]

Given this general but pointed principle,[30] and the doctrinal architecture of Blackstone's *Commentaries* and thus of American legal education for the century preceding 1868, the original public meaning of "any person" in the fundamental-rights-regarding Equal Protection Clause included living preborn humans.

3. The Three Main Criminal-Law Protections of the Unborn Child in American Common Law

a. In the Treatises

Blackstone's two sentences at 1 *Commentaries* *129–30 select just one of the three criminal-law protections of the child *in utero* that he will expound at 4 *Commentaries* 198–201. There, in one sentence tracking the sentences from Coke that his first volume had cited at *130, Blackstone will affirm[31] that both [III] and [II] are grave offenses:

> [III] To kill a child in its mother's womb, is now no murder, but a great misprision: but [II] but if the child be born alive, and dieth by reason of the potion or bruises it received in the womb it seems, by the better opinion, to be murder in such as administered or gave them [fn. 3 Inst. 50. 1 Hawk. P. C. 80. But see 1 Hal. P. C. 433.].[32]

The passage treats the opinion of Coke (before Hale) and Hawkins (after Hale) as sounder, in this instance, than Hale's[33]—all three treatises being staple authorities in Blackstone's exposition of common-law criminal law. But Blackstone promptly goes on to affirm that [I] accidentally causing the death of the pregnant woman by consensual abortion is murder, and here a judicial ruling by Hale is his primary authority. Expounding homicide with implied or transferred malice, Blackstone says, about felony murder:

> And if one intends to do another felony and undesignedly kills a man, this is also murder.[fn. i 1 Hal. P. C. 465] Thus, if one shoots at A and misses him, but kills B, this is murder.... The same is the case where one lays poison for A; and B, against whom the prisoner had no malicious intent, takes it, and it kills him; this is likewise murder. [fn. j Ibid. 466] So also, [I] if one gives a woman with child a medicine to procure abortion, and it operates so violently as to kill the woman, this is murder in the person who gave it.[fn. k Ibid., 429][34]

Notice: "a woman with child," that is, a pregnant woman—no reference to quickening. In this, Blackstone is following Hale, who—at the end of a vigorous argument concluding that physicians, even if unlicensed, are not guilty of homicide if the potion they give *intending to heal* in fact kills[35]—contrasts that position with the administration of abortifacients:

> But [I] if a woman be with child, and any gives her a potion to destroy the child within her, and she take it, and it works so strongly, that it kills her, this is murder, for it was not given to cure her of a disease, but unlawfully to destroy the child within her, and therefore he that gives a potion to this end, must take the hazard, and if it kill the mother, it is murder....[36]

"[M]ust take the hazard:" the real or pretended medical practitioner who engages in abortion does so at risk of being guilty of murder if his patient's death ensues, however skillfully he acted. For, as Hale's "unlawfully" only implies but Blackstone's exposition at 4 *Commentaries* *198 makes clear, this is a case both of felony murder—because destruction of the unborn child is *incipiently* felonious—and of transferred murderous malice ("malice aforethought")—because intent to destroy the unborn child is *incipiently* homicidal: if the aborted child is born alive and then perishes from the effects of the abortifacient, that is [II] murder.

The three types of criminal-law protection of the unborn that are expounded by Blackstone were expounded both earlier and later in the criminal-law treatises in use in America. The three offenses are set out economically in *Burn's Justice of the Peace*,[37] both the 1764 English edition, and the 1792 American edition, *Burn's Abridgment, or The American Justice; containing the whole practice, authority and duty of justices of the peace; with correct forms of precedents relating thereto, and adapted to the present situation of the United States*,[38] addressed to justices in New Hampshire, Massachusetts, and Vermont and published in Dover, New Hampshire. The chapter on homicide, in its section on murder, treats the three offenses as a single unit: Having set out Hale's ruling (H.P.C. 429) about lethal but not criminal medical mistakes, the section continues with Hale's ruling (H.P.C. 429) that [I] giving a potion "to destroy the child within her" is murder if it kills the mother; this is followed immediately by Coke's ruling (3 *Inst.* 50) that [III] "if a woman be quick with child, and by a poison or otherwise killeth it in her womb" this is "a great misprision but no murder"; and that is followed immediately by Coke's ruling that [II] it is murder if the child is born alive and dies from the abortifacient measure. A sub-paragraph reports Hale's opinion (1 H.P.C. 433) that it cannot "legally be known" whether the abortifacient killed the child or not, but gives the final word to Hawkins's (1 Hawk. 80) view that "it is clearly murder."

First published in London in 1803, Edward East's *Treatise of the Pleas of the Crown* was promptly published in Philadelphia in 1804 and 1806.[39] In the chapter on homicide, after a terse but thoughtful presentation, in passing, of rules [II] and [III], there is an extensive discussion of *transferred* malice aforethought, including homicidal malice transferred from the unborn child to the pregnant mother, a discussion brought to bear on rule [I]:

> [ch. V, sec. 17, margin note: *Malice to one which falls on another*] In these cases the act done follows the nature of the act intended to be done. Therefore *if the latter were founded in malice*, and the stroke from whence death ensued fell... upon a person for whom it was not intended, yet *the motive being malicious*, the act amounts to murder....
>
> ....
>
> ... [margin note: 1 Hale, 429] Hither also may be referred the case of one who gave medicine to a woman; and that of another who put skewers in her womb, with a view in each case to procure an abortion; whereby the women were killed. Such acts are clearly murder; though the original intent, had it succeeded, would not have been so, but only a great misdemeanor; for *the acts were in their nature malicious* and deliberate, and necessarily attended with great danger to the person on whom they were practised.[40]

The skewers case (but not the potion case) is cited in the margin: "Marg[aret] Tinckler's case, 6th Nov. 1781 by all the judges [of England]," and East summarizes it from judges' notes.[41] The abortifacient acts of the accused abortionist (insertion of skewers and tossing up and down of the pregnant woman), though all consensual, were all criminal, and so constituted murder on [the fulfilling of the condition subsequent,][42] the death of the pregnant woman—which in this case happened to be after the birth of her child (alive, but dying instantly).

East's discussion of the transferred malice in a consensual elective abortion is deployed in the affirmation of rule [I] by Russell's *Treatise on Crimes*,[43] perhaps the most important of the early-nineteenth-century English-American treatises.[44] Attempts to evade East and Russell and the major judicial ruling in *Tinckler's Case* will in 1971 play a large part in the desperate efforts of Cyril Means (whose deeply flawed historical analysis, which we will address later, was accepted uncritically by the majority in *Roe*) to avoid and efface the common law's many-faceted criminalization of elective abortion.[45]

His first article (called "Means I" by the Court in *Roe*) was written while he was general counsel of National Abortion Rights Action League, and had already been refuted.[46] The second ("Means II"), which abandoned key theses of the first, was so recent that no scholar had yet examined its sources, and so flawed that it was known to "fudge" the history even by counsel for Jane Roe who cited it.[47] Once scrutinized, its sources crumbled, as did *Roe*'s consequent assertion of a historic common-law "right to terminate a pregnancy."[48] Key elements in Means I and II are selected for examination below, exemplifying the articles' gross errors and manipulations.

b. In State Court Cases

The Brief of the United States, intervening in *Dobbs*, rightly identifies Chief Justice Shaw's judgment for the Supreme Judicial Court of Massachusetts in *Commonwealth v. Parker*[49] as the appropriate representation of what *Roe* called the "received common law in this country."[50] Relying on Bracton-Coke-Blackstone, Shaw wrote that indictments for abortion must aver that the woman "was quick with child."[51] That is the dispositive ruling in the case, a ruling superseded by statute less than six weeks before it was given.[52] It was a conservative, defendant-favorable judicial ruling,[53] but it *explicitly declined to rule* on the question "what degree of advancement in a state of gestation would justify the application of that description [quick with child] to a pregnant woman"—Shaw declined to hold that at common law a woman's "being quick with child" meant that she has "felt the child alive and quick within her."[54] He quoted with implied approval Bracton's ruling—in which *formatum et animatum* certainly did not allude to maternal sensations of fetal movement/kicking—and summarised it: until the fetus had "advanced to that degree of maturity" that it could be "regarded in law" as having a "separate and independent existence," rule [III] abortion was not indictable.[55] Moreover, Shaw reaffirmed the common-law rule [II] that if the child dies from abortion after being born alive, the abortifacient acts, however early in the pregnancy they were done, were murder.

A few weeks earlier the state's legislature had definitively swept away the whole debate about "quick with child," by making abortion at any stage punishable (variously but with at least one year's imprisonment).[56] It adopted the thrust of the Penal Code Commissioners 1844 proposal, but rejected their suggestion that being "quick with child" be relevant to penalty, and instead made the severity of penalty depend upon whether or not the mother died (thus folding a mitigated rule [I] into the newly articulated rule [III]).

Parker's limitation of the common-law rules [II] and [III] to attempts and abortions on a woman "quick with child" was rejected by the courts in Pennsylvania and Iowa.[57] It was accepted by the courts in New Jersey[58] and Maine,[59] but New Jersey's legislature instantly rejected the limitation.[60] Maine's legislature had criminalized abortion at all stages of gestation much earlier, in 1840, and so its court's 1851 ruling on the common law had little practical significance.[61]

4. The Unimportance of Quickening

The conclusion that the original public meaning of "any person" in the Equal Protection Clause included living preborn humans is not undermined by the (limited, shifting, under-determinate, and ultimately transient) relevance at common law of a child's or woman's being "quick" or "quickened."

a. Before the 1850s

Though crumbling by Blackstone's time, archaic views of human generation had some credence as late as the early nineteenth century. Such views, unchallenged from the thirteenth through the mid-seventeenth century, mostly supposed that generation involved an unformed mass, first milky then fleshy, undergoing successive "formations" (receptions of new forms—vegetable, animal, and so forth) until it was differentiated enough, at around six weeks, to acquire a distinctly human form, and substance, the *animation* of which by a rational soul (*anima*)[62] was considered to make it a *human* organism. Despite scientific advances, this widespread misunderstanding of gestation as marked by a discontinuity—by the emergence of a *human individual* at about six weeks from conception—was exacerbated in public discourse by linguistic instability and consequent further misunderstandings making the words "quick," "quicken," and their cognates unstable and ambiguous right down to the mid-nineteenth century. Although these uncertainties led some courts to leave reform of common-law abortion offenses to legislatures,[63] they did not affect the *legal* question whether prenatal humans—*whenever* science showed they existed—were "person[s]" entitled to life and security. All along, they have been, as is demonstrated by near universal talk of unborn children (rather than fetuses) and by the shape of the common law, in which *at least* type [I] homicide protection was entirely independent of quickening in any sense, and—as general opinion about gestation caught up with the science—courts and lawmakers fairly swiftly extended the long-standing type [II] and the even longer-standing type [III] protections by freeing them from any limiting notions of "quick," "quickened," and so forth.[64] The confusion was perhaps at its height during the first half of the nineteenth century, when one two-millennial paradigm was in the last phase of being definitively replaced by the new paradigm of continuous self-directed growth from conception.[65]

THREE SENSES OF "QUICK[EN]"

To make sense of the legal history, three distinct senses of "quick[en]" must be kept in view:

i. "quick with child" meant *pregnant*[66]—from pregnancy's start, conception—but was also sometimes used interchangeably with having
ii. "a quick child" (a *live child*), understood to emerge when embryonic development had yielded an individual sufficiently formed and differentiated and articulated to receive a *rational animating* principle (soul) and so from that moment be a truly human individual, "an infant" and one "*able to* stir in the womb";
iii. "quickening" (a "quickened child," etc.), from the pregnant woman's perception of a shift in the uterus's position or her child's movements, sometime between the twelfth and the twentieth week (or not at all), but normally about the fifteenth or sixteenth week.

It is essential to distinguish sense iii from sense ii (and from sense i so far as it matches sense ii). As stated in the previous paragraphs, "quick" in sense ii applied—in Bracton's mid-thirteenth century,[67] Coke's late sixteenth to early seventeenth,[68] and the educated opinion of Blackstone's time[69]—from the sixth week of pregnancy.

The importance of these meanings and of the distinctions between them derives largely from the passage of Coke that Blackstone cited to illustrate the unborn child's right to life. It is from the *Institutes*' chapter on murder, in the section about who can be murdered (answer: "*a reasonable creature, in rerum natura*"):

[III] If a woman be quick with childe, and by a potion or otherwise killeth it in her wombe; or if a man beat her, whereby the childe dieth in her body, and she is delivered of a dead childe, this is a great misprision, and no murder: but [II] if the childe be born alive, and dieth of the potion, battery, or other cause, this is murder: for in law it is accounted a reasonable creature, *in rerum natura*, when it is born alive.... And so horrible an offense should not go unpunished. And so was the law holden in Bracton's time, *Si aliquis qui mulierem praegnantem percusserit, vel ei venenum dederit, per quod fecerit abortivum, si puerperium jam formatum fuerit; et maxime si fuerit animatum, facit homicidium.* [trans.: Anyone who strikes a pregnant woman, or gives her a poison by which he induces abortion, commits [III] homicide if the infant/fetus was already formed, and especially if it was animated [ensouled].] And herewith agreeth Fleta....

Thus Coke at 3 *Inst.* 50 summed up his statement of rule [III] and [II] by arcing back to the Bracton passage later quoted by Blackstone. And by appealing to Bracton's proposition, Coke emphasizes that when he says that "it"—the "child" with which the woman was "quick"/pregnant—is, when born alive, "accounted a reasonable creature, *in rerum natura*," he means that it is counted/treated as having been alive and capable of being murdered *at the time when the lethal act was done to it*, that is, when it was unborn (at any stage of pregnancy when it was sufficiently formed to be capable of being injured in a manner reliably detectable after its live birth).

Roe uncritically reported Cyril Means's view that "Coke, who himself participated as an advocate in an abortion case in 1601, may have intentionally misstated the law."[70] That "abortion case," *R. v. Sims*, actually goes far to disproving the charge. For there it was not Coke as prosecuting or intervening attorney general but the King's Bench itself that authoritatively stated the unborn-child-protective principles at issue and the corresponding rule [II] in a form ("born alive") shaped by evidential considerations:[71]

for if it be dead born, it is no murder, for non constat [it is not provable] whether the child were living at the time of the battery or not, or if the battery were the cause of the death.

Coke, in the passage (3 *Inst.* 50) recalled by Blackstone (and depreciated by Means and *Roe*), did no more than unpack and restate the two rules. Rule [II] was stated in *Sims* but rule [III] was implicit in—or assumed by—the King's Bench's decision, because the act that would be murder if the child was born alive (and died as a result of the act) must have been felonious or quasi-felonious (misprision *as distinct from misdemeanor*) when it was done. That act occurred in all cases of attempted elective abortion, whether done by the mother or by someone else—any act done so as to kill the unborn child (whether quickened in sense iii or not). Provided the child survived to be born alive, however briefly alive, the sequence of events—beginning with that act and ending with the born child's death because of that act—counted as murder. Once born, the child was in the public realm (*"in rerum natura"*), but it had been "a reasonable creature" at the time when the lethal act was done (perhaps soon after conception) or at any rate as soon as it was formed and animated ("quick" in sense ii). In other words, the lethal act when done was murder subject to a condition subsequent: that the child be born alive.[72] To repeat: The foundation for imposing this condition subsequent was, *Sims* had ruled, an evidential one. And quickening in sense iii is nowhere alluded to.

Moreover, rule-[III] indictable abortion was not merely implicit in *Sims*, awaiting Coke's articulation of it at 3 *Inst.* 50. It was part of the working common law throughout his lifetime, increasingly as the ecclesiastical courts declined. The Means-*Roe* allegation or insinuation that he invented it is baseless.[73]

Hale became an outlier in relation to rule [II] (and perhaps also rule [III]), by taking the *Webb* evidential concerns to an extreme, as if they were a definitional part of the common law: The second consideration, that is common both to murder and manslaughter, is, who shall be said a person, the killing of whom shall be said murder or manslaughter. If a woman be quick or great with child, if she take, or another give any potion to make an abortion, or if a man strike her, whereby the child within her is kil[led], it is not murder or manslaughter by the law of England, because it is not yet *in rerum natura*, tho' it be [III] a great crime, and by the judicial law of Moses was punishable by death, NOR CAN IT LEGALLY BE KNOWN, WHETHER IT WERE KIL[LED] OR NOT [citation to Yearbook of Edward III]. So it is, if after that child were born alive, and baptized, and after die of the stroke given to the mother, this [II] is not homicide [citation to an earlier Yearbook]. (Emphasis added)[74]

The argument proves too much and was rejected, perhaps even by Hale himself,[75] certainly by Blackstone and all the American editions of criminal-law treatises before and after him.[76]

Hale's robust rule [I], on the other hand, was universally followed: causing death by elective, consensual abortion, even when skillfully performed by a registered physician, is always murder. The rule made no reference at all to quickness. Moreover, the rule implicitly deployed a condition-subsequent doctrine of murder, analogous to Coke's rule [II]: attempting abortion, at any stage of gestation, is—by transfer of homicidal malice from unborn child to mother—murder subject to the condition subsequent that the mother die from its effects. And, contrary to Means II's wild claim[77] that Hale invented it in a fit of "Restoration gallantry" towards women endangered by unskillful abortionists, rule [I] had been established and applied for centuries—as far back as Bracton's time—when Hale articulated it.[78]

What was the significance of Coke's and Blackstone's quotation of Bracton, as witness to the "ancient law"?[79] Bracton's sentence plainly addresses "quick"-ness in the *second* sense—a supposedly not-yet-human entity's change (by formation) into an organism and (by animation) into a human organism, "an individual" as Blackstone would say.[80] By quoting Bracton, both Coke and Blackstone were effectively teaching that abortions were common-law heinous misdemeanors (as *sui generis* homicides, neither murder nor manslaughter) from the sixth week of pregnancy.[81]

Roe contradicts this, launching its discussion of the common law (and of quickening in sense iii) by citing Coke and Blackstone for its claim that

> it is undisputed that at common law, abortion performed *before* 'quickening'—the first recognizable movement of the fetus *in utero*, appearing usually from the 16th to the 18th week of pregnancy—was not an indictable offense.

False. Again, Coke and Blackstone cited only Bracton, who was referring to a living child, quick in sense ii, animated by a human form or soul, months before the mother would feel "recognizable movement" around the "16th to the 18th week."[82]

Roe, later in the Court's opinion, returned to Bracton and, by relying on an English translation while ignoring the Latin, made one of its worst and most damaging errors. Having correctly observed (410 U.S. at 133–34) that early common law focused on formation and animation as defining the time from which abortion would be homicide, and that there were uncertainties about when the completion of formation by animation occurred, the Court (at 134) lurched into stark error:

> Due to continued uncertainty about the precise time when animation occurred, to the lack of any empirical basis for the 40–80-day view, and perhaps to Aquinas' definition of movement as one of the two first principles of life, Bracton focused upon quickening as the critical point.

But Bracton, writing in Latin, spoke only of the fetus being formed and animated. "Quick[ened]" is just the term unhappily chosen by

Samuel Thorne, a few years before *Roe*, to translate Bracton's *animatum*.[83] So *Roe*'s claim that Bracton was providing a resolution to uncertainties about "animation" by opting to focus on something else (or on some other term), "quickening," is simply absurd. And the absurdity gives *Roe* an illegitimately easy way to ignore sense ii of "quick" entirely, and to give sense iii and the fifteen-sixteen-week stage an illegitimate primacy or monopoly in its picture of the common law.

Roe's generalization that the common-law offense [III] required perceptible movement is not well defended by citing *State v. Cooper*.[84] It is true that New Jersey's high court, after holding that abortion involves a woman "quick with child," appeared to take sides (though it was not in issue) on when this occurs, answering: "when the embryo gives the first physical proof of life, no matter when it first received it."[85]

Yet *Cooper*'s framing of the question about "offense against the person"—as concerning when a human child is "*in esse*" (in being)— itself tells in favor of the principle that a prenatal human individual warrants protection from its first moment of existence (a principle *Cooper* acknowledges the evidence for, and does not rebut).[86] And *Cooper* made clear that it neither contested that a new human life begins before the mother perceives movement,[87] nor questioned the other legal protections for children at those early developmental stages.[88] It also explicitly chose to leave reform to the legislature,[89] and New Jersey lawmakers promptly abolished the distinction between pre- and post-"quickening" and extended prohibition of this "offense against life" to begin when a woman is "pregnant with child"—that is, at conception.[90]

b. Antebellum and Ratification Eras

The high-water mark of treating quick*ening* (felt movement) as relevant was the early nineteenth century;[91] by the last third of that century, that line was virtually gone, as it was always destined to be—denounced by the medico-legal treatises as groundless because formation and animation occur at conception.[92] The same treatises also regarded the old Bracton-Coke-Blackstone version of "quick with child" (around six weeks) as equally ridiculous.[93] With modern scientific embryology, that Bracton test was compelled, by its own rationale, to recognize personhood from conception even in the cramped, defendant-solicitous criminal law.[94] Thus, the influential and widely circulated 1803 textbook *Medical Ethics* explained that "to extinguish the first spark of life is a crime of the same nature, both against our maker and society, as to destroy an infant, a child, or a man."[95]

What these treatises taught about the unborn—many describing their destruction as murder or indistinguishable from infanticide[96]—was vigorously promoted and re-asserted in professional medical associations, legal education, and state legislatures. The American Medical Association in 1859 dismissed the fiction "that the foetus is not alive till after the period of quickening" and urged correction of any "defects of our laws, both common and statute, as regards the independent and actual existence of the child before birth as a living being."[97]

The leading American treatise on criminal law mocked the pegging of legal protection to felt quickening and effectively buried the Bracton-Coke quickening-as-animation criterion. *Wharton's Criminal Law*, from its first edition in 1846, argued that the criminal law of offenses against unborn persons should be aligned with the law of property, guardianship, and equity[98] as expounded in cases such as *Hall v. Hancock*, adopting authoritative English equity precedents which recognized unborn rights at *all* stages of development.

Thus, by 1866 Chief Justice Tenney of the Maine Supreme Court could accurately report that "the [quickening] distinction...has been abandoned by jurists in all countries where an enlightened jurisprudence exists in practice."[99]

    c. Constants

Whatever the confusions about "quick" and "quickening," the common law indisputably, always and everywhere, made any attempted abortion a serious indictable offense from roughly fifteen weeks. The Ratification Era's virtually unanimous legislative,[100] professional, and public support for this part of the nation's tradition of ordered liberty, *and* for following the science and removing any temporal limit in the criminal law's protection, has been extensively documented by scholars since *Roe* and *Casey*.[101] This confirms that "any person" in the fundamental-rights-regarding Equal Protection and Due Process Clauses includes all unborn human beings.

So does the fact that, while prevailing (though not universal)[102] nineteenth-century common law made only post-"quickening" abortion indictable, the common law *always* regarded pre-quickening abortion as "an act done without lawful purpose," as Chief Justice Shaw mildly put it in 1849,[103] so that abortions (however skillfully performed) that accidentally caused the consenting mothers' death constituted murders. As has been shown above, even pre-quickening abortion was always a kind of inchoate felony for [I] felony-murder purposes,[104] as well as always constituting the *actus reus* with *mens rea* for the crime of [II] murder subject to a condition subsequent: that the child die, however soon, after being born alive.[105]

And all along, every involvement in elective abortion was unlawful in the broader sense that was signaled by its liability to other legal penalties. Contracts for elective abortion services were void for illegality; any place used for elective abortion or for "offering medicines to destroy a child"[106] was liable to summary closure as a disorderly house, on pain of criminal penalty for non-compliance; advertising or publicly offering abortion services so described was criminal per se or a conspiracy *contra bonos mores*. The "openness" with which abortions were available in some places throughout the relevant era, an openness vaunted by pro-choice modern scholars, was analogous to the openness with which other criminal or unlawful practices were available and even respectable among some classes in some areas: to take an extreme case, of the open visitations by the Ku Klux Klan at some times and places, or at the other end of the spectrum, the availability in many places of pornography or forbidden drugs, or of alcohol under local or national prohibition.

B. Antebellum Statutes and Post-Ratification Precedents Confirm This Status

1. State Abortion Statutes

The Union in 1868 comprised thirty-seven states, of which thirty had statutory abortion prohibitions.[107] Most were classified as defining "offenses against the *person*,"[108] with twenty-eight applying before *and* after quickening in senses ii and iii—protecting, in other words, the child from the point of conception.[109] And Congress, legislating for Alaska and the District of Columbia shortly after ratification of the Fourteenth Amendment, referred to unborn children as "person[s]."[110]

Many such statutes were adopted or strengthened within a year or two of the Amendment's ratification, as in New York,[111] Alabama,[112] and Vermont.[113] In Florida, Ohio, and Illinois, the very legislatures ratifying the Amendment also banned abortion at all stages.[114] About a month after ratifying the Amendment, Ohio's senate committee concluded that given the "now...unanimous opinion that the foetus in utero is alive from the very moment of conception," "no opinion could be more erroneous" than "that the life of the foetus commences only with quickening, that to destroy the embryo before that period is not child murder."[115]

Thus, state legislators not only viewed these laws as consistent with the Fourteenth Amendment, but also—like any legally informed reader—would have understood equality of fundamental rights for "any person" to include the unborn. In relation to none of the state legislative proceedings to reform the common law of abortion, beginning at latest in New York's 1829 statute and running through to 1883 (when the forty-third of the states to do so prohibited abortion at all stages) has any suggestion been recorded that any legislator considered that these statutes were abolishing a common-law right or liberty possessed by women since colonial times. The allegation by Cyril Means and *Roe*, now made even more recklessly by Professor Aaron Tang,[116] is that that was precisely—and momentously—what the legislatures were doing. It is an allegation so devoid of evidence and historical plausibility that it appears in only a carefully muted, somewhat chastened form in the present Historians' Brief for the respondents in this case (retreating, tacitly, from the utterly discredited[117] Historians' Briefs in *Webster* and *Casey*).

2. Precedent Interpreting the Fourteenth Amendment: The Case of Corporations

The original public legal meaning of "persons" encompassed *all* human beings. On this, the legal meaning fixed by treatises and cases was confirmed by rapid expansions of prenatal protections in the early to mid-nineteenth century. And—even apart from the latter evidence—under the *Dartmouth College* principle giving legal meaning primacy over drafters' motivating concerns, the inclusion of children *in utero* could not have been blocked except by wording (easily available, but neither proposed nor adopted) such as "any person wherever born."

The plain legal meaning and sweep of a constitutional provision "is not to be restricted" by the "existing" problem it was "designed originally to prevent."[118] So declared Justice Field, on circuit in *Santa Clara County v. Southern Pacific Railroad Co.*, soon affirmed by the Supreme Court itself in its holding (in the headnote) that corporations are persons under the Due Process and Equal Protection Clauses. Field quoted Chief Justice Marshall in Trustees of *Dartmouth College v. Woodward*:

> It is not enough to say that this particular case was not in the mind of the convention when the article was framed, nor of the American people when it was adopted. It is necessary to...say that, had this particular case been suggested, the language would have been so varied as to exclude it.... The case being within the words of the rule, must be within its operation....[119]

As Marshall had explained in *Dartmouth College*, it may be:

> more than possible, that the preservation of rights of this description was not particularly in the view of the framers.... But although a

particular and a rare case may not, in itself, be of sufficient magnitude to induce a rule, yet it must be governed by the rule, when established, [absent] plain and strong reason for excluding it....[120]

The plain and original meaning of the constitutional text extended to the case, though its application had not been envisaged.[121] (Nor was there any "sentiment delivered by its contemporaneous expounders, which would justify us in making" any exception.)[122] This principle remains an axiom of constitutional (especially originalist) interpretation today.[123]

Here it controls. As a matter of plain original meaning to educated lawyers, just as the college charter considered by Marshall fell under the Contract Clause, and the railroad considered by Field was a "person" under the Equal Protection Clause, so too, but *more* certainly, prenatal humans are "persons" under the Clause, whether or not its drafters and ratifiers specifically had that in mind.[124]

Inclusion of the unborn is *more* certain because of their foregrounding in the discussion of fundamental rights to life and security in Blackstone's *Commentaries*, the formative text for educated lawyers of 1776–89 and 1866–68 (in Congress and nationwide), invoked in the introduction of a civil rights bill prefiguring or supported by the Fourteenth Amendment.[125]

Given the evil they aimed to cure, the Amendment's ratifiers may not have subjectively had in mind that the Equal Protection Clause would affect established antebellum Union rules and institutions at all.[126] But if a state in, say, 1870 had legislated to permit all elective abortions, the reasonable ratifier would have agreed that the Amendment's terms entitled guardians ad litem to obtain equitable relief for unborn children.[127] This could have been denied only on some Fourteenth Amendment–limiting theory[128]—for example, of the Amendment's race-specific motivating goals[129]—long and rightly rejected by the Supreme Court as inconsistent with the original and plain public meaning of the words of the Equal Protection Clause.

II. *Roe*'s and *Casey*'s Arguments Against Fetal Personhood Are Unsound

A. Justice Stevens' Defense in *Casey* Has Absurd Implications

Since *Roe*, the only Justice to defend *Roe*'s denial of constitutional personhood—Justice Stevens—clung to a single plank: *Roe*'s claim that unborn children's right to guardians ad litem to protect their property interests is no recognition of personhood because those interests are not perfected until birth.[130]

This plank is no affirmative case, merely a response to one counterargument, and still it fails—attempting to drum up a constitutional principle from one narrowly stated[131] sub-constitutional technical rule[132] while ignoring other rules that reflect the principle declared by Blackstone and Shaw, and by the Lord Chancellors whose rulings they cited: the unborn child "is a person *in rerum natura*" under "the civil and common law" and "to all intents and purposes[.]"[133] Thus, the child *in utero* has had substantive rights to receive income or other property by inheritance or intestate succession, and to get an injunction against waste, rights sufficiently vested to serve her seamlessly through birth and infancy.[134] Then there are the vested rights of the unborn, enforced by courts against their parents' competing rights-claims, in *parens patriae* cases ordering blood transfusions, and so forth.[135] The latter civil rights to life—which could hardly override parental rights unless the unborn were themselves persons—had to be ignored by *Roe* and verbally denied[136] by Justice Stevens. Similarly ignored were the ongoing prosecutions and convictions, now as then, for violations of unborn children's right to life as enforced in state feticide laws.[137]

B. *Roe*'s Grounds for Denying That "Any Person" Included Unborn Children Are Utterly Untenable

Roe's counterarguments merit no deference, *Roe* having disqualified itself from constitutional-settlement status by refusing to appoint a guardian ad litem or hear the contemporaneous Illinois appeal involving an unborn child so represented[138]—and its points fail anyway.

Roe produced three reasons not to recognize unborn humans as persons. Its textual reason, that "person" as used elsewhere in the Constitution gave no "assurance" of "pre-natal application," was concededly inconclusive, and in fact subverts itself by proving too much.[139] Its pragmatic reason was so implausible that it was framed in questions, not propositions.[140] And its historical reason was a cluster of gross errors drawn solely from the two articles by Cyril Means.

History "disposes of any claim that abortion was a 'common law liberty'";[141] the common-law and statutory history above already shows the claim to be preposterous, and it will be supplemented in the next section. And *Roe*'s astonishing "doubt[]" that post-quickening abortion was "ever firmly established as a common law crime"[142] contradicts the precedents and authorities since before Bracton in the 1200s. Means's attempt to explain away those precedents, an attempt repeated by *Roe*,[143] was soon refuted, not least by original records underlying the inaccurate printed accounts used by Means.[144]

C. By Following Means I and II, *Roe* Caricatured the Common Law and the Reforming Statutes

In this section we make only two of the many points that could be made about the analyses (sharply differing but overlapping in error) in Means I[145] and Means II.[146] One point concerns the putative common-law liberty of—or right to—pre-quickening abortion (the version in Means I) or abortion up to birth (the version in Means II). The other concerns the misuse, in both articles, of *State v. Murphy*[147] as principal, indeed almost sole evidence for the articles' fantastic proposition that the mid-nineteenth-century reforming statutes had *no purpose* of rejecting that imagined liberty (in either of its versions) to destroy the unborn ("fetuses"), but instead the *exclusive* purpose—now obsolete, needless and therefore unconstitutional—of protecting women against procedures dangerous to their health or life.

1. The Invented "Common-Law Liberty of Abortion"

To make even the semblance of a case that there was a common-law liberty to abort—whether at all stages or only at pre-quickening stages—Cyril Means had to surmount the settled doctrine of all the treatises used by America's frontline criminal courts, the justices of the peace. That doctrine, to repeat (see supra sections I.A.1–3), had three stable and unchallenged elements:

(i) causing the death of the mother by consensual elective abortion measures at any stage of pregnancy is murder (see Hale, Hawkins, Blackstone, *Conductor generalis*, the *American Justice*, East, Russell, the draft Massachusetts Penal Code, Chief Justice Shaw in *Parker*...);

(ii) causing the death of the child after its birth by elective abortion measures at any stage of pregnancy is murder (see Coke, Hawkins, *Conductor generalis*, the *American Justice*, the draft Massachusetts Penal Code, Chief Justice Shaw in *Parker*...);

(iii) any elective consensual abortion measure is a serious misdemeanor at least if it is taken while the mother was "quick with child" and causes the death of the child in the womb; many authorities (including probably Hale himself and certainly the Massachusetts Penal Code commissioners and American treatises such as Wharton and Bishop) treat it as a serious misdemeanor at *all* stages of pregnancy, at least if it causes the death of the child in the womb.

MEANS I: FALSIFIED BY HALE

Means's 1968 article (Means I) focused[148] on Coke's 3 *Inst.* 50 statement of [III] and [II]. Here Means was concerned to assert, without argument, that Coke's opening words, "If a woman be quick with child..." "witnessed" that

> [a]t some point between the thirteenth and seventeenth centuries, English common law developed along the line suggested by Brac-

ton's distinction between formation and animation. In so doing, it postulated the latter event as occurring at the time of quickening (i.e., toward the end of the fourth or the beginning of the fifth month of pregnancy), as witnessed by the statement of Sir Edward Coke[]....[149]

Means never gave any argument or evidence for the highly improbable claim that Coke was referring to "quickening," in the sense of an event of maternal perceptions "towards the end of the fourth or the beginning of the fifth month."[150] (Nor consequently did *Roe*, which simply changed the just-quoted assertion in Means I into the even more egregiously implausible claim that the common law's adoption of maternally perceived quickening occurred in the famous sentence of Bracton itself.)[151] It is highly probable that Coke, like everyone else between 1250 and 1650, regarded the woman as *quick with child*, if not from the beginning of her pregnancy, then at the time when the approximately six-week formation of the conceptus into a child was completed and followed, distinctly but presumptively immediately, by the distinct though secret event of animation, generally accepted as occurring at about the fortieth, forty-second, or forty-sixth day after conception.[152]

On this almost universally accepted schema, Bracton's distinction between *formatum* and *animatum* would be read as disambiguating *formatum*, "formed," which on its own could refer to any point in an eighteen-day period between the twenty-eighth and forty-sixth day. "Quickening" in the sense that interested some nineteenth-century judges, Means, and the Historians' Brief in *Dobbs*, was irrelevant to those for whom, like Bracton and Coke, the key question always was and is: From when are we dealing with *a distinct human being* in the womb? Means I's grand division of theories into "immediate animation," "mediate animation" and "birth," and the declaration of Means I at 418 (where *Roe* begins to cite Means) that "the only one of the three theories that explains absolutely nothing in our legal system is immediate animationism,"[153] totally overlooks the two different ideas of "mediate": ensoulment at around 40 days, and maternally perceptible movement at approximately 105 days. Means I proceeds, at 420, to derive from the quoted passage of Coke the proposition "an abortion before quickening, with the woman's consent, whether killing the foetus while still within the womb, or causing its death after birth alive, was...not a crime at all." This is what Means I (by contrast with Means II) will mean by the "ancient common-law liberty" to abort.[154]

But that passage in Coke (and Blackstone and the rest) dealt only with rules [III] and [II], not at all with [I], the liability of the provider of an elective abortion for murder if the mother dies from it. *Means I admits that this liability is incurred even though the abortion was done or attempted before quickening.*[155] The article does not raise the rule [I] issue at all until it has purportedly completed its demonstration that pre-quickening consensual abortion was no crime either in the woman or in her provider, and has passed on to a consideration of the subordinate question whether the consent of the husband was needed if the not-yet-quickened pregnant woman was married. (Answer: There is no evidence that it was, and the article does not for even a moment consider how improbable its liberty thesis is in relation to a "patriarchal" society—or indeed any society with a serious conception of marriage—insofar as it proposes that the common law made no objection to the married woman's secret or defiant destruction of her husband's son and heir.)

This sequencing allows Means I to argue in a vicious circle: The provider of a pre-quickening abortion was acting lawfully because the passage quoted from Coke shows that "[a]bortion before quickening was not an offense at common law at all (unless the patient died)."[156] But that passage from Coke dealt only with rules (ii) and (iii), and it neither stated nor implied that *abortion was lawful* if the mother was not yet quick with child: It merely said that if she *was* quick with child, abortion was a great misprision and was murder if the child born alive died from it.[157] Means took care to evade the implications of holding the abortionist guilty of murder if "the patient [mother] died," by avoiding—navigating around—Hale's statement of the rule, which *describes the abortion as unlawful*—"unlawfully to destroy the child within her, and therefore, he that gives a potion to this end must take the hazard...."[158] It is because the procedure is unlawful that the abortionist, however skillful, "must take the hazard" of being liable for murder if the mother dies.[159]

Hale is here making clear that there is no common-law liberty of abortion. For if the abortionists are guilty of murdering the consenting woman if she dies from the abortion, the murderous acts were none other than their abortifacient conduct, perhaps many months before her death. The common law knew nothing of an act that is lawful when and as done—which involves neither *actus reus* nor *mens rea*—but becomes criminal on the happening of some subsequent event. What it does recognize is *unlawful* acts that constitute criminal homicide if and only if some subsequent harm happens to result from that act.

So Means I deals with the issue by quoting two American judgments (*Parker* in 1845 and *Smith* in 1851) in which the judges do not quote Hale, and instead of his term "unlawfully to destroy the child" use the softer phrase "without lawful purpose" (a phrase that Means I proceeds to treat as concerned only with the common law's implied permission of therapeutic life-saving abortion).[160] The fact that one of the judgments cites Hale is buried in a footnote, without identifying the citation beyond "a posthumously published (1736) treatise by Sir Matthew Hale (1609–1670)."[161]

MEANS II: EXTREMIST ESCAPE FROM ITS AUTHOR'S DILEMMA

So Means was obliged to take seriously, and tackle, the problem concealed by Means I. He did so in Means II, with new boldness but a familiar technique.

The new boldness is part of the radical shift in stance between Means I and Means II. Quickening, the heart of Means I, has been moved almost offstage: The liberty proclaimed is not of pre-quickening elective abortion; it is "English and American women's common-law liberty of abortion at will," that is, to "terminate at will an unwanted pregnancy" "at every stage of gestation."[162] Correspondingly, the rule [I] issue is contained within the question with which Means II, on its second page, frames its whole discussion: "Did an expectant mother *and her abortionist* have a common-law liberty of abortion *at every stage of gestation?*"[163]

The familiar technique, already deployed in Means I, is to postpone all mention of rule [I] until after the discussion has reached the essential conclusion that—in the Means II version—the woman did indeed have (in England until the statute of 1803, in America "until 1830") a common-law liberty of elective abortion just as much after as before quickening. Only then is the question about "her abortionist" raised and rule [I] reconsidered.[164] The answer that Means II will give to its framing question from page 336 is delayed until page 373, and it is an answer dividing the position of "the expectant mother" from the position of "her abortionist":

> During the late seventeenth, the whole of the eighteenth, and early nineteenth centuries, English and American women were totally free from all restraints, ecclesiastical as well as secular, in regard to the termination of unwanted pregnancies, at any time during gestation. During virtually the same period (i.e., starting with Hale's decision in 1670), however, the common law had imposed a new risk on the woman's abortionist: he became the insurer of her survival.... [T]he common law said[:] ... if your patient die, you will hang for her murder. If she survive, you will have committed no offense.[165]

On the preceding page, 372, Means II states that last proposition more radically: "In Massachusetts when Shaw wrote [in *Parker*], therefore [since there was no ecclesiastical jurisdiction, only secular common law], *it would have been false to say that an abortifacient act was done 'unlawfully'*; it merely lacked 'lawful purpose.'"[166]

But in the very same sentence, Shaw had said: "the consent of the woman cannot take away the imputation of malice, any more than in the case of a duel, where, in like manner, there is the consent of the parties."[167] What is the "malice" of the provider of a consensual abortion? Means II ignores the question at this critical point (just as Means I had ignored it entirely). But earlier Means II had tried to tackle it, by casting doubt (unwarranted, as we shall soon see) on what East says about transferred malice in the justly influential passage (1 East 230) discussed above.[168] Means I and II needed to deny or evade, and did deny or evade, the fact that for Hale, East, and Chief Justice Shaw, *the malice of the consensual abortion was against the unborn child*.

Shaw's comparison with dueling[169] helps make sense of the whole question whether the abortionist was acting unlawfully even before any mother died from his elective procedures. It helps to bear in mind that the common law did not operate with a principle or general doctrine that an attempt to commit a crime (felony, misprision, misdemeanor) is itself an indictable crime.[170] But it did operate with a principle or general doctrine that there had to be an *actus reus*, the doing of which with *mens rea* defined the time and place of the committing of the offense, even if the offense's indictability depended upon a subsequent event such as a death.[171] What was done before the fulfilling (if ever) of that condition subsequent was, of course, unlawful and in a broad, important sense, criminal.[172]

How did Means II evade and disguise the implications of East's discussion? First by pretending that 1 East 230 was not a general statement of principle and law, but a commentary on *Tinckler's Case*, in which both the mother and the baby (born living for a few moments) died—allowing Means to claim that, since the defendant abortionist was not prosecuted for murdering the baby, and East did not allude to the murder of the baby, he and the Crown prosecutors and the trial judge and all the "Twelve Judges of England" must have rejected the doctrine in Coke (3 *Inst.* 50) that [II] the abortion-caused death of the aborted baby born alive is murder.[173] The whole argument is absurd (and entirely characteristic of the argumentation of Means I and II), for the following three reasons.

(1) As is reported on 1 East 355, a page which Means II quotes in its entirety, the baby when born was proved by the surgeons to be "perfect."[174] So there was no ground for prosecuting Tinckler for murder under rule [II], and all Means's inferences from that non-prosecution, and all his rhetorical flourishes in stating them, are entirely worthless. Means simply ignores what he has transcribed about the fact ("was perfect") that would have made it impossible to establish the causal link between abortive measures and death that is one of the two requirements of rule [II].

(2) 1 East 230 is not, as Means II claims,[175] a commentary on *Tinckler*.[176] It is a general exposition of a legal rule, of which *Tinckler* is one appropriate illustration. But, as the page makes unambiguously clear, *Tinckler* is only the second of two different illustrations, two precedents explicitly identified as different, the first being an unidentified case of giving an abortifacient potion causing the death of the mother (with no suggestion of a born-alive baby or a possible rule [II] murder).

(3) Means II's insistent claim that East probably disapproved of Coke's rule [III] because he certainly (says Means) disapproved of Coke's rule [II][177] is disproved not only by its illogic as a fallacious *and* groundless argument from silence (about Tinckler's baby's unprosecuted death), but above all by the plain fact, unaccountably ignored by Means, that only two pages earlier in the same discussion of homicidal malice, 1 East 227 explicitly approved and adopted precisely both of Coke's rules![178] Indeed, for good measure,1 East 228 pointed out that both Hale and Staundford (Means II's hero in the article's struggle to discredit rule [III]) *agreed with rule [III]* even though they rejected rule [II] for reasons that East, like almost everyone else, goes out of his way to say were unsound.[179]

After and seemingly because of these blunders or misfeasances, Means II simply ignores the references to malice that appear prominently in the authorities he approves: *Russell on Crimes*,[180] Shaw in *Parker*,[181] and the Maine court in *Smith* (1851).[182] Notably, Means II's commentary on *Parker* focuses entirely on Shaw's low-key phrase "without lawful purpose," ignoring what Means I had said about the same passage, and instead implausibly taking it as a sign that Shaw thought Hale treated abortion as only an ecclesiastical offense.[183] The whole commentary functions to divert readers' attention away from the real premises and logic of Shaw's argument: the consensual abortion is a malicious act, the "imputation of malice" is no more cancelled by the woman's consent than it is in the case of a duel, and the upshot is that the procedure, however skillful, is not just a homicide but a murder.

The failure of Means II's extended discussion of rule [I] further illustrates the extravagant baselessness of the article's rejection of rules [II] and [III], with its accompanying attempt to remove from the common law of abortion everything that was affirmed by Coke and by all who followed him, including Blackstone and all the treatises recalled above.

2. The Reforming Statutes' Rationale: *Murphy* Mishandled

To recall: Both Means I and Means II ascribed extraordinary, indeed unique importance to *State v. Murphy*.[184] They treated a single sentence in the New Jersey Supreme Court's opinion as their principal, indeed almost their sole evidence for their proposition that mid-nineteenth-century reforming statutes in dozens of states had no purpose of rejecting the (imaginary) common-law liberty (in either of its versions) to destroy the unborn ("foetuses"), but instead the exclusive purpose of protecting women against procedures dangerous to their health or life. The articles were entirely unconcerned with the decision in *Murphy*. It was only ever one single, oracular sentence that these articles quoted; they made not the slightest reference to the facts or the issue in the case, or to the context of the sentence in the New Jersey Supreme Court's opinion. Here is the sentence:

The design of the [New Jersey] statute [of 1849] was not to prevent the procuring of abortions, so much as to guard the health and life of the mother against the consequences of such attempts.[185]

About this sentence, Means I and Means II made the same incredible claim:

Until now [1968!], this observation, in *State v. Murphy*, had been the sole piece of contemporary evidence as to why the legislatures enacted these statutes abridging the liberty to abort before quickening, a right which women enjoyed at common law for centuries. It remains the sole *judicial* exposition of such a statute contemporary with its enactment.[186]

Towards the end of Means I, the author doubles down:

The New York Revisers' Report of 1828 and the New Jersey decision of 1858 in *State v. Murphy* are literally the only known contemporary authoritative texts explaining the reason for the enactment of any of these novel prohibitions of abortion before quickening. Both point to the life and health of the pregnant woman as the *sole* objective in legislative view.[187]

And Means II repeats all this:

The only contemporaneous judicial explanation for the enactment of any of the pre-Lister [scil. 1867 or 1884][188] abortion statutes—a decision of 1858 construing New Jersey's first such statute passed in 1849—contains [the sentence above quoted].[189]

Despite the effrontery of these false claims, they had the desired effect. They were swallowed whole by *Roe*.[190] The Court makes a show of saying that it is merely describing what "parties challenging state abortion laws" "claim" and "argue."[191] But the argument and the evidence for it is simply what Means I and Means II say about *Murphy*, and by the end of this key passage the Court is simply embracing it:

> Pointing to the absence of legislative history to support the contention [that a purpose of these laws, when enacted, was to protect prenatal life], [parties challenging state laws] claim that most state laws were designed solely to protect the woman. Because medical advances have lessened this concern, at least with respect to abortion in early pregnancy, they argue that with respect to such abortions the laws can no longer be justified by any state interest. There is some scholarly support for this view of original purpose.[fn. See discussions in Means I and Means II.] The few state courts called upon to interpret their laws in the late nineteenth and early twentieth centuries did focus on the State's interest in protecting the woman's health rather than in preserving the embryo and fetus. [fn. See, e.g., *State v. Murphy*, 27 N.J.L. 112, 114 (1858).][192]

These claims by Means I and II—that *Murphy* was the only judicial decision before 1867/1884 (Lister) or 1968 ("now" in Means I) that identified the legislative purpose of a state abortion statute—were untenable, to put it mildly. Within a year of *Murphy*, the Massachusetts Supreme Court authoritatively—and not as mere dictum—identified the purpose of that state's 1845 statute,[193] and the Vermont Supreme Court identified the purpose of that state's 1846 statute.[194] And, tellingly though unsurprisingly, neither court saw any reason to mention maternal health. Each court, independently of the other, identified the legislative purpose as filling in the gap in the common law's protection of the unborn child—the "quick with child" requirement of rule (iii).

Equally untenable was the other main claim made by Means I and II about *Murphy*: that it held or declared that protection of unborn life was not even one purpose of New Jersey's 1849 statute. Even read in isolation, the key words of the quoted sentence are "not to prevent the procuring of abortions, *so much as to* guard the health...."; the words here italicized imply, unquestionably, that preventing the procuring of abortions was *a purpose*, though not the primary one. But context is a primary determinant of meaning, and the sentence's context, totally ignored by Means and *Roe*, shows that "not to prevent the procuring of abortions" meant far less than appears in isolation. It was not intended to contrast preventing destruction of unborn life with preventing damage to maternal health, but rather to contrast what the court took to be the common law's exclusive focus on the fate of the unborn with the legislature's *additional* concern to protect women from the dangers presented by the activities and solicitations of abortionists and suppliers of abortifacients.

For the sole issue in *Murphy* was whether it was a defense to a charge of supplying abortifacient drugs that the woman had not swallowed them. The court's answer is No. That answer was obvious from the words of the statute, but the court launched itself into a redundant and convoluted justification. The mischief tackled by the statute is supply of means of inducing abortion or, more generally, is *the activities of abortionists*. Those activities endangered maternal health, *whether or not* a particular woman supplied with an abortifacient (and/or solicited to use it) did in fact incur the danger to herself [not to mention to "the embryo and fetus"!] by actually using it.

So the emphasis in the sentence selected and quoted by Means I and II was really on *procuring*, here meaning: actually bringing about an abortion. Procuring is being contrasted with *attempting* to procure, and/or with *facilitating* abortion:

> [T]he mischief designed to be remedied by the statute was the supposed defect in the common law developed in the case of *The State v. Cooper*, viz., that the procuring of an abortion, *or an attempt* to procure an abortion, with the assent of the woman, was not an indictable offence, as it affected her, but only as it affected the life of the *foetus*.

The design of the statute was not to prevent the procuring of abortions, *so much as to* guard the health and life of the mother against the consequences of such *attempts. The guilt of the defendant is not graduated by the success or failure of the attempt.* It is immaterial whether the *foetus* is destroyed, or whether it has quickened or not. In either case the degree of the defendant's guilt [under the statute] is the same.[195]

For reasons best known to itself, the court further complicates its opinion with another concern: to make clear that the statute, in saying "if any person...shall administer...or prescribe...or direct..." was criminalizing only the activities of abortionists, not of their clients. The court contrasts all this with the common law, focused as it was and is on the life of the unborn child: Unless the child was quickened and then destroyed, the actions of both mother and abortionist are unindictable at common law, however damaging they are to the woman. (The court neglects rule [I].)

Some of these defects of the common law would have been remedied had the common law incorporated a functioning general principle that it is an indictable offense to attempt or incite an offense. But not only did it lack such a principle,[196] but by its exclusive focus on the formed or quickened child, it also failed (leaving aside the mother's death and rule (I)) to penalize either successful or attempted abortions early in pregnancy, even though such acts and attempts were just as dangerous, at least to the mother, from conception onwards, and even if there had in fact been no conception. As the court put it:

> At the common law, the procuring of an abortion, or the attempt to procure an abortion, by the mother herself, or by another with her consent, was not indictable, *unless the woman were quick with child.*[197]

Thus, the legislature's remedy had two aspects: The statute criminalized, regardless of quickening,[198] (1) all elective abortifacient facilitations and incitements, regardless of their outcome (including actual consumption of abortifacients), and (2) unlike the common law, the statute [does not] make it criminal for the woman to swallow the potion, or to consent to the operation or other means used to procure an abortion. No act of hers is made criminal by the statute. Her guilt or innocence remains as at common law. Her offence at the common law is against the life of the child. The offence of third persons, under the statute, is *mainly* against her life and health. The statute regards her as the victim of crime, not as the criminal; as the object of protection, rather than of punishment.[199]

None of this in any way suggests that the statute had cancelled either the common-law abortion offenses or the common law's concern for the child.[200] The "mainly" here, like the "so much as" in the sentence quoted by Means I and II, suggests instead that the statute's reforming priority was that such protective concern for the child be extended so as to protect the life and health of women *more adequately than before*.[201]

But, absurd though it was, the Means I and II thesis that the legislative purpose of dozens of state statutes could be demonstrated by pointing to one decontextualized sentence in a single, convoluted, debatable court opinion was, as shown above, essentially adopted in *Roe*. Before long, but too late, the thesis was demolished by James Witherspoon's exhaustive survey of those statutes' actual features, and his unfolding, as exemplar, of the legislative history of Ohio's reforming statute of 1868.[202] The lively concern for the child in the womb so amply displayed in the Ohio statute's particular legislative history was present and manifested in numerous features of the design and enacting of overwhelmingly many other reforming statutes in other states (not least in the New Jersey statute under discussion in *Murphy*)—Witherspoon listed and exemplified in detail no fewer than twelve such features, and identified all the statutes that embodied them.[203] In doing so, he also showed that the legislators' pervasive concern for children *in utero* was always entirely compatible with, indeed reinforcing, and reinforced by, an equivalent lively concern for the health of women.

III. In Founding and Ratification Era Legal Thought, Constitutional Status as a Person Transcended Narrow Doctrines and Legal Fictions

A. A Preliminary Warning Example: Roscoe Pound

The attempt by Justice Stevens to narrow the constitutional-level understanding of "any person" by appeal to technical rules or doctrines inverts the logic of constitutional thought. It does so by neglecting the meanings that were public (shared) among Founding and Ratification Era constitution-makers and ratifiers, meanings conveying (and taken by those makers and ratifiers to convey) the very framework of legal thought and of the legal system. That framework they took to be articulated, in broad and solid terms, by Blackstone's *Commentaries*, deeply based as these were not only on case law, statutory developments and classic treatises, but also on prior attempts such as Matthew Hale's[204] to grasp the system of English law as a whole. Legal thought and language so framed took as foundational natural realities such as those that in 1 *Commentaries* *129–30 Blackstone takes as a starting point for that seminal passage's exposition of the natural person's right to life.

An analogous inversion is exemplified by Roscoe Pound's ambitious legal-theoretical treatment of persons and legal personality in his final magnum opus, *Jurisprudence*.[205] Pound's discussion is full enough to make clear the doctrinal or analytical incoherence that results from giving doctrines and fictions priority over realities such as the continuous identity of an individual person both before and after birth, notwithstanding birth's reasonable social and legal importance.

In section 127, "BEGINNING AND TERMINATION OF LEGAL PERSONALITY," Pound commences with the seemingly authoritative proposition: "Beginning of natural legal personality is conditioned by birth. The Romans held, and this has been adhered to ever since, that this means complete separation of a living being from the mother." There follows a page of references to various relevant points of difference between classical Roman law and later German, French,

Spanish and other doctrines or enactments. After two dozen lines of this we read: "At common law the requirement is that the child be born alive." But the only authority cited to verify this is "Coke, Third *Inst.* (1644) 50."[206]

At this point it is obvious that Pound's discussion of "persons" in law has come adrift. A technical rule of criminal law *about murder*, established in 1601 and related by Coke in a paragraph about murder without the slightest theoretical pretension, is being treated as if it were (or made manifest) a general principle of law and building-block of juristic thought. Pound's misuse of Coke is refuted by Blackstone's treatment of the unborn across the whole sweep of the law in 1 *Commentaries* *129–30, examined above throughout Section I.A.1.

One page further on, Pound suddenly admits that Roman law had a rival principle, opposite to the *not-a-person-until-birth* principle he had canonised. Now he says: "[U]nborn children are in almost every branch of the civil law regarded as clearly existing"! Pound discusses technical exemplifications of this, but makes no effort to reconcile it with the position (principle? rule? doctrine? definition?) he announced without qualification at the beginning.

Pound gets to the truth of the matter when he broadens his discussion of persons and personhood to engage with human realities, benefits and harms, not mere jigsaw pieces of old (and mostly foreign) legal rules and maxims:

> In the United States down to the Civil War, the free negroes in many of the states were free human beings with no legal rights. They were not property. But they could scarcely be called legal persons.... At common law there was civil death—loss of legal personality in one naturally alive.
>
> . . . .
>
> But there came to be a steady expansion of legal personality, a recognition of the human being as a moral and so a legal unit and extension of legal capacity, so that in the era of natural law, legal personality was

thought of as an attribute of the individual human being. The human being had certain qualities whereby he was naturally entitled to have certain things and do certain things and so was the subject of natural and therefore legal rights.

Pound does not pause to note that this "natural-law" thinking—subordinating legal doctrines and fictions to *truths* about the "attributes" and "qualities" that belong to "the human being" *prior* to a society's laws—is integral to the thinking we find crystallized in the Constitution and again in the Due Process and Equal Protection Clauses. Instead Pound goes straight on, taking for granted that academic progress has "eliminated" all that attention to natural realities and consequent moral, pre-legal responsibilities:

With the natural-law basis eliminated, there remained for analytical jurisprudence the definition [of person]: "A subject of legal rights and duties."[207]

But though you expel nature with a pitchfork, it comes back in by the rear door, and so we find Pound soon admitting, indeed on the following page, that

analytical jurisprudence has had to take account of idiots, *unborn children*, babes in arms, in Roman law children under seven years, and those lunatics whose mental disease inhibits exercise of will. *All these are commonly accounted natural persons and certainly would today be legal persons.*

In short: The part of Pound's work on persons that is of constitutional relevance is the part where natural realities are acknowledged as informing the law's most fundamental (constitutional) building blocks and prescriptions, not the part where axioms articulating legal fictions adopted in former legal systems or former doctrines of our own system are taken—too quickly, without sufficient reason—to be truths of legal ("analytical") philosophy.

B. Constitutional Terms: Neither "Common Sense" nor "Common Law" but Meanings Shared by Drafters/Ratifiers

C'Zar Bernstein's article "Fetal Personhood and the Original Meanings of 'Person'"[208] argues that an originalist interpreter, considering the original meaning of "person" in the Constitution, must choose between the original "ordinary meaning" and the original "common-law meaning." The former provides a route to acknowledging that the unborn are within the meaning of "any person" in the Fourteenth Amendment (which would, as Bernstein himself quite reasonably thinks, be the better solution in terms of policy or justice). But that route is blocked if the appropriate original meaning is the common-law meaning, which Bernstein seeks to identify across about forty pages, mostly concerning "the Born-Alive Rule" in criminal law, law of torts, and succession: In all three areas (though not with certainty in the law of succession), the born-alive rule (Bernstein argues) excludes fetuses from the scope of "person." Investigating his article's treatment of the material can shed light on our Brief's argument, and the failure of his article's good-faith critique of fetal personhood provides reassurance of the solidity of our Brief's position.

The case for holding that unborn children are persons within the original meaning of the Fourteenth Amendment *does not look to either of Bernstein's alternatives*. On the one hand, it does not inquire after an unfocused "ordinary meaning" or "ordinary understanding," or "ordinary-language public meaning," though it agrees with Bernstein about what his inquiry yields: that "person" in the Equal Protection Clause refers to any "'member of the human species,' a category that includes the unborn." The better focus of inquiry is into the *meaning of "person" that was shared or "ordinary" among legally informed members of the drafting and ratifying legislatures* when they were considering documents intended for legal deployment, including constitutional text, sub-constitutional legislation, and related judicial and administrative usage. In that context they neither excluded nor gave priority to how their electorates understood the term. The legally informed members of the relevant drafting and ratifying bodies were thoroughly familiar with the highly prominent use of the word "person" to structure the treatises foundational to their entire formation first as students and then as, in many instances, practitioners of law.

On the other hand, however, that foundational usage of "persons" as a primary building block in the thought and discourse of the *Commentaries* cannot be rightly understood as "the common-law meaning of 'person.'" For:

1. *There is and was no single common-law meaning of "person," no common-law definition of "person,"* but rather a variety of rules and stated principles identifying the categories of persons that are the subjects or objects of specific rules and doctrines, rules and doctrines that were shaped and adopted to do *justice*-according-to-law as conceived by judges, practitioners and treatise-writers (with constant reference to corrective legislation) at particular periods. These justice-seeking rules and principles have drawn major (but not unchanging) distinctions between the born and the unborn. And that line-drawing was appropriate in principle, for two reasons. One reason was the uncertainty that used to prevail, more or less insuperably until birth, about whether a particular unborn human entity was one, two, or many; alive or dead; a creature of a rational nature or a hydatidiform mole; male or female. Another reason was and is the social significance of attitudes and customs that have their root in the change that birth made and still to some extent makes: from darkness and uncertainty to the daylight of the visible, ordinary world. Some of the law's justice-seeking rules do not count the unborn among their objects or subjects, but other rules—notably, those *essential to preserving the basic interests of the unborn* at least prior to birth—*do*, or (on the rights-theory of our Constitution), *should* count the unborn the same as or very much like other persons.

2. Members of the drafting and ratifying community did not consider themselves bound to particular common-law judgments, rules, and doctrines, where these collided with their own judgments about

justice and practicality. As was outlined in section I.B.1 above, the generation that drafted and ratified the Equal Protection Clause was the generation that most profoundly and extensively reformed and replaced the common law's forms of criminal-law protection of the unborn—always increasing the level of protection. For that generation of state legislators, by and large, regarded that historic set of rules and doctrines as in some respects profoundly unsatisfactory—that is, inadequate to the truth about human beings precisely as objects of the law's protection.

1. Common-Law Succession Rules

Bernstein forces the common-law rules and doctrines onto a Procrustean bed (what he calls "the Born-Alive rule"), in which personhood is never attributed to the unborn until they are born alive, at which point it is attributed to them *by a fiction* as having been enjoyed prior to birth. So, for example, Bernstein says:

> In the succession context, there are two legal fictions. First, the legal fiction that the unborn do not exist. Second, the legal fiction that persons already born were born before they were in fact born. This second fiction—the relation of birth back to conception—was necessary only because the first fiction existed and so is evidence of the lack of legal personality of the unborn at common law.

This way of formulating the common law's rules is starkly opposed to the language and thought of 1 *Commentaries* *129–30 and of *Hall v. Hancock*. Bernstein's article never mentions *Hall v. Hancock*, though he labors on some of the cases and dicta collected in Shaw's judgment there.[209] The opposition between Bernstein's imagined common-law discourse and the real discourse of the common law is illustrated in note 209 above. To repeat: The real common law goes with the grain of reality, tracking the commonsense and scientific truth that birth, while momentous as entry into a public social world, is not at all the beginning of the child's life as a person, a life which began many months earlier. The common law's fictions, where they are adopted, run in the direction of *enhancing* protection of the unborn *in utero*—by treating them for many purposes *as if* they were born—while simplifying the disposition of the affairs and interests of the born by treating those unborn who emerge from the womb *dead* (and thus incapable of being benefited) *as if* they had never existed.

Bernstein can point to a couple of decisions in which judicial dicta speak of the unborn as if they were only fictitiously existent, or fictitiously persons. Thus the Chancellor of the Chancery Court of New York in *Marsellis v. Thalhimer* said:

> [T]he existence of the infant as a real person before birth is a fiction of law, for the purpose of providing for and protecting the child, in the hope and expectation that it will be born alive, and be capable of enjoying those rights which are thus preserved for it in anticipation.[210]

But though the case is not reported to have been cited to the court in *Hall v. Hancock*, Shaw's piling up of statements of principle looks as if it was aimed against this talk of fiction, and was concerned to emphasize that *the existence of the infant as a real person from conception to birth is acknowledged by the law, with two qualifications: (1) the protection afforded to the unborn infant's interests in life and property is afforded for its benefit only and cannot be deployed in defining the property interests of others unless and until the child is born; and (2) these protections terminate if it is born dead (or otherwise dies before birth),* and for the future the law's rules apply to those concerned (who might have benefited had it been born alive) as if the child had never lived.

The dicta about fiction in *Marsellis* were entirely unnecessary to the decision,[211] which itself and in its essential reasoning and treatment of authority is fully in line with the cases deployed four years later in *Hall v. Hancock*. All that needed to be said was said elsewhere in the judgment and in all the authorities including *Hall v. Hancock*: The law's acknowledgement of the reality and existence of the unborn human being/person is, pending birth, *for the benefit of that infant only*. It is not for the benefit of others, and so does not count for purposes of defining those others' property/succession entitlements.

Similarly with Bernstein's other succession authorities, first *Gillespie v. Nabors*,[212] which states:

> From the citations above,[213] it results that although an unborn child is treated as having an existence for certain purposes beneficial to it, yet, this existence is conditional and imperfect, and confers no rights of property, until it is born alive. When that event happens, to preserve successions, and to prevent forfeitures, it becomes, by relation and legal fiction, a separate, individual person having personal and property rights, dating back to the time of conception, when such backward step is necessary to protect a descent or devise. If, however, the foetus is never born alive, then it is treated as if it never had an existence.[214]

This is an outlier, not a convincing or representative analysis or explanation. The claim that the *existence* of the unborn is "conditional and imperfect" and that on birth the "unborn child"/"foetus" "becomes, by relation and legal fiction, a separate, individual person" is *one way* of expressing the conditionality of, and limitations upon, the law's acknowledgement and protection of the unborn person's rights and interests. But it is neither the only way, nor the best way, which is the way adopted by the weightier line of authority and exposition, exemplified by *Hall v. Hancock* and the cases it relied upon: The child *in utero* is to be considered a person entitled to legal protections, while, *in utero*, as a distinct individual with rights—subject, however, to a condition subsequent, namely that if he or she is stillborn, those prenatal rights (or many of them) are treated *as if* they had never been.

Bernstein's remaining relevant authority is Justice Field's dictum for the Supreme Court in *Knotts v. Stearns* (decided in 1875):

> The posthumous child did not possess, until born, any estate in the real property of which his father died seized which could affect the power of the court to convey the property into a personal fund, if the interest of the children then in being, or the enjoyment of the dower right of the widow, required such conversion.[215]

But Bernstein does not mention what the Court's opinion also says, later on the same page: a statement (quoted below) that supports the directly contrary premise (for reaching the same conclusion). This statement cancels every possible implication that the Court has set its face against acknowledging either the existence of the unborn child or that child's capacity while unborn to possess an estate or interest in land (even if that possession or interest could not be counterposed to the power of conversion):

> But there is another answer to the objection. Assuming that the child, before its birth, whilst still *en ventre sa mere*, possessed such a contingent interest in the property as required his representation in the suit for its sale, he was thus represented, according to the law which obtains in Virginia, by the children in being at the time who were then entitled to the possession of the estate. Parties in being possessing an estate of inheritance are there regarded as so far representing all persons, who, being afterwards born, may have interests in the same, that a decree binding them will also bind the after-born parties.[216]

In short, the Court here showed itself to be quite free of the dogmatic fictions of fetal non-existence that Bernstein asserts were "the common law."

In sum: Rather than awaiting birth and then *backdating* to conception the personhood and existence of the child born alive, the common law ascribes to the unborn child—from its actual conception and all the way along its gestation *in utero*—the status and legal protections that the child will possess once born, making just two adjustments in view of birth's significance.

The common law ascribes to the unborn child the status and protections the child will have from birth (a) to the full extent (and only to the extent) that this status and those protections are for *that child's benefit* and (b) subject to a condition subsequent: that if the child is never born alive, that status will—for many purposes *but not all*—be treated as if it had never been in place. Not all, because electively aborting the unborn child, at least once it had attained the definite individuality connoted by "quick" in sense ii, remained a serious offense, just below *capital* felony, even when the child is never born alive; and in cases where the aborted child, *even though not "quick,"* died after birth or where the mother died from the elective abortion (however skillfully and carefully performed), the inchoate felony status of the abortive acts *when done* entailed that the abortion provider was guilty of murder.

2. Common-Law Criminal Law

Bernstein's extended treatment of the common-law criminal law is less adequate than his treatment of succession (where he commendably acknowledges that some of the decisions of the great Lord Chancellors can be read as opposed to his fictions). He misunderstands the classic treatises by underestimating their subtlety, he truncates and consequently distorts their key formulations, and he misreads *Sims*. We have already, in note 82 above, addressed the central strategic claim Bernstein makes in this discussion; what follows is supplementation.

(i) Not unreasonably, Bernstein focuses on Coke's treatment of homicide and abortion. Bernstein quotes the passage from 3 *Inst.* 50 quoted above, but he omits Coke's affirmation that what has just been said agrees with the Bracton sentence (which Coke then quotes in full), and he comments:

> The important point from that passage is...that abortion COULD NOT COUNT AS MURDER precisely because the law did not regard the unborn AS PERSONS YET IN EXISTENCE [citation to a 1674 Chancery case citing this page of Coke] unlike all other natural persons (those listed [by Coke] above).

The evidence of this is as follows. [2] First, Coke addresses each element of murder in turn, including the element that the entity killed BE A PERSON IN EXISTENCE. [3] Second, both the list of natural persons within that concept's extension and his statement of the Born Alive Rule are included under his exposition of THIS ELEMENT. Third, the discussion about abortion and the Born Alive Rule follows immediately after his list of examples of NATURAL PERSONS IN EXISTENCE. [4] Fourth, the obvious reason to include feticide here is to distinguish fetuses from the other natural persons listed and to clarify that FETICIDE, unlike killing more generally, COULD NOT count as murder at common law, because it could not satisfy this element. [5] Putting all this together, Coke AFFIRMS THAT ABORTION is wrong and for that reason is criminalized, but it COULD BE NO MURDER—and this is the crucial point—BECAUSE "in law" the fetus IS NOT "accounted a reasonable creature, in [EXISTENCE], [UNTIL] it is born alive."[217]

Each of the sentences we have enumerated miscarries.

[1] Nothing in Coke's passage says abortion *cannot* or *could not* be murder, and indeed the whole or a large part of the point of the passage is to affirm that abortion (or what Bernstein also calls feticide) is murder when the aborted child's death follows, however closely, its live birth. The reason why Bernstein has things so back-to-front emerges in point [5].

[2] Again Bernstein uses the phrase "a person in existence," and he will continue to do so. But the element in the definition of murder that Coke is expounding in this passage is neither "person" nor "in existence," but rather "reasonable creature" and "*in rerum naturae.*" "Reasonable creature" is close in its reference (denotation) to "(human) person," but like Blackstone a century and a half later it keeps in view both (a) all creaturely (i.e., created) life's dependence on a Creator and (b) the distinction between human nature and the nature of other animals. Both "person" and "rational animal/reasonable creature" smoothly include the unborn human child, but the latter perhaps a shade more

obviously. As for "in existence," if it were a fully safe translation of *in rerum natura* it would surely have been used by Coke, Hale, Blackstone, and all; but it is not, so it wasn't. Literally "in-the-nature-of things," it is obviously used here in an idiomatic sense, as a term of art signifying being in a condition to participate in the ordinary world, in the palpable social world as a distinct individual of known sex, appearance, ability to communicate even if inarticulately, and so forth.[218] By substituting "person in existence" for Coke's actual terms, Bernstein makes it seem as if Coke and the common law use "person" as a building block in the law's definitions or trains of reasoning. Instead, "person" functions in Coke's discourse (when it is used at all) in much the same untheorized way as "child" (as in "child in the womb").

[3] and [4] use the same problematic verbal substitutions as [1] and [2]; and [4] makes the same entirely mistaken claim as [1]—that abortions cannot be murder.

[5] Here the verbal substitutions are within the framework of a syntactic inversion which helps obscure Coke's point from Bernstein. Coke is telling us that abortifacient blows or ingestions *are* murder whenever they result in the child's death after it is born alive, and he gives us the reason why this is conceptually possible: "for in law it is accounted a reasonable creature *in rerum natura*"—that is, it falls within *that* element in his definition of murder—"when it is born alive." For of course, *every* child *is* a reasonable creature *in rerum natura* when the child is born alive, but the law counts the child who is murdered by abortion—the child who was born briefly alive despite the abortion—as *having been* a reasonable creature when the lethal deed was done to it while it was still in the womb.

The problem that confronts Coke, and all his readers who are following the legal argument he develops across his entire exposition of the law of murder, is that *actus reus* and *mens rea* must coincide (he articulates the related classic axiom *actus non facit reum nisi mens sit rea* only four pages later). *When the death occurs* is not a problem, provided it is within a year and a day of the lethal act done with "malice aforethought;" and *when the death occurs* we can say that the murder victim *was murdered* at the time when that act—the murder!—was done, perhaps many months before the victim's death. And this holds good also in the special case of the unborn child murdered by abortion, whose death occurred after his or her live birth but who must have satisfied—and in contemplation of law did satisfy—the relevant element of the definition of murder *at the time of the lethal act—the murder*—a time when that child was in the womb. And that relevant element is, in Bernstein's phrasing: being an existing person; and in Coke's: being a reasonable creature *in rerum natura*—in the ordinary world.

So Coke owes his readers an explanation of why murder by abortion is subject to a limiting condition subsequent—that the child be born alive—since that state of affairs does not relate, whether chronologically nor causally, to either the lethal abortifacient act or the death. He was well placed to provide the explanation that Hale provides, at precisely this point in *his* exposition of why abortion though a great and lethal crime is not murder:

> The second consideration, that is common both to murder and manslaughter, is, who shall be said a person, the killing of whom shall be said murder or manslaughter. If a woman be quick or great with child, if she take, or another give her any potion to make an abortion, or if a man strike her, whereby the child within her is killed, it is not murder or manslaughter by the law of England, because it is not yet *in rerum natura*, tho it be a great crime... NOR CAN IT LEGALLY BE KNOWN, WHETHER IT WERE KILLED OR NOT [citation to Yearbook of Edward III]. So it is, if after that child were born alive, and baptized, and after die of the stroke given to the mother, this is not homicide [citation to an earlier Yearbook].[219]

As we have said, in that last sentence Hale speaks as an outlier whose opinion his successors Hawkins and Blackstone (see 4 *Commentaries* 198), and everyone subsequently, decline to follow.[220] Hale, if not blindly following the two highly questionable[221] Yearbook authorities he cites, is following the logic of his general explanation of why abortion is not homicide: not that the unborn child is not a person, or not a reasonable creature, or is non-existent, but that he or she is not yet *in rerum natura*, and that "it cannot legally be known, whether it were kil[led] or not." And that was the explanation that Coke himself, so it seems, elicited (as prosecuting or intervening Attorney-General) from Chief Justice Popham and Justice Fenner in King's Bench in *Sims*—the evidential considerations[222] quoted above at note 74. It is perhaps surprising that Coke neglects to give the explanation here, in its appropriate place, 3 *Inst.* 50. Perhaps he harbored (but did not act upon) the doubt that Hale did act upon (but perhaps in the wrong direction): the evidential argument seems to "prove too much," for if causality can be proved in the case of the victim of abortion born alive, why not in the case of the victim of abortion born dead?

Bernstein mishandles this passage of Hale in more ways than one. Immediately after point [5] in his passage about Coke, above, he goes on (page 40):

> Sir Matthew Hale was as explicit and clear on this point. [fn. omitted] [1] Here is how he describes the essential element in the law of homicide that the victim be an entity the law considers as a person: "The second consideration, that is common both to murder and manslaughter, is, *who shall be said a person*, the killing of whom shall be said murder or manslaughter." [fn. omitted] [2] Immediately after Hale describes this essential element of homicide, he says that abortion "is not murder nor manslaughter by the law of England, *because* [the fetus] is not yet *in rerum natura*." [fn. omitted] [3] According to Hale, then, the unborn fetus is not an entity "who shall be said a person" in the law against homicide. [fn. omitted] [4] It follows that the criminal law counted a natural person (in the ordinary sense) as in existence only if it is born alive, and the lesser offense of which one might be guilty for killing a fetus involved an offense against

an entity lacking the legal personality that inhered in other natural persons. [fn. omitted]

Again, the propositions we have enumerated all misfire.

[1]. Here Bernstein takes Hale to be working with a theorem or premise of the form "Only persons can be murdered," as if he were setting up the syllogism that continues: "But fetuses are not persons. Therefore fetuses cannot be murdered." But once Hale's now obsolete system of punctuation is allowed for, we can see that his thought is not that the unborn are *not persons* (as Bernstein wrongly truncates his thought in paraphrase) but that they are *not persons the killing of whom is murder*[223]—a thought for which Hale gives two reasons, neither of them in any way suggesting that the unborn are not persons or are non-existent persons: they are (a) human beings not yet *in rerum natura* and (b) human beings the cause of whose death is hidden in the profound darkness of the womb (was this dead child alive when the blow or potion went to work?).

[2]. Bernstein helps his misinterpretation on its way by inserting "the fetus" where Hale had an "it" that looked back to the beginning of the very same sentence: "the child within her." It is harder to deny that human beings are persons with (as Blackstone will say) a right to life if you are calling them children, sometimes located here, sometimes there, rather than using the term "fetus" (shared with sub-rational animals; depersonalised). Hale's English does not include "fetus" in any of its spellings.

[3]. Again Bernstein mistakenly assumes that Hale or his readers are in search of the class each of whose members is an "entity 'who shall be said a person.'" Hale's concern is with the class of *persons whose killing is criminal homicide at common law*, and he identifies the class: those persons who are *in rerum natura*: persons born alive.[224] Persons not yet born are protected by other rules of criminal law, one or more rule(s) punishing their killing as such, one or more punishing their killing or attempted killing whenever it results in their mother's death, and so on.

[4]. Though Bernstein does not formally deny this, Hale neither says nor implies that the unborn lack legal personality. He is concerned to delineate murder or homicide, and in this context he does not use "person" as his categorizing tool. *The term is here used not as a term of art deployed in legal rules, but as a scarcely theorised way of denoting human beings including infants or children both before and after birth, a legally significant line but not one bearing upon personhood as he conceives it.*

Much more could be said about Bernstein's efforts to construct a common-law doctrinal denial of fetal personhood. But there is little need, since they err in the same sorts of ways as are on display in the two passages we have discussed. We note only, in parting, that he entirely misses the evidential concerns at the core of *Sims* (supra note 71) (and of Hale's passage quoted supra note 33).

In sum: Common-law rules rarely use "person," and dictionaries of the common law that Bernstein cites to define other terms include no definition of person(s). The term is used in high-level analytical syntheses such as Hale's or Blackstone's *Analysis of the Law* (supra note 204). Though it is there extended to corporations conceptualized as artificial persons, its use in relation to natural persons is all but identical to common-language use. In these uses, which display law's most general purpose or rationale—to serve the well-being of natural persons (human beings in all their similarities and dissimilarities)—the term "person" is used by the great scholarly and judicial exponents of the common law (and makers or ratifiers of constitutions in its mould) in a manner that approximates closely to the common-sense and common-speech use that other parts of Bernstein's article successfully affirm and show *includes unborn human children.*

IV. Dobbs Amicus Briefs of the United States and Associations of Historians Fail at All Relevant Points

The *amicus curiae* Brief of the United States makes a number of submissions that contradict or cut across the positions proposed in the present

Brief. In reviewing and rebutting those submissions, we will also respond shortly to relevant assertions in the Historians' Brief in this case.

> A. The United States Brief Never Confronts the Thesis of This Article, That Roe Could and Should Be Overruled on the Ground That the Object and Victim of an Elective Abortion Is Entitled, Precisely as a Person Within the Meaning of the Due Process and Equal Protection Clauses of the Fourteenth Amendment, to Constitutional Protection Against Such a Procedure (Accepted by *Roe* Itself as a Ground That—If Sound—"Collapses" Its Entire Holding and Rationale)

For on the basis of that ground, the "absolute" or natural rights to life, limbs, and bodily integrity (and consequent rights of self-determination) that are urged by the United States at 23–26 (mainly on the sound basis of Blackstone's representative recital of them) cease to be decisive or even weighty in favor of *Roe* and its progeny. Those rights then instead entail a position essentially like that of Texas in *Roe*: elective abortions violate the corresponding absolute and constitutional rights of the child who is their object and victim, while non-elective terminations of pregnancy vindicate the absolute and constitutional rights of the pregnant woman even when they unavoidably cause the child's death.

Similarly, the position advanced by the United States at 24 that *Roe* and *Casey* simply cannot be *grievously* wrong stands and falls with its hidden premise: that *Roe* succeeded in rebutting Texas's assertion of the Fourteenth Amendment rights of the unborn child. In accepting, unequivocally, that if that assertion was sound, the case for the rule established in *Roe* collapses, the Court in *Roe* was accepting, inevitably and rightly, that if it was going wrong in rejecting Texas's assertion, it was going grievously wrong and licensing a substantial and ongoing violation of the absolute and constitutional right always acknowledged *first*, to life.

Nor does the position change when the United States' denial of grievous error is given its full formulation: A woman's liberty "to have some freedom to terminate her pregnancy.... is so closely related to bodily integrity, familial autonomy, and women's equal citizenship" that "*Roe*'s and *Casey*'s core holding that the Constitution protects some freedom to terminate a pregnancy cannot be grievously incorrect."[225] For, rhetoric and emphases aside, those interests in bodily integrity, familial autonomy, and equal citizenship were amply present to the mind of the *Roe* Court when it acknowledged that if the unborn are Fourteenth Amendment persons, its position collapses. And as soon as the destruction of *another person's* bodily integrity is acknowledged as implicated in a woman's decision to terminate her pregnancy, the ambiguity in the phrase twice used by the United States, "some freedom to terminate," becomes vividly evident, and clarification becomes an inescapable responsibility. The phrase "elective abortion" is a compressed summary of the needed disambiguation: The pregnant woman unquestionably has an "absolute" (natural) and constitutional freedom—closely connected with bodily integrity—akin to the legitimate freedom of self-defense in situations in which exercise of that liberty-right does not become illegitimate even when foreseeably lethal. So she would indeed retain, unimpaired but measured (like ordinary self-defense) by inter-personal fairness, a real "freedom to terminate" if *Roe* and *Casey* were overturned on account of the legitimate constitutional right of her child. But just as the Equal Protection Clause prevents her interest in familial autonomy and/or equal citizenship from being the constitutionally legitimate basis of a right to infanticide, so too, analogously, the Clause prevents those interests from being the constitutionally legitimate basis or measure of a right to *elective* abortion.

It scarcely needs saying that in the perspective developed in our Brief, the phrase "state interests" (deployed in a customary way by the United States on 24–25), though of course retaining the relevance it has to the state's upholding of other individuals' rights to life, ceases to be an adequate articulation of the interests and the "absolute" and *federal constitutional* rights of the person whose life is at stake in her mother's choice of elective abortion.

Similarly, the argument advanced by the United States at 25–26, that overruling *Roe* would threaten the Court's decisions in *Griswold*,

Loving, *Lawrence*, and *Obergefell*, has no force if the ground for overruling *Roe* is recognition of the neglected countervailing rights of constitutional persons erroneously denied that status. For no such denial of personal status or countervailing rights was involved in any of the cases just mentioned.

> B. At 26–27 the United States Makes a Number of Historical and Legal-Historical Claims That This Brief Shows to Be Mistaken, Along with Constitutional Claims That a More Accurate History Rebuts

At 26, going immediately to the critical issue, the United States asserts on the authority of *Roe*, 410 U.S. at 134, that at common law "there was agreement" that the fetus in the early stages of pregnancy was to be regarded as "part of the woman." But in its very next sentence, *Roe* bases both the meaning and the truth of its assertion on perhaps the most absurd of the errors in its error-strewn opinion: It says that "[d]ue to continued uncertainty about the precise time when animation occurred, to the lack of any empirical basis for the 40–80-day view, and perhaps to Aquinas' definition of movement as one of the two first principles of life, Bracton focused upon quickening as the critical point"—and thus quickening, "appearing usually from the 16th to the 18th week of pregnancy" (132), "found its way into the received common law in this country" (134). But, as noted above (at notes 82–86 supra), this asserted clarification of the law by Bracton is fantasy. For Bracton, writing in Latin, said nothing whatsoever about quickening, let alone quickening in the sense naively taken for granted by *Roe*: He spoke only of the unborn infant becoming "formed and *animatum*," where *animatum* means nothing either more or less specific than ensouled, animated in the sense of endowed with *anima*, a human soul. Nor do Bracton, Coke, Hale, Hawkins, or Blackstone speak of the pre-"quick" fetus or embryo as "part of the mother," or concede that she is entitled to treat it as simply a part. The very occasional uses of the term "part" (usually as *pars viscerum matris*) are by outlier authorities.[226]

But the United States, in its next sentence on 26, rightly identifies Chief Justice Shaw's judgment in *Parker* (supra at notes 49–61) as the appropriate representation of what *Roe* called the "received common law in this country," and summarizes it:

> Until the fetus had "advanced to that degree of maturity" that it could be "regarded in law" as having a "separate and independent existence," abortion was not prohibited. *Commonwealth v Parker*, 50 Mass. (9 Met.) 263, 266, 268 (1845).

But at 50 Mass. 268 the court said only that the acts set forth in the indictment, without averment that the woman had been "quick with child," "are not punishable at common law." At 265, having defined the issue before the court, Shaw recalls one of what our Brief has shown was many ways which "abortion" was "prohibited" in the sense of unlawful even when not itself per se indictable/punishable at common law: He reaffirms the rule that if the child dies from abortion after being born alive, the abortifacient acts, however early in the pregnancy they were done, were murder.

And at 50 Mass. 266 itself, Shaw illustrates what "separate and independent existence" means by not merely citing but quoting Bracton saying that abortion is homicide if the unborn infant is formed and *animatum*. The only authority that Shaw finds identifying "quick with child" with "quickened" in the *Roe* sense is *Phillips* (supra note 62), interpreting "quick with child" "in the construction of this [English] statute." And Shaw immediately (267) declines to rule on ("decide") the question "what degree of advancement in a state of gestation would justify the application of that description," that is to say, "quick with child," "to a pregnant woman," at common law. Nor did he ever have to, since a few weeks earlier the state's legislature had definitively swept away the whole debate about "quick with child," by making abortion at any stage punishable (variously but with at least one year's imprisonment).[227]

It follows that the next sentence of the United States Brief is mistaken in citing *Parker* at 267 to verify its claim that "at common law, the fetus was generally considered to have a legally 'separate existence' [only] after quickening—when the woman could feel its movement *in utero*."[228] More pointedly: The only common-law authority advanced by the United States to support *Roe*'s entire "quickening" doctrine is, if anything, an authority against it.

And even if that were not so, the definitive evolution or rectification of Massachusetts law in the same early months of 1845 is a sign of the constitutional irrelevance of quickness in any but its central sense, the child's being alive. That evolution in Massachusetts, subsequent to New York, Ohio, Maine, Alabama, and Iowa (and on one view Illinois), manifested a reform (accomplished completely by the end of 1868 in twenty-seven states and substantially in twenty-eight) that is of more immediate constitutional significance than the common law, whose entrapment in unresolved uncertainties concerning ambiguous sources and physiologically explored concepts obscured its basic and enduring recognition of the unborn child's status as a person with a right to life— the status implicit in Bracton's word *homicidium*, killing of a human being, so carefully and otherwise needlessly quoted by Coke, Blackstone, and Shaw along with the same Bracton sentence's focus not on maternal perceptions but on the fetus/child's reality as *formatum et animatum*.

In retailing, in its Brief's next sentence on 26, *Roe*'s preposterous claim that it is doubtful whether abortion of a quick child "was ever firmly established at common law" and *Roe*'s associated assertion of the "paucity of common-law prosecutions for post-quickening abortion," the United States overlooks the probable relative rarity of abortions until the early nineteenth century (a rarity established with some clarity in the affirmations made and sources quoted and cited not only by Joseph Dellapenna's Amicus Brief in *Dobbs* at 13–16)[229] but also by *Parker* itself, an appeal from just such a prosecution and conviction and referring to a Massachusetts conviction (similarly overturned on appeal for reasons found obscure by Shaw) in 1810. Conspicuously, the United States does not repeat *Roe*'s central claim that at common law there was a legal "liberty" or "right" to early abortion; it makes the already-noted assertions, refuted by its chosen authority *Parker*, that such abortion was "legal," and for the rest limits itself to the vague and dubious social-historical claims that "women generally could terminate an abortion" (27) or "abortion was generally available" (27n.4).

> C. Similarly, the Historians' Brief in This Case Marks a Notable Retreat from Some of the Most Confidently Advanced Legal Errors in its Predecessor Amicus Briefs—Signed by Individual Historians, Unlike the Present One (Signed by Counsel)—Errors Made by Those Predecessors in Endorsing Roe's Invented Common-Law "Liberty" and "Right."

As to the historic law relating to abortion, the present Historians' Brief rightly abstains even from the word "free," let alone "liberty" or "right." The most it will venture are the hazy formulations "opportunity to make this choice" (3, quoting *Roe*) and "under the common law, a woman could terminate a pregnancy at her discretion prior to physically feeling the fetus move." (7) (This is the same "could" as the United States ventured while scrupling to add the equivocal and misleading "at her discretion.")

Instead, the Historians offer a new, romanticized version of the common law as focused upon an alleged "female-centric principle" (5), a "subjective standard decided by the pregnant woman alone," and a legal standard "not considered accurately ascertainable by other means" (2). The evidence offered for this last proposition proves on inspection to be no evidence at all: A sentence quoted (6) from Taylor's *Medical Jurisprudence* (1866) with the innuendo that it concerns evidence for ascertaining and determining the fact of quickening for legal purposes turns out on inspection to be in a section of the book entirely concerned with informing clinicians for clinical purposes. The sentence relied upon has nothing whatever to do with law or legal proceedings, actual or potential. The Brief undeniably misuses it.

The footnote on the same page (6) misuses *Russell on Crimes* (1841) almost as severely, quoting a proposition that asserts that "quick with child" means "the woman has felt the child within her" as if it were the author's affirmation of a common-law principle—the Historians come up with no other affirmation comparably clear—when in fact it is no more than a marginal note summarizing (as a kind of running index for rapid readers) the content of the adjacent paragraph, which is transcribing the reported trial direction in *Phillips* (supra note 62). Simply for brevity (as throughout the volume), the marginal note (in no case offered to make an authorial affirmation) omits the essential qualification made by the trial judge: that his interpretation of "quick with child" is for the purposes of applying the English statute (Lord Ellenborough's Act) of 1803. About the common law neither the judge nor the author/editor of the marginal note said anything.

The Historians' Brief, at 9, offers an inept formulation of "the common law principle" said to be "consistently enunciated" by "legal treatises":

> Like Blackstone, these sources explained that the reason for this principle was the legal belief that a fetus was not considered a cognizable life for purposes of the law until quickening. See, for example, [*Roscoe on Evidence*, 3rd ed 1846 p. 652 [in fact 694]]. ("A child in the womb is considered *pars viscerum matris* ... and not possessing an individual existence, and cannot therefore be the subject of murder.")

The proposition in *Roscoe on Evidence*, being about "a child in the womb," manifestly does nothing to verify "until quickening" in the previous sentence. Nor does it manifest a "legal belief," but only a legal fiction. Nor does it say anything about "a cognizable life for purposes of the law." The fiction is merely to account—in the non-explanatory way that fictions do—for the legal rule that abortion, even when a serious criminal offense,[230] is not murder or manslaughter. And this fiction is particularly inept, because it leaves the criminality of abortions, at least when done to a woman "quick with child," entirely unexplained.

Seeking to discredit Wharton, whose treatises on criminal law, like those of Joel Bishop, were of greater weight than those cited with approval by the Brief, the Brief alleges (10) that he "opposed allowing any abortion." But in fact Wharton writes, in his chapter on abortion at common law: "Of course it is a defence that the destruction of the child's life was necessary to save that of the mother."[231]

The later parts of the Historians' Brief continue at the same low level of accuracy, balance, and coherence.

V. Recognizing Unborn Children as Persons Entitled to Equal Protection Coheres with Their Mothers' Similar Entitlement, and Requires No Irregular Remedies or Unjust Penalties

Recognizing unborn personhood would be a natural exercise of courts' power to bind parties to a case by applying the law to the facts, disregarding unconstitutional laws, directing lower courts, and enjoining unlawful executive actions.[232] Such a holding would bar lower courts from enjoining prosecutions or vacating convictions of abortionists. Injunctions would lie against officials asked to facilitate elective abortions, as in cases like *Garza v. Hargan*,[233] where guardians ad litem could be appointed for the unborn with a view to protecting them against elective abortion, as before *Roe*.[234]

While state homicide laws would need to forbid elective abortion,[235] here too courts would be limited to customary remedies. Most states have laws tailor-made for "feticide;"[236] any carve-outs for elective abortion would be disregarded by courts as invalid.[237] New laws, or prosecutorial practice, that reduced criminal-law protection of the unborn below the constitutionally mandated minimum would face legal challenge like any statute *today* that decriminalized homicides of some class—say, the cognitively disabled.[238] State regimes invalidated for denying minimal prenatal protection would, absent amendment, revert to the default, general homicide law; states would thus have strong incentives to establish a just balance—a balance consistent with the constitutional command of equal protection of the laws.

Equal protection allows states to treat different cases differently, for legitimate ends.[239] States may consider degrees of culpability as mitigating factors or altogether immunize from prosecution certain participants in wrongful killings. Here such policy choices serve legitimate purposes by taking fairly into account ("balancing") the child's humanity and her unique physical dependence and impact on her mother, another person entitled to equal protection. By analogy with the right of self-defense, the mother's constitutional rights could require states to allow urgent or life-saving medical interventions even when these would unavoidably result in the child's death.[240]

If states failed in their duties of protection or enforcement, a responsibility would also fall to Congress, which could follow a personhood holding with proportional legislation under Section 5 of the Fourteenth Amendment to protect the unborn.[241]

CONCLUDING POSTSCRIPT

The Amicus Brief that this chapter expands and supplements is cited in footnote 24 of the Opinion of the Court in *Dobbs v. Jackson Women's Health Organization*, 142 S. Ct. 2228 (2022), in relation to the "debate[d]" question that the Opinion frames as one about "the exact meaning of 'quickening.'" As we demonstrated in the Brief and have shown again here, the debate is really about whether the common-law term "quick," as in "quick with child" or (less commonly) "with quick child," should be taken to have referred at all to quickening in the sense intended by the Opinion. But in any event, the Court in *Dobbs* judged that it had no need to "wade into this debate." More important was the prominence that the Opinion—on the way to its fundamental ruling that "a right to abortion is not deeply rooted in the Nation's history and traditions"—gives to what the Brief (at pages 3, 22) called "a kind of inchoate felony for felony-murder purposes" (rule [I]), and the Opinion at page 2250 suitably refers to as "a proto-felony-murder rule":

That the common law did not condone even prequickening abortions is confirmed by what one might call a proto-felony-murder rule.

This finding, like the associated findings about the common law in parts 2a, 2b, and 2c of the Opinion, is supported by the many authorities cited in the Brief, including the main authorities we cited for rule [I]. It is a very significant finding, disposing decisively of the myths of "abortional freedom" that were so assiduously cultivated in Means I and Means II, in *Roe*, and in the Historians' Brief and the Brief for the United States in *Dobbs*. It is a finding not challenged in the *Dobbs* dissent.

Our Brief's main thesis, about the constitutionally proper and original public meaning of "any person" in the Equal Protection Clause, was dismissed in footnote 7 of the dissent ("a revolutionary proposition: that the fetus is itself a constitutionally protected 'person,' such that an abortion ban is constitutionally *mandated*") and rejected in the concurring opinion of Justice Kavanaugh ("Some *amicus* briefs argue that the Court today should…hold that the Constitution *outlaws* abortion throughout the United States. No Justice of this Court has ever advanced that position But [the position is] wrong as a constitutional matter, in my view.").

What about the Opinion of the Court? Between the two actual parties in *Dobbs*, it was common ground that the Constitution does not require states (or Congress) to prohibit even elective abortions.[242] That common ground allowed the Court to remain silent about the question, and it did, neither affirming nor questioning that common ground. Even the Court's declaration that it is "return[ing] the power to weigh those [policy] arguments to the people and their elected representatives" does not strictly entail that it is affirming Justice Kavanaugh's position (in a concurrence joined by no other Justice) that the Constitution is neutral about abortion. "Our opinion is not based on *any* view about if and when prenatal life is entitled to any of the rights enjoyed after birth" (emphasis added).[243]

The Court's verbally unqualified rhetoric of return to the people is silently subject to qualifications it articulates elsewhere in the Opinion: For example, the people's legislature must have a rational basis for thinking its enactments serve legitimate state interests.[244] Nowhere, however, does the Opinion articulate anything to qualify the appearance it gives of mistakenly assuming that prenatal children are not persons protected by the Equal Protection Clause. Nevertheless, the judgment of the Court, in which the Chief Justice too concurred, makes no finding or ruling on the matter, *and neither depends nor could depend on the mistaken assumption.* For the decision in *Dobbs* was to reverse the Fifth Circuit and require courts to uphold Mississippi's prohibition of abortion after fifteen weeks' gestation. The Court's position that that prohibition is constitutionally valid is not, and could not conceivably be, supported by the proposition that unborn children are not entitled to Equal Protection.

Without departing from the strict rules of *stare decisis*, therefore, a future Court could (as it should) hold that prenatal children are constitutional persons, protected by the Equal Protection Clause, without challenge to anything in *Dobbs* save the breadth of the logically superfluous, constitutionally overbroad rhetoric of entirely returning abortion's permissibility to the people. A future decision of the Supreme Court could adopt everything that, on the arguments of our Brief and this chapter, is required by fidelity to constitutional text and history in order to do justice to the rights given constitutional status in 1868, rights (as we have argued) both of persons prior to their birth and of their mothers.

CHAPTER TEN

Constitutional Structures and Civic Virtues

Those of us who are citizens of democratic republics do not refer to those who govern as "rulers." It is our boast that we rule ourselves. And there is truth in this, inasmuch as we participate in choosing those who do rule. So we prefer to speak of them not as our rulers, but as servants—public servants, or at least as people in "public service." Of course, these so-called servants are nothing remotely like the servants in *Downton Abbey*. The extraordinary prestige and usually the trappings attaching to public office, in just about all times, and in just about all places, would by themselves be sufficient to distinguish, say, the Mayor of Knoxville, or the Governor of Michigan, or the President of the United States from Carson the butler. But that prestige signals an underlying fact that discomfits our democratic and egalitarian sensibilities, namely, the fact that even in liberal democratic regimes high public officials are rulers. They make rules, enforce them, and resolve disputes about their meaning and applicability. To a very large extent, at the end of the day, what they say goes.

Of course, our rulers rule, not by dint of sheer power, the way the mafia might do in a territory over which it happens to have gained control, but rather lawfully.[1] Constitutional rules specify public offices and settle procedures for filling them. Whether the constitution exists in the form of a specific document, such as the Constitution of the United States or the Constitution of California or of West Virginia, or in some other form, as in the United Kingdom and New Zealand, it constitutes, in a sense, the set of rules governing the rulers—rules that both empower office-holders to make and execute decisions of various sorts and limit their powers. So, though they are rulers, they are not absolute rulers. Constitutional rules set the scope, and thus the limits, of their jurisdiction and authority. They are rulers who are subject to rules—rules they do not themselves make and cannot easily or purely on their own initiative revise or repeal. They rule in limited ways, and ordinarily for limited terms (which may or may not be indefinitely renewable at the pleasure of voters). They rule by virtue of the democratic processes by which they came to hold office. They can be removed or significantly disempowered at the next election if the people are not happy with them. Still, they rule.

Now, my point is not to hoot at the idea of those holding governmental offices and controlling the levers of governmental power as "servants." On the contrary, I want, in the end, to defend the idea that rulers truly can be servants. I want to establish, however, that if these people we call public servants are, indeed, servants, they are servants in a special sense, a sense that is compatible with their at the same time being rulers. They are people who serve us by ruling. They serve us well by ruling well. If they rule badly, they serve us poorly—indeed, they disserve us.

There are, of course, lots of ways that rulers can disserve those whom they have a moral obligation to serve by ruling well. Most obviously, there is incompetence. Then, of course, there is corruption. And at the extreme, there is tyranny. So what does it mean for the ruler to truly be a servant? What does it mean for someone holding political office and exercising public power to rule well?

RULING FOR THE COMMON GOOD

It means making and executing decisions for the sake of the common good. Such decisions will necessarily be compatible with the requirements of justice and at the same time embody justice. If we understand the concept of the common good properly—and I will say a word about that in a moment—then we will see that no decision that violates a requirement of justice is truly for the common good; and no decision that genuinely upholds and serves the common good will fail to advance the cause of justice.

It is also important to note that decisions can fail to serve the common good and can, indeed, damage the common good, even when they are not unjust. Even honorably motivated and well-intentioned people, including rulers, can make decisions that harm the common good because they are inexpedient, imprudent, or unwise. Holders of public office, like anyone else, can make poor, even disastrous, decisions even when acting on the purest and best of motives. Poor decisions by well-intentioned public officials can trigger or prolong a great depression; lead a nation into an unnecessary and even disastrous war, or prevent a nation from going to war to protect its people and their vital interests when it should have done; undermine or weaken the marriage culture and with it family life and everything in a society that depends on the health and vibrancy of marriage and the family.

It is worth adding here that reasonable people of goodwill can, and obviously do, disagree about what the common good requires and forbids, and what is, in truth, just and unjust.[2] Honorable people exercising public power can commit injustices—even grave injustices—while seeking, in good faith, to do justice, and believing in good faith that they are doing it. Not all injustices are the result of malice, ill-will, or like vices. Still, all injustices, even if committed by officials who are sincerely trying to do the right thing, harm the common good. For justice is itself *a* common good and a central aspect of *the* common good of the political community. It is to the benefit of each and every citizen to live in a just social order; and harm to that order is therefore a loss for everyone, and not merely for the immediate and obvious victims of any particular injustice. Indeed, it is a loss even for the ostensible beneficiaries of injustices, and, indeed, even for their perpetrators—though, naturally, true evildoers don't see it that way. Corruption of character narrows their vision of the good, blinding them to the profound respects in which wrongdoing harms what is, in truth, *their* interest in living in a just society, as well as everyone else's.

The common good requires that there be rulers and that they actually rule. To grasp this is to begin to see the sense in which good rulers are also servants. Members of societies face a range—sometimes a vast range—of challenges and opportunities requiring both means-to-ends and persons-to-persons coordination, including, in the case of complex societies, coordination problems presented by the large number and the complexity of the other coordination problems. Since such problems cannot, as a practical matter, be addressed and resolved by unanimity, *authority*—political authority—is required.[3] Institutions will have to be created and maintained, and persons will need to be installed in the offices of these institutions, to make the choices and decisions that must be made, and to do the things that need to be done, for the sake of protecting public health, safety, and morals; upholding the rights and dignity of individuals, families, and non-governmental entities of various descriptions; and advancing the overall common good.

This would be true even in a society of perfect saints, where no one ever sought more than his fair share from the common stock, or violated the rights of others, or deliberately acted in any manner that was contrary to the common good. Even in such a society, effective coordination for the sake of common goals, and, thus, for the good of all, would be required; and seeking unanimity, assuming a large and fairly complex society, would not be a practical option.[4] So authority would be required, and that means persons exercising authority—rulers, ruling.

But the moral justification for the rulers' ruling is service to the good of all, the common good. And the common good is not an abstraction or platonic form hovering somewhere beyond the concrete well-being—the flourishing—of the flesh-and-blood persons constituting the community. It just is the well-being of those persons and of the families and other associations of persons—Burke's "little platoons" of civil society—of which they are members. The right of legitimate rulers to rule is rooted in the duty of rulers to rule in the interest of all—in other words, the basis of the *right* to rule is the *duty* to serve. And the realities that constitute the content of service are the various elements of the common good. By doing what is for the common good, and by avoiding doing anything that harms the common good, rulers fulfill their obligations to the people over whom they exercise authority, thus serving their interests, their welfare, their flourishing—in a word, them.

I don't know how to improve on the definition of the common good proposed by John Finnis in his magisterial book *Natural Law and Natural Rights*. The common good, Finnis says, is to be understood as "a set of conditions which enables the members of a community to attain *for themselves* reasonable objectives, or to realize reasonably *for themselves* the value(s) for the sake of which they have reason to collaborate with each other (positively and/or negatively) in a community."[5] Now every community—from the basic community of a family, to a church or other community of religious faith, to a mutual aid society or other civic association, to a business firm—will have a common good. The common good of some communities is fundamentally an intrinsic good rather than an instrumental good. That is true, for example, of the community of the family. Although families serve many valuable, and some indispensable, instrumental purposes, the point of the family is not exhausted by these purposes, nor do they define what the family is. The most fundamental point of being a member of the family is, simply, being a member of the family—enjoying the intrinsic benefit of being part of that distinctive network of mutual obligation, care, love, and support. The same is true, in Christian and Jewish thought, at least, of the common good of the community of faith. Though communities of faith characteristically serve many valuable instrumental purposes, the most fundamental purpose of Israel or the Church is to be the people of God. Things are obviously different when it comes to, say, business firms. Although there are ordinarily many opportunities for principals and employees of companies to realize intrinsic or basic human goods (including goods that are fundamentally social, such as the good of friendship) in their collaborations in pursuit of the firms' objectives, those objectives are the ends to which the firm and the cooperation of those working in and for it are means.

Now, what about the common good of the political community—the common good served by good rulers (and to which citizens also have responsibilities)? Is it fundamentally an intrinsic good or an instrumental good? There is, in what Sir Isaiah Berlin referred to as the central tradition of Western thought[6] about morality, including political morality, a powerful current of belief that the common good of political society is an intrinsic good. This seems clearly to have been the view of Aristotle, and many self-identified Thomists are firmly convinced that it was the view of Aristotle's greatest interpreter and expositor, St. Thomas Aquinas. Finnis, however, argues that the common good of political society, though, to quote Aristotle, "great and godlike" in its range and importance, is nevertheless fundamentally an instrumental, not an intrinsic, good.[7] And he further argues that the instrumental nature of the common good of political society entails limitations of the legitimate scope of governmental authority—limitations that, though not in every case easily articulable in the language of rights, are requirements of justice. Although I have a difference, at the margins, with Professor Finnis, who (along with Joseph Raz) was my graduate supervisor in Oxford, on the question of just what the limits are (and in particular whether they exclude in principle moral paternalism), I agree that the common good of political society is fundamentally an instrumental good and that this entails moral limits on justified governmental power.[8]

The way we have come to think of these limits is in terms of what is usually called the doctrine of subsidiarity. This is a sound doctrine, though the label has now been appropriated by some people who, for whatever reason, want the use of the word without actually signing on to the doctrine. Without implying bad faith on anyone's part, this amounts to an abuse, and destabilizes the word's meaning in a way that may eventually render it useless. Still, we have no better word or label at the moment, so let's just try to be clear in our minds about what the doctrine actually holds. A bit over ninety years ago, Pope Pius XI, in the encyclical letter *Quadragesimo Anno* (1931), explained the basic idea:

> Just as it is wrong to withdraw from the individual and commit to a group what private initiative and effort can accomplish, so too it is wrong... for a larger and higher association to arrogate to itself functions which can be performed efficiently by smaller and lower associations. This is a fixed, unchanged, and most weighty principle of moral philosophy.... Of its very nature the true aim of all social activity should be to help members of a social body, and never to absorb or destroy them.

Now, this principle of justice and the common good reflects a particular understanding of the nature and content of human flourishing. Flourishing consists in *doing things*, not just in getting things, or having desirable or pleasant experiences, or having things done for you. The good, as Aristotle taught, consists in activity.[9] Human goods are realized by acting—one *participates* in them—thus enriching one's life and even ennobling oneself as one exercises and fulfills one's natural human capacities (for example, one's capacities for friendship, knowledge, critical aesthetic appreciation).

And so the common good, is, as Finnis remarked, best conceived as a *set of conditions*. But, we must ask, conditions for what? Well, let's recall Professor Finnis's definition: conditions for enabling members of a community to attain *for themselves* reasonable objectives, or to realize reasonably *for themselves* the value(s) for the sake of which they have reason to collaborate with each other in a community. The common good is, in this sense, facilitative. Its elements are what enable people to do things, individually and in cooperation with others, the doing of which to a significant degree constitutes their all-round or integral flourishing. Under favoring conditions, people can more fully and more successfully carry out reasonable projects, pursue reasonable objectives, and, thus, participate in values—including some values that are inherently social in that they fulfill persons in respect of capacities for non-instrumental forms of interpersonal communion—that are indeed constitutive of their well-being and fulfillment.

Properly understood, then, the common good requires, as a matter of justice, limited government—government that respects the needs and rights of people to pursue objectives and realize goods *for themselves*. The fundamental role of legitimate government, and thus the responsibility of legitimate rulers—rulers who serve—is not to be doing things for people that they could do for themselves; it is, rather, to be helping to establish and maintain conditions that favor people's doing things for themselves, and with and for each other. Governments should do things *for* people (as opposed to letting them do things *for themselves*) only where individuals and the non-governmental institutions of civil society cannot do them or cannot reasonably be expected to do them for themselves. Finnis used the word "enable," and it is the right word here: Government's legitimate concern is with the establishment and maintenance of the *conditions* under which members of the community are *enabled* to pursue the projects and goals by and through which they participate in the goods constitutive of their flourishing.

Now, this facilitative conception of the common good does not require a doctrinaire libertarianism in the domain of either political economy or social morality; but it clearly excludes corporatist and socialist policies that, to recall those words from Pius XI, "withdraw from the individual and commit to the group what private individual and effort can accomplish," or which remove from the family or religious or civic association and commit to government what can be accomplished by non-governmental collaborative effort. Surely a conception of the common good that is serious about the principle of subsidiarity will respect private property and take care to maintain a reasonably free system of economic exchange—that is to say, as a practical matter, a market economy. "Social" (that is, comprehensive or even widespread state) ownership of the means of production is plainly incompatible with subsidiarity's concerns and objectives, as is anything resembling a command economy. And this would be true even if the record of socialist states were benign when it came to respect for civil liberties and political freedom—which, on the whole, it certainly is not.

And it would be true even if, again contrary to the historical record, private property and the market system were not necessary as checks against the excessive concentration and abuse of power in the hands of public officials. But, as I've noted, the historical record demonstrates that private property and the market system, while not sufficient as guarantees against the concentration and abuse of political power, are for all intents and purposes necessary conditions for civil liberty and limited government. And there is a profound lesson in this for those of us who are interested in ensuring that rulers remain servants ruling in the interest of citizens, and do not reduce citizens to a condition of dependency or servitude. For it is critical to the effective limitation of governmental power that there be substantial non-governmental centers of power in society. Private property and the market economy not only provide the conditions of social mobility, which is important to the common good in any modern or dynamic society, but also ensure that there are significant resources (and thus opportunities for people and the private associations they form) that are not in the control of governmental officials or the apparatus of the state. This diffusion of power benefits society as a whole, and not only those who immediately benefit economically from the possession of property or the ability to profit in the market. And here I am not simply talking about general prosperity, though that is yet another benefit of private property and the market system. I am talking about the benefit to all—in terms of liberty, opportunity, and security—of the diffusion of power.

This goes well beyond economics. If we understand the common good, if we have a grasp of what constitutes or is conducive to the flourishing of human beings and what is not, we will recognize that limited government is also important because it permits the functioning and flourishing of non-governmental institutions of civil society—those little platoons again, families, churches, and so forth—that perform better than government ever conceivably could the most essential health, education, and welfare functions and which play the primary role in transmitting to each new generation the virtues without which free societies cannot survive—basic honesty, integrity, self-restraint, concern for others, and respect for their dignity and rights, civic-mindedness, and the like.[10] These non-governmental authority structures represent another crucial way in which power is properly diffused and not concentrated in the hands of the state and its officials. They can play their role only when government is limited—for unlimited government always usurps their authority and destroys their autonomy, usually recruiting or commandeering them into being state functionary organs—and where they are playing their proper role they help to create conditions in which the ideal of limited government is much more likely to be realized and preserved, and its benefits enjoyed by the people.

A CONCERN FOR CONSTITUTIONAL RESTRAINTS

I will return to the role of the institutions of civil society towards the end of this chapter, but now let me shift the discussion to the question of constitutional structural constraints on the powers of government. Historically, political theorists have focused on the need for such constraints as the most obvious and important way to ensure that governmental power remains limited and that rulers serve the people and do not become tyrants. And I myself think that constraints of this nature are important in this cause, though I will eventually get round to saying that they are likely to be effective only when they are a part of a larger picture in which they are supported by, and in turn support, other features of social life that help to keep government within its proper bounds for the sake of the common good. So, as important as they are, I would warn against placing too great an emphasis on constitutional structural constraints. The danger here is ignoring the other essential features.

The Constitution of the United States is famous for its "Madisonian system" of structural constraints on powers of the central government. More than two hundred years of experience with the system gives us a pretty good perspective on both its strengths, which are considerable, and its limitations, which do exist. The major structural constraints are: 1) the doctrine of the general government as a government of delegated and enumerated, and therefore limited, powers; 2) the dual sovereignty of the general government and the states—with the states functioning as governments of general jurisdiction exercising generalized police powers (a kind of plenary authority), limited under the national constitution only by specific prohibitions or by grants of power to the general government, in a federal union; 3) the separation of legislative, executive, and judicial powers within the national government, creating a so-called "system of checks and balances" that limits the power of any one branch and, it is hoped, improves the quality of government by making the legislative and policy-making processes more challenging, slower, and more deliberative; and 4) the practice (nowhere expressly authorized in the text of the Constitution, but lay that aside for now) of constitutional judicial review by the federal courts.

Now, I often ask my students at the beginning of my undergraduate course on civil liberties how the framers of the Constitution of the United States sought to preserve liberty and prevent tyranny. It is, alas, a testament to the poor quality of civic education in the United States that almost none of the students can answer the question correctly. Nor, I suspect, could the editors of the *New York Times* or other opinion-shaping elites. The typical answer goes this way:

> Well, professor, I can tell you how the framers of the Constitution sought to protect liberty and prevent tyranny. They attached to the

Constitution a Bill of Rights to protect the individual and minorities against the tyranny of the majority; and they vested the power to enforce those rights in the hands of judges who serve for life, are not subject to election or recall, cannot be removed from office except on impeachment for serious misconduct, and are therefore able to protect people's rights without fear of political retaliation.

This is about as wrong as you can get. But it is widely believed, and, as I say, not just by university students. None of the American founders, even among those who favored judicial review and regarded it as implicit in the Constitution, which not all did, believed that it was the central, or even a significant, constraint upon the power of the national government. Nor did they believe that the enforcement of Bill of Rights guarantees by courts would be an important way of protecting liberty. The Federalists—in the original sense of those who supported the proposed Constitution—generally opposed the addition of a Bill of Rights because they feared it would actually undermine what they regarded as the main structural constraints protecting freedom and preventing tyranny, namely, (1) the conception and public understanding of the general government, not as a government of general jurisdiction, but as a government of delegated and enumerated powers; and (2) the division of powers between the national government and the states in a system of dual sovereignty.[11] When political necessity forced the Federalists to yield to demands for a Bill of Rights (in the form of the first eight amendments to the Constitution), they took care to add two more amendments—the ninth and tenth—designed to reinforce the delegated-powers doctrine and the federalism principles that they feared would be obscured or weakened by the inclusion of a Bill of Rights.

As for the way judicial review has functioned as a structural constraint in American history, suffice it to say that the practice has given the distinguished contemporary political philosopher Jeremy Waldron, a fierce critic of judicial review, plenty of ammunition in making his case around the world against permitting judges to invalidate legislation on constitutional grounds.[12] The federal courts, and the Supreme Court in particular, have had their glory moments, to be sure, such as in the racial de-segregation case of *Brown v. Board of Education* in the 1950s, but they have also handed down decision after decision—from *Dred Scott v. Sandford* in the 1850s, which facilitated the expansion of slavery, to *Lochner v. New York* in 1905, which struck down state worker-protection laws limiting working hours in industrial bakers to sixty hours per week, to *Roe v. Wade* in the 1970s, which legalized abortion throughout the United States—in which the justices have overstepped the bounds of their own authority and unconstitutionally imposed their personal moral and political opinions on the entire nation. Quite apart from whatever anyone's views happen to be on slavery or worker-protection laws or abortion, these decisions are usurpations of the authority of the democratically constituted people to govern themselves.

Moreover, since the 1930s, the courts have done very little indeed by way of exercising the power of judicial review to support the other constitutional structural constraints on the exercise of central governmental power. A very small number of isolated decisions have struck down this or that specific piece of federal legislation as exceeding the delegated powers of the national government or trenching upon the reserved powers of the states, but that is about it.[13] In 2012, the Supreme Court found a way, by a bare majority, to uphold a rather obvious instance of constitutional overreaching by the national government—the imposition of an individual mandate requiring citizens to purchase health insurance coverage as part of President Obama's signature "Patient Protection and Affordable Care Act."[14] The government defended the mandate as a legitimate exercise of the expressly delegated power to regulate commerce among the several states. The trouble, of course, is that on its face the mandate does not appear to *regulate* commerce at all; rather, it forces people into commerce—a particular kind of commerce—on pain of a financial penalty. Now, the Court's four liberal justices at the time were willing to stick to what has become longstanding tradition for those in their ideological camp, namely, counting virtually anything the national government proposes to do as a legitimate exercise of the power to regulate interstate commerce if that's what the government says it is. The five more conservative justices were willing to say that whatever is going on with the imposition of a mandate to purchase health insurance, it is not regulating interstate commerce. One of the five, however, Chief Justice Roberts, decided to reinterpret the penalty as a *tax*. He then joined the four liberals to uphold the mandate and the legislation as a whole as constitutionally permissible.

That's odd, to say the least, in view of the fact that the Obama administration and its supporters in Congress had repeatedly and vociferously denied that the penalty was a tax during the debate leading up to the passage of the "Patient Protection and Affordable Care Act." And there are other constitutional questions that arise, and that were not addressed by the Chief Justice, if one regards the penalty as a tax.

The truth is that the matter should not have ended up in the courts at all. Congress itself, and President Obama, should have recognized and honored the fact that the Constitution does not empower the national government to impose a mandate on the people to purchase products, including health care coverage. Whether one agrees with that position or not, it should remind us that one of the problems with judicial review in general is that its practice tends to encourage the belief among legislators (and, worse still, among citizens more broadly) that the constitutionality of proposed legislation is not the concern of the people's elected representatives; if a proposed piece of legislation is unconstitutional, they say, then it is up to the courts to strike it down. But this is a travesty. For structural constraints to accomplish what they are meant to accomplish, for them to constrain the power of government as they are meant to do, the question of the constitutionality of legislation in light of those constraints is *everybody's* business—judges exercising judicial review, yes, but also legislators, executives, and the people themselves.

A PEOPLE WORTHY OF FREEDOM

And that brings me to the critical, yet oddly neglected, subject of political culture and civic virtue. I mentioned Professor Waldron earlier. A few years ago, he visited his native New Zealand to read his countrymen the riot act about what he condemned as the abysmal quality of that nation's parliamentary debate. The bulk of his lecture was devoted to an analysis and critique of a range of factors leading to the impoverishment of legislative deliberation, warranting the stinging title he assigned to his lecture: "Parliamentary Recklessness." Its penultimate section, entitled "Parliamentary Debate," offers a thoroughly gloomy appraisal. But instead of ending there, offering no grounds for hope, he concludes with a section entitled "The Quality of Public Debate," in which he points to the possibility that the deficiencies of parliamentary debate may be at least partially compensated for by a higher quality of *public* debate, and even hints that a higher quality of public debate could prompt the reforms necessary to at least begin restoring the integrity of parliamentary debate. But he warns that things could also go the other way. The corruption of parliamentary debate could "infect[] the political culture at large," driving public debate down to the condition of parliamentary debate—a condition he chillingly described in the following terms:

> Parliament becomes a place where the governing party thinks it has won a great victory when debate is closed down and measures are pushed through under urgency; and the social and political forum generally becomes a place where the greatest victory is drowning out your opponent with the noise that you can bring to bear. And then the premium is on name-calling, on who can bawl the loudest, who can most readily trivialize an opponent's position, who can succeed in embarrassing or shaming or if need be blackmailing into silence anyone who holds a different view.

So, in a sense, it is up to the people to decide whether they will rise above the corruption that has demeaned parliamentary politics or permit it to "infect the political culture at large." But "the people" are not some undifferentiated mass; they are *people*, you and me, individuals. Of course, considered as isolated actors there is not a lot that individuals can do to affect the political culture. But individuals can cooperate for greater effectiveness in prosecuting an agenda of conservation or reform, and they can create associations and institutions that are capable of making a difference—advocacy groups, think tanks, and the like.

A critical element in any discussion of the quality of democratic deliberation and decision-making will be the indispensable role that non-governmental institutions of civil society—those little platoons, yet again—play in sustaining a culture in which political institutions do what they are established to do, do it well, and stay within their limits. And so we must be mindful that bad behavior on the part of political institutions—which means bad behavior on the part of the people who exercise power as holders of public offices—can weaken, enervate, and even corrupt these institutions of civil society, rendering them for all intents and purposes impotent to resist the bad behavior and useless to the cause of political reform.

My point, and this is why I promised to return at the end to the importance of institutions of civil society, is that this is true generally, and it is certainly true with respect to the bad behavior of public officials who betray their obligations to serve by transgressing the bounds of their constitutional authority and the limits embodied in the doctrine of subsidiarity. Constitutional structural constraints are important, but they will be effective only where they are effectually supported by the people—that is, by the political culture. The people need to understand them and value them—value them enough to resist usurpations by their rulers even when unconstitutional programs offer immediate gratifications or the relief of urgent problems. This, in turn, requires certain virtues—strengths of character—among the people. But these virtues do not just fall down on people from the heavens. They have to be transmitted through the generations and nurtured by each generation. Madison said that "only a well-educated people can be permanently a free people." And that is true. It points to the fact that even the best constitutional structures, even the strongest structural constraints on governmental power, aren't worth the paper they are printed on if people do not understand them, value them, and have the will to resist the blandishments of those offering something tempting in return for giving them up or letting violations of them occur without swift and certain political retaliation. But it is also true that virtue is needed, and that's not merely a matter of improving civics teaching in homes and schools. The Constitution of the United States was famously defended by Madison in Federalist Paper Number 51 as "supplying, by opposite and rival interests, the defect of better motives." He made this point immediately after observing that the first task of government is to control the governed, and the second is to control itself. He allowed that "a dependence on the people is, no doubt the primary control on the government, but experience has taught mankind the necessity of auxiliary precautions"—hence, the constitutional structural constraints, among other things. But even in this formulation they do not stand alone; indeed, they are presented as secondary. What is also necessary, and, indeed, primary, is healthy and vibrant political culture—"a dependence on the people" to keep the rulers in line.

But that brings us back to the role and importance of virtue. John Adams understood as well as anyone the general theory of the Constitution. He was the ablest scholar and political theorist of the founding generation. He certainly got the point about "supplying the defect of better motives," yet he also understood that the health of political culture was an indispensable element of the success of the constitutional enterprise—an enterprise of ensuring that the rulers stay within the bounds of their legitimate authority and indeed be servants of the common good, servants of the people they rule. He remarked that "our Constitution is made for a moral and religious people" and "is wholly inadequate to the government of any other."[15] Why? Because a people lacking in virtue could be counted on to trade liberty for protection, for financial or personal security, for comfort, for being looked after, for being taken care of, for having their problems solved quickly. And there will always be people occupying or standing for public office who will be happy to offer the deal—an expansion of their power in return for what they can offer by virtue of that expansion.

So the question, then, is how to form people fitted out with the virtues making them worthy of freedom and capable of preserving constitutionally limited government, even in the face of strong temptations, which inevitably come, to compromise it away. Here we see the central political role and significance, I believe, of the most basic institutions of civil society—the family; the religious community; private organizations of all types that are devoted to the inculcation of knowledge and virtue; private (often religiously based) educational institutions; and the like that are in the business of transmitting essential virtues. These are, indeed, as is often said, mediating institutions that provide a buffer between the individual and the power of the central state. It is ultimately the autonomy, integrity, and general flourishing of these institutions that will determine the fate of limited constitutional government. And this is not only because of their primary and indispensable role in transmitting virtues; it is also because their performance of health, education, and welfare functions is the only real alternative to the removal of these functions to "larger and higher associations," that is, to government. When government expands to play the primary role in performing these functions, the ideal of limited government is soon lost, no matter the formal structural constraints of the Constitution. And the corresponding weakening of the status and authority of these institutions damages their ability to perform all of their functions, including their moral and pedagogical ones. With that, they surely lose their capacity to influence for good the political culture which, at the end of the day, is the whole shootin' match when it comes to whether the ruler can truly be a servant.

A final word about "American Greatness." At the foundation of America's greatness are the virtues of her people. It is those virtues that sustain the principles and practices of constitutional government. But it is not, or not primarily, those principles and practices that impart the virtues on which they depend. It is first and foremost "the little platoons"—above all, the family. Do you want to make America great? Good. That's what we should all want. But the American family has suffered massive disintegration in recent decades, disintegration that has devastated the poorest and most vulnerable sectors of our society. That disintegration has weakened us morally and spiritually. All the material wealth and military power in the world cannot make up for that. So let us make no mistake: American greatness will not be restored without the restoration of strong and healthy families—marriage-based families. American greatness ultimately depends on the greatness of American families, for they and they alone can transmit the virtues on which all else depends.

CHAPTER ELEVEN

Catholicism and the American Civic Order

What should those of us who are Catholics be teaching our children about the United States of America, and about their rights and responsibilities as citizens?

American Catholics have faced this question from the time of the American founding. Most Catholic citizens, and most American Catholic leaders, including bishops and clergy, have affirmed the American republic and endorsed its founding principles and constitutional structures. Most have treated Protestant—and now secular progressive—concerns about the ability of faithful Catholics to be loyal Americans as rooted in bigotry or, more charitably, as reflecting a misunderstanding of either Catholicism or American ideals and institutions (or both). But there have always been, and are today, Catholics, including American Catholics, who shared and share the belief that good Catholics cannot unreservedly affirm the principles of the American regime—a regime that they view as defective from a faithfully Catholic vantage point.

We have in America a separation of church and state. The phrase itself does not appear in the Constitution—and the nature of the separation is wildly misunderstood by many people, especially among secular progressives—but we do have a regime in which the church and the state are separated institutionally. And so, for example, no one holds political office in virtue of an ecclesiastical appointment, and no one holds ecclesiastical office in virtue of a political appointment. What's more, we have constitutionally protected freedom of religion. The First Amendment to the Constitution states that "Congress shall make no law respecting an establishment of religion or prohibiting the free exercise thereof." The Constitution also protects religious liberty by prohibiting religious tests for public office. People are free to be—and may not be discriminated against by government for being—Catholic; but people are equally free to be, and protected from discrimination for being, Protestant, Jewish, Muslim, Buddhist, Hindu, Sikh, agnostic, atheist, or anything else. And, of course, the United States of America is a democratic republic. We resolve our differences of opinion in the broad realm of politics ultimately by voting.

None of this is a problem for most Catholics today. Nor has it been a problem for most American Catholics in earlier generations. But there have been, and are today, some Catholics who view the separation of church and state, religious freedom, and democracy as, at a minimum, less than ideal. They believe that in a fully just state, in an ideal state, the Catholic faith would be constitutionally recognized as the true faith, and the Catholic Church would be the established religion. Furthermore, they believe that in an ideal state the spreading of religious falsehoods—that is, ideas that are in conflict with the teachings of the Catholic Church—would be forbidden. And in such a state, we would not ultimately resolve our political disagreements by allowing everyone (or everyone who had attained a certain age) to vote.

Catholics who share these concerns recall the teachings of nineteenth-century popes expressing skepticism, to put it mildly, about the separation of church and state, freedom of religion, and democracy. These popes worried that separation of church and state and freedom of religion would have the effect of encouraging religious skepticism or indifferentism and creating an environment inhospitable to the gospel and the work of evangelization. They were concerned that democracy would lead people to believe that right and wrong, truth and falsehood, are to be determined, and perhaps even established, by voting—and therefore lack the objectivity they have always been claimed by the Church to have. Contemporary Catholic critics of American ideals and institutions fear that the worries and concerns of these popes have proven to be fully justified. They look at a contemporary landscape in which religious indifferentism and skepticism and moral subjectivism and relativism are flourishing, and faith is foundering, and say, "See, the old popes were right!"

Of course, the contemporary magisterium of the Church expresses no objections to the separation of church and state, understood as I described it earlier (in contrast to the understanding promoted by contemporary secular progressives, which is something more on the order of French *laïcité*), and positively affirms the right to religious liberty and the legitimacy—even desirability—of democracy. How do Catholic critics of these ideas come to terms with that?

Some believe that recent popes, beginning with Pope Saint John XXIII, have simply taken the Church down the wrong path. They think, for example, that the great Declaration on Religious Freedom of the Second Vatican Council—*Dignitatis Humanae*—affirming a robust view of religious freedom that embraces the right of people to promote their beliefs about religious questions even when they are in error, was a grave mistake and should be abrogated. (Some, of course, think that the entire Council was a mistake.) Similarly, they think that Pope Saint John Paul II's global advocacy of democracy, and his endorsement of the principles of the Declaration of Independence and the Constitution of the United States during his visits to our country, were misguided.

How should Catholics think about all this—which is just another way of asking the question with which I began: What should Catholic parents (and, I might add, teachers in Catholic schools) be teaching our young people about the United States of America and their role as citizens of this nation? Perhaps the place to begin is with those nineteenth-century popes, men like Gregory XVI and Blessed Pius IX. The critics often point to the teaching of these figures to illustrate what they claim to be discontinuities between the larger Catholic tradition and the teaching of the Church at and in the aftermath of the Second Vatican Council, as expressed in *Dignitatis Humanae*, the other Council documents, and the teachings of the post-conciliar popes. Do the teachings of pre-conciliar popes represent an indictment of the entire American project, inasmuch as American ideals and institutions are intertwined with allegedly "liberal," "modernist," or "indifferentist" political ideas such freedom of religion and democracy? If indeed the pre-conciliar popes condemned ideas like democracy and religious freedom wholesale, that would seem to pose a problem for Catholic parents seeking to teach their children to be responsible citizens and to respect American ideals and institutions. But is it truly the case that the American project is fundamentally irreconcilable with traditional Catholic political and social doctrine?

Leaving aside the point that, from the perspective of the Catholic faith, the teaching authority of an ecumenical council such as Vatican II is superior to the non–ex cathedra teaching of an individual pope—something that would resolve the matter in the event there were a contradiction—we must consider whether such a contradiction exists. I propose to do that by charitably examining what the pre-conciliar popes actually taught—and, crucially, by situating their words within their historical and rhetorical contexts.

Pope Gregory XVI, in his 1832 encyclical letter *Mirari Vos* on the subject of "liberalism and religious indifferentism," decried the "perverse opinion" that "it is possible to obtain the eternal salvation of the soul by the profession of any kind of religion, as long as morality is maintained." Pope Gregory wrote that such a "shameful font of indifferentism gives rise to that absurd and erroneous proposition which claims that liberty of conscience must be maintained for everyone" through means such as freedom of the press and what he described as the "license of free speech." These ideas, Pope Gregory argued, were promoted by "shameless lovers of liberty" whose "unbridled lust for freedom" also compelled them to "break the mutual concord between temporal authority and the priesthood"—to seek, in other words, a subjugation of the church by the state. In a similar vein, in his 1864 encyclical *Quanta Cura*, Gregory's successor Pope Blessed Pius IX denounced the notion that "liberty of conscience and worship is each man's personal right, which ought to be legally proclaimed and asserted in every rightly constituted society; and that a right resides in the citizens to an absolute liberty, which should be restrained by no authority whether ecclesiastical or civil, whereby they may be able openly and publicly to manifest and declare any of their ideas whatever, either by word of mouth, by the press, or in any other way." In an attached document, the famous "Syllabus of Errors," Pope Pius bluntly condemned the proposition that "[t]he Roman Pontiff can, and ought to, reconcile himself, and come to terms with progress, liberalism, and modern civilization."

Here, we must first acknowledge the historical context in which Popes Gregory and Pius wrote. At the front of their minds, and at the front of the minds of the entirety of the Church's leadership—which was during this period overwhelmingly European—was the French Revolution, along with the political, religious, cultural, and social consequences that ideas associated with the French Revolution were continuing to have in European countries where the Church's hierarchy had once enjoyed enormous political influence. It is not an exaggeration to say that the nineteenth-century Catholic Church was under attack—by radical ideologies including skepticism, religious indifferentism, moral relativism, subjectivism, extreme anti-clericalism, demands for liberation from traditional moral constraints, and calls for subjugation of the church to the state.

In France, the Revolution at the conclusion of the eighteenth century had seen the widespread suppression and violent subjugation of churches and monasteries, as well as the martyring of priests, consecrated religious, and faithful Catholic laymen who refused to swear to the Civil Constitution of the Clergy or otherwise adhere to the revolutionary government's rabidly anti-clerical and Rousseauvian religious policies. The Revolution's effects did not stop with the fall of the revolutionary government: In the decades following, the doctrines of French revolutionary ideology continued to fester within the Church; both Gregory and Pius were forced to contend with prominent French Catholics—among both the clergy and the laity—who publicly and persistently argued that French revolutionary principles were reconcilable with Catholic doctrine.

The predominant ideology of the French Revolution was Jacobinism—what Father John Courtney Murray, SJ, the American Jesuit commonly acknowledged to have shaped the development of the Church's teaching on religious freedom at Vatican II, termed "sectarian Liberalism." Its "cardinal thesis" was the primacy of the political. For the Jacobins, the only place for the Church was under the state—in other words, the Church must be subjugated to serve the needs of the state. That is precisely what they sought to do with the Civil Constitution of the Clergy, which essentially created a "department of church" whose clergy owed their ultimate fidelity to the revolutionary government, as well as through their various innovations to try to eliminate the institutional Church altogether—the Cult of Reason, for example, and the infamous Cult of the Supreme Being.

The Jacobin revolutionaries were eager students of Rousseau and his conception of civil religion—it was within the purview of the state to determine the *how*, *when*, *where*, and *what* of permissible religious worship and participation for its citizens. Remember: This is the historical context in which the pre-conciliar popes wrote, and this is undoubtedly the context in which their thinking was shaped. Jacobinism and its associated ideologies were what contemporary popes predominately had in mind when they warned against "progress" and "liberalism." It was this system—not the tenets later prescribed in *Dignitatis Humanae*—that the Church's leaders were pushing back against when they denounced "separation of church and state" and "religious liberty."

Indeed, the opinion that Gregory XVI condemned as "perverse" in 1832—the notion, rooted in a liberal understanding of freedom of conscience, that "it is possible to obtain the eternal salvation of the soul by the profession of any kind of religion"—is bread-and-butter religious indifferentism, and is something that is certainly not affirmed by *Dignitatis Humanae* in its defense of religious freedom. Quite the opposite. *Dignitatis Humanae* strongly opposes indifferentism in its affirmation of the eternal truth that there is "one true religion" which "subsists in the Catholic and Apostolic Church, to which the Lord Jesus committed the duty of spreading it abroad among all men." (At the same time, to be sure, the Second Vatican Council, in the document *Nostra Aetate*, recognizes and commends "all that is true and holy" in other religious traditions, including non-Christian traditions, such as Judaism and Islam.)

Dignitatis Humanae rejects understandings of religious freedom that are grounded in the view that all religions are *equally* true (or untrue), or in the view that religious truth is a purely subjective matter. It rejects the familiar liberal idea that religious freedom is to be justified as a necessary means for maintaining social peace and stability in the face of entrenched religious pluralism. *Dignitatis Humanae* also rejects the liberal view that religious liberty is an abstract right grounded in "personal autonomy" or a concept of "fairness" floating free of any consideration of the human good. These arguments all incline, to varying degrees, toward some form of public and governmental agnosticism concerning the ultimate or integral well-being and fulfillment of human persons—what in academic political theory goes by the label "anti-perfectionism."

Instead, *Dignitatis Humanae* grounds the importance of, and right to, religious freedom in the role it plays in enabling and facilitating the sincere and earnest truth-seeking in religious matters that all persons are called to undertake, insofar as the pursuit of religious truth (and the conformity of one's life to the precepts of religious truth as it is discovered) constitutes a unique and fundamental aspect of human flourishing. The declaration pairs its acknowledgement of objective religious truth—its affirmation that "all men are bound to seek the truth, especially in what concerns God and His church, and to embrace the truth they come to know, and to hold fast to it"—with the explicit acknowledgment that "[t]he truth cannot impose itself except by virtue of its own truth, as it makes its entrance into the mind at once quietly and with power." *Dignitatis Humanae* teaches that "as the truth is discovered, it is by a personal assent that men are to adhere to it."

The wise and philosophically sound defense of religious freedom articulated in *Dignitatis Humanae*—and one that is entirely consistent with the patrimony of Church teaching, never having been condemned by the eighteenth- and nineteenth-century popes—does not appeal, explicitly or implicitly, to any form of religious indifferentism, relativism, subjectivism, or to the instrumentalization of religion for political purposes. It is not religious freedom of the Rawlsian anti-perfectionist liberal sort, grounded in philosophies of abstract right or of "justice as fairness." Serious Catholics would be correct in rejecting any defense of religious freedom grounded in such premises.

The right to religious freedom recognized by *Dignitatis Humanae* is grounded in the intrinsic value of religion—a good whose realization begins with the sincere quest for religious truth and the resolution to order one's life in conformity with the truth as best one grasps it. This good cannot be realized or well-served by external coercive imposition by the civil state or any other authority—again "the truth cannot impose itself except by virtue of its own truth." Any attempt by the state to coerce religious faith and practice, even *true* faith and practice, will at best be futile and would likely damage people's authentic participation in the good of religion. Indeed, coercion can only serve to impair or impede the possibility of an authentic religious faith—necessary for authentic realization of a fundamental aspect of human flourishing—because it damages free and sincere religious discernment by hijacking the person's interior deliberations with completely different concerns: for example, the avoidance of suffering, physical harm, mental anguish, material loss, and the loss of rights, privileges, or liberties of various sorts.

On the Catholic understanding of faith, finding and maintaining communion with the Lord Jesus Christ, the saints in Heaven, and his Church on Earth is analogous to communion with our fellow human beings in authentic friendship in its *reflexivity*; it cannot constitute authentic communion unless it represents a free self-giving—unless it is the fruit of a genuine choice to enter into the relationship. Such a relationship simply cannot, by its very nature, be established by coercion.

Religious freedom, however, is not absolute—*Dignitatis Humanae* notes that religious communities "rightfully claim freedom" only so long as "the just demands of public order are observed." Governments may legitimately restrict religious freedom—as, I should note, our government does, and the Constitution of the United States allows for—when failure to do so would imperil the common good. For instance, if a neo-Aztec cult wanted to practice human sacrifice (even if it was supposedly "consensual") to please the Sun God, the government could—and surely would—prohibit this practice, and would do so without violating the principles outlined in *Dignitatis Humanae*. This is true even when those acts are asserted by adherents to be religiously required and even where the restriction implies or entails that the religious propositions which gave rise to the common good-imperiling act are false (for example, even if the neo-Aztec cult claimed to believe that regular human sacrifices were required to satisfy the Sun God's bloodlust and prevent him from destroying the world).

As *Dignitatis Humanae* teaches, "[S]ociety has the right to defend itself against possible abuses committed on pretext of freedom of religion." It is with this principle that we can dispatch, for example, contemporary liberal claims that certain religions "require" the killing of unborn children via abortion and that abortion access is thus a matter of religious freedom. It is also true with what superficially might seem to be muddier religious freedom claims—a liberal mainline Protestant denomination's argument that their revisionist beliefs about marriage mean that the law must define or redefine marriage to include unions other than those between one man and one woman, for example, which they might claim "doesn't harm anyone" but in fact attacks the common good by lying about the nature of marriage and undermining the conditions of a healthy marriage culture.

Of course, it may be asserted, perhaps by the critics, that the understanding of religious freedom I have just outlined marks a fundamental shift in Catholic thinking and teaching away from the responsibility of the state to promote all aspects of the common good—of which individual citizens maintaining right religion and right relationship with God would be a significant part. But such an objection misses the point. The state, if it is doing what *Dignitatis Humanae* requires, *is* promoting the common good; it is creating the conditions of human flourishing.[1]

Under the guidelines presented by *Dignitatis Humanae*, the state, recognizing the value of religion as a fundamental aspect of human flourishing, as well as the crucial importance of religion for the common good, actively works to promote religion, religious practice, and the place of religious values in the public square. It does this in part, and perhaps above all, by respecting and protecting religious freedom, including the full and generous recognition of the freedom (including the freedom to evangelize) of the Catholic Church—as our Constitution does, I should add. Moreover, it may foster and promote religion by providing for the protection and accommodation of its free exercise—once again, as our Constitution does.

With respect to our Constitution, there's no evidence to suggest that the popes of the eighteenth and nineteenth centuries had much knowledge of its structure, its protections of various civil liberties, or the American political system—sufficient knowledge to, say, understand the First Amendment's prohibition of sectarian religious establishment, its enshrinement of a strictly *institutional* separation of church and state, and the robust protection of the free exercise of religion for all persons, as distinct from French Revolutionary-style religious indifferentism, relativism, and state secularism. As Europeans shaped by a particular historical experience (and in many ways shielded from the rest of the world—the first pope in centuries to step foot outside of Europe was Paul VI in 1964), they tended to understand the idea of religious freedom as it was manifested in French Revolutionary ideology; they did not bring clearly into focus features that distinguish it from the very different conception of religious freedom developed largely by Anglophone thinkers and statesmen, manifested to significant degree in the words and deeds of the American founders, and later, of course, integrated into the Church's teaching).

What about the other four of the "five freedoms" protected by the First Amendment—freedom of speech, of the press, of assembly, and the right to petition the government? Well, we must note that *Dignitatis Humanae* teaches that "religious communities rightfully claim freedom in order that they may govern themselves according to their own norms, honor the Supreme Being in public worship, assist their members in the practice of the religious life, strengthen them by instruction, and promote institutions in which they may join together for the purpose of ordering their own lives in accordance with their religious principles." The declaration further professes that religious communities "also have the right not to be hindered in their public teaching and witness to their faith, whether by the spoken or by the written word."

What we can say is that the precise laws regulating speech, the press, and assembly that a Catholic is called to support remain in large part a matter of prudential judgment, so long as the rights of members of non-Catholic religions are respected. And, of course, progressive conceptions of "free speech" as protecting libertine excesses such as pornography and obscenity must be rejected as not only not protected speech (just as defamation, deliberate incitement to imminent violence, and false advertising are forms of expression unprotected by the First Amendment right to free speech) but, particularly in the case of pornography, actively destructive of the common good and therefore within the state's responsibility to legislate and act against. Still, there's nothing within the Church's magisterium that condemns or rejects the freedoms protected in the First Amendment as the First Amendment was understood and interpreted up until the Warren Court Era when, for example, pornography began to be treated by liberal judges as protected free speech; quite to the contrary, the conditions of religious freedom called for by

Dignitatis Humanae would seem to be served well by robust protections of free speech, a free press, and the right to peaceably assemble.

The truth is that our Constitution and our founding documents are not grounded in relativistic or subjectivist principles—or modern progressive innovations such as abstract right or Rawlsian antiperfectionism. The Declaration of Independence famously proclaims the "self-evident truth" that all men are "endowed by their Creator with certain unalienable rights"; the Constitution, while admittedly not citing a precise philosophical grounding for the free exercise of religion it defends, certainly does not ground or sustain its free-exercise protections in the French Revolutionary doctrines condemned by magisterial authority in the nineteenth century. Indeed, a responsible and charitable interpretation of our Constitution would not result in the conclusion that the rights it protects are somehow incompatible or irreconcilable with Catholic doctrine. The strong pronouncements of Gregory XVI and Pius IX were well-considered and represented a forceful attempt to confront the challenges the largely European Church was facing at the time—but they included no condemnations fairly applicable to our Constitution or our nation's founding principles.

We should also note again that since the conclusion of Vatican II, there have been many papal endorsements of the principles of American civic life and the American system of republican democracy—and certainly no pronouncements that, for example, the free exercise of religion protected under the First Amendment is in conflict with the Church's teaching on religious freedom and the civil state's duty to protect it. Pope John Paul II was particularly effusive in his praise for what he described as the "American democratic experiment." He noted that in "[r]eading the founding documents of the United States, one has to be impressed by the concept of freedom they enshrine: a freedom designed to enable people to fulfill their duties and responsibilities toward the family and toward the common good of the community." He commended our founding fathers for asserting their claims to freedom and independence on the basis of "self-evident truths about the human person"—not on the basis of any "unbridled lust for freedom," to quote Gregory XVI. The concept of freedom John Paul recognized that our Constitution and our democratic system rightly affirm is not freedom for freedom's sake (the "freedom" of "if it feels good, do it") —to the contrary, he noted that our founding fathers "clearly understood that there could be no true freedom without moral responsibility and accountability."

Indeed, true freedom is not freedom understood as liberation from supposedly outdated and oppressive moral constraints. It is the freedom to choose the good—to engage in morally worthy choosing and pursue human goods in the particular ways God calls us to pursue them. Freedom of religion is among the instrumentally necessary conditions enabling us to participate in the good of religion and pursue religious truth—and with God's grace, arrive at its fullness. Freedom of speech, assembly, and petition are similarly conditions and tools that enable us to pursue truth and proclaim and promote it in the public square.

It is in this spirit that I again return to the question with which I began: What should Catholic parents and teachers be teaching children about our country and their role as citizens of this nation? The answer, it seems to me, is clear: We must teach our children to understand our country's history, cherish and maintain its founding principles, and recognize that when we have gone wrong as a nation, it has been on those occasions when we have acted in defiance of those principles or failed to honor them. We should teach young men and women to value our Constitution because the freedoms it protects allow us to pursue truth and goodness and nurture and sustain our families, our communities, and our country's civic order. And we must affirm to our children and our students that there is no reason at all they should feel as though they must choose between being a faithful Catholic and being a patriotic American.

Of course, the Church does not teach that democracy is always required or that it is the highest or best form of government—the Church does not make judgments that there is any single best form of government, though it rejects, emphatically, certain forms of government, especially totalitarian political systems such as fascism and communism. But democracy at its best does give expression—perhaps unique expression—to the principle of equal human dignity that the Church always and everywhere proclaims. As John Paul noted, "[T]he continuing success of American democracy depends on the degree to which each new generation, native-born and immigrant, makes its own the moral truths on which the Founding Fathers staked the future of your Republic." We must continuously pray—and work—for the health and strength this nation, "under God," as Lincoln's stressed, that our laws and our leaders truly honor that North Star principle—the ur-principle, as I sometimes describe it—of all sound morality: the principle of the profound, inherent, and equal dignity of each and every member of the human family.

During his visit to the United States in 1995, Pope John Paul II delivered in Baltimore a speech in which he addressed directly the subject of this chapter. I close by recalling his exhortation:

> Catholics of America! Always be guided by the truth—by the truth about God who created and redeemed us, and by the truth about the human person, made in the image and likeness of God and destined for a glorious fulfillment in the Kingdom to come. Always be convincing witnesses to the truth. 'Stir into a flame the gift of God' that has been bestowed upon you in Baptism. Light your nation—light the world—with the power of that flame!

CHAPTER TWELVE

The Baby and the Bathwater
with Ryan T. Anderson

Among the most prominent lines of argument in political theory in the past several years has been a sharp critique of "liberalism" as essentially incompatible with pre-liberal ideals of human flourishing. Scholars advancing this critique object to the notion commonly asserted by progressives, usually in the name of "liberalism," that liberal ideals require laws that are "neutral"—by which they mean laws that do not embody and are not predicated upon any substantive view of what is humanly and morally valuable or what is right and wrong—and that only laws that elevate unlimited personal choice in matters like abortion and sexuality can pass that test. Any political arrangement that insists on such neutrality is misbegotten and harmful, the critics argue.

Such arguments are right about what many influential progressives have made of "liberal" political and social theory. But could it be that an order that might be called "liberal"—namely, the sort of thing sometimes described as "liberal democracy"—is morally defensible? We believe so, while agreeing that "neutralist" liberalism is misguided. Indeed, we think that the contemporary critique of neutralist liberalism itself points toward a defense of a certain (very different) sort of liberalism, or at least to a defensible social and political order in which certain "liberal" principles and institutions are key parts of the picture. The supposed neutrality or (to use John Rawls's term) "anti-perfectionism" of contemporary progressive liberalism is indeed illusory. Appeals to moral neutrality, however sincerely offered, have functioned in practice as smoke screens to disguise the smuggling in of a certain controversial conception of the good—one that progressives hold and just about everyone else rejects.

Rejecting anti-perfectionist liberalism need not commit one to rejecting all forms or aspects of what might legitimately be called "liberalism," even if one judges—as we do—much of Enlightenment liberal philosophy, including its most influential contemporary forms (Rawlsianism, for example), to be misguided. As two scholars who have deployed and sought to contribute to the development of the Aristotelian-Thomistic moral tradition, we see no reason to view Lockean liberalism—or Kantian or Rawlsian liberalism—as philosophical advances (whatever might be learned from them). Indeed, we have good reasons to judge them unsound in fundamental ways. And yet we are prepared to defend, for our own reasons, what are sometimes labeled "liberal" political institutions. (Of course, there is no magic in the word "liberalism," and it need not be used if one regards it as so bound in common social usage to neutralism that its use risks misleading people.)

Many "liberal" political ideals and institutions predate liberal philosophy and, more to the point, have proven effective at promoting the common good. Some such ideals and institutions have much stronger (in the sense of more credible) justifications in the Aristotelian-Thomistic tradition than in Lockean or Rawlsian liberal theory. None of them rests upon or presupposes the necessity, desirability, or even possibility of neutrality about the human good. Representative government, separation of powers, constitutionalism, limited government, and respect for the autonomy and integrity of institutions of civil society (beginning with the marriage-based family), jury trial, freedom of speech, freedom of religion, and other basic civil liberties all pre-date John Locke. They are more than defensible (and are indeed better defended) without invoking Lockean philosophical ideas.

We should not do away with any of them, for they are the political ideals and institutions that, compared to the alternatives, best promote and protect the common good—even when we conceive of the common good in a manner quite alien to some central principles of Enlightenment or contemporary progressive liberalism.

THE SHAPE OF THE DEBATE

Debates about political ideals and institutions are now too often framed as presenting two extreme and unappealing options. On the one hand is a radical commitment to foundational, philosophical liberalism of a Lockean-Rawlsian sort, with all that that presupposes and entails for philosophical anthropology, official "neutrality" about the good, the sidelining of religion, and the exclusion of religious arguments from public debate. On the other hand is illiberalism, where liberty itself is devalued even as an instrumental good or a condition for the realization of human goods by free choice and action. According to this view, civil liberties such as freedoms of speech and religion ought to be extensively pared back on the ground that "error has no rights," and political authority should be subordinated in a more or less comprehensive way to spiritual authority.

This description oversimplifies the shape of our public disputes, but only a little. The problem with framing the debate in these terms is that the two rival positions expect far too much from philosophy and theology, and they assume that this is an either/or proposition, rather than a matter of gradations and variations. They assume that there is more rational determinacy about these matters than is really available. While some ways of organizing civic life are per se rationally excluded as contrary to the integral human good at all times and in all places, a lot in political theory (let alone political practice) depends on circumstances, experience, prudence, and technical expertise. To say so isn't relativism; no less an anti-relativist than Thomas Aquinas says that lawmakers must often choose between or among reasonable options, none of which is excluded by absolute moral principles. These are choices between morally good, or at least acceptable, but mutually incompatible options.

This truth reveals a flaw in much of today's political discourse. Because the *philosophical* Lockean-Rawlsian-liberalism-versus-full-bore illiberalism set of alternatives presents a false pair of options (or, perhaps better, a pair of false options), the debate is suffering from a deep structural flaw—namely, people are assuming that an argument against any single component of one view counts as a good argument against *all* the elements of that view, and a sufficient argument for all the elements of the alternative. So, for example, some critics of moral neutrality automatically count their (sound) criticisms of that idea as a good argument against "liberal" institutions or principles such as freedom of speech or religion. This is plainly a non sequitur. We need to disambiguate the elements and appreciate the spectrum of options between the extremes, which might mix and match the elements in a rationally coherent and unified way.

One such mix is particularly appealing. Like many critics of liberalism, we're perfectionists (in the political-theory sense), and deny that freedom is the ultimate good or that government can or should be neutral about what makes for or detracts from a valuable and morally worthy way of life. Like many liberals, we think liberty is good (if generally instrumentally and conditionally so), and that basic civil liberties like freedom of speech and religion are worthwhile for their contributions to human well-being. Moreover, we support certain "liberal" institutions (representative democracy, due process, private property, freedoms of religion and speech, and the like) precisely for perfectionist reasons. But those perfectionist reasons mean that, like many critics of liberalism, we think there are legitimate limits on liberty that go beyond what can be accounted for by simply invoking the need to protect the liberty or rights of others.

What's more, in rejecting Lockean-Rawlsian liberalism and in recognizing the substantive value of religion, we more than welcome religion in the public square and public life, and believe that political society should promote the free exercise of religion and the flourishing of religious life. At the same time, we think that much about the way to order public life is rationally underdetermined—including on church-state issues. So, while we hold that the coercion of religion as such and a public stance of hostility to religion are both wrong per se, we also believe that some forms of religious establishment can be permissible—though not required.

All of that said, we certainly do not favor the establishment of religion in the United States, where the historical and sociological circumstances and national self-understanding would make any religious establishment a hindrance to the common good rather than a help to it. In other words, just as there can be moral reasons not to legislate a particular moral principle, there can be pro-religion reasons not to adopt this or that particular formally pro-religion political-*institutional* arrangement. Prudence is key. And prudence can be very much at home in a certain sort of "liberal" regime.

POLITICS IS PRACTICAL

Political philosophy is a practical science. It is concerned with identifying what concrete choices will best promote—or at least will promote acceptably well—the flourishing of people and the communities they form. Devising sound political institutions and crafting good public policy isn't simply a matter of direct derivation from first principles of philosophy (or theology). Rather, it requires what Aquinas referred to as a *determinatio*: an application of true moral principles to the particularities of one's time and place; a choice not only between morally good and bad options, but also between (or among) several morally acceptable, but incompatible, possibilities. This requires both sound philosophy *and* the wisdom acquired from historical experience, sober reflection, and, in some cases, a measure of technical expertise.

It also requires the evaluation and comparison of (and hence an ability to identify) live options—along with an appreciation of the fact that every one of the options will have *some* downsides or costs. There is no single best political regime. Thus, to conclude that a particular regime or institution has unacceptably high costs, one needs to know: Compared to what? Final judgments in practical disciplines such as political philosophy are always conducted in terms of practical possibilities. Abstract (general and universally applicable) ideals may be starting points, but they can't be conclusions, for political deliberation needs to render a judgment about how we should govern our lives together here and now, where particular human beings with a particular history and profile of faults and strengths will exercise political power.

As we think through these questions, we must always be mindful that fallen human beings will be the ones who wield governmental power. The difficulty is not simply that various political communities have their own histories and cultures and thus politics needs to be adaptive; it's also that *every* political community will be governed by fallen creatures—fallible men and women. And so it is essential, in every time and place, to think about how to organize and structure government power to minimize the abuse of legitimate authority. Recognizing the *limits* of government—even when it wants to promote a sound conception of the common good—is as important as recognizing the *goals* of government to promote that good.

Thomas Aquinas famously taught that the law should not command every virtue or prohibit every vice. Attempts—in the name of the human good—to penalize every form or instance of immorality would actually *undermine* the human good (by, for example, giving power to governments that is too easily abused, or intruding improperly into the lives of families and other institutions of civil society, or imposing a legal burden that is too heavy for most to bear). And so, he taught, the state should limit itself to punishing the graver forms of immorality, those that do the most harm, and those against which the force of law can be effective. Thus, we see in Aquinas one "pre-liberal" limit on government power: Government should not attempt to promote the common good in ways that are likely to undermine or harm it. Indeed, sometimes restricting the liberty to do wrong—a liberty to which no one has a moral right—can actually harm the common good rather than promoting it. It was in light of this insight and others like it, not Lockean or other forms of modern liberal philosophy, that our tradition of civil liberty emerged and was crucially shaped. With the benefit of experience, political communities learned how best to structure political power to effectually promote the common good.

Civil liberties such as freedom of speech and private property rights are not abstract absolutes that spring forth directly from human nature. They are political rights that are justified by—and thus inherently limited by—the demands of human well-being and the common good. Political communities have structured speech rights and property rights in various ways precisely with an eye to structuring and limiting political power to best—or at least adequately—promote human well-being and the common good. To see the ways in which speech and property can both contribute to and hinder the flourishing of people requires an understanding of human nature and human flourishing. It also requires an understanding of human fallibility—to see the ways in which fallen human beings can use and abuse governmental authority to promote or undermine the common good.

And so, from the natural-law perspective, there is no single uniquely correct political arrangement—no "ideal regime." There is simply no one best legal system of regulating speech or property. These can take a variety of morally appropriate forms given the particularities of culture, of a people's circumstances, history, traditions, needs, and challenges. Of course, *certain* options are strictly ruled out as in principle contrary to the overall human good: for example, strict philosophical libertarianism (in which the only legitimate actions of government are those to prevent harm to non-consenting persons or to protect negative liberties) and genuine socialism (in which private property is abolished or severely limited and government or "society" owns or controls the means of production, with all major economic decisions made by "central planners"). But apart from these extreme positions, there is a certain amount of room for prudence and *techne* regarding which institutional arrangements and which specific policies would best promote the common good of this or that political community.

SPEECH AND PROPERTY

Still, the natural-law tradition does not embrace moral or political relativism. The "pluralistic perfectionist" theory of civil liberties toward which it points relies on what Aristotelians call *eudaimonistic* (or human-flourishing) grounds for the limitation of certain governmental powers—and, not unrelatedly, the protection of certain civil liberties. The judgment is that these limitations tend, overall and in the long run, to best protect integral human well-being. They do this in large part by preserving the autonomy and integrity of basic institutions of civil society, which have the primary obligation and authority to provide for people's health, education, and welfare, and to transmit to rising generations the virtues needed to lead successful lives and be decent citizens. It is precisely out of concern for human flourishing that constitutions, be they written or unwritten, should limit the scope of governmental power (and the authority of governments to usurp the just authority of institutions of civil society, beginning with the family) and protect certain fundamental liberties and political rights.

We can illustrate this by looking at two examples of liberal institutions that are frequently criticized by "post-liberal" voices and that are frequently absolutized by philosophical liberals. Both the criticism and absolutism turn out to be mistakes.

First, consider government regulation of speech. Limiting the authority of the state to regulate speech based on the government's judgment about the *truth or falsity* of the speech seems to be the approach that best allows for the pursuit, attainment, and appropriation of truth in the context of robust debate. Perhaps paradoxically, it is precisely out of concern for real human flourishing—not out of a belief in or commitment to moral neutrality—that the state limits its own judgments about truth in the context of speech regulation, and protects within broad limits a "neutral" space for communication (in an overused metaphor, "the marketplace of ideas").

This isn't to embrace—or back into—relativism, moral or otherwise. And it is not to pretend that respecting freedom of speech cannot impose real costs. There are indeed universal and objective moral principles, but people are more likely (though by no means guaranteed) to grasp them, embrace them, and integrate them into their lives (especially when it comes to beliefs that do not enjoy the favor of the governing class or the majority) when the government isn't empowered to police speech based on its own judgments about truth or falsity. Nor is there any reason to assume that government agents, or majority vote, will always track with "truth." On the other hand, because the value of freedom of speech is instrumental and conditional, certain limits may be justified. These will include not only so-called "time, place, and manner" restrictions, but regulations of slander, libel, conspiracy, false advertising, and incitement to violence, to cite a few important examples. And, of course, pornography shouldn't be viewed as speech at all, and regulations on smut are entirely consistent with a commitment to the free pursuit of truth.

Then again, liberals seem to have the support of historical experience when they suggest that restricting speech about important moral, political, religious, scientific, and related matters on the ground that it is erroneous tends to entrench orthodoxy, encourage conformism and groupthink, discourage inquiry into legitimately disputed questions, and incentivize inauthenticity—thus impeding the pursuit and appropriation of the very truths it aims to vindicate. And so a regime of free speech should be crafted based on all of these considerations about human flourishing and human fragility and fallibility. (It is an irony worth noting that today it is often progressive "liberals" who are stifling speech on campuses and elsewhere, thus entrenching orthodoxies and encouraging conformism and groupthink.)

Second, something similar is true with respect to property rights and duties and government regulation of economic activity. From the natural-law perspective, there is no single uniquely correct economic system. Those systems that are strictly ruled out—such as radically individualist or social Darwinist philosophical libertarianism and radically collectivist socialism—are ruled out because they are in principle incompatible with the flourishing of human beings and their communities. But between these extremes lie many plausible regimes of property and market relations. Decent governments create and structure various systems of ownership rights and contract law with an eye to what will best serve the common good of their particular societies, taking moral principles of solidarity and subsidiarity seriously. Solidarity teaches that we should actively promote the well-being of our neighbors and our communities. And subsidiarity teaches that people should bring about their own flourishing through participation in activities and organizations, while "higher" organizations assist—but do not replace—the proper activities of "lower" organizations (again, beginning with families and religious associations) and of individual persons.

Government regulation of the market isn't inherently wrong, though it can be misguided or counterproductive, or even violate basic moral principles and for that reason undermine the common good. The only way to conclude that a particular regulation or set of regulations is indeed wrong is to engage the question on the merits. Sound philosophy tells us to be attentive to the ways in which property ownership can advance—and, in certain cases, undermine—human flourishing, and to be attentive to the ways in which government regulations can advance—or, again, undermine—human flourishing. The wisdom acquired through experience and reflection leads many, including ourselves, to support robust property rights and relatively free markets, but neither private property nor free markets, desirable as indeed they are for the sake of the common good, should be deified or treated as absolutes.

And so appeals to economic rights can't be used as trumps to justify market activity that actually undermines the common good. (An example that most people agree would undermine the common good would be allowing a free market in which children available for adoption would be sold to the highest bidders—something Richard Posner once suggested.) Nevertheless, certain general legal principles can be embraced precisely because limiting government action in certain spheres tends to protect and promote human well-being.

None of these conclusions—about a regime of free speech or a regime of property rights—is derived simply by sitting in an armchair and thinking philosophically. They require true practical wisdom—insight into the human good coupled with sound judgments about the likely long-term consequences of various institutions.

RELIGION AND THE LIBERAL SOCIETY

Something similar is true when it comes to church-state relations. There isn't a single uniquely correct way of structuring the relationship between church and state. The right answer for any particular society depends on the conditions of the people, as shaped by their history and circumstances, in light of which practical judgments must be made as to what effectively promotes and what would hinder the common good, including the flourishing of religion (and, of course, the traditions and institutions of faith in which that good is, in part, concretely embodied). The answers vary from time to time and from place to place, and are rather obviously dependent on the religious beliefs of the citizenry.

As a result, anyone who says that theology requires a specific political arrangement or proposes an "ideal" arrangement is claiming too much. What sound philosophy and theology require is for the state to effectively promote the common good, taking fully and ungrudgingly into account the fact that the integral good of human beings includes their religious good and spiritual well-being, just as it includes their physical, intellectual, emotional, and social well-being.

And so, Pope Francis today and Pope Leo XIII more than a century ago were both articulating *necessarily* contingent judgments when they made claims about confessional states. Ecclesial favor of laws and patronage could end badly, as Francis suggests, or could produce the beneficial results Leo hoped for. It's a contingent, prudential judgment—not a timeless truth of philosophy or theology.

That said, *certain* political arrangements or acts *are* excluded. Possessing legitimate authority over a religious community shouldn't alone be taken as a sign or criterion of legitimate authority over temporal, secular affairs. Meanwhile, political authority shouldn't undertake managerial direction of religious institutions, and it shouldn't coerce religious acts (though it may and should coercively forbid certain acts that may happen to be religious, such as the slaughter of children). This is because the political common good does not directly concern personal holiness or heavenly beatitude.

The Second Vatican Council teaches that the political common good is not the highest good, but rather is about earthly and temporal affairs. Political authority is directed to—and limited by reference to—the temporal common good:

> The religious acts whereby people, by their personal judgments, privately or publicly direct their lives to God transcend by their very nature the order of earthly and temporal affairs. The civil power therefore, whose proper responsibility is to attend to the temporal common good, ought indeed to recognize and favor the religious life of the citizenry, *but must be said to exceed its limits if it presume to direct or inhibit religious acts.* (Emphasis added).[1]

While the political community should foster the religious lives of its citizens (provided their way of life does not violate the rights of persons, public morality, or public peace), it must not "direct or inhibit" religious acts because its jurisdiction is limited, as the council fathers teach, to the "temporal common good." The key point from the council—one that Thomas Aquinas developed many centuries before—is that the common good that the Church is charged with promoting is distinct from (though not, of course, entirely detached from) the common good that the state has authority over. And that is entirely consistent with holding that the political order should "recognize and favor the religious life of the citizenry" and, indeed, create conditions in which they can and most likely will, acting in freedom, pursue the highest good.

There's really no *single* and unitary common good within the reach of politics, for each community has its own common good, even if all are ultimately facets of the common good that embraces all others. Seeing the distinction between the particular and higher common goods is vitally important for politics. As legal philosopher John Finnis explains in a penetrating analysis,

> Taking common good in its widest extension, it is for the common good of the members of a political community that they find the truth about divine creation and redemption, live in accordance with that truth, and so enter and remain forever in the altogether fulfilling fellowship of the divine family extending from this world into eternity. But the state is responsible only for temporal common good, and correspondingly the coercive jurisdiction of state government and law has as its defining objective not the widest common good which might include salvation itself, but what the Council calls a (or the) "basic component of the common good," namely *public* order.[2]

The political common good is a *component* of the larger, more comprehensive common good. The state is not *directly* responsible for directing man to that more comprehensive common good, though the state should act in ways that are compatible with human good in its fullest sense, the common good most comprehensively understood. This does indeed include favoring and fostering the religious life of the people.

And so, where does this leave us in thinking about the state's relation to religion? Finnis suggests six conclusions. First, "the state's government and law cannot justly teach that no religion is true. For such a teaching would be false, and false on a matter closely affecting a basic aspect of human wellbeing." Second, "there is certainly an obligation not to hold out as true any religion that is not essentially the true one." Third, "there is a duty not to make subscription to a particular religion, or to one of the many religions, a prerequisite for public offices or benefits." Fourth, "there is a duty not to seek to *direct* the true religion by claiming a power to appoint its functionaries (say, bishops) or to give or withhold ratification of its doctrinal pronouncements or ecclesiastical arrangements." Fifth, "voters and legislators can rightly and should take into account the firm moral teachings of a religion if it is the true religion, so far as its teachings are relevant to issues of law and government." And finally,

> with the third duty firmly acknowledged as excluding *positive* religious tests for voting or other public office, and with the negative duties to abstain from coercion all firmly in place, it does not seem to be contrary either to what experience shows are the exigencies of authenticity in religious inquiry, or to what seem likely to be the conclusions of revelation as well as philosophy about limits to the state's coercive jurisdiction and temporal authority, to hold that in establishing their constitutional arrangements a people might without injustice or political impropriety record their solemn belief about the identity and name of the true religious faith and community.[3]

Note well that each step depends on whether or not government action would indeed promote the common good. Certain things are ruled out—a strict wall of separation at one extreme, and throne-and-altar unity at the other—but what in-between position is to be chosen needs to be decided not by abstract philosophical reasoning but through wisdom concerning what, in the circumstances and conditions of the society, best fosters and favors the religious life of the citizens.

And note well that nothing in this argument supports or encourages progressive liberalism's strictures against religious believers acting in the public square to advocate for just and humane public policy. It does require equal liberty for religious communities as a political matter in circumstances of pluralism like ours. But it does not require a naked public square where religious believers must leave behind their substantive beliefs about the human good.

Indeed, religious traditions are sources of wisdom, and citizens owe it to one another to draw deeply from these wells of wisdom when deliberating about essential aspects of justice and the common good. This is not, contrary to certain fears, to embrace theocracy—the authority of church and state are distinct. As Richard John Neuhaus never tired of saying, the alternative to the naked public square isn't the sacred public square but the *civil* public square in which citizens of all religious persuasions (or "comprehensive views") can deliberate together about how we should order the life of the community we constitute.

LIBERALISM, PROPERLY UNDERSTOOD

It is good for conservatives to once again think about which institutions and policies truly and effectively promote the political common good. We should be aware of the demons in democracy, as philosopher Ryszard Legutko points out, and be sensitive to negative trajectories built into the logic of Lockean and other forms of Enlightenment liberalism, as Patrick Deneen argues.

But to suggest, as Rod Dreher's summary statement of Deneen's thesis does, that "classical liberalism strikes out" goes too far. While classical liberalism (or important elements of it) may not have hit a home run, it certainly hasn't struck out. Politics is a practical discipline aimed at effectively promoting the common good. Noting the philosophical defects of liberalism (as we ourselves have done) and recognizing the limitations of even morally defensible and desirable "liberal" institutions is important. But by itself, it does not tell us what in effect will best promote the common good of any particular community.

That judgment requires practical wisdom as well as a steady grip on foundational philosophical truths. Our "liberal" institutions deserve better than to be dismissed a priori based on abstractions. They deserve to be admired when they enable the common good, and improved (or in some cases replaced) when they don't.

PART THREE

Culture and Education

CHAPTER THIRTEEN

Markets, Morality, and Civil Society

The market economy, or what some people call "democratic capitalism," is, in my opinion, eminently defensible. That said, the market economy cannot be defended or even *understood* without reference to considerations of integral human well-being—in other words, moral considerations. Indeed, any effort to de-link the market economy from such considerations, or to prescind from them in making the case for the market economy, distorts our understanding of both.

The risk of that distortion is not an abstract or merely theoretical risk. In fact, the desire to separate economics from morality is rampant in our politics. That kind of separation is in particular held up as a path to "consensus" and middle ground. One will sometimes hear people say, for example, "Let's leave behind the 'social issues' and just worry about getting the economy moving."

I want to explain, however, why this separation is both impossible and undesirable. We can see why in a few distinct ways. The first way is the simplest, though also perhaps the least instructive for our purposes here. Simply put, economics cannot be separated from morality because nothing can be separated from morality. Everything we do, as human individuals and as societies, should be understood at least in large part in terms of the idea of the intelligible value—the human good—that it seeks to advance. So to ask about our economic system—the means by which we build our national wealth, allocate resources, address people's material needs, reward hard work and risk-taking—can't possibly be separated from the deepest moral questions that we as a society confront.

But I want to focus here on two other respects in which the question of the market economy in our free society is inevitably a moral question: one reason having to do with the nature of the system of free enterprise and exchange, and the other with the nature of our free society.

The economic system we today typically refer to as "capitalism" (and characteristically distinguish from communism and other species of command economy) is of course an economic system; but it is crucial to see that at its roots, at its origins, it was always at the same time understood as a moral system. Adam Smith, whom we think of as perhaps the father of free-market theory, was a moral philosopher. And his economic system, as laid out in *The Wealth of Nations*, was intended as an element of a larger moral system, a moral system that Smith understood as essential to our kind of free society.

Smith believed that a free society required more than just rules that limited the power, scope, and intrusiveness of government and secured people's rights—essential as those obviously are. A free society required, above all, men and women fit for freedom. What that meant was people who had the right kind of moral formation to be trusted with an enormous amount of liberty and choice—people who would respect the rights of others, would live orderly and peaceful lives, could exercise reasonable and sound judgment, would be responsible and reliable, honest and charitable—in a word, *decent*. We think of these kinds of virtues as democratic virtues, maybe bourgeois virtues, and Smith argued that they were essential to life in a free society.

Smith's idea of liberty—which is of course central to his case for the market economy—was not unbridled license but ordered social life, in which the people's basic rights are protected as well as respected by government, and the people's self-discipline and regard for one another's dignity limits (though, of course, it cannot eliminate) the need for state coercion.

The market system that Smith envisioned in his economic writings is made possible by this kind of social order; but it also acts to reinforce that order and to strengthen it.

Smith believed the market-based commercial society he contemplated would be a good society, for several reasons. To begin with, he argued, the generation and preservation of wealth is necessary for a good society, because it reduces the misery of the poor and it allows everyone to be more sympathetic and generous. "[I]f our own misery pinches us very severely," he argued, "we have no leisure to attend to that of our neighbor."

But at least as important, the market is not just a mechanism for wealth production, but also a civilizing institution. It makes human relations more dignified, Smith argued. The market system of exchange, as opposed to the feudal system of owner and tenant or the southern European system of patron and client, allows even the less privileged to address society in terms of *what they have to offer*, rather than *what they need*. The dignity of work helps us to see the dignity of people—all people.

The fundamentally popular or democratic character of the system he proposed was also an important moral point for Smith. "No society can surely be flourishing and happy of which the far greater part of the members are poor and miserable," he wrote. His system would allow those who lived off wages, not property, to benefit more than any other economic arrangement could.

And finally, the commercial society would encourage people to behave responsibly. Market players have a powerful incentive to consider what others will think of their actions, since they have to appeal to those others as employers, employees, or customers. And the virtues most valued in sellers and buyers are the moderate virtues essential to life in a free society: prudence and thrift, honesty and reliability, civility and good order—again, those crucial democratic and bourgeois virtues.

The maintenance of the market system, as Smith saw it, is made possible by these virtues and also acts to reinforce them, provided it is governed and regulated with these aims in mind. It demands and rewards habits of peaceful order, and can spread these into the larger society. The market economy at its best can therefore promote prosperity and compassion, dignity and fellow-feeling, and a sense of responsibility. Properly conceived and governed, it makes for a suitable companion for the free society, precisely on moral grounds.

To see why that may be right, we should turn to the second, and deeper, case for the moral character of our economic system—which is a case about the character of our free society and the preconditions for its freedom.

Any healthy society, any decent society, will rest upon three crucial pillars. The first is respect for the human person—the individual human being and his dignity. Where this pillar is in place, the formal and informal institutions of society, and the beliefs and practices of the people, will be such that every member of the human family—irrespective of race, sex, or ethnicity, age, size, stage of development, or condition of dependency—is treated as a person: that is, as a subject bearing profound, inherent, and equal worth and dignity.

A society that does not nurture respect for the human person will sooner or later come to regard human beings as mere cogs in the larger social wheel whose dignity and well-being may legitimately be sacrificed for the sake of the collectivity. Some members of the community, or those in some conditions, will come to be regarded as disposable, and others—those in severe circumstances of dependency, for example—will come to be viewed as intolerably burdensome.

In their most extreme modern forms, totalitarian regimes reduce the individual to the status of an instrument to serve the ends of the fascist state or the future communist utopia. When liberal democratic regimes go awry, it is often because a utilitarian ethic reduces the human person to a means rather than an end to which other things including the systems and institutions of law, education, and the economy are means.

In cultures in which religious fanaticism has taken hold, the dignity of the individual is typically sacrificed for the sake of tragically misbegotten theological ideas and goals. By contrast, a liberal democratic ethos, where it is uncorrupted by utilitarianism, supports the dignity of the human person by giving witness to basic human rights and liberties. As we have seen, the market system at its best serves this goal too—by dignifying work and by enabling our charitable impulses.

The second pillar of any decent society is the institution of the family. It is indispensable. The family is the original and best department of health, education, and welfare. Although no family is perfect, no institution matches the healthy family in its capacity to transmit to each new generation the understandings and traits of character—the values and virtues—upon which the success of every other institution of society, from law and government to educational institutions and business firms, vitally depends.

Where families fail to form, or too many break down, the effective transmission of the virtues of honesty, civility, self-restraint, concern for the welfare of others, justice, compassion, and personal responsibility is imperiled. Without these virtues, respect for the dignity of the human person, the first pillar of a decent society, will be undermined and sooner or later lost—for even the most laudable formal institutions cannot uphold respect for human dignity where people do not have the virtues that make that respect a reality and give it vitality in actual social practices.

Respect for the dignity of the human being requires more than formally sound institutions; it requires a cultural ethos in which people act from conviction to treat each other as human beings should be treated: with respect, civility, justice, compassion. The best legal and political institutions ever devised are of little value where selfishness, contempt for others, dishonesty, injustice, and other types of immorality and irresponsibility flourish. Indeed, the effective working of governmental institutions themselves depends upon most people most of the time obeying the law out of a sense of moral obligation, and not merely out of fear of detection and punishment for law-breaking. And perhaps it goes without saying that the success of business and a market-based economic system depends on there being reasonably virtuous, trustworthy, law-abiding, promise-keeping people to serve as workers and managers, lenders, regulators, and payers of bills for goods and services.

The third pillar of any decent society is a fair and effective system of law and government. This is necessary because none of us is perfectly virtuous all the time, and some people will be deterred from wrongdoing only by the threat of punishment. More important, contemporary philosophers of law tell us the law coordinates human behavior for the sake of achieving common goals—the common good—especially in dealing with the complexities of modern life. Even if all of us were perfectly virtuous all of the time, we would still need a system of laws (considered as a scheme of authoritatively stipulated coordination norms) to accomplish many of our common ends (safely transporting ourselves on the streets, to take a simple and obvious example).

The success of business firms and the economy as a whole depends vitally on a fair and effective system and set of institutions for the administration of justice. We need judges skilled in the craft of law, free of corruption, and disciplined enough to respect the limits of their own authority in the constitutional system. We need to be able to rely on courts to apply legal rules and principles faithfully to settle disputes, including disputes between parties who are both in good faith, and to enforce contracts and other agreements and enforce them in a timely manner. Indeed, the knowledge that contracts will be enforced is usually sufficient to ensure that courts will not actually be called on to enforce them. A sociological fact of which we can be certain is this: Where there is no reliable system of the administration of justice—no confidence that the courts will hold people to their obligations under the law—business will not flourish and everyone in the society will suffer.

A society can, in my opinion, be a decent one even if it is not a dynamic one, if the three pillars are healthy and functioning in a mutually supportive way (as they will do if each is healthy). Now, conservatives of a certain stripe believe that a truly decent society cannot be a dynamic one. Dynamism, they believe, causes instability that undermines the pillars of a decent society. So some conservatives Europe and even the United States opposed not only industrialism but the very idea of a commercial society, fearing that commercial economies inevitably produce consumerist and acquisitive materialist attitudes that corrode the foundations of decency. And some, such as some Amish communities in the U.S., reject education for their children beyond what is necessary to master reading, writing, and arithmetic, on the ground that higher education leads to worldliness and apostasy and undermines religious faith and moral virtue.

Although a decent society need not be a dynamic one (as the Amish example shows) dynamism need not erode decency and (as we've seen Adam Smith suggested) can support and reinforce it. A dynamic society need not be one in which consumerism and materialism become rife and in which moral and spiritual values disappear. Indeed, dynamism can play a positive moral role and, I would venture to say, a truly sustainable dynamism almost certainly will play such a role.

Dynamism is sustained by two sets of institutions in particular: first, institutions of research and education in which the frontiers of knowledge across in the humanities, social sciences, and natural sciences are pushed back, and through which knowledge is transmitted to students and disseminated to the public at large; and second, business firms in a fundamentally free and competitive market, and associated institutions supporting them or managed in ways that are at least in some respects patterned on their principles, by which wealth is generated, widely distributed, and preserved.

We can therefore think of universities and business firms, along with respect for the dignity of the human person, the institution of the family, and the system of law and government, as the five pillars of decent *and* dynamic societies. The university and the business firm depend in various ways for their well-being on the well-being of the others, and they can help to support the others in turn. At the same time, of course, ideologies and practices hostile to the pillars of a decent society can manifest themselves in higher education and in business, and these institutions can erode the social values on which they themselves depend not only for their own integrity, but for their long-term survival.

It is all too easy to take the pillars for granted. So it is important to remember that each of them has come under attack from different angles and forces. Operating from within universities, persons and movements hostile to one or the other of these pillars, usually preaching or acting in the name of high ideals of one sort or another, have gone on the attack.

Attacks on business and the very idea of the market economy and economic freedom coming from the academic world are, of course, well known. Students are sometimes taught to hold business, and especially businessmen, in contempt as heartless exploiters driven by greed. In my own days as a student, these attacks were often made explicitly in the name of Marxism. One notices less of that after the collapse of the Soviet empire, but the attacks themselves have abated little.

Needless to say, where businesses behave unethically, they play into the stereotypes of the enemies of the market system and facilitate their effort to smear business and the free market for the sake of transferring greater control of the economy to government.

Similarly, attacks on the family, and particularly on the institution of marriage, have been common in the academy. The line here is that the family, at least as traditionally constituted and understood, is a patriarchal and exploitative institution that oppresses women and imposes on people forms of sexual restraint that are psychologically damaging and inhibiting of the free expression of their personality.

Now, some will counsel that commercial businesses and businesspeople "have no horse in this race." They will say that these are moral, cultural, and religious disputes about which businesspeople and people concerned with economic freedom need not concern themselves. But this strikes me as fundamentally wrong. I think there is a reason that hard-left movements, such as Leninism, that seek to undermine the market-based economic system and replace it with statist control of vast areas of economic life also, at the same time, seek to weaken and instrumentalize the family, reducing marriage to a contract and transferring important elements of traditional parental roles and authority to the state or its instrumentalities. They perceive a link between the market and the family, and I think they are right to perceive it, however much I believe they are wrong to seek to undermine these institutions and shift power to the central state.

In my view, the weakening of the family imposes costs that are counted in ruined relationships, damaged lives, and all that follows in the social sphere from these personal catastrophes. In many poorer places in the United States, and I believe this is true in many other countries, families are simply failing to form and marriage is disappearing or coming to be regarded as an optional "life-style choice"—one among various optional ways of conducting relationships and having and rearing children. Out-of-wedlock birthrates are very high, with the negative consequences being borne less by the affluent than by those in the poorest and most vulnerable sectors of society.

In 1965, Daniel Patrick Moynihan, then a young Harvard professor who was working in the administration of President Lyndon Johnson as it was launching its Great Society initiatives, shocked Americans by reporting findings that the out-of-wedlock birth rate among African Americans in the United States had reached nearly 25 percent. He warned that the phenomenon of boys and girls being raised without fathers in poorer communities would result in social pathologies that would severely harm those most in need of the supports of solid family life. His predictions were all too quickly confirmed. The widespread failure of family formation portended disastrous social consequences of delinquency, despair, violence, drug abuse, and crime and incarceration. A snowball effect resulted in the further growth of the out-of-wedlock birth rate. It is now over 70 percent among African Americans. It is worth noting that at the time of Moynihan's report, the out-of-wedlock birth rate for the population as a whole was almost 6 percent. Today, that rate is over 40 percent.

The economic consequences of these developments are evident. Consider the need of business to have available to it a responsible and capable workforce. Business cannot manufacture honest, hard-working people to employ. Nor can government create them by law. Businesses and governments depend on there being many such people, but they must rely on the family, assisted by religious communities and other institutions of civil society, to produce them. So business has a stake—a massive stake—in the long-term health of the family. It should avoid doing anything to undermine the family, and it should do what it can where it can to strengthen the institution.

As an advocate of dynamic societies, I believe in the market economy and the free-enterprise system. I particularly value the social mobility that economic dynamism makes possible. Indeed, I am a beneficiary of that social mobility. A bit over a hundred years ago, my immigrant grandfathers—one from southern Italy, the other from Syria—were coal miners. Neither had so much as remotely considered the possibility of attending a university—as a practical economic matter, such a thing was simply out of the question. At that time, Woodrow Wilson, the future President of the United States, was the McCormick Professor of Jurisprudence at Princeton. Today, just two generations forward, I, the grandson of those immigrant coal miners, am the McCormick Professor of Jurisprudence at Princeton. And what is truly remarkable is that my story is completely unremarkable. Something like it is the story of millions of Americans. Perhaps it goes without saying that this kind of upward mobility is not common in corporatist or socialist economic systems; but it is very common in market-based free-enterprise economies.

Having said that, I should note that I am not a supporter of the laissez-faire doctrine embraced by strict libertarians. I believe that law and government do have important and, indeed, indispensable roles to play in regulating enterprises for the sake of protecting public health, safety, and morals; preventing exploitation and abuse, and promoting fair competitive circumstances of exchange. But these roles are compatible, just as Adam Smith suggested, with the ideal of limited government and the principle of subsidiarity according to which government must respect individual initiative to the extent reasonably possible and avoid violating the autonomy and usurping the authority of families, religious communities, and other institutions of civil society that play the primary roles in building character and transmitting virtues.

Something else that is too often lost on strict libertarians is the fact that limited government—considered as an ideal that is as vital to business as to the family—cannot be maintained where the culture collapses and families fail to form or easily dissolve. Where these things happen, the health, education, and welfare functions of the family will have to be undertaken by someone, or some institution, and that will sooner or later be the government. Freedom cannot be sustained without a population made fit for it by moral formation. To deal with pressing social problems, bureaucracies will grow, and with them the tax burden. Moreover, the growth of crime and other pathologies where family breakdown is rampant will result in the need for more extensive policing and incarceration and, again, increased taxes to pay for these government services. If we want limited government, as we should, and a level of taxation that is not unduly burdensome, we need healthy institutions of civil society, beginning with a flourishing marriage culture supporting family formation and preservation.

Advocates of the market economy and supporters of marriage, family, and traditional virtues, from honesty to chastity, therefore have many common aims and many common adversaries. But their union is not, and must not be regarded as, a mere marriage of convenience. The reason they have common adversaries is that they have common principles: namely, respect for the human person, which grounds our commitment to individual liberty and the right to economic freedom and other essential civil liberties; belief in personal responsibility, which is a pre-condition of the possibility and moral desirability of individual liberty in any domain; recognition of subsidiarity as the basis for effective but truly limited government and for the integrity of the institutions of civil society that mediate between the individual and the centralized power of the state; respect for the rule of law; and recognition of the vital role played by the family and by religious institutions that support the character-forming functions of the family in the flourishing of any decent and dynamic society.

The two greatest institutions ever devised for lifting people out of poverty and enabling them to live in dignity are the properly regulated market economy and the institution of marriage. I believe that these institutions will, in the end, stand or fall together. Those who doubt their fundamental goodness or effectiveness and who wish to transfer more power over the economy and child-rearing to the state seem fully to understand the connection between them. My plea is that people who share my own view that these institutions need to be strengthened, not weakened, and that state power should be lessened a bit rather than further expanded, should see the connection no less clearly. We should understand the moral dimension of our economic debates, and of our economic system, and work to establish and preserve a prosperous, dynamic, and virtuous society.

CHAPTER FOURTEEN

Is There a Cure for Campus Illiberalism?

Colleges and universities that are dedicated to liberal arts ideals have three fundamental purposes: the pursuit, preservation, and transmission of knowledge. Of course, there are other desirable ends that these institutions—and the schools that feed students into them—legitimately seek to achieve, but those are their fundamental and defining purposes. Other things that such institutions do (in the arts, for example, or in professional training, athletics and the like) are, in a sense, founded upon them; and anything they do that undermines these purposes they should not be doing.

A grave threat to their pursuit today is posed by the politicization of the academy (and sometimes of its feeder schools). The problem is most vividly manifest in the phenomenon of campus illiberalism. By that I mean the unwillingness of so many members of college and university communities to entertain, or even listen to, arguments that challenge the opinions they hold, whether those opinions have to do with climate science; racial or ethnic preferences; abortion; welfare policy; sexual morality; immigration; U.S. foreign policy; the international economic order; or the origins of human consciousness.

At many institutions, speaking invitations are not even issued to dissenters from campus orthodoxies. If they are issued, dissenting speakers are sometimes "disinvited" under pressure from opponents of their views. Or, if not disinvited, they are pressured to withdraw under the threat of disruptive protest. Or, if they do not withdraw, they may be interrupted, shouted down, even subjected to violent assault. But it's not just outside speakers who are at risk. Faculty and student dissenters within campus communities are subjected to abuse and intimidation (as we have seen at Evergreen State and other places).

I do not wish to paint with too broad a brush. The situation is better or worse at different institutions. As it happens, it is not at all bad at my own institution. I have taught for more than three decades at Princeton, where I have never been subjected to intimidation or abuse (though I've had threats from off campus, one of which landed the perpetrator in a federal prison, and threats have been made against Princeton for having me on its faculty.) But everyone knows the cases I have in mind at colleges around the country.

I described this form of illiberalism as the "most vividly manifest" version of the problem I am discussing, for what gets public attention are denials and withdrawals of speaking opportunities, the disruption of meetings, and the shouting down of dissenting speakers. But these are merely some *manifestations*. The core of the problem is this: Many institutions, both postsecondary and K–12, are subverting the transmission of knowledge by failing to ensure that their students at every level are confronted with, and have the opportunity to consider, the best that is to be said on competing sides of all questions that are in dispute among reasonable people of goodwill. Instead, they permit prevailing opinions on campus to harden into dogmas, dogmas that go largely unchallenged, leaving students with the false belief that there are in fact *no disputes* on these matters among reasonable people of goodwill. At the problem's core is the toxic thing that provides an environment in which illiberalism flourishes, namely, the phenomenon of groupthink.

Liberal arts education goes beyond learning facts and acquiring skills. It requires the engagement of the knowledge seeker with competing perspectives and points of view. It also requires certain virtues, including open-mindedness, respect for what John Stuart Mill called "liberty of thought and discussion," intellectual humility—humility of the sort one can possess only insofar as one accepts one's own fallibility—and love of truth. It is the task of colleges and schools, as institutions of learning, to expose students to competing points of view and to foster in them those virtues. That is necessary not because there are no truths to be known, but, rather, because the pursuit of truth and the deeper appropriation of truths and their meaning and significance require it.

Whatever is to be said about the predominance of certain views and their proponents on campuses, and the exclusion of others, the problem I am calling attention to here is less about unfairness to conservatives or others than about the need to avoid and, where it has set in, overcome groupthink. We owe that to our students—whether they like it or not.

It is a scandal when students graduate from a liberal arts program—or any educational program at any level—with no understanding (or, worse yet, grotesque misunderstandings) of the arguments advanced by serious scholars and thinkers who dissent from campus orthodoxies on issues such as those mentioned above. Even if the opinions that students may acquire in an environment of groupthink happen to be true, their ignorance of the arguments of dissenters will prevent them from understanding the truth as deeply as they should and *appropriating* it—that is to say, understanding *why* it is so and why competing views have nevertheless attracted the attention and even the allegiance of serious thinkers.

The great twentieth-century jurist Learned Hand famously said that "the spirit of Liberty is the spirit of being not too sure one is right." In making that point, he was not endorsing radical skepticism or relativism or anything of the sort. Rather, he was pointing to the need for intellectual humility in light of the inescapable reality of human fallibility. But what he says about the spirit of liberty is also true of the spirit of truth-seeking. A sense of one's own fallibility, that one could be wrong, even in one's most fundamental beliefs, an openness of mind, a willingness to entertain criticism and to engage critics—all these things are essential to the truth-seeking project. And that means that they must be cultivated in institutions whose mission includes the pursuit and transmission of knowledge.

That is not to say we should not be advocates for our views or not be engaged politically. I myself am highly engaged politically and have been so throughout my career in the academy. But politically engaged scholars and teachers, like all scholars and teachers, need to be highly cognizant of their own fallibility—even on matters about which they care deeply and causes in which they are profoundly emotionally invested. One must never imagine that one cannot possibly be wrong about this or that cherished conviction, or that one's political adversaries and intellectual critics cannot possibly be right. That is fatal to the truth-seeking enterprise.

I think the proper attitude for us to hold is the attitude Plato teaches us to adopt, especially in the *Gorgias*. We must always be on the lookout for, and be open to, the person who will confer upon us the inestimable benefit of showing us that we are in error, where in fact we are in error. Such a person, in correcting our mistakes, does us the very best service. We need to see that, and we need to help our students to see it. One who sees his intellectual adversary as an enemy to be defeated, rather than as a friend joined with him dialectically in the pursuit of a common aim, namely, knowledge of the truth, is already off the rails. He is in grave danger of falling into the ditch of sophistry.

A spirit of openness to argument and challenge, where it flourishes in an academic culture, is what immunizes academic institutions against groupthink and chases the groupthink away when it comes knocking at the door.

Part of the problem, of course, is that once groupthink has taken hold, those who are caught up in it don't recognize the problem. When is the last time you met somebody who said, "Yeah, you know what, my problem is that I'm caught up in groupthink. I tend to just think like everybody else around me thinks." The trouble with groupthink is that—like a fish swimming in water—when you're in it, you generally don't know you're in it. You may realize that not everyone shares your views, but you will suppose that those who dissent from them are irrational or ill-motivated. You will imagine that anyone who disagrees with you is a bigot or tool of nefarious interests—a fool or a fraud. When someone is in groupthink, he could pass a lie detector test claiming that he is not in groupthink. But that doesn't mean he's not in groupthink. And wherever ideological orthodoxies settle into place, we have to worry about groupthink setting in. That's true whether or not campus illiberalism visibly manifests itself in dissenting speakers being excluded from campus or shouted down.

Viewpoint diversity has value as a kind of vaccine against groupthink, and as antidote to groupthink when it begins to set in. Diversity of views, approaches, arguments and the like is the cure for campus illiberalism. People who have the spirit of being "not too sure they are right," people who want to be challenged because they know that challenging and being challenged are integral and indispensable to the process of knowledge-seeking, such people (whatever their own personal views) will want intellectual diversity on campus in order for the institution to accomplish its mission.

We all know that it's hard to get this intellectual diversity. And I think there are several reasons for that, reasons that go well beyond deliberate discrimination in hiring and promotion against people who dissent from the regnant orthodoxies. I don't think such blatant discrimination (though, regrettably, it does occur) is the heart of the problem. The more fundamental—and difficult—challenge is that we human beings, frail creatures that we are, have trouble appreciating meritorious work and even good arguments when they run contrary to our own opinions, especially when we're strongly emotionally attached to those opinions.

As I see it, this isn't just a progressive or left-wing problem—it's a human-nature problem. Any time an intellectual or political orthodoxy has hardened into place—it doesn't matter whether a left-wing or right-wing orthodoxy—it becomes very difficult for many people to draw the distinction between "work I disagree with despite its being really very good and challenging, and interesting, and important" and "work that goes contrary to what I just know to be true on issues that are important and critical to me and bound up with my sense of who I am as a [fill in the blank] progressive, conservative, feminist, libertarian, Christian, atheist, or whatever. People will perceive challenges to the dominant opinions as outrageous attacks on truth, indecent assaults on essential values, threats to what is good and true and right and just, intolerable violations of the norms of "our" community.

So, what to do? First, I address my friends in academia who are on the progressive side of the political divide, and who perceive the problem as I do, and who think something needs to be done about it: We need to expose, and protest, any *overt* discrimination based on viewpoint. Honorable progressives themselves need to be in the forefront of calling it out the moment it appears. Period. By both precept and example, we also need to strongly encourage our colleagues and students to be rigorously self-critical in ways that would enable them honestly to say, as I might say about the work of, for example, my colleague at Princeton, Peter Singer. "Well, you know, I'm really scandalized by his defence of the moral permissibility of infanticide, but there's an argument he makes that's got to be met. And the burden is on me to make the argument that our dignity as human beings comes by our humanity—our status as beings possessing, at least in root form, even in the earliest stages of development, the capacities for the types of characteristically human activities that give human beings a special kind of standing and inviolability. In other words, the burden is on me to meet his challenge.

I want my progressive colleagues to take the same position about work by more conservative scholars, especially in these hot-button areas. But I acknowledge that it's hard to do, especially when dogmas and orthodoxies have hardened into place and one is not even hearing arguments against one's own positions. For when we are not hearing them, and everybody we know tends to think the same thing about that body of issues, no matter how much diversity there is on other matters, we're likely headed for groupthink.

Working up the motivation to think more critically gets much easier when, in the normal course of things, one is regularly challenged by thoughtful people who do not always see things just as one does oneself. So it's best for us not to get ourselves into this fix in the first place.

A growing number of prominent university leaders around the country—Robert Zimmer, president of the University of Chicago; Michael Roth, president of Wesleyan University; Christopher Eisgruber, president of Princeton; Carol Christ, chancellor of the University of California, Berkeley; Ronald Daniels, president of Johns Hopkins University; among others (most of whom are, by the way, self-proclaimed political progressives)—are publicly acknowledging the groupthink or "echo chamber" problem in American higher education and are asking for help in doing something about it. Here alumni and friends of American education who want to help make a difference have a golden opportunity. They can join efforts to found or support campus initiatives aimed at bringing a wider diversity of views into the discussion and turning campus monologues into true dialogues. Centers and institutes have already been created at many top universities in the U.S. and Britain to do just that. And they are already having an impact.

Allow me a couple of examples of the value of intellectual diversity, drawn from my own experience. One is the James Madison Program at Princeton, which I have the honor to direct. Founded nineteen years ago, its impact on the intellectual culture of Princeton, precisely by bringing viewpoint diversity into our community in a serious way, has been remarkable. It gives me enormous satisfaction that this opinion is shared by many of my liberal colleagues who share none of my other opinions. They have praised the Madison Program for expanding the range of ideas and arguments heard on campus—and benefitting everybody in the process. The presence of such an initiative on campus ensures that there are people around who represent a wide spectrum of views.

That means that in general discussions across the university, not just at the Madison Program's own events, people cannot simply suppose that everybody in the room shares the same assumptions or holds the same opinions. People know they must defend their premises—because they will be challenged. That makes for a different, and much better, and more serious, kind of engagement, which profoundly enriches the intellectual life of the entire community.

A second example, again from my experience, has been teaching together with my friend and colleague Cornel West. Understand that Professor West and I have deep disagreements (he's a democratic socialist, I'm a traditional conservative)—but what happens in our joint seminars is magical and the impact on our students is amazing. We collaborate across the lines of ideological and political difference in the common project of truth-seeking, knowledge-seeking, wisdom-seeking, engaging with each other and our students in a serious, respectful manner, striving to understand and learn from each other, treating each other not as enemies but as partners in the dialectical process of seeking truth, knowledge, wisdom.

And here is the thing that really matters: The students learn, and they learn how to learn. They learn to approach intellectual and political matters dialectically—critically engaging the most compelling points to be adduced in favour of competing ideas and claims. They learn the value and importance of mutual respect and civility. They learn from two guys with some pretty strong opinions, neither of whom is shy about stating them publicly, that the spirit of truth-seeking, like the spirit of liberty, is open to the possibility that one is in error.

What Cornel and I do is, I believe, part of the cure for campus illiberalism. Now, I've always prided myself as a teacher on being able to represent, accurately and sympathetically, moral and political views I myself do not share. So if I'm teaching about abortion, or something having to do with affirmative action, or marriage, or religious freedom, or campaign finance and the First Amendment, or the Second Amendment right to bear arms, or whatever it is, in my constitutional interpretation or civil liberties classes, I like to think that if someone came in who happened not to know which side I was on, they wouldn't be able to figure it out from my presentation of the competing positions and the arguments for and against them. That's not because I think professors should hide their views—and outside the classroom I do nothing of the sort! But I don't think classrooms should be used to proselytize or push a moral or political agenda or recruit adherents for one's causes. That is why, no matter how much I care about an issue, I strive in class to present the very best arguments, not only for my own positions but for positions I strongly reject.

What I have learned in teaching with Cornel, however, is that, as good as I think I am at this, I am not good enough. The evidence is simply that time after time in the course of our seminars I have found Cornel saying something, or making a compelling point in response to a point that I or one of the more conservative students has made, that simply would not have occurred to me—a point that needs to be seriously considered and engaged. Had Cornel not been there, even though I was doing my best to represent his side, the point would not have been made, and the benefit to be conferred on all of us in grappling with it would not have been gained.

Cornel tells me that he has had precisely the same experience, time and again. He has found me making points or developing lines of argument that he says he has never considered and that simply would not have occurred to him, even though he shares my aspiration to represent as fully and sympathetically as possible positions and arguments from across the spectrum.

A healthy intellectual milieu is one in which students and scholars regularly encounter competing views and arguments, where intelligent dissent from dominant views is common and the value of dissent is understood and appreciated, where beliefs that can be supported by arguments and advanced in a spirit of goodwill are common enough that they do not strike people as reflections of ignorance, bigotry, or bad will and people who do not share them do not experience them as personal assaults or outrages against community values.

It's great to have competing views among instructors in the classroom. Yet that is a luxury that many institutions cannot afford to provide on a regular basis. But diversity among faculty on campus, even if not in the same classroom, helps to cure campus illiberalism. It voids the tendency of people—students and faculty alike—who hold positions that happen to be dominant to suppose that the college or university is only for people like them, not for people who disagree with them. It sends a message that all who seek knowledge of truth and wish to pursue it in a spirit of civility and mutual respect are welcome here as insiders sharing the truly constitutive values and goals of the community, not outsiders who are, at best, merely to be tolerated.

Am I advocating "affirmative action" for conservatives? Not at all. I am pleading for attitudes and practices that will cure campus illiberalism without the need to give conservative scholars preferences in hiring and promotion. If conscious and unconscious prejudice against people who dissent from prevailing orthodoxies were defeated, if intellectual diversity were truly valued for its vital contribution to the cause of learning, the hiring and promoting problems would take care of themselves. We would not have departments of sociology or politics or history with forty-three liberals and one conservative (or, more likely, one libertarian). Nor would we have the embarrassments, and (as at Middlebury) the tragedy, of campus illiberalism.

Let me close with a plea to teachers, administrators, school board members, parents, and anyone else who is in a position to influence what goes on in K–12 and, especially, high school education. You are sending those of us who teach at the college level increasingly diverse students, and that's great. It's especially wonderful to see so many young men and women who are of the first generation in their families to go to college, and to see many, many children of immigrants from nations and cultures spanning the entire globe. Bravo! That's what we want.

But I'm also seeing something else, and it's not what we want or should want—students who are diverse in myriad ways and yet alike in their viewpoints and perspectives, students who have absorbed what I sometimes call the *New York Times*–editorial board view of the world. They think what, evidently, they think they are supposed to think if they are to be regarded as urbane, sophisticated, "woke." They seem to have absorbed progressive ideology uncritically, and they embrace it zealously, obediently and, alas, dogmatically as a faith, a kind of religion. Challenging its presuppositions and tenets is regarded not merely as wrong or even as heretical but, in many cases, as quite literally unthinkable. In other words, they come to us already in groupthink. (I suppose that makes the job of any left-wing professors who actually do want to indoctrinate their students easy: They come pre-indoctrinated.)

This is bad. Sure, it makes it fun for people like me to shock and scandalize the youngsters, in the way I suppose it was fun for secular liberal professors of an earlier era to shock and scandalize students from devout Evangelical backgrounds by teaching Darwinian evolution or introducing them to the historical-critical approach to understanding the Bible. But that's scarcely comforting. If teachers or schools are doing the indoctrination, they really must stop. And even if they aren't, schools need to teach students to question dominant or prevailing opinions among their peers and in their communities, and equip them with the tools of critical thinking and logical reasoning that will make such questioning intellectually fruitful for them.

For starters, kids need to be taught that whatever they and their peers believe and take as what all "right-thinking" people believe is actually contested by fellow citizens of theirs who are no less reasonable people of goodwill than they themselves are. My experience with students in recent years tends to support the thesis that many are ignorant of this fact. Sure, they know that there are people who don't share the views of the editorial board of the *New York Times* (or the people on stage at the Academy Awards), but they are inclined to think that such people must be bigots or ignoramuses. By saying that students need to "be taught" that there are reasonable people who do not share their outlook, I mean they must be taught *by example* as well as by precept. Teachers and schools need to model the tolerance, open-mindedness, willingness to challenge and be challenged, and other values that we need to see more of in our students at all levels and in our citizens. Young men and women in, say, New York public or private schools, or in San Francisco, or Chicago, should not have to wait for college to encounter libertarian, neoconservative, and socially conservative arguments, authors, guest speakers, or for that matter teachers. I have a sense that there are many schools in which conservative teachers are as rare and (if they exist at all) exotic as they are in universities. Whatever the reason for this state of affairs, it is not good.

A final word for schools and teachers. Especially in the domains of civic and moral education, students need to be equipped with a fund of basic knowledge including, notably, a knowledge of American and world history, and with the skills to think deeply, critically, and for themselves. If schools are doing their jobs properly, they will be sending us students who can spot bias in, say, history textbooks, even if the bias is in a direction they themselves favor. Our job then will be to help them deepen their knowledge and further refine their critical thinking skills. Kids will come to us from high school already on their way to being independent thinkers, life-long learners, and their own best critics. And that means they will also be on their way to being responsible citizens, fit to enjoy, and equipped to play their role in sustaining and passing along to future generations, the rich blessings of living in a democratic republic.

CHAPTER FIFTEEN

Universities Shouldn't Be Ideological Churches

After the Supreme Court of the United States handed down its decision in *Dobbs v. Jackson Women's Health Organization* in June 2022, Princeton University's Program in Gender and Sexuality Studies issued a statement fiercely condemning the ruling. The director stated that the program stood "in solidarity" with the people whose rights had been allegedly stripped away by five conservative justices doing the "racist" and "sexist" bidding of the "Christian Right," causing women to endure "forced pregnancies," and waging an "unprecedented attack on democracy."

I have no doubt that the statement reflected the views of a large majority of those associated with the Program in Gender and Sexuality Studies. But was the director, speaking on behalf of an official unit of the university, right to declare an institutional stance on the *Dobbs* decision?

I am myself the director of an academic program at Princeton—the James Madison Program in American Ideals and Institutions. A majority of those associated with the Madison Program believe that elective abortion violates the rights of unborn children. So: Would it have been appropriate for the program to put out the following statement?

The James Madison Program of Princeton University applauds the Supreme Court of the United States for rectifying a long-standing constitutional and moral atrocity. The so-called constitutional right to abortion, which had been imposed on the nation by the Supreme Court nearly fifty years ago in *Roe v. Wade*, lacked any basis in the text, logic, structure, or original understanding of the Constitution of the United States. It was "an act of raw judicial power," to quote Justice Byron White's dissent in *Roe*, which deprived the American people of their right to work through constitutionally prescribed democratic procedures to protect innocent children in the womb from the lethal violence of abortion. The Supreme Court has, finally, relegated a tragic error to the ash heap of history alongside such similarly unjust and ignominious decisions as *Dred Scott v. Sanford*, *Plessy v. Ferguson*, *Buck v. Bell*, and *Korematsu v. U.S.*

The Madison Program put out no such statement. Nor did I, as director, consider even for a moment issuing such a statement or asking my colleagues to do so. My understanding of what is proper was and is that, although I may certainly speak for myself, and identify myself as a Princeton faculty member while doing so, it would be wrong for me and my colleagues to identify the university or one of its units with a view of the rightness or wrongness of the *Dobbs* decision, or to make sweeping pronouncements on the justice or injustice of abortion on behalf of the institution.

The reason is as simple as it is clear: These are matters on which reasonable people of goodwill in our community disagree. One should feel welcome at Princeton—in the Madison Program and any other unit of the university—whether one is pro-life, as I am, or pro-choice, as a great many others in our community are; whether one thinks of *Roe v. Wade* as a violation of human rights or as a vindication of human rights.

No one in the university or any of its departments should be made to feel like an "insider" or "outsider" depending on his or her views about abortion or the moral status of unborn human life. No one should be counted as "orthodox" or "heretical" in the Madison Program or in any other department or program of the university for his or her views—whatever they happen to be. We are, after all, *a university*—an academic institution—not a political party, or a church, or the secular ideological equivalent of a church. And especially in a moment when American society is deeply polarized and people of different political perspectives are more likely to demonize than to engage one another, universities like Princeton must provide a model for a healthy community where people of different viewpoints can engage each other in a civil manner and coexist.

There are, of course, religiously affiliated universities. Princeton, however, is *not* such a university, and has not been one for a long time. It is a nonsectarian institution. At Princeton, our role is to provide, in the words of our president, Christopher Eisgruber, "an impartial forum for vigorous, high-quality discussion, debate, scholarship, and teaching." To me, this means that we as faculty members and students should strive to engage one another on controversial questions in a robust, civil, truth-seeking manner, and that we should be free to do so without the university placing its thumb on the scales of debate.

As it happens, Princeton, like some other nonsectarian institutions, is currently deliberating about what rules we should adopt regarding statements made by the university's various departments and offices regarding political questions that are not directly related to the teaching and research mission of the university—questions such as abortion, U.S. policy toward Israel, defunding the police, and reparations for slavery. What should those rules be? What principles are to be considered in devising limitations on institutional pronouncements?

To my mind, the University of Chicago arrived at the right answer more than fifty years ago, when it adopted, in the midst of the Vietnam War controversy and other matters of contention, the report of a committee chaired by the law professor Harry Kalven. The Kalven Report committed the university and its various units to *institutional neutrality* on political questions, encapsulating its rationale in the helpful dictum:

"The University is the home and sponsor of critics; it is not itself the critic." The Kalven Report did not forbid faculty, students, or staff in their individual capacities from stating their opinions publicly, or even from identifying themselves by their academic titles and affiliations when doing so. It did, however, generally forbid anyone from committing the university or its departments and offices to particular points of view on controversial political questions.

The Kalven Report embodies a particular understanding of the role of the nonsectarian university and of the conditions required for it to play that role. The university and its departments serve the cause of truth-seeking by providing a forum for members of the community to have full, fair, and open debates on fundamental issues without any institutional influence. Political tribes or sects can form within the university and its departments, but no tribe or sect may take control and make itself, in effect, the established religion on campus.

Still, why *not* authorize departments or other units to make statements when their members feel strongly about an issue and where there exists—let us imagine—an unmistakable consensus on the matter? Of course, there is a distinction between consensus on *matters of empirical and verifiable fact*, and consensus on *normative questions* of the sort that are not, and cannot be, resolved simply by establishing the facts. I would warn, however, that even in the natural sciences, history is replete with examples of scholars reaching a consensus on matters of alleged fact about which they turned out to be wrong. This, it seems to me, is a conclusive argument in support of freedom of thought, inquiry, and discussion, and for encouraging viewpoint diversity.

It is also a strong argument against committing the university and its units to a particular position unless doing so is absolutely necessary. (That would be a rare occurrence, perhaps in the case of a state law forbidding universities from hiring people who hold certain views or banning, say, the "promotion"—or teaching—of certain ideas. It would not extend to such matters as the Israel-Palestine dispute; the Ukraine War; abortion; the death penalty; how a jury ought to decide, or ought to have decided, in a criminal or civil trial; marriage and sexual morality; fracking; or whether to defund the police, legalize drugs, move to a single-payer health-care system, or abolish the FBI—all issues on which departments at Princeton or other nonsectarian institutions have released statements in recent years.)

History is also replete with examples of scholars making claims in the name of science that were, in truth, driven by normative beliefs and commitments. Sometimes the scientific community, or particular segments of it, reached a "consensus" (or something approaching one) on such matters. The case that should bear heavily on our consciences and serve as a warning to us—particularly in the academic world and the broader intellectual culture—is eugenics. As the historian Thomas Leonard has shown, eugenics was embraced and promoted by the academic establishment as if it were gospel—and with very little dissent.

Where there is a consensus on normative matters, or where a consensus is more or less clearly driven by normative beliefs and commitments, such consensus provides *no* justification for the university or one of its units to publicly commit itself to a political position. If anything, it raises the question of *why* there is a consensus on difficult moral or other normative issues on which, broadly in our society, reasonable people of goodwill disagree. Where are the dissenting voices? Has groupthink set in—in a unit, or perhaps in an entire field? What message does the lack of representation of dissenting voices send to students? Has there been discrimination or favoritism based on viewpoint? If so, is it continuing? Has this affected hiring and promotion decisions, or created what is broadly known to be a hostile environment for people who dissent from established orthodoxies?

And there are more questions: Will discrimination result from, or be exacerbated by, the practice of academic units taking positions in political disputes? Might the practice motivate, or further encourage, people to take into account candidates' moral or political beliefs for academic appointment or tenure? Will people hoping to be appointed to such positions be impelled to censor themselves, lest they jeopardize their applications? The dangers of the corruption of fair and ideologically nonpartisan hiring and promotion procedures are glaring.

Let me linger a bit on this last point. If academic units are permitted to make statements on political issues, then the following will be the case: When considering a job or tenure candidate, voting faculty members will anticipate that he or she, if appointed, will vote on future political statements. So they will perfectly reasonably want to know, and will take into account, the candidate's ideological leanings and political views and affiliations in deciding whether to support or oppose the appointment. Of course, this is something that faculty are not supposed to do under existing academic norms for nonsectarian institutions. It is condemned, for example, by the American Association of University Professors. But a policy that permits departments and other units to take political stands and issue political statements undermines this prohibition. After all, if departments are authorized to vote on political statements and choose to act on that authorization, then voting on political statements will be one of the things a faculty member is, as a practical matter, hired to do.

Of course, we should draw a careful distinction between the university and its official subunits and other entities, such as student associations, that exist within the broader university community. Student clubs certainly should have the right to devote themselves to causes (political, moral, religious, and so forth) and take positions and put out statements advocating whatever they stand for. The key here is for the university to be nondiscriminatory in recognizing and making resources available to the clubs. The Democratic Club should be treated the same as the Republican Club. The pro-choice club should be treated no better and no worse than the pro-life club. The Islamic Society should be treated exactly as the Jewish Center or Baptist Chaplaincy is treated. And so forth. Funding should be distributed without discrimination, and any institutional support should be evenhanded.

Institutional neutrality protects the university's fundamental mission of pursuing, preserving, and transmitting knowledge. This mission requires not only academic freedom and viewpoint diversity, but also principles and policies that enable us to avoid contests among people of competing ideological stripes for control of the university and its individual units. The university must belong to everyone in our community, not simply those who are on the allegedly "right" side of contested issues.

As I noted, Princeton was once a sectarian college: Until almost a century ago, it was affiliated with Presbyterian Christianity. Today, as a nonsectarian university, its mission no longer includes the propagation of sectarian doctrines. It is, in this crucial respect, unlike Notre Dame, Brigham Young, Baylor, Yeshiva, and Zaytuna. I have nothing against such institutions. In fact, I think they do great work. I've lectured at all of them. And I'm glad they are available to students and families for whom religiously based education is important.

But I believe that it is valuable for there also to be great nonsectarian universities such as Princeton, the University of Chicago, the University of Michigan, and the rest, in which people are united not by shared commitments to religious or secular ideological dogmas but by, *and only by*, a commitment to the pursuit, preservation, and transmission of knowledge—and an understanding that the cause of knowledge-seeking can be mightily advanced only by encouraging the critical engagement of ideas among people who have fundamental disagreements on normative and other important matters.

CHAPTER SIXTEEN

Christianity and Paganism: Then and Now

The great twentieth-century Jewish public intellectual and man of letters Milton Himmelfarb famously defied those of his co-religionists who claim that Judaism cannot be defined. His definition was *via negativa*: "Judaism is against paganism." This approach to understanding Judaism—and that other great Jewish religion known as Christianity—is anything but flippant, for at its foundation and heart is the most un-pagan—indeed, anti-pagan—of all teachings, namely, that man, though made from the mere dust of the earth, is fashioned in the very image and likeness of God.

What could such a teaching mean? In other words, how are we mortal, material human beings *God-like*? It cannot mean that God has five fingers on each of two hands and hair on his head and a nose. God, if he exists, is immaterial. Rather, it means this: That we human beings, albeit mortal and material, possess the (literally) *awesome* God-like powers of reason and freedom. Like God, as he is presented in the book of Genesis, we are able to envisage states of affairs that do not obtain; grasp the value—the intelligible point—of bringing about those states of affairs; and act freely, based on our rational grasp of the intelligible point of bringing them into existence, and not on mere impulse or instinct in the manner of a brute animal, to bring them about.

And in so acting—freely and on reasons—we do more than alter states of affairs in the world external to us. We also shape our own characters. Our agency makes us morally self-constituting creatures, responsible for acting virtuously (fully practically reasonably, to borrow Aristotle's language) even when doing so requires us to resist powerful feelings or emotions tempting us to do otherwise. So, again unlike brute animals, we are creatures who are capable of self-transcendence, self-mastery.

Among the moral truths we can grasp (albeit only with difficulty and in certain ways dimly) by rational inquiry, deliberation, and judgment is the truth that each and every member of the human family—no matter how small, weak, vulnerable, poor, disabled—is the bearer of profound, inherent, and equal dignity. If that stunningly un-pagan and anti-pagan moral proposition is true, then the respect called for by that dignity demands something that is as alien to paganism as it can possibly be, namely, a genuine reverence for human beings—for human life. It requires that we, in the words of Immanuel Kant, "treat humanity, whether in the person of oneself or others, always as an end and never as a means only." It requires us to abjure practices that paganism valorizes and even glorifies, from unchastity to abortion and infanticide to slavery, conquest, and domination. And it requires us to abjure these practices even when our own circumstances, desires, and self-interest tempt us to embrace and try to rationalize them.

Of course, the greatest thinkers of pagan antiquity grasped, or partially grasped, moral truths that put them in some ways in adversarial postures towards accepted practices of their times and places, including forms of unchastity and homicide. But none fully grasped—and grasped the moral implications of—the principle of profound, inherent, and equal dignity. Indeed, even Jews, Christians, and others who affirm the principle as a matter not only of reason but of divine revelation often fail to grasp its full implications. Paganism is perennially an internal—not merely an external—challenge to Jewish and Christian faith. Jews and Christians are constantly falling into, or back into, pagan ideologies and practices. Today, entire denominations have declared themselves in support of neo-pagan practices of various sorts that are explicitly in conflict with the biblical witness.

But for anyone who truly grasps the principle, and has some conception of its full moral implications, the question naturally arises: How is it that human beings have the powers they have, grounding the dignity they possess, possess equally (despite obvious differences of strength, intelligence, beauty, talent, wit, charm, wealth, social rank, and so forth), and possess in virtue of nothing other than their nature as rational creatures, nothing other than their *humanity*? It is difficult—indeed, it seems to me impossible—to find a credible competitor to the account set forth Genesis 1, the *imago Dei*, the proposition that man is made in the very image and likeness of the good and loving God who is creator and ruler of all that is. But if that is so, then the question "Should I be religious, or should I be secular?" answers itself…and the spiritual quest—the quest for the fullness of religious truth—begins.

And another question naturally arises: How shall we order our lives together—how shall we conceive and pursue the common good—in ways that are consistent with the dignity of the human person?

Secular liberal political theorists of the late twentieth century generally answered that question by insisting that sound principles of justice require that law and government be neutral as between competing conceptions of the human good, that is, of what makes for or detracts from valuable and morally worthy ways of life.

Critics, including me, argued that the "neutrality" to which the orthodox secularist liberalism of the period aspired (or at least purported to aspire) was neither desirable nor possible. That political philosophy was, we argued, built on premises into which had been smuggled controversial substantive ideas—liberal secularist ideas—about human nature, the human good, human dignity, and, indeed, human destiny—ideas as substantive and controversial as those proposed by Catholicism, Judaism, and other so-called "comprehensive doctrines," be they secular or religious.

Today, little effort is made by secular liberals (or "progressives," as many prefer to be labeled) to maintain the pretense of neutrality. Now that they have gained the advantage, in many cases have prevailed (at least for now) on battle front after battle front in the modern culture war, and have achieved hegemony in elite sectors of the culture (for example, in education at every level, in the news and entertainment media, in the professions, in corporate America, and even in much of religion), there is no longer any need to pretend.

Take, as an example, the issue of marriage. Today virtually no one on either side doubts that marriage as redefined by the Supreme Court embodies substantive ideas about morality and the human good—ideas that differ profoundly from those embodied previously in marriage law, ideas that, according to partisans of the redefinition of marriage, are to be preferred to competing ideas, such as the biblical and natural-law understandings of marriage, precisely because they are superior to the ideas they have supplanted.

So now that the pretense of neutrality has been more or less abandoned, and is on its way to being forgotten, what is the substance of the perspective (or ideology or, perhaps, religion) that is now fully exposed to view—and not merely to the view of its critics? Professor Steven Smith and Louise Perry say that it is a revived, revitalized, and modernized paganism. And I think they're right.

Now, this label is, of course, provocative. Professor Smith's and Ms. Perry's reasons for choosing it, however, go well beyond a mere desire to provoke. What they correctly perceive is that contemporary social progressivism reflects certain core (and constitutive) ideas and beliefs—ideas and beliefs that partially defined the traditions of paganism that were dominant in the ancient Mediterranean world and in certain other places up until the point at which they were defeated, though never quite destroyed, by the Jewish sect that came to be known as Christianity.

Of course, some progressives will suppose that we are deploying the term "pagan" as an epithet. But we mean something quite specific by the word—we use it to characterize ideas and beliefs that a great many people today, especially those in the ideological vanguard, have in common with people of, for example, pre-Christian Rome. This does not mean that contemporary secular progressivism shares *all* the ideas and beliefs of ancient Romans (such as belief in gods like Jupiter, Neptune, and Venus), but rather that *some* of the central ideas and beliefs that distinguish secular progressives from orthodox Christians and Jews today are ideas and beliefs they have in common with the people whose ideas and beliefs Judaism and Christianity challenged in the ancient world.

Secular progressives, no less than people of other faiths, hold cherished, even identity-forming beliefs about what is meaningful, valuable, important, good and bad, right and wrong. They may not believe in God, or a transcendent and personal deity, but certain things are nevertheless *sacred* to them—things they live for and would be willing to fight and even die for (for example, what they regard as racial justice, LGBT rights, environmental responsibility, and so forth). They have *faith*—and *a faith*. Just look at the child-preacher Greta Thunberg. But what is it about the secular progressive faith that warrants our labeling it "pagan"? After all, though not theistic, it is certainly not (in any literal sense) polytheistic. Professor Smith explains:

> Pagan religion locates the sacred *within* this world. In that way, paganism can consecrate the world from within: it is religiosity relative to an *immanent* sacred. Judaism and Christianity, by contrast, reflect *transcendent* religiosity; they place the sacred, ultimately, *outside* the world.[1]

Now, Smith concedes that this characterization oversimplifies things a bit. But the oversimplification is mainly in the description or characterization of Judaism and Christianity, not secular progressivism (or wokeism). The biblical faiths conceive God as transcendent, to be sure, but not in a way that excludes elements of divine immanence. In Jewish and Christian doctrine, a transcendent God sanctifies the world of human affairs by entering into it, while still transcending it. And God's transcendence means that, for the believer, this world is not one's ultimate home—we are, in a sense, "resident aliens." Smith contrasts Jews and Christians with pagans on precisely this point: "The pagan orientation...accepts this world as our home, and does so joyously, exuberantly, and worshipfully."[2]

Now, Christianity, had it been a religion of pure and exclusive transcendence, might have simply rejected this world and not concerned itself with its affairs. The authorities of pagan Rome might then have left Christianity alone, treating it as one more odd or exotic religion. There were many of these in the Roman empire. But it's not that kind of faith. It took an interest in the world's affairs and developed ideas about such things as authority, obligation, law, justice, and the common good—ideas that challenged pagan ideas and practices in a variety of areas, some of them profoundly important. A central area was sex.

As Smith notes, within the pagan "matrix of assumptions, the Christian view of sexuality was not only radically alien, it was close to incomprehensible."[3] This is certainly true historically. But consider that the Christian view of sexuality is today, within the "matrix of assumptions" of secular progressivism, perfectly aptly described as "not only radically alien, but close to incomprehensible." Consider again the debate over marriage, as just one of many possible examples. The biblical and natural-law conception of marriage as *conjugal*, that is, as the one-flesh union of sexually complementary spouses, is not only "alien" to secular progressives, who understand "marriage" merely as a form of sexual-romantic companionship or domestic partnership, but nearly incomprehensible to them—except, that is, as what they suppose is bigotry against people who are attracted to and wish to marry (as progressives understand the term) people of their same sex. Or consider the view that non-marital sexual conduct and relationships, including homosexual ones, are inherently immoral. That, too, is regarded by a great many secular progressives as not only unsound, but unreasonable, outrageous, scandalous, even hateful. They can account for it, if at all, only as religious irrationalism, bigotry, or, as many today now claim, a psychopathology.

As the historian Kyle Harper notes in his important book on the transformation of beliefs about sexuality and morality in the ancient world, sexuality "came to mark the great divide between Christians and the world." Christian ideas, rooted in Jewish thought, about sexual norms (rejecting fornication, adultery even by men, homosexual acts, pornographic displays, and so forth) were revolutionary; and the pagan establishment was no more welcoming of revolutionaries—even non-violent ones—than any other establishment is. So paganism could not, and did not, tolerate the Christians—even when Christianity was far too weak to pose any real challenge to political authority. It was not that Roman authorities refused to allow minority religions of any kind in the empire; those that could co-exist with the dominant paganism were allowed to do just that. But the Romans had always found the Jews to be troublesome, and they perceived Christianity—a convert-seeking religion—as a grave threat. And Christian ideas about sex (and, in consequence, about Roman sexual practices) figured significantly in that perception. The Roman pagans feared that Christianity would, in Steven Smith's evocative phrase, "turn the lights out on the party." And that, of course, is what Christianity eventually did.

But in our own time the lights have been turned back on and the party is going again. In the 1940s, Alfred Kinsey convinced a lot of people that sexual satisfaction is a human need—that psychological health and wholeness generally require frequent regular sexual activity, which may be inside or outside of marriage, and that Judaeo-Christian norms of sexual morality, when embraced, result in stilted, even twisted, personalities. In the 1950s, Hugh Hefner persuaded people that pornography was, or could be, innocent fun and that the "Playboy philosophy" of sexual indulgence was the way for up-to-date, sophisticated people to lead their lives. The "gay rights" or "LGBT" movement has made the affirmation of homosexual conduct and relationships the "civil rights cause" of our day. Dissent is not permitted. Claims to religious freedom are dismissed as mere excuses for discrimination. "Bake the cake, you bigot!"

Observant Christians and Jews, and other traditional religious believers, have been knocked back on their heels. Reversing the Sexual Revolution (despite the growing evidence, showcased by Louise Perry among many others, of its baleful social consequences, especially for children) seems nearly inconceivable. Few believe that its forward march can be paused or even meaningfully slowed down. The vast majority of religious believers think that the most they can hope for in this new epoch of pagan ascendancy are some protections for their own liberty to lead their lives as *they* see fit, in conformity with their faith, and not to be forced to facilitate or participate in activities that they cannot in good conscience condone. Progressives say, after all, that they are all for individual autonomy and liberty. In pushing the redefinition of marriage, they insisted that all they were seeking was "live and let live." Of course, that claim has already proven to be, if I may borrow a phrase from Hillary Clinton, "no longer operative." Many religious people despair even of the possibility of protecting their children from being indoctrinated into the beliefs of the governing elite, the new ruling class (or what perhaps might better be described as the old, but re-paganized, ruling class). They believe we have entered a new Diocletian age. They not unreasonably suppose that it is precisely this reality that is being signaled when progressive intellectuals, such as Mark Tushnet of Harvard Law School, say things like this:

> The culture war is over; they lost, we won.... Taking a hard line ("You lost, live with it") is better than trying to accommodate the losers, who—remember—defended, and are defending, positions that liberals regard as having no normative pull at all. Trying to be nice to the losers didn't work well after the Civil War, nor after *Brown*. (And taking a hard line seemed to work reasonably well in Germany and Japan after 1945.) I should note that LGBT activists in particular seem to have settled on the hard-line approach, while some liberal academics

defend more accommodating approaches. When specific battles in the culture wars were being fought, it might have made sense to try to be accommodating after a local victory, because other related fights were going on, and a hard line might have stiffened the opposition in those fights. But the war's over, and we won.

So there you are. The neo-pagans are in no mood to be "accommodating." Dissenters from progressive dogmas can expect "the hard-line approach." We are to be treated like the defeated Germans and Japanese after World War II.

For faithful religious folk who dissent from neo-pagan orthodoxy, then, the question is "what is to be done?" How should we respond to the "hard-line" approach—an approach that will indeed be, and in fact is being, implemented by people who want to ensure that we never again get near the light switch and that we are properly punished for having switched off the lights to the party in the first place?

Some religious folk, including entire denominations, have already taken the path of capitulation and acquiescence. They maintain the visible forms of faith while yielding its moral substance. They have made themselves the "useful idiots" of neo-paganism (to borrow Stalin's famous characterization of the anti-anti-Communist liberals of his time). They have made themselves the wokest of the woke. Obviously, that is not an option for serious believers. So: What do we do?

Often the question is posed as "flight or fight?" I've never been completely clear about what Rod Dreher has in mind by the "Benedict Option." He has described it as a "strategic retreat," but also says that it doesn't mean that we should not stay involved in the world. I certainly agree that we need to stay involved in the world—we have an obligation as believers to bear faithful witness to the values and principles we know are integral to justice and human flourishing— but I don't see what we should be retreating from, even strategically. And to what—or where—could we retreat? To our families, religious communities, civil society associations? That won't work. They'll hunt us down and dismantle our institutions. The liberal Texas politician and skateboarder Beto O'Rourke, in his characteristically charmingly hapless way, let the cat out of the bag on that point in the Democratic presidential debate in 2016, and none of his rivals contradicted him. (O'Rourke proposed that churches and other religious groups who refuse to go along with same-sex marriage have their tax-exempt status revoked as a punishment.) They are determined that our children or at least our grandchildren will think the way they think, not the way we think; so permitting us to retreat to the functional equivalent of the monasteries where we can quietly tend the gardens of our own families, and transmit to our children our own values, is not an option for them. Again, remember that we are to be treated like the defeated Japanese and Germans after World War II.

So flight, really, is not an option; we have no choice but to fight. And in this era of "woke" ideology, our fight is not simply to uphold our values pertaining to such matters as marriage and the sanctity of human life; it is to protect basic principles of republican civic life that people on the left once claimed to champion and, even (implausibly) to have discovered, but are now prepared to cast aside and even trample—principles such as freedom of speech, freedom of religion, freedom of the press, the right of peaceful assembly, limited government, democratic participation, the rule of law, the rights to due process of law and the equal protection of the laws, even the right of parents to direct the upbringing and education of their children.

This fight will not be easy; on the contrary it is, and will continue to be, hard. There will be casualties. Lots of them. People will be cancelled. They will be denied educational opportunities and opportunities for professional advancement. Some will lose their employment. Many will be ridiculed, shamed, defamed, vilified. The cost of true discipleship is, and always has been, a heavy cost—and it has only gotten, and will get, heavier. We observant Christians and Jews are back in the position of our forebears in imperial Rome. If we are true to our faith—if we are true to ourselves—then we are quite literally intolerable, as far as the Mark

Tushnets and Beto O'Rourkes of the world are concerned. And they are legion. And they hold massive cultural, political, and economic power.

So, the question and challenge we face is simply this: Can we muster the courage to be faithful, to boldly bear witness to truths that are unpopular among those controlling the levers of cultural, political, and economic power? Are we willing, if necessary, to pay the costs—the heavy costs—of discipleship? Of course, without God's help, nothing of this kind would be possible. Yet we have it on good authority that God's grace is superabundant. No one who asks for the courage to bear faithful witness will be denied it.

So, shall we flee from the battle? No. Quite the opposite. Onward, Judaeo-Christian soldiers.

CHAPTER SEVENTEEN

Catholic Teaching on Jews and Judaism

One of the great stains on the history of the Catholic Church is the contempt—and sometimes worse—that some Catholics, including some leaders of the Church, have over the centuries expressed for Jews and Judaism. Catholics were never required as a matter of doctrine to hold anti-Jewish attitudes or support, much less participate in, the persecution of Jews. For centuries, however, the posture of the Church as an institution toward the Jewish faith and the Jewish people was decidedly negative—often hostile.

In the wake of the Holocaust, this began to change. No doubt part of the explanation is that Catholics, especially those in leadership positions in the Church, rightly perceived that, though the Nazis were anti-Catholic and anti-Christian, the long history of European Christian hostility to Jews helped to shape the conditions that made the murder of Jews on an industrial scale by Hitler and his thugs possible.

To their credit, Catholics and Church leaders were represented among those who courageously protected, and in many cases rescued, Jewish victims of the Holocaust. Many of the Jews who survived attribute their survival to Catholics, ranging from peasants and laborers who took in

Jewish neighbors to the pope himself, on whose orders Jews were hidden in convents and other religious houses.

The post-Holocaust period leading up to the Second Vatican Council became a time of deep reflection for the Church and the occasion for a profound examination of conscience—and of the historical record. This bore fruit in the sections on Jews and Judaism of the conciliar document known as *Nostra Aetate*, the declaration on the Church's understanding of, and relationship with, non-Christian religions.

Nostra Aetate once and for all repudiated the idea of Jewish collective guilt and the outrageous slander that "the Jews" killed Christ or were "accursed" or "rejected by God" because the Jewish people as a whole did not accept Jesus as the Messiah. It condemned, categorically, all forms of anti-Semitism and discrimination against Jews. What's more, it expressly affirmed that there is a "common patrimony" and, indeed, a "spiritual bond"—something not merely historical, though rooted in historical reality—uniting Christians ("the people of the New Covenant") with Jews ("Abraham's stock"). Perhaps most important, quoting the Jewish Christian St. Paul, it refers to the Jewish people as the "well-cultivated olive tree onto which have been grafted the wild shoots, the Gentiles."[1]

Nostra Aetate turned out to be only the beginning of the development of Catholic teaching on Jews and Judaism. Within a decade and a half of its ratification and promulgation by Pope Paul VI as the official teaching of the Church, Karol Wojtyła, the Archbishop of Cracow in Poland, would become pope. As John Paul II, he would use *Nostra Aetate* as the foundation for further elaboration of the Church's teaching, working out the fuller implications of the Vatican Council's declaration.

It is important to understand that what concerned John Paul in this matter was above all *theological*, not sociological or political. He sought to understand, and to teach, the truth about how the Church properly understands and relates herself to Jews and Judaism. There were options on the table here—judgments to be made, if the topic was to be addressed at all. And John Paul made his judgments, exercising his full authority to declare the mind of Christ as Christ's Vicar, Supreme Pontiff of the Universal Church.

One option would have been to say that God's covenant with the Jews had been abrogated when the Jewish people as a whole did not join the Christian Church, but we should be nice to Jews anyway, and avoid speaking disparagingly of their religion, since after all, we've been awfully cruel to them over the centuries, and we'd have a better chance of winning them over by being kind.

This was not the path he took or the judgment he made. This was not the mind of Christ.

Rather, he spoke of the Jews as "the people of the original Covenant." Indeed, his exact words were "our *kindred* nation of the original Covenant." To make himself even clearer, John Paul formally declared that God's covenant with the Jews "has never been revoked." In 1986, speaking to leaders of the Australian Jewish community during a visit to that country, John Paul went still further, declaring the covenant to be not only still in force, but *irrevocable*.

> The Catholic faith is rooted in the eternal truths of the Hebrew Scriptures and in the irrevocable covenant made with Abraham. We, too, gratefully hold these same truths of our Jewish heritage, and look upon you as our brothers and sisters.[2]

The references to "our Jewish heritage" and to the Jewish people as "our brothers and sisters" are particularly noteworthy.

In one of the most important acts of his long and remarkably consequential pontificate, both those concepts would again be center stage when John Paul made his historic visit, also in 1986, to the Great Synagogue of Rome—the first by any pope—where he made the following profound declaration:

> The Jewish religion is not "extrinsic" to us, but in a certain way is "intrinsic" to our own religion. With Judaism we have a relationship

we do not have with any other religion. You are our dearly beloved brothers, and in a certain way, it could be said that you are our elder brothers.[3]

Driving the point home, John Paul greeted Jewish rabbis in a meeting in Assisi in 1993 as "our dearly beloved brothers of the ancient covenant *never broken and never to be broken."*

Benedict XVI and Francis have, of course, stood by the teachings of *Nostra Aetate* and of John Paul II—the teachings of the Church. So will their successors. These are magisterial teachings—declarations of the mind of Christ.

Obviously, contemporary Judaism and Christianity have important differences—above all the question whether Jesus of Nazareth is or is not the Messiah promised to Israel, the incarnate Son of God who suffered and died in atonement for our sins and who by his cross and resurrection triumphs over sin and death. Neither the Second Vatican Council nor John Paul II and his successors deny these differences, paper them over, or treat them as insignificant.

Those differences have led some Catholics to suppose that if, as Catholics of course believe, the Church is right on these questions, then Judaism as such, as it is practiced today, is of no special spiritual standing or importance, that "living Judaism" has no role or mission, that God is no longer in that special form of relationship called "covenant" with the Jews, that the Jewish religion has been "superseded" by Christianity.

This is not the teaching of the Catholic Church—and faithful Catholics, by definition, want to be guided by the teaching of the Church. Faithful Catholics will therefore affirm, with the Council and with the papal magisterium, that the Jewish people are indeed.the well-cultivated olive tree onto which have been grafted the wild shoots, the Gentiles," that God's original Covenant with his chosen people is unbroken and unbreakable, that our bond with the Jewish people is a spiritual bond, rooted in a common spiritual patrimony, and that our Jewish neighbors are indeed our brothers and sisters in faith.

What is more, no faithful Catholic, no Catholic who believes, and is loyal to, the gospel as proclaimed by the Church, will bear in his or her heart any hostility to people because they are Jewish or any contempt for the Jewish people and their religion. Nor will he or she quietly tolerate expressions of animosity or hatred for Jews and Judaism.

Obviously, this does not mean that a faithful Catholic may not criticize individuals who happen to be Jewish on the same grounds that he would criticize anyone else. Nor does it mean that Catholics must agree with, or may not criticize, policies of governments of Israel. Jews themselves, including Israeli Jews, do not refrain from criticizing such policies when they believe criticism is merited. At the same time, a faithful Catholic will be very careful never to accept anti-Jewish animus masquerading as policy differences with governments of the Jewish state.

Once again I quote John Paul II:

> In the face of the risk of a resurgence and spread of anti-Semitic feelings, attitudes and initiatives, of which disquieting signs are to be seen today.... we must teach consciences to consider anti-Semitism, and all forms of racism, as sins against God and humanity.[4]

It was under John Paul II that the Catholic Church established full diplomatic relations with the State of Israel, something Israel had sought from the founding of the modern state in 1948, but that had not been achieved because of disputes over non-theological questions. Here is what the Pope said when interviewed by Tad Szulc for an American magazine:

> It must be understood that the Jews, who two thousand years ago were dispersed among the nations of the world, decided to return to the land of their ancestors. This is their right... recognized from the outset by the Holy See, and the act of establishing diplomatic relations is simply an international affirmation of that relationship.[5]

Does the Pope's teaching here bind the consciences of Catholics to agree with him that the Jewish people have, strictly speaking, a right to establish a modern state in their ancestral homeland? Like John Paul II, I myself support the state of Israel. But I cannot claim that Catholics are bound by his words to agree. In this context, he was speaking as a head of state, not proclaiming theological truths. He himself would have, I have no doubt, acknowledged that, and with it the right of Catholics who in good conscience see that matter differently to dissent.

Even for such Catholics, however, I reiterate the point I made a moment ago. While criticism of Israel, or any political entity, is in bounds, hostility or contempt for Jews and living Judaism, masquerading as mere political differences with the Israeli government or state is out of bounds.

CHAPTER EIGHTEEN

Gnostic Liberalism

The idea that human beings are non-bodily persons inhabiting non-personal bodies never quite goes away. Although mainstream Christianity and Judaism long ago rejected it, what is sometimes described as "body-self dualism" is back with a vengeance, and its followers are legion. Whether in the courts, on campus, or at boardroom tables, it underwrites the expressive individualism and social liberalism that are ascendant.

Christianity's rejection of body-self dualism answered the challenge to orthodoxy posed by what was known as "Gnosticism." Gnosticism comprised a variety of ideologies, some ascetical, others quite the opposite. What they held in common was an understanding of the human being—an anthropology—that sharply divides the material or bodily, on the one hand, from the spiritual or mental or affective, on the other. For Gnostics, it was the immaterial, the mental, the affective that ultimately mattered. Applied to the human person, this principle means that the material or bodily is inferior—if not a prison to escape, then a mere instrument to be manipulated to serve the goals of the "person," understood as the spirit or mind or psyche. The self is a spiritual or mental substance; the body, its merely material vehicle. You and I, as persons, are identified entirely with the spirit or mind or psyche and not at all (or in only the most highly attenuated sense) with the body that we occupy (or are somehow "associated with") and use.

Against such dualism, the anti-Gnostic position asserts a view of the human person as a dynamic unity: a personal body, a bodily self. This rival vision is found throughout the Hebrew Scriptures and Christian teaching. This is not to suggest that Christian teaching rules out the view that the individual is numerically identical with his or her immaterial soul. Contemporary Christian thinkers are divided on whether the separated soul is numerically distinct from the human person, or is just the person in radically mutilated form. They agree, however, on the essential point, namely, that the body is no mere extrinsic instrument of the human person (or "self"), but is an integral part of the personal reality of the human being. Christ is resurrected bodily.

Aristotle, who broke with his teacher Plato on the point, defends one form of this "hylomorphism," as it has come to be called. Without denying the existence of the soul, it affirms that the human person is a material being (though not only material). We do not occupy or inhabit our bodies. The living body, far from being our vehicle or external instrument, is part of our personal reality. So while it cannot exist apart from the soul, it is not inferior. It shares in our personal dignity; it is the whole of which our soul is the substantial form. The idea of the soul as the substantial form of the body is orthodox Christianity's alternative to the heretical conception of the soul as a "ghost in a machine." One can separate living body from soul in analysis but not in fact; we are body-soul composites.

So we are animals—rational animals, to be sure, but not pure minds or intellects. Our personal identity across time consists in the endurance of the animal organisms we are. From this follows a crucial proposition: The human person comes to be when the human organism does, and survives—*as a person*—at least until the organism ceases to be.

Yet we are not *brute* animals. We are animals with a *rational nature*—organized from the start for conceptual thought, and for practical deliberation, judgment, and choice. These intellectual powers are not reducible to the purely material. Creatures possessing them are able, with maturity and under favoring circumstances, to grasp intelligible (not just sensible) features of options for action, and to respond to those reasons with choices not determined by antecedent events. It is not that we act arbitrarily or randomly, but that we choose based on judgments of value that incline us toward different options without compelling us. There is no contradiction, on the hylomorphic view, between our animality and our rationality.

If we take the Gnostic view, then human beings—living members of the human species—are not necessarily persons, and some human beings are non-persons. Those in the embryonic, fetal, and early infant stages are *not yet* persons. Those who have lost the immediate exercise of certain mental powers—victims of advanced dementia, the long-term comatose, and the minimally conscious—are *no longer* persons. And those with severe congenital cognitive disabilities aren't now, never were, and never will be persons.

The moral implications are clear. It is *personal* life that we have reason to hold inviolate and protect against harm; by contrast, we can legitimately use other creatures for our purposes. So someone who buys into a Gnostic anthropology that separates person and body in the way I have described will find it easier to speak of those with undeveloped, defective, or diminished mental capacities as non-persons. They will find it easier to justify abortion; infanticide; euthanasia for the cognitively impaired; and the production, use, and destruction of human embryos for biomedical research.

By the same token, such an anthropology underwrites social liberalism's rejection of traditional marital and sexual ethics and its vision of marriage as a male-female union. That vision makes no sense if the body is a mere instrument of the person, to be used to satisfy subjective goals or produce desirable feelings in the person-as-conscious-subject. If we are not our bodies, marriage cannot essentially involve the one-flesh union of man and woman, as Jewish, Christian, and classical ethics hold. For if the body is not part of the personal reality of the human being, there can be nothing morally or humanly important about "merely biological" union, apart from its contingent psychological effects.

Presupposing body-self dualism makes it harder to appreciate that marriage is a natural (pre-political and even pre-religious) human good with its own objective structure. If sexuality is just a means to our subjective ends, isn't it whatever we want it to be? How could it be oriented to procreation, or require permanent exclusivity, by its *nature*?

We can make sense of this one-flesh-union conception of marriage only if we understand the body as truly personal. Then we can see the biological union of a man and woman as a distinct union of persons—achieved, like the biological union of parts *within* a person, through coordination toward a single bodily end of the whole. For the couple, that end is reproduction. The body's orientation to family life thus has human and moral, not "merely biological," significance. Spouses, in their bodily unity, renew the all-encompassing union that is their marriage. This reality helps us to make sense of the natural desire to rear one's own children and the normative importance of committing to do so whenever possible, even at great personal cost. (A mother desires to be sent home with the baby she actually delivered, and not with one assigned to her randomly from the pool of babies born during her stay in the maternity center.) This instinct reinforces a sound sexual ethic, which specifies the requirements of faithful conjugal and parental love, an ethic that seems pointless and cruel to contemporary social liberals.

For them, after all, what matters is what goes on in the mind or consciousness, not the body. True personal unity, to the extent that it is possible at all, is unity at the affective level, not the biological one. "Marriage" tends to be seen, then, as a socially constructed institution that exists to facilitate desirable romantic bonds and to protect and advance the various feelings and interests of people who enter into such bonds. It is not a conjugal partnership at all, but rather a form of sexual-romantic companionship or domestic partnership. Procreation and children are only contingently related to it. There is no sense, even an indirect one, in which marriage is a procreative partnership or a partnership whose structure and norms are shaped by the inherent orientation of our sexual natures to procreation and the rearing of children. The conjugal conception of marriage as a union of the sort that is naturally fulfilled by the spouses having and bringing up children together strikes the ear of the neo-Gnostic as unintelligible and even bizarre.

Indeed, as contemporary social liberalism presents the matter, sex itself is not an inherent aspect of marriage or part of its meaning; the idea of marital consummation by sexual intercourse also seems bizarre. Just as, for social liberals, two (or more) people can have perfectly legitimate and valuable sex without being married to each other, so two (or more) people can have a perfectly valid and complete marriage without sex. It's all a matter of the partners' subjective preferences. Consensual sexual play is valuable just insofar as it enables the partners to express desired feelings—such as affection or, for that matter, domination or submission. But if they happen not to experience desire for it, sex is pointless even within marriage. It's merely incidental and therefore optional, much like owning a car, or having joint or separate bank accounts. Different strokes for different folks. The essence of marriage is companionship, not sex, to say nothing of procreation.

All of this explains, of course, why contemporary liberal ethics endorses same-sex marriage. It even suggests that marriage can exist among three or more individuals in polyamorous sexual (or non-sexual) groups. Because marriage swings free of biology and is distinguished by its emotional intensity and quality—the true "person" being the conscious and feeling self—same-sex and polyamorous "marriages" are possible and valuable in the same basic ways as the conjugal union of man and woman. For partners in these other groupings, too, can feel affection for each other and even believe that the quality of their romantic partnership will be enhanced by mutually agreeable sex play (or not, as the case may be). If that's what marriage is all about, then denying them marital status means denying "marriage equality."

And then there are transsexualism and transgenderism. If we are body-mind (or body-soul) composites and not minds (or souls) inhabiting material bodies, then respect for the person demands respect for the body, which rules out mutilation and other direct attacks on human health. This means that, except in extraordinarily rare cases of congenital deformity to the extreme of indeterminacy, our maleness or femaleness is discernible from our bodies. Sex is constituted by our basic biological organization with respect to reproductive functioning; it is an inherent part of what and who we are. Changing sexes is a metaphysical impossibility because it is a biological impossibility. Or very nearly one. It may become technologically possible to change the sex of a human individual at a very early stage of embryonic development—either by changing the genome, or in the case of an embryonic male by inducing, say, androgen insensitivity early enough that all sexual development proceeds as it would in a woman. Of course, it would be immoral to do it, since it would involve a radical bodily intervention without consent and with grave risks.

But sex changes are biologically impossible past the point when it becomes true that to change the person's sexual capacities down to the root would require reversing so many already-differentiated organs and other sexual traits that one wouldn't end up with the same organism. (I suspect that that point is reached *at least* quite early in utero.) As Paul McHugh has argued, desiring to change sexes is a pathology—a wish to cease being oneself and to be someone else. It is not to will one's good, but to will one's non-existence as who one is.

By contrast, on the contemporary liberal view, no dimension of our personal identity is truly determined biologically. If you feel as though you are a woman trapped in a man's body, then you are just that: a ("transgender") woman. And you may legitimately describe yourself as a woman, despite the fact that you are biologically male, and take steps—even to the point of amputations and hormone treatments—to achieve a feminine outward appearance, especially where you think doing so will enable you more fully to "feel" like a woman.

Even this way of putting it might concede more than is warranted. What is a pre-operative "male-to-female" transgender individual *saying* when he says he's "really a woman" and desires surgery to confirm that fact? He's not saying his *sex* is female; that's obviously false. Nor is he saying that his gender is "woman" or "feminine," even if we grant that gender is partly or wholly a matter of self-presentation and social presence. It is clearly *false* to say that this biological male is *already* perceived as a woman. He wants to be perceived this way. Yet the pre-operative claim that he is "really a woman" is the premise of his plea for surgery. So it has to be prior. What, then, does it refer to? The answer cannot be his inner *sense*. For that would still have to be an inner sense *of something*—but there seems to be no "something" for it to be the sense *of*.

Yet for the neo-Gnostic, the body serves at the pleasure of the conscious self, to which it is subject, and so mutilations and other procedures pose no inherent moral problem. Nor is it contrary to medical ethics to perform them—indeed, it might be unethical for a qualified surgeon to refuse to perform them. At the same time, the neo-Gnostic insists that surgical and even purely cosmetic changes aren't *necessary* for a male to be a woman (or a female a man). The body and its appearance do not matter, except instrumentally. Since your body is not the real you, your (biological) sex and even your appearance need not line up with your "gender identity." You have a right, we are now told, to present yourself however you feel yourself to be.

And since feelings, including feelings about what or who you are, fall on a spectrum, and are even fluid, you are not limited to only two possibilities on the question of gender identity (you may be "gender non-conforming"), nor are you permanently locked into any particular gender. There is the full Facebook fifty-six, or fifty-eight, or whatever the number now is, and you can find your gender changing over time, or abruptly. It may even be possible to change genders by acts of the will. You might change genders temporarily, for example, for political reasons or for the sake of solidarity with others. Of course, most of these observations about gender identity can extend to the concept of "sexual orientation," and the practice of self-identifying in terms of sexual desire—a concept and practice well served by a view of the human being as a non-bodily person inhabiting a non-personal body.

The anti-dualist position historically embraced by Jews and by Christians (Eastern as well as Western, Protestant as well as Catholic) has been forcefully rearticulated by Pope Francis:

> The acceptance of our bodies as God's gift is vital for welcoming and accepting the entire world as a gift from the Father and our common home, whereas thinking that we enjoy absolute power over our own bodies turns, often subtly, into thinking that we enjoy absolute power over creation. Learning to accept our body, to care for it and to respect its fullest meaning, is an essential element of any genuine human ecology. Also, valuing one's own body in its femininity or masculinity is necessary if I am going to be able to recognize myself in an encounter with someone who is different. In this way we can joyfully accept the specific gifts of another man or woman, the work of God the Creator, and find mutual enrichment. It is not a healthy attitude which would seek "to cancel out sexual difference because it no longer knows how to confront it."[1]

The pope, who recently outraged partisans of social liberalism by denouncing the practice of teaching children that gender is chosen rather than given as a matter of biological sex, is not engaging in idle or purely speculative philosophizing. He is responding to the specific challenge to Christian orthodoxy represented by the modern revival of a philosophical anthropology against which the Church struggled in its formative early battles with Gnosticism. He knows that this anthropology is now itself a kind of orthodoxy—the orthodoxy of the particular form of liberal secularism that, following Robert Bellah, I have referred to as "expressive individualism," one that has secured dominance among Western cultural elites. It provides the metaphysical foundation of the social practices and ideological challenges against which Orthodox

Jews and faithful Christians (as well as many Muslims and others) find themselves contending today: abortion, infanticide, euthanasia, sexual liberation, the redefinition of marriage, and gender ideology.

Are we right to resist? Might the dualistic understanding of the human person have been right all along? Perhaps the person is not the body, but only inhabits it and uses it as an instrument. Perhaps the real person *is* the conscious and feeling self, the psyche, and the body is simply material, the machine in which the ghost resides. To think so, however, is to ignore the fact that our entire experience of ourselves is the experience of being unified actors. Nothing gives us reason to suppose that experience to be illusory. Even if body-self dualism could be made coherent—which I doubt—we would have no more reason to believe it than we have to suppose that we are now dreaming, or stuck in the Matrix.

But there is more. Consider the most common of human experiences: sensing (hearing or seeing, for example). Sensing is, obviously, a *bodily* action performed by a living being. The agent performing an act of sensing is a bodily creature, an animal. But it's clear that in human beings, as rational animals, it is one and the same agent who both senses and understands or seeks to understand (by mental activity) what it is that he or she is sensing. The agent performing the act of understanding, therefore, is a bodily entity, not a non-bodily substance using the body as some sort of quasi-prosthetic device. Were it otherwise, we would never be able to explain the communication or connection between the thing doing the sensing and the separate thing doing the understanding.

To see the point more clearly, perhaps, let me invite you to consider what you are doing right now. You are perceiving—seeing—words on a page or screen. And you are not only perceiving, considered as an act of receiving impressions (a kind of data) through the medium of vision, you are *understanding* what it is you are perceiving: First, you are understanding that what you are seeing are words (and not, say, numbers, or blotches, or something else), and second, you are understanding what the words themselves mean (as individual words and strung together as sentences). Now what, exactly, is the entity—namely, you—that is simultaneously doing the perceiving and understanding? And, more to the point, is it one entity or two? Perception or perceiving is indeed a bodily act, but is it not the same actor (namely you, as a unified being) that is seeing the words and understanding that they are words and what they mean? It would make no sense to suppose that the body is doing the perceiving and the mind, considered as an ontologically separate and distinct substance, is doing the understanding. For one thing, it would generate an infinite regress of explanations in trying to account for the relationship between the separate substances. We wouldn't be able to make sense of the idea that you are doing the understanding, but an instrument you are using, not you yourself as a unified agent, is doing the perceiving.

Or consider a simple case of predication and thought. You approach your desk and judge that what lies on it—*that thing there*—is a book. That's a single judgment, and both parts of it (subject and predicate) must have a *single* agent: a being that does both the seeing and the thinking, that both *sees* the particular, concrete thing and *understands* it by applying an abstract concept (*book*). How could it be otherwise? How could any being hold both parts together in a single judgment—the sensory image and the abstract concept—if he weren't exercising both sensory and intellectual abilities?

Furthermore, the agent sensing the particular—*that thing there*—must be an animal, a body with perceptual organs. And the predication that goes with perception is a personal act; the agent applying a universal concept (*book*) must be a person. (A non-rational creature, such as a dog, might perceive, but lacking rationality of the sort that makes possible the formation of universal concepts, it would not understand what it is perceiving to be a particular instance of a universal.) It follows that the subject performing the act of judging—*that thing there is a book*—is one being, personal and animal. We are not two separate entities. Nor can "person" plausibly be just a stage in the life of a human animal. If it were, after all, then a categorical difference in moral status (person versus not) would be based on a mere difference in *degree* (rather than a difference in the *kind* of thing the being is), which is absurd. We are, at every moment of our existence as human beings, bodily selves and personal bodies.

In the domain of moral thought and practice, there are few projects more urgent than recovering the commonsense view that human persons are indeed dynamic unities, creatures whose bodies are not extrinsic instruments, but parts of our very selves. Contemporary social liberalism rests on an error, the tragic mistake behind so many efforts to justify—and even immunize from moral criticism—acts and practices that are, in truth, contrary to our profound, inherent, and equal dignity.

PART FOUR

Seekers of Truth
and Bearers of Witness

CHAPTER NINETEEN

Aleksandr Solzhenitsyn's Plea to the West

On June 8, 1978, a man with a craggy face and a beard came to Harvard University, where I was then a graduate student, to give the annual commencement address. The man was not a Harvard graduate. He was not a professor. He was not an American. He did not speak English. His address, given in his native Russian with simultaneous English translation, was not universally well received. I suspect that some Harvard officials regretted their decision to invite him to speak.

The man's name was Aleksandr Solzhenitsyn. He was a brilliant novelist who had spent several years as a political prisoner in the gulag in the Soviet Union. He was a strong Orthodox Christian and a fierce critic of atheistic communism and Soviet tyranny. His writings had exposed the corruption, cruelty, and injustice of the communist regime that had come to power in Russia in the Bolshevik Revolution of 1917 and would remain in power until 1991—a regime that had enslaved its own people and reduced those of many other nations to serfdom under puppet governments. It was a regime as totalitarian and as murderous as the Nazi regime in Germany, which the U.S. and Britain had allied with the Soviets in World War II to defeat.

In 1978, the Cold War was raging, and the U.S. was still reeling from its humiliation in the disastrous war in Vietnam. Anti-Americanism was flourishing both abroad and at home. Many Americans—particularly young Americans—had lost faith in their country, its institutions, its principles, its culture, its traditions, its way of life. Some proposed communism as a superior system; many suggested what came to be known as "moral equivalency" between American democracy and Soviet communism. By 1978, to suggest such equivalency had become a mark of sophistication, something to distinguish one from the allegedly backward folks—the "hicks" and "rubes"—who believed in the superiority of the American to the Soviet system. There were many such "sophisticated" people at Harvard. And Aleksandr Solzhenitsyn came to Harvard to confront them and others.

His speech was not, however, an encomium to America or the West. On the contrary, it was a severe critique—one might even say a prophetic rebuke—and a warning. Of course, Solzhenitsyn did not argue for the moral equivalency, much less the superiority, of the Soviet system. He hated communism in all its dimensions, and he loathed the gangsters who ruled the Soviet empire. What he faulted America, and the West more generally, for was their abandonment of their own moral and, especially, spiritual ideals and identity.

He viewed the West's weakness, including its weakness in truly standing up to Soviet aggression, as the fruit of the materialism, consumerism, self-indulgent individualism, emotivism, and narcissism—in a word, the immorality—into which we had allowed ourselves to sink. Solzhenitsyn, the (by then) legendary human-rights activist, warned America and the West that we had become too focused on rights and needed to refocus on obligations. We had come to embrace a false idea of liberty, conceiving of it as doing as one pleases, rather than as the freedom to fulfill one's human potential and honor one's conscientious duties to God and neighbor.

At the heart of this moral confusion and collapse, Solzhenitsyn argued, was a loss of faith, and with it the loss of a particular virtue—the virtue of courage.

Here are Solzhenitsyn's own words:

> A decline in courage may be the most striking feature, which an outside observer notices in the West in our days. The Western world has lost its civil courage, both as a whole and separately, in each country, each government, each political party, and, of course, in the United Nations. Such a decline in courage is particularly noticeable among the ruling groups and the intellectual elite, causing an impression of loss of courage by the entire society. Of course, there are many courageous individuals, but they have no determining influence on public life.[1]

I submit to you today that, despite the American victory in the Cold War (for which we should all be grateful) and the collapse and disappearance of the Soviet Union, nothing has changed that would diminish the force or relevance of Solzhenitsyn's words. The virtue we lack—and it is an indispensable virtue—is courage. And we must recover it. Our young men and women must regain it—not to defend us from a hostile foreign power armed with nuclear weapons, but to protect us from a far more dangerous foe, a truly deadly enemy: our own worst selves.

At all times and in all places, all of the virtues are needed. No virtue is superfluous or dispensable. But it seems that at any given time in any particular society there is a particular virtue that is lacking and therefore desperately needed. Moreover, because the virtues are integrally connected to one other—they are like a network—the loss of any one virtue tends to weaken and imperil all the others. Or worse, the loss of a given virtue threatens to turn other virtues into engines of vice.

Take, for example, the virtue of compassion. It is an essential virtue—like the others. It can move us to work selflessly and even heroically for the good of our fellow human beings—especially those who are needy or suffering. We cannot do without it. We rightly praise the compassionate for their good deeds in caring for the least, the last, and the lost. But consider what can happen when compassion remains strong but other virtues, such as love of truth and justice, have eroded or disappeared. Operating by itself, in isolation from the other virtues, compassion can motivate every manner of evil—from the killing of the unborn in abortion to the killing of the disabled and the frail elderly in euthanasia. We can convince ourselves that kindness calls for these things.

Well before the Nazis gave eugenics a bad name, well-intentioned, decent, compassionate people in places such as Germany, England, and the U.S. embraced eugenics, precisely out of a sense of compassion. It was they, not the Nazis, who invented the doctrine of *lebensunswertes Leben*—"lives unworthy of life." Because they did not want people to suffer, they supported mandatory sterilization for some classes of persons and even "mercy killing" for those whose lives they considered so burdensome as to be "not worth living."

We live at a time of great moral confusion. If anything, our situation is worse today than it was when Solzhenitsyn visited Harvard in 1978. There has been, to borrow a concept from Friedrich Nietzsche, a "transvaluation of values" in many spheres. What is good—such as marriage considered precisely as the conjugal union of husband and wife—has been redefined as bad. What is bad—such as sexual immorality of a wide range of types—has been redefined as good. To defend the conjugal understanding of marriage and traditional ideas about sexuality and morality today is to be accused of "hatred" by people on one side of the political divide. To welcome the migrant and the refugee is to court being accused of disloyalty to your country by some on the other side. To stand up for the sanctity of human life in all stages and conditions, beginning with the defense of the precious and vulnerable child in the womb, is to risk being labeled a "misogynist." To speak out for religious freedom and the rights of conscience is to invite being smeared as a "bigot."

It is not pleasant to be subjected to these types of abuse and defamation. And these days it goes well beyond unpleasantness. To speak moral truth to cultural power is to put at risk one's social standing, one's educational and employment opportunities, one's professional advancement; it is to place in jeopardy treasured friendships and sometimes even family relationships. And the more people, in reaction to these threats, acquiesce or go silent, the more dangerous and therefore more difficult it becomes for anyone to speak the truth out loud, even if they know it in their hearts. Anyone who succumbs to the intimidation and bullying—anyone who acquiesces or goes silent out of fear—not only harms his or her own character and fails in his or her duty to bear faithful witness to truth, he or she also makes things harder for others. We owe it not only to ourselves to be courageous, but to our brothers and sisters too. And because we owe it to ourselves and others, we owe it to God.

Our own worst selves are our unvirtuous selves. Our own worst selves are our selves when we lack the self-mastery that possession of the virtues—including the virtue of courage—makes possible. Our own worst selves are slaves—not to alien masters, but to our own weaknesses and wayward desires. Our own worst selves are what we are encouraged by so much of our culture today to be. When we are our own worst selves, what we seek are ephemeral and ultimately meaningless things, such as pleasure, status, social acceptability, wealth, power, celebrity—things that are not bad in themselves, since they can be used for good ends, but things which are not intrinsically good either. And they can lure us into supposing that—and acting as if—they were.

When we are our own worst selves, we fail in our duty to bear faithful witness because a desire for ephemeral things and a fear of losing them paralyze us. When we are our own worst selves, we lead lives that are marked by those vices against which Solzhenitsyn railed forty-six years ago: materialism, consumerism, self-indulgence, narcissism. We place the focus on doing as we please, no matter what we please; getting what we want, no matter what it is we happen to want. Instead of seeking what is true because it's true, what is good because it's good, what is right because it's right, we seek what we desire, for no better reason than our happening to desire it; indeed, we fall into the profound moral and philosophical error of imagining that the human good consists in the satisfaction of human desires.

Thus it is that we rationalize our failing to behave like rational creatures—creatures blessed with the powers of reason and freedom—and our behaving instead like brute animals, slaves of our passions. By definition, slaves to passions can never be masters of themselves; and no one who lacks self-mastery can practice and exemplify the virtue of courage. Courage always presupposes a willingness to sacrifice oneself for others or for something higher; someone who is not master of himself, someone who cannot rise above his own wants, desires, and passions, can never give himself to, or live for, others, or give himself to, or live for, something higher. Self-mastery is a precondition of the willingness and ability to live self-sacrificially. One cannot give oneself to others if one is not first master of oneself. Lacking self-mastery, one simply has nothing to give.

I have suggested that Solzhenitsyn saw a connection between the decline of courage and a loss of faith. Five years after his Harvard address, in a 1983 speech accepting the Templeton Prize in Religion, he stated this in the most explicit terms. The title of the speech could not have made the point more clearly. That title was "Men Have Forgotten God."

Forty-one years later, who can deny the truth of Solzhenitsyn's lament? Today, the cultured despisers of Christianity and Judeo-Christian values do not speak of communism or its ideals—communism having been discredited by Soviet gangsterism. They speak instead of "liberation" or of "equality," by which they seek to marginalize and stigmatize the principles of Judeo-Christian morality and justify acts and practices that contravene those principles. And they are certainly aggressive—moving, to cite just one of many examples, from the legalization of abortion, to the demand for its approval and even public funding, to the insistence that people or institutions—including religious institutions such as Catholic hospitals—who refuse to perform or refer for abortions be made to suffer professional or civic penalties or disabilities.

What is behind all this? According to Solzhenitsyn, the moral decline of the West has behind it the same factor that produced the horrors of communism, namely this: "Men have forgotten God." People worship themselves, deify their own desires, fall into an idolatry of the self, because they have forgotten that there is something—indeed someone—higher. They have forgotten God. And absent faith in God, how can they—how can we—muster the courage to bear bold witness, as Solzhenitsyn himself did, to Christian values in an increasingly hostile culture and world? How can there be courage in the absence of faith? Fear is a powerful emotion—a very powerful emotion indeed. Faith alone can finally and decisively overcome it.

There are, to be sure, honorable, truth-seeking, indeed courageous, atheists. When, however, people forget God, when they come to suppose that they don't need him or his grace and guidance, when they fall into the hubristic error of imagining that they are too smart and sophisticated to believe in him, we human beings teeter on the edge of catastrophe.

This was no novel insight or discovery of Solzhenitsyn's. It is the central teaching and theme of the prophets—all prophets, and not just the Biblical ones.

In March of 1863 another man with a craggy face and a beard spoke to the American people words of critique and prophetic warning of precisely the sort spoken by Solzhenitsyn at Harvard and in his Templeton Address. Abraham Lincoln, reflecting on the catastrophe of the Civil War and on its causes, issued a Proclamation of a National Day of Prayer and Fasting. What he said in that proclamation was, in a sense, echoed by Solzhenitsyn, and we would do well to heed it today. Indeed, we fail to heed it at our mortal peril. Here are Lincoln's words:

> Whereas it is the duty of nations as well as of men, to own their dependence upon the overruling power of God, to confess their sins and transgressions, in humble sorrow, yet with assured hope that genuine repentance will lead to mercy and pardon; and to recognize the sublime truth, announced in the Holy Scriptures and proven by

all history, that those nations only are blessed whose God is the Lord. And, insomuch as we know that, by His divine law, nations like individuals are subjected to punishments and chastisements in this world, may we not justly fear that the awful calamity of civil war, which now desolates the land, may be but a punishment, inflicted upon us, for our presumptuous sins, to the needful end of our national reformation as a whole People? We have been the recipients of the choicest bounties of Heaven. We have been preserved, these many years, in peace and prosperity. We have grown in numbers, wealth and power, as no other nation has ever grown. But we have forgotten God. We have forgotten the gracious hand which preserved us in peace, and multiplied and enriched and strengthened us; and we have vainly imagined, in the deceitfulness of our hearts, that all these blessings were produced by some superior wisdom and virtue of our own. Intoxicated with unbroken success, we have become too self-sufficient to feel the necessity of redeeming and preserving grace, too proud to pray to the God that made us![2]

It has been 162 years since Lincoln wrote those words. And yet it is as if he wrote them yesterday and directed them to us today. Yes, as a culture, as a people, we have forgotten God. That is reflected in our laws, in our public policies, in our news and entertainment media, in our schools and universities, in our economic and cultural institutions, on the streets of our cities, and even, alas, in many homes. We "have vainly imagined, in the deceitfulness of our hearts," that our "blessings were produced by some superior wisdom and virtue of our own." And, as a result, we find ourselves in the condition so accurately and brutally diagnosed by Solzhenitsyn.

But what has been forgotten may be remembered. What has fallen into decay can be renewed. What has been lost can be rediscovered. But for these things to happen, those who remember God and sincerely seek to do his will must look to him for the grace necessary to be his courageous and faithful witnesses—to be, in the words of another modern prophet,

Pope John Paul II, "signs of contradiction" to a world that has forgotten God. This, allow me humbly to say to young men and women reading these words, is your mission. You must remember God to a world that has forgotten him. By the example of your lives, as well as by the words of your mouths, you must repair what is broken and point the way to true freedom for those who have fallen into forms of slavery that are all the more abject for masquerading as liberation.

CHAPTER TWENTY

Heinrich Heine's Prophecy of Nazism

As we mark the sixty-fifth anniversary of *National Review*, was there ever a more appropriate time to stand athwart history yelling, "Stop"?

We're in the midst of a worldwide pandemic whose economic and social consequences have been as devastating as its impact on public health. Our nation is ideologically polarized and culturally tribalized to the point at which each half of the country views the other half as enemies rather than fellow citizens with whom they happen to have disagreements. And this did not begin yesterday, or in 2016.

We have rioting, complete with burning and looting, in the streets and rampaging mobs on social media "canceling" people in academia and elsewhere who have the temerity to raise even the mildest and most tentative questions about their cherished dogmas.

Conspiracy-theorizing has become rampant—and even the objectively wildest of the alleged conspiracies take on a patina of plausibility in light of the crazy things that "respectable" people and "leading authorities" have come to believe, and to insist on other people's believing. Just ask J. K. Rowling or Abigail Shrier.

Cultural changes, many undermining core values of our civilization, come with astonishing swiftness, altering even foundational institutions such as marriage and the family. Increasingly people doubt that our nation and civilization can survive—and some wonder whether they are even worth saving.

All of this has gotten me thinking about the nineteenth-century German-Jewish Christian poet Heinrich Heine.

Heine predicted in 1834 what came to pass in the 1930s and '40s in Germany. How could a man in 1834 have foreseen the rise of violent totalitarians and the plunging of Europe into vicious tyranny and the world into war a hundred years later? Well, let me quote Heine's prophecy. Then I'll say a word about why I think this is so relevant to us, and state the lesson that we need to glean from it. Here is what Heine wrote in 1834:

> Christianity—and this is its greatest merit—has to some extent tamed that brutal Germanic lust for battle, but could not destroy it; and if ever that restraining talisman, the cross, breaks, the savagery of the old fighters will rattle forth again, the absurd frenzy of the berserker, of which the Nordic poets sing and tell so much. That talisman is brittle, and the day will come when it breaks apart miserably. The old stone gods will then emerge from their forgotten ruins and rub the dust of millennia from their eyes. Thor, with the giant hammer, will spring up at last, and destroy the Gothic domes. When you hear stone crashing and glass shattering, be careful, you children next door, and do not mix yourself up in the business we are taking care of at home in Germany. It might not agree with you. Take care not to light such a fire or to extinguish it. You could easily burn your fingers on the flames. Do not take my advice lightly, the advice of a dreamer who warns you about Kantians, Fichteans, and *Naturphilosophen*. Do not take lightly the fantastic poet, who expects in the realm of appearance the same revolution which has happened in the province of the spirit. Thought goes before deeds as lightning before thunder.

German thunder is certainly German; it is not very agile and begins to rumble very slowly. But it will come and when you hear crashing, as it has never crashed before in all of world history, you will know, German thunder has finally reached its goal. With this sound, eagles will fall dead from the sky, and lions in the most distant desert in Africa will put their tails between their legs and crawl into their royal caves. A play will be enacted in Germany which will make the French Revolution look like a harmless idyll.[1]

Try to imagine in 1834 foreseeing something worse than the French Revolution with all the bloodshed of the terror and guillotine. The mass madness and mass murder. The mind-numbing inhumanity. Yet Heine said that the day would come when the abolition of the Christian worldview—the destruction of the biblical and natural-law understanding of humanity, of human nature, of the human good, of human dignity, of human destiny—would result in something that would make the French Revolution look like a "harmless idyll." Which is exactly, of course, what Hitler and the Nazis did in Germany and across Europe—revalorizing Teutonic, pagan "virtues" and even expressly reviving ancient pagan symbols, practices, and rituals.

They broke "that subduing talisman, the cross," and Thor "destroyed [ed] the Gothic domes" of the cathedrals. Of course, Heine didn't identify somebody named "Hitler" or a party called the "Nazis," but he foresaw that something like them would arise. His key insight was this: He understood that what happens in the domain of the *invisible*—in the minds, the hearts, the souls of people—eventually plays itself out in the realm of the *visible*. "Thought goes before action as lightning before thunder."

What we are seeing in the streets now and more broadly in the culture—from the schools and universities to the news media and entertainment industry to the "woke" corporate boardrooms—didn't and doesn't just happen. There is an ideology, a set of beliefs, a worldview—a way of looking at and interpreting the world—an anthropology, a moral philosophy, that has long been in place in the minds and hearts of opinion-shaping elites and influencers that now plays out in the realm of the visible. The time to have fought it was long ago, in the realm of the intellect, the invisible domain of the spirit.

But we mustn't despair. Quite the opposite. Because two can play at this game. Transformations in intellect—in the mind, in the heart, in the spirit—can have good as well as bad consequences. Good thinking, good education, good formation can produce good results every bit as much as bad thinking, bad ideas, bad formation will produce evil results.

Our task is difficult. I don't deny it—quite the contrary. It is, nevertheless, our task. For those of us who educate—whether in classrooms or in print or online—it is our calling, our vocation. Our mission is to provide that true education—that good, deep, critical, independent thinking—that exposes tyranny when it presents itself in the garb of "liberation" or "equality," and helps people to overcome what is destructive, what is inhuman and degrading, what undermines the fulfillment and flourishing of human beings and human communities at every level.

Our work now, if we do it well, will produce down the line, in the domain of the visible, the fruit of transformations in the realm of the invisible.

CHAPTER TWENTY-ONE

Joseph Raz: Philosopher of Freedom

A handful of books made a deep impression on me when I was a student at Harvard Law School in the late 1970s and early 1980s. One was *The Concept of Law*, by the great Oxford legal philosopher H. L. A. Hart. I first encountered it in a jurisprudence course taught by Charles Fried, then again in a seminar taught by Ronald Dworkin, who was teaching in the Department of Philosophy at Harvard as a visiting professor, and who was Professor Hart's successor in the Chair in Jurisprudence at Oxford. Dworkin was widely regarded as the leading critic of Hart's "legal positivism" (a concept on which I say a bit more below). Two other books were by writers who were famous for published debates with Professor Hart: Lon L. Fuller, *The Morality of Law*, and Patrick Devlin, *The Enforcement of Morals*. Three others were by former students and Oxford colleagues of Hart's: Dworkin, *Taking Rights Seriously*, John Finnis, *Natural Law and Natural Rights,* and Joseph Raz, *Practical Reason and Norms.*

Reading these books and discussing them in courses and seminars led me to want to study legal philosophy more deeply and to do it at Oxford University—perhaps with a view to making my career as a scholar and teacher in the field. I applied and was fortunate enough to be accepted. I was particularly interested in Finnis's work and the tradition of natural-law theory, which he was revitalizing and in certain respects reforming, so I asked to be assigned to him for supervision. That request was granted, but Dr. Finnis was on leave when I arrived in Oxford, so I was assigned to Dr. Raz. He left a note in my mailbox at New College (which had been new in 1379) welcoming me and asking me to send along an essay on any topic in philosophy of law that interested me, and then arrange for a meeting (known in Oxford as a "supervision") with him to discuss it. I had been further developing a paper on "legalism" that I had written for a course at Harvard, so I dropped off a draft in Raz's mailbox at Balliol College, where he was a fellow, together with a note saying that I was available to meet at any time convenient to him. He set a day and time, and I showed up, eager to hear what he had to say.

He greeted me kindly but minced no words about my paper. "Mr. George—Robert, is it?—there are places where the kind of paper you have written would count as philosophy, but Oxford is not one of those places." I was stunned. I had gotten an A at Harvard on the shorter, less developed version of the paper. He continued, his soft voice (almost a whisper) and thick Israeli accent prompting me to lean in so I could understand: "Your claims are very broad, grandiose. I don't know whether I agree with them or not, because I'm not sure what they mean. You need to state a proposition that I can agree or disagree with, then provide the reasons why I should agree with it and rebut the reasons I might suppose I have for disagreeing with it." I was crushed. I had, I suppose, expected to be patted on the head and told how fine my work was. Dr. Raz was clearly not a mean man, and I knew that he was a brilliant and extraordinarily accomplished one—in the very field I was hoping to enter. And he was telling me that what I had written wasn't just poor philosophy, it wasn't philosophy at all—at least as philosophy is understood in Oxford. I was thinking, "I'm obviously in the wrong place. I should return to Harvard or someplace like it where the kind of philosophical work I'm accustomed to doing is at least considered acceptable."

He perceived that I was stunned and hurt. Taking out a blank sheet of paper and drawing a vertical line down the middle of it, he said, "look, I want you to think of a proposition—one that some people deny but you think should be affirmed. It doesn't matter what it is. Then I want you to list the reasons for affirming it on the left side of the line and the reasons for denying it on the right. Come back next week, and we'll discuss the competing reasons. Then you can write your paper."

THE ANALYTIC TRADITION

That's how Joseph Raz, the master of analytic philosophy of law, introduced me to the analytic tradition—a way of doing philosophy that puts a premium on logical rigor, precision, and clarity. Of course, as someone interested in natural-law theory, I also recognized that he was simply requiring me to do what Thomas Aquinas and the other great scholastic thinkers did—namely, *reason* your way to a conclusion by considering the evidence and best arguments to be marshaled on both or all sides of a disputed question. It's what Raz himself did—brilliantly—in *Practical Reason and Norms* and his other writings. It is what Hart and Finnis did, too. It wasn't long before I was a convert to the faith, not simply because my teacher was demanding that I take a certain approach, but because I came to see and deeply appreciate its value.

When Dr. Finnis returned from leave, he reinforced what I was learning from Dr. Raz. Working with the two of them was as exhilarating as it was demanding. Getting a dubious argument, however clever or rhetorically attractively packaged, past one of them was a Herculean feat. Getting a dubious argument past both of them was impossible. This is something Professor Dworkin learned on many occasions in the lively seminars the three of them offered together in the 1980s, occasionally joined by the then-retired but still engaged Professor Hart. These meetings would often begin with Dworkin putting a proposition and set of arguments on the table, then Raz and Finnis would go to work pinpointing where he had slipped the rabbit into the hat.

Whether in those seminars or in supervisions with graduate students like me, Raz and Finnis examined the most significant assertion or assertions from every conceivable angle, forcing their interlocutors and students to consider everything it presupposed and entailed. They taught us—by precept and example—to be exceptionally careful in affirming any proposition, because in affirming it one is also affirming whatever it presupposes and all that it entails—a lesson I drive home to my own students.

There are many knocks against analytic philosophy generally and analytical jurisprudence in particular: It's all just nitpicking; it's arid logic-chopping; it's dry and bloodless; it's of no practical use; it ignores big questions or, by breaking them up into smaller questions, evacuates their human significance. Those criticisms are not entirely without merit when directed at certain analytic philosophers. But Raz, along with Finnis and some of their predecessors such as Herbert Hart, Elizabeth Anscombe, and Philippa Foot, showed that analytical methods can be profoundly illuminating of issues of genuine human significance—including the big questions.

Joseph Raz and I became and remained friends. He was an accomplished amateur photographer and kindly allowed me to use architectural photographs he had taken on the covers of three of my books. He also contributed original essays to collections of writings on matters of philosophy of law that I edited for Oxford University Press.

Joseph was secular and liberal, while I am Catholic and socially conservative. But these differences caused no difficulties between us. He had other friends and academic colleagues who were religiously observant (including some who were Catholic, like Professor Finnis), and some other leading Anglophone philosophers of the time were, or would soon become, very publicly Catholic, including Elizabeth Anscombe, Michael Dummett, Charles Taylor, Peter Geach, Alasdair MacIntyre, Nicholas Rescher, and Bastiaan van Fraassen. Most of them weren't brought up with religious faith but were converts from secularism. Joseph would sometimes ask me questions about what was going on in the Church.

Naturally, he was especially interested in how the Church was handling or thinking about this or that controversial moral issue (for example, human cloning, nuclear deterrence, the Iraq War). He was by no means unaware that Catholicism valued philosophical reflection and had over the centuries nurtured what Sir Isaiah Berlin called "the central tradition" of thought about ethical and other philosophical questions in the West.

LEGAL POSITIVISM

Raz's fundamental intellectual commitments were to "positivism" in legal theory (though he deprecated labels) and to a "perfectionist," autonomy-based conception of liberty in political theory. By the former, I mean the idea that law can be identified as such by reference to its sources, independently of its moral evaluation. On this point, he sided with Professor Hart against Professor Dworkin in their famous dispute. In making his case, Raz developed the extremely helpful concept of "exclusionary reasons"—that is, as he put it in *Practical Reason and Norms*, "second-order reason[s] to refrain from acting for some reason." One may have a reason to do something but also a "second-order" reason to refrain from acting on, or considering, that (first-order) reason. Laws often guide behavior precisely by providing second-order reasons for action or restraint. Legal norms can provide conclusive reasons to stop deliberating among various, perhaps competing, first-order reasons and perform a particular act. That may seem obvious, but understanding and explaining how legal norms guide the actions of citizens and officials by providing second-order reasons was a breakthrough insight that shed light on a host of related matters pertaining to the nature and functions of law.

The normativity and authority of law were central concerns of Raz's from the beginning of his career to the end of his life. His own teacher, Professor Hart, who had encouraged the young Joseph Raz to study at Oxford after meeting Raz during a visit to Israel—Raz pointed out to Hart an error in Hart's work—had always regarded his own treatment of the nature of legal authority and obligation as less than fully satisfactory. As a legal positivist, Hart did not want to conceive legal obligation as a species of moral obligation. But in what sense, then, was it an obligation? Exactly what kind of reasons for action and restraint, if they are not moral reasons, do valid laws provide? Raz famously set out and defended the "service conception" of authority (and thus the authority of law). On this account, authority's function is to provide the service of enabling reasonable persons to successfully do or achieve what they already have a moral duty to attempt to do or achieve. Consequently, laws have authority inasmuch—or insofar—as they identify what those whom they subject to legal requirements should do, more reliably and fruitfully than they could or would do acting on their own deliberation and judgment without the benefit of law's prescription (or proscription). We can rightly judge that we ought to obey the law, or these laws, or at least consider them presumptively binding, because we have reason to suppose that by allowing the law to guide us we will generally do better than acting in each case on the basis of our own judgment, independent of the law's guidance.

THE CENTRALITY OF AUTONOMY

Raz's theory of political morality was set forth in his most influential book, *The Morality of Freedom*, in which he argued that law and policy should reflect a vision of the human good, with the good of personal autonomy—enabling people to be "authors of their own lives"—at its heart. Raz rejected equality-based, or equality-focused, and "antiperfectionist" forms of liberalism that were propounded by the leading liberal theorists of the day, especially John Rawls and Ronald Dworkin. Anti-perfectionism is the idea that in designing institutions and making law and policy, particularly where we are considering placing limitations on individual liberty, we should avoid acting on (or we should be neutral as between competing) controversial conceptions of the human good—of what constitutes or detracts from a valuable and morally worthy way of life. Raz proposed instead a "perfectionist" liberalism.

What made Raz's perfectionism "liberal" was precisely the centrality of autonomy, which Raz regarded as itself an intrinsic value: something good in itself, valuable for its own sake. Yet he held that autonomy has value only when exercised in morally good ways. There is no value in exercising autonomy in a morally wrongful manner.

Raz and I had a long-running debate on autonomy and its value. We agreed that autonomy, when exercised immorally, is valueless. To me, this revealed that autonomy is not something intrinsically good. In fact, it is not, strictly speaking, a value at all, but rather a condition for the realization of other values, including what, following John Finnis, I call the (intrinsic) value of practical reasonableness. Although I failed to persuade Raz to shift his view of the matter, he worked with me to help make my argument against his position as strong and compelling as possible. He was a true—*a Socratic*—philosopher: a truth-seeker. He had convictions, many of them strongly held, but he never sought to immunize them against criticism, nor did he allow himself to fall so deeply in love with his opinions that he valued them above truth itself.

Although Raz was not a libertarian or a utilitarian—indeed, he was a forceful critic of utilitarianism, principally (and rightly, in my view) because it falsely presupposes a commensurability of basic values as they figure in options for morally significant choosing—he is often compared with the great nineteenth-century liberal philosopher of freedom John Stuart Mill. Raz's defense of liberty, like Mill's, eschewed anti-perfectionism and celebrated liberty as central, indeed indispensable, to human well-being. The right to liberty, or more precisely, to the particular liberties to which people have rights, is not an "abstract right," generated by, for example, a formal principle of equality or fairness. Respect for liberty is necessary, not because a principle demanding respect for liberty (or this or that set of liberties) would be among the principles chosen in Rawls's "original position" behind a "veil of ignorance," where one had no knowledge of one's beliefs about the human good (or of anything else that made one different from other people), but rather because autonomy—being the author of one's own life—is a central element of the all-around flourishing of any and every human being.

Joseph Raz, philosopher of freedom, was born to Jewish parents in Mandatory Palestine on March 21, 1939. He died in London on May 2, 2022. He is remembered with admiration and gratitude by his academic colleagues and, especially, by those of us fortunate enough to have been his students. His writings are his monument. They will outlast any granite or marble.

CHAPTER TWENTY-TWO

Rabbi Jonathan Sacks: A Moral Voice

A few years ago, my wife and I had the honor of hosting the Rabbi Lord Jonathan Sacks and his wife Elaine as our houseguests in Princeton. The morning after their arrival, Rabbi Sacks and I were up early, ahead of our wives, and met in the kitchen. I, bleary-eyed, began making coffee. Jonathan, fully awake and alert, was eager for a serious conversation. "You recall," he said, "what Hobbes says in the chapter on intellectual virtues?" I did, sort of, but it was early in the morning and I was struggling with the coffee maker. "For the thoughts are to the desires as scouts and spies, to range abroad and find the way to the things desired," he (accurately) recalled. "But it's not like that, is it?"

We agreed that Hobbes's purely instrumental conception of practical reason—that is, the idea that what we ultimately want is a matter of brute desire, and the role of the intellect is merely to enable us to figure out how to get what we want—is seductive, but wrong. We know that our lives are not like that. In the most important parts of our lives—love or learning, for instance—reason does not function simply as what Hume, following Hobbes, described as "the slave of the passions." Sometimes we want things because, or in virtue, of our rational grasp of their intelligible value as intrinsically fulfilling and, as such, worthwhile. We grasp with our minds what fulfills us—what is objectively humanly good—as the complex (physical, rational, affective, relational, morally responsible) creatures we are, and we desire what is good precisely as aspects of our flourishing as human beings.

Rabbi Sacks noted that this account of our reasons for action (and of the human goods providing those reasons) is implicit in the biblical story of creation. Genesis tells us that human beings, though mere dust of the earth, are fashioned in the very image and likeness of the divine Creator and Ruler of all that is. Of course, we are not God. In fact, we are so far below him as to make his even noticing us a matter of wonderment. "What is man," the psalmist asks, "that you have been mindful of him, mortal man that you have taken note of him?"

Yet, by God's design, we are *like God*, albeit in limited and imperfect ways. By our God-given nature, we possess and come to exercise the Godlike capacities of reason and freedom—we are *agents*; God has given us a role, a certain sharing in his creative power and activity. Like God, we can envisage states of affairs that do not (yet) exist, understand the point—the advantage, the value, the goodness—of bringing them into existence, and act freely on the reasons provided by our understanding. Such understanding is not merely a "scout" or "spy" to "find the way to the things desired."

In virtue of our being made in the divine image (*imago Dei*), we are bearers of profound, inherent, and equal dignity. Even the poor, the weak, the vulnerable, the physically or cognitively disabled, the unloved, indeed the despised, the "defective," the "useless," the self-debased, the sinner, the dying, are of immeasurable value. Each is and, as a matter of strict moral obligation, must be regarded and treated as an end, never as a mere means. That is why Jews and Christians were scandalized by infant sacrifice and are appalled today by the harvesting of transplantable vital organs from severely cognitively disabled persons or even from convicted criminals, as is done in China. Any ideology that reduces the human person to the status of a cog in the collective wheel, or sacrifices his or her dignity on the altar of "the greatest good of the greatest number," stands condemned under the biblical standard of morality.

Morality is the title of the last book my beloved friend Jonathan Sacks published in his lifetime. It was released in the United States in September of 2020, and he died in November of that year, at age seventy-two. Its subtitle is *Restoring the Common Good in Divided Times*, which brings us back to Hobbes's mistake and Genesis's depth. Rabbi Sacks's argument was ultimately that a shared human nature means that there are certain basic aspects of human well-being and fulfillment that, when rightly understood, provide the basis for human solidarity.

There is a common good because shared human goods provide reasons for human beings to cooperate in various forms of community, from families and communities of faith to national political communities and even the community of mankind. Some of the reasons people have to form bonds, relationships, and communities are not merely instrumental; some communities—for example, the community of husband, wife, and children in the marriage-based family, or communities of faith—fulfill human beings in respect of the inherently relational aspects of our nature. This is a point that did not go unnoticed by the great Greek philosophers––consider, for example, Aristotle's treatment in the *Nicomachean Ethics* of the inherent goodness of true friendship. But what really establishes this point in the great Western civilizations is the biblical witness.

Although Rabbi Sacks was a fine philosopher and a deep exegete, *Morality* is neither a work of moral philosophy nor a book of biblical interpretation. It is a defense of the Judeo-Christian worldview (a phrase and concept Rabbi Sacks did not hesitate to use) for the common reader, for whom the tenets of that tradition can no longer be presumed. At the same time, it is a response to and powerful critique of competing worldviews—the various forms of individualism, collectivism, and identitarianism—that vie in this era of extreme ideological partisanship and polarization to displace and succeed the biblical vision of morality.

The fundamental problem Rabbi Sacks identifies in *Morality* is that those of us living in modern Western societies and shaped by the ethos dominant within them have become fixated on the individual—on me, myself, and I—and the satisfaction of our own desires. We have, to one degree or another, embraced the ideology of individualism. As a result, we have lost our sense of the importance of the common good—of we, ourselves, and us—and of the value(s) of the communities to which we belong and in which alone we can find our true fulfillment. We must move from what Sacks calls the "I society" back to a "We society."

What Rabbi Sacks wants us to see is that we can avoid the errors of individualism and collectivism—and the trap of identity politics, which combines and feeds on the errors of both—if we correctly understand the nature of the human person. Individualism is false, teaches Rabbi Sacks (in line with the great tradition) because human beings, though packaged as individuals, flourish in significant part by virtue of intrinsically valuable—that is, not merely instrumentally useful—relationships with others, including by participating in communities, beginning with the family, whose value and dignity are indeed inherent. These are communities whose worth cannot be understood or accounted for purely by reference to services (or the quality of services) they provide. Among such communities are, as I noted, communities of faith. This is certainly the self-understanding of the Jewish community and of Christian communities, too.

To some extent, of course, we need others for the instrumental benefits they provide, and neither Rabbi Sacks nor other thinkers in the Judeo-Christian tradition suppose otherwise. For example, we need the services of the auto mechanic, the doctor, the farmer, the lawyer. But our fulfillment also includes, and requires, our participation in non-instrumental forms of relationship—being a spouse, a friend, a parent or grandparent, a coreligionist—in which we love and are loved, in which we will the good of the other for the sake of the other and the other wills our good for our sake, in which we act together for the sake of goods that are not "mine" and "yours" but are truly *ours*—common goods and a common good.

Rabbi Sacks joins the distinguished Harvard political philosopher Michael Sandel in rejecting the idea that a human being is, or comes into the world as, an "unencumbered self." Our connectedness to others, far from being an incidental fact about us, is integral to who we are. We enter life as someone's son or daughter and grandson or granddaughter. Often, we are born into communities of which our parents are, and perhaps our forebears were, members—including communities of faith. We will eventually make choices, including choices of relationships and communities to be part of. Still, we have unchosen relationships and unchosen obligations—including unchosen obligations we have in virtue of our membership in communities we did not choose to join.

To get where we need to be, we must understand that the dignity of the human person and the centrality of the common good are two sides of the same coin. This will require our embracing and exercising virtues of character as well as those of intellect and recognizing, as Sacks does, that reasons are not mere "scouts and spies, to range abroad and find the way to the things desired."

For twenty-two years (1991–2013), Rabbi Sacks served with enormous distinction as chief rabbi of Britain's United Hebrew Congregations of the Commonwealth. In that capacity, he was a teacher of Judaism, a judge on the rabbinic court, and what might be described as British Jewry's ambassador to Jews throughout the world. But Rabbi Sacks was not merely the leader of the United Kingdom's *Jewish* community. In an Anglican nation with a large Catholic minority and only a tiny Jewish presence, it was a rabbi to whom believers in general—Christian no less than Jewish—looked to explain and defend in the public square belief in God and allegiance to the moral principles of "the Judeo-Christian tradition." He was, by virtue of his character, intellect, and eloquence, the leading spokesman for religious believers of all stripes—not only in the United Kingdom but throughout the world.

Rabbi Sacks's stature as a moral leader for the world comes through at several moments in *Morality*. In one of them, he describes visiting a center for juvenile offenders while he was making a television documentary for the BBC on the state of the family:

> They were all from broken, and many from abusive, families. When I tried to get them to talk about their childhoods, they refused to do so, out of loyalty to their families. So I changed the approach. I said, "One day you will have children. What kind of father would you like to be?" That is when they started crying. They said things like, "I'd be a tough father, but I'd make sure that there were rules, and whenever the children needed me, I would be there for them." I found the experience deeply moving, and distressing.... I believe that the injustice done to them by society is hard to forgive. A generation imbibed the idea of sex without responsibility and fatherhood without commitment, as if there were no victims of that choice.[1]

What one hears in these lines is not merely a man of empathy and insight but someone who has taken responsibility for his society and its failures—and striven through sermons, books, radio, and television to turn it back toward the common good.

I have said that *Morality* is a work of neither moral philosophy nor biblical interpretation, but Rabbi Sacks was indeed a fine philosophical exegete, and, thankfully, sometimes he could not resist the urge. Toward the end of the book, he remarks that his doctoral supervisor, the great philosopher Bernard Williams, made an important distinction:

> The most primitive experiences of shame are "connected with sight and being seen," but... "guilt is rooted in hearing, the sound in oneself of the voice of judgment; it is the moral sentiment of the word."[2]

Sacks goes on to suggest that this explains the story of Adam and Eve, which, he says, is not about sex or forbidden fruit or even original sin. "It is about the respective roles in the moral life of seeing and hearing." The first reference to shame in the Bible, he notes, is that Adam and Eve were initially not ashamed of their nakedness. When the couple eat the forbidden fruit, their eyes are opened, and they seek to cover their nakedness out of shame. So far, Sacks notes, every element in the story is visual, but it is precisely at that point that a moral voice enters:

> Far and away the most interesting line is the one that reads: "They heard God's voice walking in the garden with the wind of the day. The man and his wife hid themselves from God among the trees of the garden" (Gen. 3:8). Everything about this verse is strange. Voices don't walk. And you can't hide from God.[3]

Note, by the way, the unaffected lapidary brilliance of Sacks's writing. Why, then, do Adam and Eve perceive God's voice to be walking and imagine that they can hide from it? Sacks posits that they are still governed by sight and shame, but the Bible's gift to the world is the moral voice. Sacks writes:

> Judaism, with its belief in an invisible God who created the world with words, is an attempt to base the moral life on something other than public opinion, appearance, honor, and shame. As God tells Samuel, "The Lord does not look at the things people look at. People look at outward appearance, but the Lord looks at the heart." (I Samuel 16:7)[4]

As Rabbi Sacks understood, in a world obsessed with image and likes, retweets, and subtweets, this biblical message is as timely and vital as it ever was. How profoundly I miss my friend's wisdom and inimitable moral voice. Thank God he left us his writings.

CHAPTER TWENTY-THREE

Ralph Stanley: Traditionalist

Bluegrass music isn't ancient. It's not even old. However "traditional," or even "antique," it may sound, it's worth reflecting that lots of people alive today were already young adults when the genre came into being.

It all began in December of 1945 when an innovative young musician named Earl Scruggs was hired by Kentucky native Bill Monroe to be the banjo player for his acoustic country music band known as the "Bluegrass Boys." What was different about Scruggs was that he did not play in the "clawhammer" banjo style of most other mountain players, including his immediate predecessor in Monroe's band, David Akeman (who went by the stage name "Stringbean"). Rather, Scruggs had perfected a three-finger way of playing the five-string banjo that enabled him to produce impressively fast-moving, hard-driving solos with much more room for improvisation than the clawhammer style permitted. The crowds loved it. His success, and the success of bluegrass music, was instantaneous.

So Bill Monroe (whose instrument was the mandolin) and Earl Scruggs were founding fathers of bluegrass. But they were not alone. Nor was Scruggs alone as the father of bluegrass banjo playing. For as Scruggs was developing the three-finger style, so was another young five-string picker named Don Reno. What was distinctive about Reno's work was that it incorporated elements of jazz, which had sprung into existence a few decades before bluegrass, as well as some of the popular music of the day. Major and minor seventh chords, sixth chords, and ninth chords, which rarely, if ever, appeared in Monroe's music or Scruggs's picking, were deployed in Reno's work—giving it a jazzy feel. He would also cut loose regularly with single-string solos of the sort that might have been produced using a flat pick, in the mode of the four-string "plectrum banjo" players, though Reno produced them by thumb-forefinger alternation. Scruggs never did that.

But there was one more founding father of bluegrass banjo playing, and that was Ralph Stanley—*Doctor* Ralph Stanley, as he liked to be called after receiving an honorary doctorate from Lincoln Memorial University in Tennessee in 1976 (he would later receive one from Yale). If Reno took the three-finger style of five-string banjo playing away from the more traditional or "old timey" mountain sound towards jazz and pop music, Stanley did the opposite. His music hewed closer even than Scruggs's to the traditional sound of the folk music of the Appalachian hills. Indeed, Stanley preferred the label "old-time country music" to "bluegrass," though there is no denying that his three-finger banjo playing was in the Scruggs (hence bluegrass) style, rather than the clawhammer style that, for example, Lucy Stanley—Ralph's mother—had played and which Ralph himself played before hearing Scruggs. But there is also no doubt that Stanley's sound was unique, and it has influenced countless bluegrass musicians. The same is true of Stanley's vocal style and the overall sound of the Clinch Mountain Boys—the band he founded with his brother Carter and kept going for fifty years after Carter's death. Now Ralph himself has died. The last of the founding fathers of bluegrass banjo—and, indeed, bluegrass music—has "gone to be with the Lord."

That's not a throwaway line. What has been missing in the stories about and tributes to Ralph Stanley that have been pouring out since his death a week ago is just how profoundly everything about the man was shaped by his belief in God and his sense of God's active presence in the affairs of man. The failure of people to pick up on this fact is scarcely his fault. He would tell anyone who would listen, or ask him a question about himself or his music. It's just that most of the people writing the stories and tributes, even those who are themselves religiously affiliated, can't quite get hold of how faith quite literally *suffuses* the lives of people like Ralph Stanley. But those of us who grew up in Appalachia get it. And so would people from, say, Orthodox Jewish or Muslim communities, no matter how distant in geography or theology from the Primitive Baptist Church (that's actually the name of the tradition) in which Stanley was formed as a Christian believer.

But whence the stories and tributes? Why so much public attention—even an obituary in the *New York Times*—over the death of a bluegrass musician?

The explanation is simple: Stanley developed a remarkably wide and even somewhat cultish following among people, many of whom had little previous interest in bluegrass or old-time mountain music, when he was a featured artist in the Coen brothers' 2000 film *O Brother, Where Art Thou?* He sang a haunting—one might even say *chilling*—unaccompanied version of the dirge "O Death," capturing countless new fans and scoring a Grammy Award in 2002. Shortly after the Grammy was awarded, Stanley was interviewed about his music and life by Jeffrey Brown of the *PBS NewsHour*. To understand my point about the centrality of Stanley's religious faith to everything about him, including his music, and to see how hard that is for many people today to grasp, one only needs to watch that interview and note *both* Stanley's unaffected candor about religion *and* Brown's nearly cringe-inducing efforts to follow him without smirking.

Now, none of this means that someone has to share Ralph Stanley's faith, or even his belief in God, to appreciate and enjoy his music. But if you want to know where the man was coming from, what he was doing, what made him tick, and what inspired his work, and, above all, if you really want to *understand* his music, you need to be able to at least sympathetically imagine what it is like to view the world as he did, and live a life suffused by a sense of the presence of God.

When Ralph Stanley sang "O Death," he was not merely entertaining us. He was instructing us. More to the point, he was warning us. He meant it. Death was a-coming for us all, and we had better lead our lives with that in mind. Life is short, and lived in the shadow of death. And with death comes judgment. God is merciful but just. He is not mocked, and we ignore him or break his commandments at our peril. He makes the rules, we don't. He has given us gifts—"everything we have," as Stanley instructs Jeffrey Brown in the *PBS NewsHour* interview—and he expects those gifts to be used to do good; they are not for mere self-gratification. We are sinners, but redeemed. We can choose to walk in the Lord's ways—or not. We're constantly tempted and we often stray. We are never truly prepared for death, for we are never fully prepared for judgment.

O death.
O death.
Won't you spare me over just another year?

None of this is to suggest that Ralph Stanley and his music were morbid or "preachy," or that all or even most of it was overtly religious. It's true that he had a huge repertoire of hymns, recorded several bluegrass gospel albums, and always included sacred numbers (often his classic "Over in the Glory Land") in his live performances; but he also sang love songs, songs about things like livestock ("I've got a pig, home in a pen . . .") and poverty ("Lord have mercy on this sharecropper's son"), and even songs about bootleg liquor ("Mountain Dew") and slightly racy numbers ("How Mountain Girls Can Love"). One of the numbers he is best known for is a song about a broken romance in which the wayward woman is holding a dram glass in her hand—"Little Maggie." In addition, he wrote, recorded, and regularly performed some now classic bluegrass banjo instrumentals (such as "Clinch Mountain Backstep").

But everything, even the secular aspects of his work and music, was shaped by and reflected his belief in the presence of God in the world. If you don't understand that, then you can't understand him or his music.

Another of Stanley's signature numbers was "I Am a Man of Constant Sorrow," and he was often called onto the performing stage by an announcer who invited the audience to welcome "the man of constant sorrow, Grammy Award winner Dr. Ralph Stanley!" But though, like the rest of us, his life was touched by tragedy and sadness (notably the untimely death of his brother Carter from alcoholism), he was not a man who lived constantly in sorrow or abject fear. Precisely on account of his faith, and with it the awareness of living as a redeemed sinner in the shadow of death, he lived in gratitude—feeling as though he had been blessed beyond measure—and in "the sure and certain hope" that he would someday go to be with the Lord—"over in the glory land." It's hard to imagine his being turned away.

ACKNOWLEDGMENTS

It is a pleasure to express my gratitude to the many friends who helped in a variety of ways in the preparation of this book. Two of my star former students at Princeton, Myles McKnight and Matthew X. Wilson, provided indispensable research assistance. My faithful executive assistants, Jane Hale and Kathleen Mitchell, supported me in countless ways, as did my colleagues in the leadership of the James Madison Program at Princeton: Bradford Wilson, Shilo Brooks, Debra Parker, and Adam Thomas. I have relied, as well, on the moral support of my friends at the Witherspoon Institute, Luis Tellez, R. J. Snell, and Kelly Hanlon. Some of the ideas in this book were developed in courses I taught at Princeton, working alongside my course administrators, David R. Oakley, Matthew Franck, and David Tubbs; others were developed in dialogues with academic friends working in philosophy of law, moral and political philosophy, constitutional law, bioethics, and theology and religion, especially Mary Ann Glendon, Hadley Arkes, William L. Saunders, Rabbi David Novak, John Keown, Leon Kass, John DiIulio, Gilbert Meilaender, Donald Landry, Yuval Levin, Cornel West, Gerard V. Bradley, Adrian Vermeule, Melissa Moschella, Carter Snead, Daniel Mark, Micah Watson, Josh Craddock, Rabbi Meir Soloveichik, José Joel Alicea, Father Kevin Flannery, SJ, John Peter DiIulio, Andrew Walker, and the late Daniel N. Robinson, Joseph M. Boyle Jr., Germain Grisez, Jean Bethke Elshtain, Father Richard John Neuhaus, Elizabeth Fox-Genovese, Roger Scruton, Robert Jenson, and Rabbi Jonathan Sacks. Above all, I wish to thank my colleagues who co-authored some of the essays published in this volume: Ryan T. Anderson, John Finnis, Sherif Girgis, Christopher Kaczor, Patrick Lee, and Christopher O. Tollefsen.
— Robert P. George

NOTES

CHAPTER ONE: THE NATURE AND BASIS OF HUMAN DIGNITY

1. Boethius's definition, especially as interpreted by St. Thomas Aquinas, is still valid: "An individual substance (that is, a unique substance) of a rational nature." So neither a nature held in common by many nor a part is a person. But every whole human being performing his or her own actions, including actions such as growth toward the mature stage of a human being, *is* a person. See Boethius, "De Duabus Naturis," in *Patrologia Latina*, ed. J.-P. Migne (Paris: Migne, 1891), 1354–412, and Thomas Aquinas, *Summa Theologiae* (Christian Classics, 1981), part 1, question 29, article 1.
2. Jenny Teichman, *Social Ethics: A Student's Guide* (Blackwell, 1996).
3. Jeremy Bentham, *An Introduction to the Principles of Morals and Legislation* (Oxford, 1948), chapter 17.
4. Peter Singer, *Animal Liberation*, 2nd ed. (New York Review of Books, 1990), 7.
5. Jeff McMahan, whose view is in other respects more complex than Singer's, still holds that only interests are of direct moral concern, and explicitly recognizes, and accepts, this logical consequence. See Jeff McMahan, *The Ethics of Killing: Problems at the Margins of Life* (Oxford University Press, 2002), 205–06.
6. Singer, *Animal Liberation*, 19.
7. Richard Arneson, "What, If Anything, Renders All Humans Morally Equal?," in *Singer and His Critics*, ed. D. Jamieson (Blackwell, 1999), 105.
8. Paul Taylor, "The Ethics of Respect for Nature," in J. P. Sterba, ed., *Morality in Practice*, 4th ed. (Wadsworth, 1993), 488.
9. Could it be true of every being, living or not? It is hard to see what the good or fulfillment of a non-living being is, since on that level it is hard to know just what are the basic, substantial entities as opposed to aggregates of entities. Thus, when we breathe we convert oxygen and carbon molecules into carbon dioxide molecules—have we destroyed the oxygen in that process, or have we only rearranged the atoms in their constitution? It is difficult to say.
10. Louis Lombardi, "Inherent Worth, Respect, and Rights," *Environmental Ethics* 5, no. 3 (2000): 257–70.
11. David S. Oderberg, *Applied Ethics: A Non-Consequentialist Approach* (Blackwell, 2000), 101.
12. See, for example, Taylor, "The Ethics of Respect."
13. Peter Singer acknowledges that he is "not convinced that the notion of a moral right is a helpful or meaningful one, except when it is used as a shorthand way of referring to more fundamental considerations."
14. We are laying aside here the issue of capital punishment.
15. Thus, the pleasures of the sadist or child molester are *in themselves* bad; it is false to

say that such pleasures are bad only because of the harm or pain involved in their total contexts. It is false to say: "It was bad for him to cause so much pain, but at least he enjoyed it." Pleasure is secondary, an aspect of a larger situation or condition (such as health, physical and emotional); what is central is what is really fulfilling. Pleasure is not a good like understanding or health, which are goods or perfections by themselves, that is, are good in themselves even if in a context that is overall bad or if accompanied by many bads. Rather, pleasure is good (desirable, worthwhile, perfective) if and only if attached to a fulfilling or perfective activity or condition. Pleasure *is* a good: A fulfilling activity or condition is better with it than without it. But pleasure is *unlike* full-fledged goods in that it is not a genuine good apart from some other, fulfilling activity or condition. It is a good if and only if attached to another condition or activity that is already good.

16 It is worth noting that not only do nonhuman animals themselves regularly engage in killing each other, but many of them (lions and tigers, for example) seem to depend for their whole mode of living (and so their flourishing), on hunting and killing other animals. If nonhuman animals really did have full moral rights, however, we would have a *prima facie* obligation to stop them from killing each other. Indeed, we would be required to invest resources presumptively protecting zebras and antelopes from lions, sheep and foxes from wolves, and so on.

17 See Patrick Lee and Robert P. George, *Body-Self Dualism and Contemporary Ethics and Politics* (Cambridge University Press, 2007), chapter 5.

18 Aristotle, *De Anima* (Clarendon, 1961), book 3, chapter 4.

19 Joel Wallman, *Aping Language* (Cambridge University Press, 1992), esp. chapters 5 and 6.

20 Cf. Richard J. Connell, *Logical Analysis: An Introduction to Systematic Learning* (Bellwether, 1981), 87–93; John Haldane, "The Source and Destination of Thought," in *Referring to God: Jewish and Christian Philosophical and Theological Perspectives*, ed. P. Helm (St. Martin's, 2000); Mortimer Adler, *Intellect: Mind over Matter* (Macmillan, 1990); Russell Pannier and Thomas D. Sullivan, "The Mind-Maker," in *Theos, Anthropos, Christos: A Compendium of Modern Philosophical Theology*, ed. R. A. Varghese (P. Lang, 2000); James F. Ross, "Immaterial Aspects of Law," *Journal of Philosophy* 89, no. 3 (March 1992): 136–50.

21 True, something extrinsic could preserve it from death, but it is the sort of thing that is, by its nature, subject to death. This is the basis for the major premise in the classic example of a syllogism: All men are mortal; Socrates is a man; therefore, Socrates is mortal.

22 Another example will illustrate this point. When children arrive at the age at which they can study logic, they provide evidence of the ability to grasp a nature or property held in common by many. They obviously do something qualitatively distinct from perceiving a concrete similarity. For example, when studying elementary logic, the child (or young man or woman) grasps the common pattern found in the following arguments:

   A. If it rains then the grass is wet.
       The grass is not wet.
       Therefore, it is not raining.
   B. If I had known you were coming, I would have baked you a cake.
       But I did not bake you a cake.
       So, (you can see that) I did not know you were coming.

We understand the difference between this type of argument, a *modus tollens* argument, and one that is similar but invalid, namely, the fallacy of affirming the consequent: If A then B, B, therefore A. But, what is more, we understand *why* the fallacy of affirming the consequent is invalid—namely, some other cause (or antecedent) could be, or could have been, present to produce that effect. A computer, a mechanical device, can be programmed *to operate according to* the *modus tollens* and to react differently to (give a different output for) words arranged in the pattern of the fallacy of affirming the consequent. But *understanding* the arguments (which humans do) and merely *operating according to* them because programmed to do so (the actions of computers) are entirely different types of actions. The first does, while the second does not, require the understanding or apprehending of a form or nature as distinct from its instances. (This is not to say that the nature exists separately from the individuals instantiating it, or as a universal, outside the mind. We hold that the nature exists in the mind as universal, but outside the mind as multiplied and individuated. Of course in propositional knowledge the mind apprehends the particular as well as the universal.

23 Mortimer Adler (1990) noted that, upon extended observation of other animals and of human beings, what would first strike one is the immense uniformity in mode of living among other animals, in contrast with the immense variety in modes of living and customs among human beings.

24 Roger Scruton, *Sexual Desire: A Moral Philosophy of the Erotic* (Free Press, 1986).

25 James B. Reichmann, *Evolution, Animal "Rights," and the Environment* (Catholic University of America Press, 2000), chapter 2; see also John Campbell, *Past, Space, and Self: Representation and Mind* (Edinburgh University Press, 1994).

26 Lynne Rudder Baker, *Persons and Bodies: A Constitution View* (Cambridge University Press, 2000), chapter 3; Campbell, *Past, Space, and Self*.

27 The genetic structure orients them toward developing a complex brain that is suitable to be the substrate for conceptual thought; that is, it is capable of providing the kind of sense experience and organization of sense experience that is suitable for data for concepts. Since the object of conceptual thought is not restricted to a particular place and time, this is evidence that the power of conceptual thought is non-material. So we hold that human beings have a non-material aspect, the powers of conceptual thought and free choice.

28 It is not essential to the defense of human dignity to argue that *only* humans have this power of conceptual thought and (to be discussed in a moment) free choice. However, there is not evidence of such conceptual thought or free choice in other animals. It is sometimes argued that perhaps some nonhuman animals do have minds like humans do, only at a diminished level. Perhaps, it is speculated, it is only the complexity of the human brain, a difference only in degree, that distinguishes humans from other animals. Perhaps other primates are intelligent but they have lacked the opportunities to manifest their latent intelligence. But such speculation is misguided. While intelligence is not directly observable, it is unreasonable to think that an intelligence of the same type as human intelligence, no matter how diminished, would not manifest itself in at least some of its characteristic effects. If a group of beings possesses a power, and possesses that power over many years (even decades or centuries), it is implausible to think that such a power would not be actualized.

29 Robert Kane, *The Significance of Free Will* (Oxford University Press, 1998).

30 It is not essential to the defense of human dignity to argue that *only* humans have this power of conceptual thought and (to be discussed in a moment) free choice. However, there is not evidence of such conceptual thought or free choice in other animals. It is sometimes argued that perhaps some nonhuman animals do have minds like humans do, only at a diminished level. Perhaps, it is speculated, it is only the complexity of the human brain, a difference only in degree, that distinguishes humans from other animals. Perhaps other primates are intelligent but they have lacked the opportunities to manifest their latent intelligence. But such speculation is misguided. While intelligence is not directly observable, it is unreasonable to think that an intelligence of the same type as human intelligence, no matter how diminished, would not manifest itself in at least some of its characteristic effects. If a group of beings possesses a power, and possesses that power over many years (even decades or centuries), it is implausible to think that such a power would not be actualized.

31 A more extended argument can be seen in Joseph M. Boyle Jr., Germain Grisez, and Olaf Tollefsen, *Free Choice: A Self-Referential Argument* (University of Notre Dame Press, 1976); see also Peter van Inwagen, *An Essay on Free Will* (Oxford University Press, 1986) and Peter van Inwagen, "Free Will Remains a Mystery," in *The Oxford Handbook of Free Will*, ed. R. Kane (Oxford University Press, 2002).

32 The argument here is indebted to Aquinas (see, e.g., *Summa Theologiae*, part I–II, question 10, articles 1–2).

33 Hume contended that practical reason begins with given ends which are not rationally motivated. However, this view cannot, in the end, make sense of the fact that we seem to make objective value judgments, not contingent on, or merely relative to, what this or that group happens to desire—for example, the judgments that murder and torture are objectively morally wrong. Moreover, the Humean view fails to give an adequate account of how we come to desire certain objects for their own sake to begin with. A perfectionist account, on the contrary, one that identifies the intrinsic goods (the objects desired for their own sake) with objective perfections of the person, is able to give an account of these facts. For criticisms of the Humean notion of practical reason see Joseph Boyle, "Reasons for Action: Evaluative Cognitions That Underlie Motivations," *American Journal of Jurisprudence* 46 (2001): 177–97; J. R. Wallace, "How to Argue about Practical Reason," *Mind* 99 (1990): 355–87; Christine Korsgaard, "Skepticism about Practical Reason," in Christine Korsgaard, *Creating the Kingdom of Ends* (Cambridge University Press, 1996); David Brink, "Moral Motivation," *Ethics* 107 (1997): 4–32; John Finnis, *Fundamentals of Ethics* (Georgetown University Press, 1983), 26–79; Joseph Raz, *The Morality of Freedom* (Oxford University Press, 1986), 288–368.

34 The idea is this: What is to be done is what is perfective. This seems trivial, and perhaps is obvious, but it is the basis for objective, practical reasoning. The question, What is to be done? is equivalent to the question, What is to be actualized? But what is to be actualiz*ed* is what actualiz*es*, that is, what is objectively perfective. For human beings this is life, knowledge of truth, friendship, and so on.

35 This claim is derived from Thomas Aquinas, and has been developed by Thomists and Aristotelians of various types. It is not necessary here to assume one particular development of that view against others. We need only make the point that the basic principles of practical reason come from an insight—which may be interpreted in

various ways—that what is to be pursued, what is worth pursuing, is what is fulfilling or perfective of me and others like me. For more on this see Germain Grisez, Joseph Boyle, and John Finnis, "Practical Principles, Moral Truth and Ultimate Ends," *American Journal of Jurisprudence* 33 (1988): 99–151; John Finnis, Joseph M. Boyle, and Germain Grisez, *Nuclear Deterrence: Morality and Realism* (Oxford University Press, 1987), chapters 9–11; Finnis, *Fundamentals of Ethics*; John Finnis, *Aquinas: Moral, Political, and Legal Theory* (Oxford University Press, 1998); T. D. J. Chappell, *Understanding Human Goods: A Theory of Ethics* (Edinburgh University Press, 1998); David S. Oderberg, *Moral Theory: A Non-Consequentialist Approach* (Blackwell, 2000); Ralph McInerny, *Aquinas on Human Action: A Theory of Practice* (Catholic University of America Press, 1992); Mark C. Murphy, *Natural Law and Practical Rationality* (Cambridge University Press, 2002).

36 Once one apprehends such conditions or activities as really fulfilling and worthy of pursuit, the *moral* norm arises when one has a choice between one option the choice of which is fully compatible with these apprehensions (or judgments) and another option that is not fully compatible with those judgments. The former type of choice is fully reasonable, and respectful of the goods and persons involved, whereas the latter type of choice is not fully reasonable and negates, in one way or another, the intrinsic goodness of one or more instances of the basic goods one has already apprehended as, and recognized to be, intrinsically good.

37 The argument presented here is similar to the approaches found in Louis G. Lombardi, "Inherent Worth, Respect, and Rights," *Environmental Ethics* 5 (1983): 257–70; Michael Goldman, "A Transcendental Defense of Speciesism," *Journal of Value Inquiry* 35 (2001): 59–69; and William J. Zanardi, William J., "Why Believe in the Intrinsic Dignity and Equality of Persons?," *Southwest Philosophy Review* 14 (1998): 151–68.

38 The position that the criterion for full moral worth cannot be an accidental attribute, but is the rational *nature*, that is, being a specific type of substance, is defended in Patrick Lee, "The Pro-Life Argument from Substantial Identity: A Defense," *Bioethics* 18 (2004): 249–63. See also Dean Stretton, "Essential Properties and the Right to Life: A Response to Lee," *Bioethics* 18 (2004): 264–82 and Patrick Lee, "Substantial Identity and the Right to Life: A Rejoinder to Dean Stretton," *Bioethics* 21 (2007): 93–97.

39 Stretton, "Essential Properties."

CHAPTER TWO: THE SOUL: NOT DEAD YET

1 Roger Scruton, "If We Are Not Just Animals, What Are We?," *New York Times*, March 6, 2017, https://www.nytimes.com/2017/03/06/opinion/if-we-are-not-just-animals-what-are-we.html,

2 Trenton Merricks, *Objects and Persons* (Oxford University Press, 2003).

CHAPTER THREE: DUALISTIC DELUSIONS

1 Keith L. Moore and T. V. N. Persaud, *The Developing Human: Clinically Oriented Embryology*, 5th edition (W. B. Saunders, 1993); see also William J. Larsen, *Essentials of Human Embryology*, 3rd ed (Elsevier Health, 2001); Scott F. Gilbert, *Developmental Biology*, 7th edition (Sinauer Associates, 2003); and Ronan O'Rahilly and Fabiola Muller, *Human Embryology and Teratology*, 3rd edition (Wiley-Liss, 2001).

CHAPTER FOUR: NATURAL LAW

1 On the first principle of morality and its specifications, see John Finnis, Joseph M. Boyle, Jr., and Germain Grisez, *Nuclear Deterrence: Morality and Realism* (Oxford University Press, 1987), 281–87.
2 Aristotle, *Nicomachean Ethics*, book 1, chapter 2, page 1094b, line 10.
3 For such a critique by an eminent contemporary theorist of natural law, see John Finnis, *Fundamentals of Ethics* (Oxford University Press and Georgetown University Press, 1983), chapter 4.
4 By the phrase "our humanity" I mean to refer more precisely to the nature of humans as rational beings. The nature of human beings is a rational nature. So in virtue of our human nature, we human beings possess a profound and inherent dignity. The same would be true, however, of beings other than humans whose nature is a rational nature, if indeed there are such beings. In the case of humans, even individuals who have not yet acquired the immediately exercisable capacities for conceptual thought and other rational acts, and even those who have temporarily or permanently lost them, and, indeed, even those who do not possess them, never possessed them, and (short of a miracle) never will possess them, possess a rational nature.
5 Having said this, I do not want to suggest a sharper difference than can be justified between positive and negative rights. Even in the case of negative rights, it is sometimes relevant to ask how a right should be honored and who, if anyone, has particular responsibility for protecting it. Moreover, it can be the case that there is not a uniquely correct answer to questions about what place the protection of the right should occupy on the list of social priorities. Consider, for example, the right not to be subjected to assault or battery. While it is obvious that individuals have the obligation to respect this right, and equally obvious that governments have an obligation to protect persons within their jurisdiction from those who would violate it, different communities reasonably differ not only as to the means or mix of means that are used to protect persons from assault and battery, but also as to the level of resources they allocate to protecting people against violations of the right. I am grateful to Allen Buchanan for this point.
6 Yves R. Simon, *A General Theory of Authority* (University of Notre Dame Press), 1962.
7 See, e.g., *Nicomachean Ethics* book 3, chapter 5.
8 It is worth elaborating the point: We each are aware that there are others out there, who, like us, can flourish as human persons. We are also aware that there are practical limitations (scarcity, war, violence, disease, etc.) that threaten to stand in the way of fulfillment for everyone. One of the requirements of practical reasonableness is reasonable impartiality between persons. And so, in dealing with the problems (scarcity, etc.) we must will that they be dealt with in a way that is fair, that gives equal concern to the interests of all. So we must will the common good, which means dealing with these problems fairly, for the sake of human flourishing—not just our personal flourishing, but everyone's. And that "everyone" includes all human persons—not just in our political community, but around the world. And, in fact, the establishment of particular political communities that have special care over their own citizens is intelligible, defensible, only because such a set of arrangements is good for the true common good... which belongs to all of humanity. For this point, and much else, I'm grateful to my former student and research assistant (and now Harvard Law student) Myles McKnight.

9. Thomas Aquinas, *Summa Theologiae*, part 1-2, question 96, article 1.
10. Ibid., question 90, article 4.
11. Ibid, question 95, article 2.
12. On the incoherence of these Benthamite notions, see John Finnis, *Natural Law and Natural Rights*, 2nd ed. (Oxford University Press), 112–18.
13. See John Finnis, "Natural Law and Legal Reasoning," in Robert P. George, ed., *Natural Law Theory: Contemporary Essays* (Clarendon Press, 1992), 134–57, especially 138–43.
14. See Ronald Dworkin, *Law's Empire* (Harvard University Press, 1986).
15. See Robert H. Bork, *The Tempting of America: The Political Seduction of the Law* (The Free Press, 1990), esp. 251–59.
16. Hans Kelsen, "The Natural-Law Doctrine Before the Tribunal of Science," in *What is Justice? Justice, Law, and Politics in the Mirror of Science: Collected Essays by Hans Kelsen* (Berkeley: University of California Press, 1957), 144.
17. Aquinas, *Summa*, part 1-2, question 96, article 4.
18. See Finnis, *Natural Law and Natural Rights*, 12–18.
19. Aquinas, *Summa*, part 1-2, question 96, article 4.
20. Ibid.
21. Ibid. Note, however, that, according to Aquinas, one may never obey a law requiring one to do something unjust or otherwise morally wrong. And sometimes *disobedience* is required to avoid causing (or contributing to) "demoralization or disorder." On issues relevant to the translation of Aquinas's phrase "scandalum vel turbatio," see John Finnis, *Aquinas: Moral, Political and Legal Thought* (Oxford University Press, 1998), 223 at note 23, 273 at note 112, and 274 at note d.)
22. See Aquinas, *Summa*, part 1-2, question 60, article 5.
23. Ibid.
24. H. L. A. Hart, *The Concept of Law*, 3rd ed. (Clarendon Law Series, 2012).
25. H. L. A. Hart, *Essays on Bentham: Jurisprudence and Political Theory* (Clarendon Press, 1982), 252–55.
26. This criticism of Hart (and Raz) is carefully developed by Finnis: see *Natural Law and Natural Rights*, 12–18. On Hart's misinterpretation of Aquinas on these matters, see ibid., chapter 12.

CHAPTER FIVE: THE NATURAL-LAW FOUNDATIONS OF MEDICAL LAW

1. For a recent account of the foundational principles of natural-law ethics, see Christopher Tollefsen, "Natural Law, Basic Goods, and Practical Reason," in George Duke and Robert P. George, eds., *The Cambridge Companion to Natural Law Jurisprudence*, (Cambridge University Press, 2017), 133–58.
2. For discussion of the prescriptive nature of the first principles of the natural law, see Germain Grisez, "The First Principle of Practical Reason: A Commentary on the *Summa Theologiae*, 1–2, Question 94, Article 2," *Natural Law Forum* 10, no. 1 (1965): 168–201.
3. See Patrick Lee and Robert P. George, *Body-Self Dualism in Contemporary Ethics and Politics* (Cambridge University Press, 2008), responding to dualist theories such as those in Derek Parfit, *Reasons and Persons* (Oxford University Press, 1989) and Jeff

McMahan, *The Ethics of Killing: Problems at the Margins of Life* (Oxford University Press, 2003).

4   For discussion of the first principle of morality, see Joseph Boyle, "On the Most Fundamental Principle of Morality," in John Keown and Robert P. George, eds., *Reason, Morality, and Law: The Philosophy of John Finnis* (Oxford University Press, 2013), 56–72.

5   For a more in-depth treatment of the derivation of such intermediate norms, see Germain Grisez, *The Way of the Lord Jesus, Vol 1: Christian Moral Principles* (Franciscan Herald Press, 1983), chapter 8.

6   John Finnis, *Natural Law and Natural Rights*, 2nd ed. (Oxford University Press), chapter 6.

7   For further discussion of the concept of vocation and its importance, see Grisez, *The Way of the Lord Jesus*, 77–130.

8   For a recent and thorough treatment of inviolability and medical law, see John Keown, *The Law and Ethics of Medicine: Essays on the Inviolability of Human Life* (Oxford University Press, 2012).

9   For an extended and more detailed discussion on this point, see Robert P. George and Christopher Tollefsen, *Embryo: A Defense of Human Life*, 2nd ed. (Witherspoon, 2011). For a thorough discussion of the moral arguments surrounding abortion, see also Christopher Kaczor, *The Ethics of Abortion: Women's Rights, Human Life, and the Question of Justice*, 2nd ed. (Routledge, 2015).

10 On the question of the scientific consensus, see Christopher O. Tollefsen, Patrick Lee, and Robert P. George, "Marco Rubio Was Right: The Life of a New Human Being Begins at Conception," The Public Discourse (August 15, 2015), http://www.thepublicdiscourse.com/2015/08/15520/.

11 For helpful discussion of this issue, with references, see Alfonso Gómez-Lobo, *Bioethics and the Human Goods: An Introduction to Natural Law Bioethics* (Georgetown University Press, 2015); see also, for critical engagement with a biologist who denies the humanity of the early embryo, Patrick Lee, Christopher Tollefsen, and Robert P. George, "The Ontological Status of Embryos: A Reply to Jason Morris," *Journal of Medicine and Philosophy* 39 (2014) 483–504.

12 Judith Jarvis Thomson, "A Defense of Abortion," *Philosophy and Public Affairs* 1, no. 1 (autumn 1971): 47–66.

13 On natural obligations founded on biological relatedness, see Melissa Moschella, *To Whom Do Children Belong? Parental Rights, Civic Education, and Children's Autonomy* (Cambridge University Press, 2016); for the argument of unfairness, see Patrick Lee and Robert P. George, "The Wrong of Abortion," in Andrew I. Cohen and Christopher Heath Wellman, eds., *Contemporary Debates in Applied Ethics* (Blackwell, 2005), 13–26.

14 See Christopher Tollefsen, "Double Effect and Two Hard Cases in Medical Ethics," *American Catholic Philosophical Quarterly* 89, no 3 (summer 2015): 407–20.

15 The history of the nineteenth-century physicians' crusade against abortion is related in Frederick N. Dyer, *The Physicians' Crusade Against Abortion* (Science History Publications, 2005).

16 See Rachel Lu, "Why Pro-Lifers Don't Support Punishing Women for Abortion", The Federalist, April 5, 2016, http://thefederalist.com/2016/04/05/why-pro-lifers-dont-support-punishing-women-for-abortion.

17 Joseph Boyle explores these implications of the natural-law idea of the sanctity or inviolability of life in "Sanctity of Life and Suicide: Tensions and Developments within Common Morality" in Baruch A. Brody, ed., *Suicide and Euthanasia* (Kluwer, 1989), 221–50.
18 For further discussion of justice in the natural-law tradition, see Finnis, *Natural Law*, chapter 7; as Finnis points out at 161–63, justice "embraces three elements" in the natural-law tradition: it is other directed, it designates what is owed, and it involves some form of equality.
19 See John Finnis, "Euthanasia and the Law," in *Human Rights and Common Good, Collected Essays* (Oxford University Press, 2011), vol. 3, 251–70 for discussion of these and related points.
20 An important body of literature now exists arguing that current laws permitting physician assistance in dying notably fail as regards both the content and the enforcement of such protocols. See, for example, John Keown, "Euthanasia in the Netherlands: Sliding down the Slippery Slope?," *Notre Dame Journal of Law, Ethics & Public Policy* 9, no. 2/3 (1995): 407– 48; Neil M. Gorsuch, *The Future of Assisted Suicide and Euthanasia* (Princeton University Press, 2006).
21 Ezekiel J. Emanuel, "Four Myths about Doctor Assisted Suicide," *New York Times*. October 27, 2012, https://archive.nytimes.com/opinionator.blogs.nytimes.com/2012/10/27/four-myths-about-doctor-assisted-suicide/.
22 John Keown pursues these implications in volume 3 of *The Law and Ethics of Medicine*.
23 For further discussion, see RyanAnderson, "Always Care, Never Kill: How Physician-Assisted Suicide Endangers the Weak, Corrupts Medicine, Compromises the Family, and Violates Human Dignity and Equality," The Heritage Foundation, March 24, 2015, http://www.heritage.org/health-care-reform/report/always-care-never-kill-how-physician-assisted-suicide-endangers-the-weak.
24 See John Finnis, *Moral Absolutes: Tradition, Revision, and Truth* (Catholic University of America Press, 1991).
25 For further articulation of this position, see Joseph Boyle, "Who Is Entitled to Double Effect?," *Journal of Medicine and Philosophy* 16, no. 5 (October 1991): 475–94 and "Intention, Permissibility, and the Structure of Agency," *American Catholic Philosophical Quarterly* 89, no. 3 (summer 2015): 461–78.
26 The origins of the Principle are standardly traced back to St. Thomas Aquinas's discussion of killing in self-defense, in his *Summa Theologiae*, part 2-2, question 64, article 7; for further commentary, see Joseph Boyle, "'Praeter Intentionem' in Aquinas," *Thomist* 42, no. 4 (1978): 649–65.
27 For such a formulation, see Gomez-Lobo, *Bioethics and the Human Goods*, 59–60. Our simpler formulation captures parts 2 and 3 in the requirement that the bad effect not be intended, by which we mean "intended as an end or as a means." But an act in which the bad effect is intended is one that is impermissible in itself, so part 1 is encompassed in our simple formulation as well. Both formulations share the requirement that there be a proportionate reason, that is, that bad side effects be proportionate to the good sought.
28 *Vacco v. Quill* 521 US 793 (1997). Gorsuch defends the importance of the intend-foresee distinction for end-of-life issues in *The Future of Assisted Suicide*, chapter 4.
29 See, e.g., Tom L. Beauchamp and James F. Childress, *Principles of Biomedical Ethics*, 7th ed. (Oxford University Press, 2013).

30 See the discussion of two "models", one paternalistic, one autonomy-focused and consumerist, in Mark Siegler, "Searching for Moral Certainty in Medicine: A Proposal for a New Model of the Doctor-Patient Encounter," *Bulletin of the New York Academy of Medicine* 57, no. 1 (January–February 1981).
31 See Finnis, *Natural Law*, chapter 9.
32 For further elaboration of this claim, see Grisez, *The Way of the Lord Jesus*.
33 By "obligations of charity," we mean simply obligations to give; such obligations are obligations in justice. No contrast between charity and justice is supposed here.
34 For recent natural-law accounts of private property, see Finnis, *Natural Law*, 169 and Adam J. MacLeod, *Property and Practical Reason* (Cambridge University Press, 2015). Both accounts are indebted to that of Aquinas in *Summa*, part 202, question 66, article 1.
35 For a nuanced account of Aquinas's concept of superflua, see John Finnis, *Aquinas: Moral, Political and Legal Theory* (Oxford University Press, 1998), 191–96.
36 See Jason Boyle, "Fairness in Holdings: A Natural Law Account of Property and Welfare Rights" *Social Philosophy and Policy* 18, no. 1 (2001): 206–26.
37 With regard to some undeveloped countries, it will make little sense to speak of the right to health care of the citizens against their own state. We prescind here from the question of what health-related rights such states might have as regards more developed countries; that issue is addressed from a natural-law perspective in Thana Cristina de Campos, *The Global Health Crisis: Ethical Responsibilities* (Cambridge University Press, 2017).
38 See Germain Grisez, "Health Care Technology and Justice," in Christopher O. Tollefsen, ed., *Bioethics with Liberty and Justice: Themes in the Work of Joseph M. Boyle* (Springer, 2011), 221–41.
39 See the discussion in Joseph Boyle, "Limiting Access to Healthcare: A Traditional Roman Catholic Analysis," in H. Tristram Engelhardt Jr. and Mark J. Cherry, eds., *Allocating Scarce Medical Resources* (Georgetown University Press, 2002), 89–91.
40 For instances and discussion of the controversies, see the contributions by C. Lustig and J. Boyle to C. Tollefsen, ed., *Bioethics with Liberty and Justice: Themes in the Work of Joseph M. Boyle* (Springer, 2011).
41 See the discussion in Kevin Wm. Wildes, "Creating Critical Care Resources: Implications for Distributive Justice," in H. Tristram Engelhardt Jr. and Mark J. Cherry, eds., *Allocating Scarce Medical Resources* (Georgetown University Press, 2002), 200–11.
42 For articulation of such criticisms, se Julian Savulescu and Udo Schüklenk, "Doctors Have No Right to Refuse Assistance in Dying, Abortion, or Contraception," *Bioethics* 31 (2016): 162–70.
43 See the discussion by Ryan Anderson and Sherif Girgis in John Corvino, Ryan T. Anderson, and Sherif Girgis, *Debating Religious Liberty and Discrimination* (Oxford University Press, 2017).
44 See Chrisopher O. Tollefsen, "Conscience, Religion, and State," *American Journal of Jurisprudence* 54 (2009): 93–116.

CHAPTER SIX: HUMAN EMBRYOS ARE HUMAN BEINGS

1 Ruth Marcus, "Thank the Alabama Supreme Courty for Its IVF Decision. I'm Serious," *Washington Post*, March 6, 2024, https://www.washingtonpost.com/opinions/2024/03/06/fetal-personhood-embryo-ivf-alabama-supreme-court-backfire/.
2 Michael Sandel, "Embryo Ethics," *Boston Globe*, April 8, 2007.

CHAPTER SEVEN: DEATH WITH DIGNITY: A DANGEROUS EUPHEMISM

1 For a more in-depth explanation of the first three senses of the term, see Daniel P. Sulmasy, "Dignity and Bioethics: History, Theory, and Selected Applications," in Adam Schulman, Edmund D. Pellegrino, and Thomas W. Merrill, eds., *Human Dignity and Bioethics: Essays Commissioned by the President's Council on Bioethics*, (US Independent Agencies and Commissions, 2008), 469–501. The fourth sense of the term is suggested by Ruth Macklin, who holds that dignity can be reduced to respect for autonomy. See Ruth Macklin, "Dignity Is a Useless Concept," *British Medical Journal* 327 (2003): 1419–20.
2 Sulmasy, "Dignity and Bioethics," 473.
3 Ibid.
4 Ibid.
5 Macklin, "Dignity Is a Useless Concept," 1420.
6 Perhaps the best-known defense of Macklin's claim is Steven Pinker's "The Stupidity of Dignity," *New Republic* May 27, 2008, 238. A critique of their views can be found in the first chapter of Christopher Kaczor, *A Defense of Dignity: Creating Life, Destroying Life, and Protecting the Rights of Conscience* (University of Notre Dame Press, 2013).
7 Patrick Lee and Robert P. George, *Body-Self Dualism in Contemporary Ethics and Politics* (Cambridge University Press, 2007).
8 Immanuel Kant, *Grounding for the Metaphysics of Morals*, trans. James W. Ellington, 3rd ed. (Hackett, 1993), 36.
9 For more on this distinction, see John Keown, *The Law and Ethics of Medicine: Essays on the Inviolability of Human Life* (Oxford University Press, 2012), chapter 1.
10 Kant, *Grounding for the Metaphysics of Morals*, 35.
11 Ibid., 36.
12 Ibid., 37.
13 Ronald Dworkin et al., "Assisted Suicide: The Philosopher's Brief," *New York Review of Books*, March 27, 1997, 41–47.
14 Colin Bird, "Dignity as a Moral Concept," *Social Philosophy & Policy* 30, no. 1–2 (2013): 150–176.
15 Alan Gewirth, *Self-Fulfillment* (Princeton University Press, 2009), 168–169.
16 Ibid., 169.
17 John Keown, "A New Father for Law and Ethics of Medicine," in John Keown and Robert P. George, eds., *Reason, Morality, and Law: The Philosophy of John Finnis* (Oxford University Press, 2013), 300.
18 John Finnis, *Human Rights and Common Good. Collected Essays of John Finnis: Volume III* (Oxford University Press, 2011), 226.

CHAPTER EIGHT: WHAT *OBERGEFELL* SHOULD HAVE SAID: GIRGIS AND GEORGE, DISSENTING

1   This estimate reflects the number of votes for ballots approving traditional marriage laws between 1996 and 2012, based on official state reports.
2   Andrew Koppelman, *Beyond Levels of Scrutiny:* Windsor *and "Bare Desire to Harm,"* 64 Case. W. Res. L. Rev. 1045, 1048 (2014). Given that this chapter is in the form of a judicial opinion, the authors have used Bluebook style for all citations.
3   *See* Washington v. Davis, 426 U.S. 229, 242 (1976) (holding that a disparate impact claim alone does not "trigger the rule, that racial classifications are to be subjected to the strictest scrutiny and are justifiable only by the weightiest of considerations" (citation omitted)).
4   *See* Koppelman, *supra* note 2, at 1049.
5   The majority might object that desire for particular contours of group sexual bonds and the absence of sexual desire don't constitute identities, unlike desire for same-sex relationships. But as a previous case of ours has noted and as Justice Eskridge today repeats, "the 'concept of the homosexual as a distinct category of person' emerged only at the end of the nineteenth century" (Eskridge, J., concurrence) (citing Lawrence v. Texas, 539 U.S. 558, 568 (2003)). So there's no "natural" divide between patterns of desire that do and don't constitute an identity.
6   *See, e.g.*, Massachusetts Board of Retirement v. Murgia, 427 U.S. 307, 313 (1976) (suggesting that strict scrutiny applies in cases involving groups with a "'history of purposeful unequal treatment'" (quoting San Antonio Sch. Dist. v. Rodriguez, 411 U.S. 1, 28 (1973)).
7   United States v. Virginia, 518 U.S. 515, 533 (1996).
8   *Id.*
9   Hence, perhaps, the Court's ambivalence about sex classifications. *See, e.g.*, Craig v. Boren, 429 U.S. 190, 200 (1976) (opting for intermediate scrutiny, three years after a plurality of the Court had applied heightened scrutiny in Frontiero v. Richardson, 411 U.S. 677 (1973)).
10 City of Cleburne v. Cleburne Living Ctr. Inc., 473 U.S. 432, 441 (1985).
11 Nev. Dep't of Human Res. v. Hibbs, 538 U.S. 721, 731 (2003).
12 J. M. Balkin, *The Constitution of Status*, 106 Yale L.J. 2313, 2361 (1997).
13 For claims along these lines by women across the political spectrum, see, for example, Helen M. Alvaré, Gonzales v. Carhart: *Bringing Abortion Law Back into the Family Law Fold*, 69 Mont. L. Rev. 409, 444 (2008) ("Denying that women are drawn to their unborn children, as well as to spending considerable time and effort rearing born children, only results in policies reinforcing an outdated and largely male model of social life and employment—a model in which no institution need 'flex' or change to allow women and men to meet children's needs. On the other hand, recognizing that both men and women feel keen obligations to their children at the same time that they have work or school obligations to meet is both more realistic and a more likely premise for a successful argument in favor of family-friendly work and education policies." (footnote omitted)); Elizabeth Fox-Genovese, *Wrong Turn: How the Campaign to Liberate Women Has Betrayed the Culture of Life, in* Life and Learning XII: Proceedings of the Twelfth University Faculty for Life Conference 11, 19 (Joseph W. Koterski ed., 2003) (lamenting the claim that "to enjoy full dignity and rights as an individual, a woman must resemble a man as closely as possible. It is

difficult to imagine a more deadly assault upon a woman's dignity as a woman. For this logic denies that a woman can be both a woman and a full individual."); Robin West, *Concurring in the Judgment, in* What *Roe v. Wade* Should Have Said: The Nation's Top Legal Experts Rewrite America's Most Controversial Decision 121, 141–42 (Jack M. Balkin ed., 2005) (arguing that the equal citizenship argument for abortion rights "legitim[izes], and with a vengeance, the inconsistency of motherhood and citizenship itself").

14 Erika Bachiochi, *Embodied Equality: Debunking Equal Protection Arguments for Abortion Rights,* 34 Harv. J.L. & Pub. Pol'y 889, 941 (2011).
15 It is basic or radical (i.e., root) in that other, contingent conditions (of health, age, timeliness, other circumstances, and certain actions) need to be met for it to be realized fully in any particular case.
16 Nguyen v. INS, 553 U.S. 53, 68 (2001).
17 The rational-basis test, which we have argued applies here, is judges' way of applying the Equal Protection Clause while deferring to lawmakers' normative and policy choices wherever these are reasonable, whether or not ultimately *sound*. It is another question whether the U.S. Congress, pursuant to its enforcement power under Section 5 of the Fourteenth Amendment, has more leeway to impose its own normative and policy judgments, including by requiring States to recognize same-sex civil marriages. *See, e.g.,* John F. Manning, *The Supreme Court 2013 Term—Foreword: The Means of Constitutional Power,* 128 Harv. L. Rev. 1, 5 & n.19 (2014) (suggesting that Congress may have more discretion than the courts in enforcing the Reconstruction Amendments).
18 Lochner v. New York, 198 U.S. 45, 75 (1905) (Holmes, J., dissenting).
19 *Id.*
20 Evan Wolfson, *Why Marriage Matters: America, Equality, and Gay People's Right to Marry* (2005).
21 *Lochner,* 198 U.S. at 75 (Holmes, J., dissenting).
22 *Id.* at 76.
23 *Id.*
24 *See generally* John Rawls, Political Liberalism (1993).
25 Loving v. Virginia, 388 U.S. 1, 7 (1967) (quoting Naim v. Naim, 87 S.E.2d 749, 756 (Va. 1955)). Nancy F. Cott provides historical support for this conclusion:
    It is important to retrieve the singularity of the racial basis for these laws. Ever since ancient Rome, class-stratified and estate-based societies had instituted laws against intermarriage between individuals of unequal social or civil status, with the aim of preserving the integrity of the ruling class.... But the English colonies stand out as the first secular authorities to nullify and criminalize intermarriage on the basis of race or color designations. [Their laws] did not concern all mixed marriages. They aimed to keep the white race unmixed...and thus only addressed marriages in which one party was white.
    Nancy F. Cott, Public Vows: A History of Marriage and the Nation 41 (2000) (footnote omitted).
26 *See, e.g.,* G. Robina Quale, A History of Marriage Systems 2 (1988) ("Marriage, as the socially recognized linking of a specific man to a specific woman and her offspring, can be found in all societies. Through marriage, children can be assured of being born

to both a man and a woman who will care for them as they mature."); *see also* Edward Westermarck, A Short History of Marriage 1 (1926) (recognizing that marriage across cultures "involves certain rights and duties both... of the parties entering the union and... of the children born of it" and "implies the right of sexual intercourse").

27 *See, e.g.*, Plato, The Laws of Plato 232, 840c—841a (Thomas L. Pangle trans., 1988) (writing favorably of legislating to have people "pair off, male with female... and live out the rest of their lives" together).

28 For Aristotle, the foundation of political community was "the family group," by which he "mean[t] the nuclear family." Alberto Maffi, *Family and Property Law, in* The Cambridge Companion to Ancient Greek Law 254, 254 (Michael Gagarin & David Cohen eds., 2005). For Aristotle, indeed, "[b]etween man and wife friendship seems to exist by nature." Aristotle, Nicomachean Ethics bk. VIII, at 1162a15–19 (W. D. Ross trans., 1925) (ca. 350 BCE), *reprinted in* 2 The Complete Works of Aristotle 1836 (Jonathan Barnes ed., 1984).

29 He said that a "husband and wife... should come together for the purpose of making a life in common and of procreating children, and furthermore of regarding all things in common between them,... even their own bodies," viewing this form of affectionate and bodily union—and not only its fulfillment in procreation—as desirable. Musonius Rufus, *Discourses* XIIIA, *reprinted in* Cora E. Lutz, *Musonius Rufus, "The Roman Socrates," in* 10 Yale Classical Studies 3, 89 (Alfred R. Bellinger ed., 1947).

30 According to Plutarch, Solon saw marriage as a union of life between man and woman "for the delights of love and the getting of children." Plutarch, Life of Solon ch. 20, § 4, *reprinted in* 1 Plutarch Lives 403, 459 (G. P. Goold ed., Bernadotte Perrin trans., Harv. Univ. Press. 6th prtg. 1993). Plutarch himself wrote of marriage as a distinct form of "friendship," specially embodied in "physical union" of intercourse (which he called a "renewal" of marriage). Plutarch, The Dialogue on Love § 769, *reprinted in* 9 Moralia 307, 427 (Edwin L. Minar Jr. trans., T. E. Page et al. eds., Harv. Univ. Press, 1961).

31 And they all denied that any sexual acts but coitus, even between a married man and a woman, could seal a truly marital relationship. *See* John M. Finnis, *Law, Morality, and "Sexual Orientation,"* 69 Notre Dame L. Rev. 1049, 1062–68 (1994).

32 Petitioners contend that this point is undermined by the States' recognition of infertile opposite-sex partnerships. But it's reasonable for the States to hold that recognizing infertile conjugal unions would have at least fewer of the costs of recognizing same-sex bonds. First, petitioners argue, it does less to focus the public vision of marriage on romantic attachment alone—as opposed to conjugal unions conspicuously and naturally oriented to family life. So to the extent that that focusing is what undermines traditional marital norms, it's reasonable to expect it to do less harm. Second, many couples believed to be infertile end up having children, who are served by their parents' marriage; and trying to determine fertility would require unjust invasions of privacy. Moreover, a policy limited to fertile opposite-sex unions might lead couples to see marriage as *merely* instrumental to child-rearing, which might well destabilize their bond, thus harming the public interest in giving children a stable home with both parents.

33 Andrew J. Cherlin, Marriage-Go-Round: The State of Marriage and the Family in America Today 29 (2009).

34 *Id.* at 31 (emphasis added).

35 W. Bradford Wilcox & Jeffrey Dew, *Is Love a Flimsy Foundation? Soulmate versus Institutional Models of Marriage*, 39 Soc. Sci. Res. 687, 697 (2010).
36 Lenore J. Weitzman, *The Divorce Law Revolution and the Transformation of Legal Marriage, in* Contemporary Marriage: Comparative Perspectives on a Changing Institution 301, 305 (Kingsley Davis ed., 1985).
37 William J. Goode, World Changes in Divorce Patterns 144 (1993).
38 *See* Douglas W. Allen & Maggie Gallagher, *Does Divorce Law Affect the Divorce Rate? A Review of Empirical Research, 1995–2006,* iMAPP (July 2007), http://www.marriagedebate.com/pdf/imapp.nofault.divrate.pdf.
39 *Beyond Same-Sex Marriage: A New Strategic Vision for All Our Families & Relationships,* BeyondMarriage.org (July 26, 2006), http://beyondmarriage.org/BeyondMarriage.pdf.
40 Ellen Willis, *Can Marriage Be Saved?*, The Nation, July 5, 2004, at 16 ("[C]onferring the legitimacy of marriage on homosexual relations will introduce an implicit revolt against the institution into its very heart.").
41 Elizabeth Brake, *Minimal Marriage: What Political Liberalism Implies for Marriage Law,* 120 Ethics 302, 303 (2010).
42 *See* Quale, *supra* note 26, at 2.
43 J. David Velleman, "Family History," 34 Phil. Papers 357, 375 (2005). *Id.* at 375.
44 *See, e.g.*, Elizabeth Marquardt et al., Instit. for Am. Values, My Daddy's Name Is Donor: A New Study of Young Adults Conceived through Sperm Donation 5 (2010) (seeking "to learn about the identity, kinship, well-being, and social justice experiences of young adults who were conceived through sperm donation").
45 Kristin Anderson Moore, Susan M. Jekielek, & Carol Emig, *Marriage from a Child's Perspective: How Does Family Structure Affect Children, and What Can We Do about It?*, Child Trends Research Brief (June 2002): 1–2, 6, http://www.childtrends.org/files/MarriageRB602.pdf.
46 Jack M. Balkin, *The Constitution of Status,* 106 Yale L.J. 2313, 2324 (1997).
47 *See* Jack M. Balkin, *Windsor and the Constitutional Prohibition against Class Legislation,* Balkinization (June 26, 2013), http://balkin.blogspot.com/2013/06/windsor-and-constitutional-prohibition.html ("Class legislation is legislation that picks out a group of people for special benefits or special burdens *without adequate public justification*.... All laws classify and have some kind of differential impact; whether a law singles out a group for special and unjustified burdens or stigma is an interpretive question and a question of values.").
48 *See, e.g.*, United States v. O'Brien, 391 U.S. 367, 383 (1968) ("It is a familiar principle of constitutional law that this Court will not strike down an otherwise constitutional statute on the basis of an alleged illicit legislative motive.").
49 Andrew Koppelman, *Why Scalia Should Have Voted to Overturn DOMA,* 108 N.W. L. Rev. Colloquy 131, 142–43 (2013), http://www.law.northwestern.edu/lawreview/colloquy/2013/12/LRColl2013n12Koppelman.pdf (footnotes omitted) (quoting Antonin Scalia & Brian A. Garner, Reading Law: The Interpretation of Legal Texts 33 (2012)). We note that while in this last sentence, Koppelman argues that DOMA's purpose was to injure and disparage gay people, in the very next he says, "The impact on gay people was far from Congress's mind when [DOMA] was enacted." *Id.* at 143.

50 The case is not far from real life. President Barack Obama and congressional Democrats sought to limit and eventually end congressional support for tuition vouchers to low-income families in the District of Columbia. Bill Turque & Shailagh Murray, *Obama Offers Compromise on D.C. Tuition Vouchers*, Washington Post, May 7, 2009, http://www.washingtonpost.com/wp-dyn/content/article/2009/05/06/AR2009050603852.html.

51 *See, e.g.*, Griswold v. Connecticut, 381 U.S. 479 (1965) (the use of contraceptives by spouses); Eisenstadt v. Baird, 405 U.S. 438 (1972) (the use of contraceptives by the unmarried); Roe v. Wade, 410 U.S. 113 (1973) (abortions); Webster v. Reprod. Health Serv., 492 U.S. 490 (1989) (same); Planned Parenthood of Se. Pa. v. Casey, 505 U.S. 833 (1992) (same); Lawrence v. Texas, 539 U.S. 558 (2003) (consensual sex).

CHAPTER NINE: EQUAL PROTECTION AND THE UNBORN: A *DOBBS* BRIEF

1 Roe v. Wade, 410 U.S. 113, 156–57 (1973); *see also* Thornburgh v. Am. Coll. of Obstetricians & Gynecologists, 476 U.S. 747, 779 (1986) (Stevens, J., concurring). Both *Roe* and *Lawrence* overlooked a three-judge district court majority's cogent defense of fetal constitutional personhood in Steinberg v. Brown, 321 F. Supp. 741, 746–47 (N.D. Ohio 1970). Because of the nature of this chapter as an adapted amicus brief, the authors have elected to retain some in-text citations as opposed to notes and have used Bluebook style for all citations, whether in-text or in notes. The original texts of our *Enhanced Amicus Brief in* Dobbs *and our Supplement to an Enhanced Amicus Brief in* Dobbs are available online at https://pa pers.ssrn.com/sol3/papers.cfm?abstract_id=3955231 and https://papers.ssrn.com/sol3/papers.cfm?ab stract_id=3973183, respectively.

2 These rulings include McDonald v. City of Chicago, 561 U.S. 742 (2010); District of Columbia v. Heller, 554 U.S. 570 (2008); and Crawford v. Washington, 541 U.S. 36 (2004).

3 Hall v. Hancock, 32 Mass. (15 Pick.) 255, 257–58 (1834).

4 *See* discussion *infra* section I.A.4.a, THREE SENSES OF QUICK[EN].

5 *See infra* note 90.

6 *See* Santa Clara County v. S. Pac. R.R. Co., 118 U.S. 394 (1886).

7 U.S. CONST. amend. XIV, § 1 (emphasis added).

8 *Cf.* District of Columbia v. Heller, 554 U.S. 570, 605–16 (2008) (interpreting original public meaning based on Ratification Era treatises, antebellum case law, and Civil War–Era legislation).

9 Congress, though not limiting itself to this purpose, drafted the Fourteenth Amendment to sustain the Act of 1866. See Kurt T. Lash, *Enforcing the Rights of Due Process: The Original Relationship Between the Fourteenth Amendment and the 1866 Civil Rights Act*, 106 GEO. L.J. 1389, 1391 (2018).

10 CONG. GLOBE, 39th Cong., 1st Sess. 1118 (March 1st, 1866).

11 *Id.* at 1118 (col. iii); *see also* 1 WILLIAM BLACKSTONE, COMMENTARIES ON THE LAWS OF ENGLAND *123 (stating that "absolute *rights*" are those that "would belong to their persons merely in a state of nature, and which every man is entitled to enjoy"). (Blackstone uses "man" synonymously with "human being.") In this usage, rights are called *absolute* because they are *not conditional* either upon

recognition and specification by positive law (whether common law or statute, or Civil or other laws), or upon relationships entered into with other individuals. *Id.* The Amicus Brief of the United States rightly acknowledges the unequalled primacy of these pages of Blackstone as demonstrating the rights recognized "[a]t the Founding," precisely as "absolute rights" vested in persons "by the immutable laws of nature." Brief of the United States as Amicus Curiae Supporting Respondents at 22, Dobbs v. Jackson Women's Health Org., 142 S. Ct. 2228 (2022) (No. 19-1392) (citing pages *120, *125 and *130, but significantly omitting *129).

Present in the background is the fact rightly recorded in the Amicus Brief of the American Historical Association and the Organization of American Historians at 7, Dobbs v. Jackson Women's Health Org., 142 S. Ct. 2228 (2022) (No. 19-1392): Blackstone's "works constituted the preeminent authority on English law for the founding generation." Alden v. Maine, 527 U.S. 706, 715 (1999). James Wilson, who crafted the preamble to the U.S. Constitution, quoted and endorsed Blackstone's words in his seminal lectures of 1790: "In the contemplation of law, life begins when the infant is first able to stir in the womb." James Wilson, *Natural Rights of Individuals* (1790), *reprinted in* 2 THE WORKS OF JAMES WILSON 316 (James DeWir Andrews ed., Chi., Callaghan & Co. 1896).

The cited passage from Justice Wilson's 1790 lecture reads, more fully:
With consistency, beautiful and undeviating, human life, from its commencement to its close, is protected by the common law. In the contemplation of law, life begins when the infant is first able to stir in the womb. By the law, life is protected not only from immediate destruction, but from every degree of actual violence, and, in some cases, from every degree of danger.

2 THE WORKS OF JAMES WILSON 596–97 (Robert G. McCloskey ed., 1896).

12 BLACKSTONE, *supra* note 11, at *129–30 (footnote omitted). Nothing in Blackstone or Coke, Hawkins, and other classic writers on the common law suggests that the phrase "able to stir" meant "felt by the mother to stir," as the Amicus Brief of the American Historical Association and the Organization of American Historians, *supra* note 11, asserts at 5 (opening paragraph of its Argument) and *passim*, erroneously stating: "At common law, as explained by authorities such as Coke and Blackstone, life was deemed legally to begin only when a pregnant woman sensed the fetus stirring in her womb." Nothing would have been easier to say, but Coke, Blackstone, and the others neither say nor imply it. From Bracton through the American founding era, common-law criminal law fixed its attention almost entirely on the unborn child's formation and animation—that is, its life as a distinct individual, and its consequent *ability* to move or stir—not on the mother's usually much later experiences of the child's making its presence felt by its stirring and kicking. *See infra* at notes 67, 69, 81.

13 American editions of 1 COMMENTARIES, based on Edward Christian's 1793 edition, here insert a note stating that if the child is born alive and dies from the abortion it will be murder, and those who administered the potion or advised the woman to take it will be liable as accessories before the fact to the same punishment. See for example the 1822 and 1860 editions mentioned *infra* note 14, or the 1818 edition by publishers in Boston, Philadelphia, Baltimore, Washington City, and Georgetown, D.C.

14 For the passage from Coke (3 INST. 50) and the sentence that both Coke and Blackstone quote from Bracton, see text *infra* after note 69. Note that the quotation above is from 1 COMMENTARIES's first edition, Oxford 1765, pp. 125–26; in its second edition, 1768, and thereafter the editions in Blackstone's lifetime—including the first American edition, Boston 1774—these paragraphs are at pp. 129–30 and the first paragraph's last sentence reads: "But *Sir Edward Coke doth not look upon this Offence* in quite so atrocious a light, but merely as a heinous misdemeanor" (emphasis added). (In later American editions such as the second American edition, Boston 1799, the 1822 New York edition, or George Sharswood's many editions, *e.g.*, Philadelphia 1860, it reads: "But the modern law doth not look on this offence in quite so atrocious a light, but merely as a heinous misdemeanor.") The change makes it evident that by 1768 Blackstone had decided that he would not articulate the "present" position in his own voice until his full treatment of homicide in vol. 4, the first edition of which was in 1769. There he deals with type [III] protection of unborn life not as a misdemeanor but, more serious, "a great misprision," and—as with types [I] and [II]—makes (unlike Coke) no reference to the quickness or otherwise of the unborn child. See *infra* note 31.

15 See *infra* section I.A.3.a, and notes 34, 88, 103.

16 Blackstone uses "it" of born children as well as unborn. See BLACKSTONE, *supra* note 11, at *300 ("[T]he child, by reason of its want of discretion...").

17 *Id.* at *129–30 (some footnotes omitted). Footnote 11(s) reads, translated: "Those who are *in utero* are understood in Civil law to be 'in the real world' [*in rerum natura esse*], when it is a matter/question of their benefit" (citing Justinian's *Digest* 1.5.26, save the last five words, which in fact give the gist of 1.5.7). Blackstone has cut two words to universalize the principle, which in his source had read: "in *almost the whole [toto paene] of* the Civil law."

18 *See id.* at *133 ("This natural life...cannot legally be disposed of or destroyed by any individual...merely upon their own authority.").

19 *See, e.g., id.* at *270 ("[I]n contemplation of law [the King] is always present in court."). Legal fictions are found on a spectrum ranging from legally stipulated definitions close to ordinary-language conceptions of natural or other realities, through more or less technical and artificial terms of art, to outright contra-factual (fictive) propositions of law such as the one just quoted. See further *infra* section III.C.1 and notes 79, 132, 209, 213.

20 For the phrase, not then a legal term of art, see *infra* note 62.

21 *See* BLACKSTONE, *supra* note 11, at *130 (citing Coke for "reasonable creature"); *id.* at *300 (using that phrase for human being or person).

22 *See infra* section I.B.2.

23 *See, e.g., id.* at *123, *467. 1 COMMENTARIES concludes with a chapter on the rights of "artificial persons," corporations.

24 32 Mass. (15 Pick.) 255 (1834).

25 (1740) 26 Eng. Rep. 472, 2 Atk. 114, 116.

26 (1795) 126 Eng. Rep. 617; 2 H. Bl. 399.

27 *Hall*, 32 Mass. at 257–58.

28 *Id. See also in rerum natura*, BLACK'S LAW DICTIONARY (11th ed. 2019) ("In the nature of things; in the realm of actuality; in existence."). The idiomatic sense in

these contexts often approximates to "in the ordinary world," for instance, the "world" outside the darkness and anonymity of the womb, where the child is in "a world of its own," even its sex unknown to all, and unable to communicate or be communicated with even in a rudimentary fashion. For more on this routine phrase, always kept, elusively, in a foreign language, see *infra* notes 72, 79, and especially 218.

Lord Hardwicke's parallel decision in Millar v. Turner (1748) 27 Eng. Rep. 971, 1 Vesey Sr 85, shows how these cases correct the inference, adverse to the unborn, that might be drawn from Coke's statement, at 3 *Inst.* 50, that children are accounted *in rerum natura* when born alive. Hardwicke cites 3 *Inst.* 50 to support his statement that an unborn child "is considered as *in esse*," "the destruction of him is murder; which shews the laws [*sic*] considers such an infant as a living creature." *Millar*, 1 Vesey Sr at 86. The deliberate doing of the destructive act, though completed while the child in *in utero*, is murder, subject only to a condition subsequent: that the child be living, however temporarily and unviably, when delivered.

29 See Morrow v. Scott, 7 Ga. 535, 537 (1849) (posthumous child's share in estate on intestacy). Following 1 COMMENTARIES *130, Kent and Hardwicke in *Wallis* and *Clarke*, and Shaw in Hall v. Hancock, the Georgia Supreme Court quotes from the latter the rule that "in general, a child is to be considered as *in being*, from the time of its conception, where it will be for the benefit of such child to be so considered," and adds: "This rule is in accordance with the principles of justice, and we have no disposition to innovate upon it, or create exceptions to it. Let the judgment of the Court below be reversed." *Id.*

30 See Botsford v. O'Conner, 57 Ill. 72, 76 (1870) (holding that a child *in ventre sa mere* is a "person" who "must have an opportunity of being heard, before a court can deprive such person of his rights"); *see also Wallis*, 26 Eng. Rep. at 473; Beale v. Beale (1713) 24 Eng. Rep. 373; 1 P. Wms. 244.

31 The context is Chapter 14, "Of Homicide," in BLACKSTONE, 4 COMMENTARIES (beginning at page *176). At page *188, sec. III., Blackstone explains that "[f]elonious homicide" is "the killing of a human creature, of any age or sex, without justification or excuse." Later, at page *194 and following, Blackstone discusses "deliberate and wilful *murder*.":

> In order also to make the killing murder, it is requisite that the party die within a year and a day after the stroke received, or cause of death administered; in the computation of which, the whole day upon which the hurt was done shall be reckoned the first. [fn. 1 Hawk. P. C. 79.] Further; the person killed must be "*a reasonable creature in being, and under the king's peace,*" at the time of the killing. Therefore to kill an alien, a Jew, or an outlaw, who are all under the king's peace and protection, is as much murder as to kill the most regular-born Englishman; except he be an alien enemy in time of war. [fn. 3 Inst. 50. 1 Hal. P. C. 433.] To kill a child in its mother's womb.... BLACKSTONE, 4 COMMENTARIES *197–98.

32 4 COMMENTARIES (8th ed. 1778) 198. For the key passage here cited, 3 INST. 50, see *infra* p. 145.

33 SIR MATTHEW HALE, HISTORIA PLACITORUM CORONAE: THE HISTORY OF THE PLEAS OF THE CROWN 432–33 (1743) [hereinafter HALE, H.P.C.]:

[T]he second consideration, that is common both to murder and manslaughter, is, who shall be said a person, the killing of whom shall be said murder or manslaughter. If a woman be quick or great with child, if she take, or another give her any potion to make an abortion, or if a man strike her, whereby the child within her is *killed*, it is not murder or manslaughter by the law of *England*, because it is not yet *in rerum natura*, tho it be [III] a great crime, and by the judicial law of Moses(*g*) was punishable with death, nor can it legally be known, whether it were kil[led] or not, [citation to Yearbook of Edward III] so it is, if after such child were born alive, and baptized, and after die of the stroke given to the mother, this [II] is not homicide [citation to an earlier Yearbook]. (emphasis added).

Hale's first two sentences do not deny that the child *in utero* is a person. They deny only that it is a person *of the kind* whose killing is homicide as distinct from [III] "a great crime" (Coke's great misprision). *See infra* text accompanying note 224. But the last sentence does deny that killing the child after abortion is a type [II] indictable homicide, and in this view Hale is virtually alone and will be explicitly rejected by all the subsequent authoritative eighteenth and nineteenth century treatises circulating in America. *See infra* at notes 73–76.

34 4 COMMENTARIES *200–01.
35 HALE, H.P.C., supra note 33, at 429.
36 *Id.* at 429–30 (emphasis added) (adding that he had given this ruling "at the assizes at *Bury* in the year 1670").
37 RICHARD BURN, JUSTICE OF THE PEACE, AND PARISH OFFICER (1764), 228–29.
38 RICHARD BURN, BURN'S ABRIDGMENT, OR THE AMERICAN JUSTICE; CONTAINING THE WHOLE PRACTICE, AUTHORITY AND DUTY OF JUSTICES OF THE PEACE; WITH CORRECT FORMS OF PRECEDENTS RELATING THERETO, AND ADAPTED TO THE PRESENT SITUATION OF THE UNITED STATES (1792), 226 [misprinted 216]. An edition published in Boston in 1773 had referred only to Hale's opinion on types [II] and [III].
39 1 EDWARD HYDE EAST, A TREATISE OF THE PLEAS OF THE CROWN (Philadelphia 1806).
40 *Id.* at 230 (emphases added).
41 *Id.* at 230, 354–56 (ch. V, sec. 124). Notice that though this case was tried before one of the King's judges on assize and was later considered by "all the judges," it is entirely unreported and would be unknown but for the (extensive) account of it in East's treatise.
42 For this analysis, see *infra* notes 28, 76–77, 105, and *supra* pp. 156–57, 166–67.
43 1 SIR WILLIAM OLDNALL RUSSELL, A TREATISE ON CRIMES AND MISDEMEANORS (Lincoln's Inn, 1819). Its first American Edition was by Daniel Davis in his third decade as Solicitor-General of Massachusetts, published by Wells and Lilly of Court Street, Boston, in 1824. By 1841 it was in its fourth American edition, incorporating the notes, supplementations and excisions made by Davis, by Theron Metcalf (later a judge of the Supreme Court of Judicature), and by George Sharswood, and published in Philadelphia. 1 SIR WILLIAM OLDNALL RUSSELL,

A TREATISE ON CRIMES AND MISDEMEANORS (Philadelphia 4th ed. 1841). The American editions use Russell's text and supplement or comment on it in footnotes.

44 Russell deals with [I] in Book III, ch. 1 (Murder), sec. IX, which begins on p. 759 with the general proposition that the rest of the section will particularize:

> If an action, *unlawful in itself,* be done deliberately, and with *intention of mischief or great bodily harm to particulars,* or of mischief indiscriminately, fall where it may, and death ensue against or beside the original intention of the party, it will be murder.

Id. at 759 (emphasis added) (capitalization adapted).

Thus Russell moves abortion "felony-murder" into the context of transferred malice: the abortion was intended to do (lethal) mischief to one individual, the actual or supposed unborn child, but resulted in (lethal) mischief to another, the (actual or supposed) mother: result, murder. He continues on p. 760:

> [margin note: *Murder in attempting to procure an abortion*] So, where a person gave medicine to a woman to procure an abortion [fn. 1 Hale, 429], and where a person put skewers into the womb of a woman for the same purpose [fn. Tinckler's case, 1 East. P. C. c. 5, s. 17, p. 230, and s. 124, p. 354], by which in both cases the women were killed, these acts were held clearly to be murder; for, though the death of the women was not intended, the acts were of a nature deliberate and malicious, and necessarily attended with great danger to the persons on whom they were practised.

Id. at 760.

"The persons on whom they were practised" included, it seems, both the women and the unborn children they were or were believed to be carrying.

45 *See infra* text near note 170.
46 *See* GERMAIN GRISEZ, ABORTION: THE MYTHS, THE REALITIES, AND THE ARGUMENTS 382–92, 395, 434 (1970).
47 A 1971 memorandum circulated among *Roe*'s legal team said Means's "conclusions sometimes strain credibility" and "fudge" the history but "preserve the guise of impartial scholarship while advancing the proper ideological goals." DELLAPENNA, *infra* note 73, at 143–44, 683–84.
48 *Roe*, 410 U.S. at 140–41.
49 50 Mass. (9 Met.) 263, 267 (1845). The judgment, at 267, alludes in passing to Hall v. Hancock, in which the common-law rule reaffirmed in *Parker* was foundational in the unsuccessful argument (of Metcalf) for the appellant defendant, and was dealt with by Chief Justice Shaw thus: "We are also of opinion, that the distinction between a woman being pregnant, and being quick with child, is applicable mainly if not exclusively to criminal cases; and that it does not apply to cases of descents, devises and other gifts; and that, generally, a child will be considered in being, from conception to the time of its birth, in all cases where it will be for the benefit of such child to be so considered."

Hall v. Hancock, 32 Mass. (15 Pick.) 255, 257–58 (1834).
50 Roe v. Wade, 410 U.S. 113, 134 (1973).
51 *Parker*, 50 Mass. (9 Met.) at 265.

52 Massachusetts had made the question moot (for future litigation) on January 31, 1845, by a statute prohibiting any attempt to "procure the miscarriage of a woman." *An Act to Punish Unlawful Attempts to Cause Abortion*, ch. 27, Mass. Acts 406 (1845).

53 The Massachusetts Penal Code Commissioners who reported in February 1844, REPORT OF THE PENAL CODE OF MASSACHUSETTS (Boston 1844), had made it clear that, *in the common law* as they understood it, indictability or criminal liability for abortion did not depend on whether the woman was or was not "quick" with child. Their proposal retained the term "quick" only in relation to severity of punishment. Nothing related to maternal *perceptions* of the life and motion of the child made any appearance in their discussion, *id.*, ch. VII, at 19–20, of the common law, and even the word "quicken" appeared in that discussion only in relation to Bracton, where they twice use "quickened" to translate his word *animatum*. Nor is "quick[en]" part of their proposed definition of the offence of abortion, which prohibits the action of any one who:

> maliciously, without lawful justification, *with intent to cause the miscarriage of a woman then with child*, administers to her, or causes or procures to be administered to or taken by her, or knowingly aids or assists in administering to her, or causing or procuring to be administered to or taken by her, any poison or noxious thing, or shall maliciously use any instrument or other means with like intent. . . .

Id., ch. XIII at 1 (emphasis added).

The commissioners then go out of their way to re-emphasize that their provision states what they believe to be the existing common law: both in criminalizing elective abortion at all stages of pregnancy and in respecting the mother's need to terminate a pregnancy that threatens her life. For footnote (a) says:

> *This is a crime by the common law.* (Deac[on] Cr. Law [London 1831], 9; 1 Russ[ell *On Crime*,] 796, 8th Ed.[by Daniel Davis, S-G Mass., 1841]; 3 Chit[ty], Cr. Law, 798 [Mass. 1841]; [Daniel] Davis's Justice[s of the Peace, Boston 1828] 262; Bang's C[ase] 9 Mass, R. 387 [181]).... Where the potion is given, or other means of causing abortion are used, by a surgeon, *for the purpose of saving the life of the woman*, the case is free of malice and has a lawful justification, and so does not come within the above provision.

Id. n.(a) (emphases added).

Thus, at the time of Chief Justice Shaw's opinion in *Parker*, a significant section of legal opinion considered that the common law's type [III] rule was not tied to "quick with child" (let alone "quickening") but was concerned only with the existence of a child capable of being killed in the womb. The commissioners in effect sided with those such as Daniel Davis, for more than thirty years solicitor general of Massachusetts, who came to think that the *Bangs* ruling, Commonwealth v. Bangs, 9 Mass. 387 (1812), erred in requiring that indictments for abortion allege that the woman was quick with child. *See* DANIEL DAVIS, PRECEDENTS OF INDICTMENTS: TO WHICH IS PREFIXED A CONCISE TREATISE UPON THE OFFICE AND DUTY OF GRAND JURORS 34 n.3 (Boston, 1831) ("There is no authority referred to in [*Bangs*] . . ."); *id.* at 36 n.1 (form of indictment for administering savin-based drug to a woman "with child but not quick with child" with intent to procure miscarriage, taken

from 3 Chitty, *Criminal Law* *798 "upon the presumption that the facts therein stated would amount to a misdemeanour at common law.").
54 *Parker*, 50 Mass. (9 Met.) at 267. The only authority that Shaw finds identifying "quick with child" with "quickened" in the maternal-perceptions sense is *Phillips* (*infra* note 62), interpreting "quick with child" "in the construction of this [English] statute."
55 *Id.* at 266, 268.
56 *See supra* at note 49; Commonwealth v. Wood, 77 Mass. (11 Gray) 85 (1858).
57 Mills v. Commonwealth, 13 Pa. 631, 632–33 (1850); State v. Moore, 25 Iowa 128, 135 (1868).
58 State v. Cooper, 22 N.J.L. (2 Zab.) 52, 54 (1849).
59 Smith v. State, 33 Me. 48, 51 (1851).
60 *Infra* note 90 (quoting State v. Murphy, 27 N.J.L. 112 (N.J. 1858)).
61 *Infra* note 200.
62 Scientists into the seventeenth century relied on ARISTOTLE, HISTORIA ANIMALIUM 7.3.583b (cited by *Roe* at 133 in its muddled footnote 22) for the view that, at approximately forty days (at least for males) this mass becomes articulated and the first fetal movement occurs. (So too Blackstone's "able to stir in the womb.") Bracton probably held the view Aquinas contemporaneously articulated in SUMMA CONTRA GENTILES II c. 89, summarized in JOHN FINNIS, AQUINAS: MORAL, POLITICAL AND LEGAL THEORY 186 (1998): It takes about six weeks for generation to yield a body sufficiently elaborated (*complexionatum*) and organized (*organizatum*) for animation (receiving the rational, human soul). For the most widely read treatment contemporaneous with both Bracton and Aquinas, see *infra* note 67.
63 *Infra* note 89.
64 *Supra* section I.A.3.b.
65 Crucial in fomenting if not initiating the final-phase confusion was Rex v. Phillips (1811) 3 Camp. 73, 77, 170 Eng. Rep. 1310. This seems to have been the first reported case of an indictment under that section of the 1803 English statute 43 Geo. III c. 58, which made abortion of a woman quick with child a capital offense. The medical witnesses, significantly, "differed as to the time when the foetus may be stated to be quick, and to have a distinct existence," and the woman swore "that she had not felt the child move within her before taking the [abortifacient] medicine, and that she was not then quick with child." The medical witnesses, despite their own (differing) medical views, "all agreed that in common understanding, a woman is not considered to be quick with child till she has herself felt the child alive and quick within her, which happens with different women in different stages of pregnancy, although most usually about the fifteenth or sixteenth week after conception." The trial judge, Lawrence J., said that this was the interpretation that must be put on the words *quick with child* IN THE STATUTE; and as the woman in this case had not felt the child alive within her before taking the medicine—he directed an acquittal." The full account of the case in JOHN. A. PARIS & JOHN FONBLANQUE, 3 MEDICAL JURISPRUDENCE 86–90 (1823) (a treatise cited by counsel for the appellant in Hall v. Hancock) is followed immediately by the comment (90): "It cannot be necessary here to repeat that the popular idea of quick or not quick with child is founded in error." An edition of Campbell's Nisi Prius reports including *Phillips* was published in New York and Charleston, South Carolina, in 1821.

66 See R. v. Wycherley (1838) 173 Eng. Rep. 486, 8 C. & P. 263 (approved in FRANCIS WHARTON, A TREATISE ON THE CRIMINAL LAW OF THE UNITED STATES 457 (2d ed. 1852)). Even *Wycherley*, however, having emphasized the primacy of sense i (as to a capitally condemned pregnant woman's right to reprieve during pregnancy), confuses sense ii with iii. Bracton had stated the reprieve principle in terms of pregnancy: "If a woman has been condemned for a crime and is pregnant, execution of sentence is sometimes deferred after judgment rendered until she has given birth." 2 BRACTON ON THE LAWS AND CUSTOMS OF ENGLAND 429 (Thorne trans., 1968) (emphasis added). On such a "plea of pregnancy," the charge to the jury of matrons came to be expressed as determining whether the condemned was "quick with child," and in Blackstone's view the question evidently was not whether the mother or child had quickened in sense 3, but whether the child was quick in sense 2 such that, without reliance upon the mother's testimony or the use of ultrasound or even a stethoscope, they could determine that there was present a *living* (not dead) child. See BLACKSTONE, 4 COMMENTARIES, *supra* note 32, at 395: "if they bring in their verdict *quick with child* (for barely, with child, *unless it be alive in the womb*, is not sufficient) execution shall be stayed..." (emphasis added). Hale, perhaps an outlier on this matter, had stated that the jury of matrons must find the condemned woman "with child of a quick child," and at the very end of the discussion of the peculiar case where she is mistakenly found to be in that condition but later becomes pregnant Hale indicates, in Latin, that the *foetus* is *vitalis* usually about 16–18 weeks though as medical opinions indicate it may be significantly earlier. See HALE, H.P.C., *supra* note 33, at 368–69.

67 What Bracton meant by "formed and animated/ensouled" is made clear by the extremely influential encyclopedic work composed in the same decades as his own treatise on English law: *On the Properties of Things* [*De Proprietatibus Rerum*] by Bracton's contemporary Bartholomaeus Anglicus (between 1230 and 1250); the English translation made by John Trevisa in 1398/99 was first printed in 1497 and again in 1582 (thus linking Bracton's time and culture with Coke's): we can read the 1398/99 translation in modernized spelling in 1 ON THE PROPERTIES OF THINGS: JOHN TREVISA'S TRANSLATION OF "BARTHOLOMAEUS ANGLICUS DE PROPRIETATIBUS RERUM": A CRITICAL TEXT 296–97 (Oxford, 1975) (bk. 6, on the creation of the infant [*creatione Infantis*]):

> The child is bred forth...in four degrees. The first is when the seed has a milk-like appearance. The second is when the seed is worked into a lump of blood (with the liver, heart and brain as yet having no distinct shape). The third is when the heart, brain and liver are shaped [*formatis*], and the other or external members [head, face, arms, hands, fingers, legs, feet and toes] are yet to be shaped and distinguished. The last degree is when all the external members are completely shaped [*formantur*]. And *when the body is thus made and shaped* [*organizato*] *with members and limbs, and disposed to receive the soul* [*ad susceptionem animae*]*, then it receives soul and life* [*vivificat*]*, and begins to move itself* [*incipit se movere*] and sprawl with its feet and hands [better: kick with its feet: *peditu calcitrare*....]
>
> In the degree of milk it remains seven (7) days; in the degree of blood it remains nine (9) days; in the degree of a lump of blood or unformed flesh

it remains twelve (12) days; and *in the fourth degree, when all its members are fully formed, it remains eighteen (18) days....*

So from the day of conception to the day of complete disposition or formation [completionis] and first life of the child [vivificationis fetus] is forty-six days. (emphases added).

At this point, the work refers to the biblical-theological significance that St. Augustine of Hippo, over eight centuries earlier, had found in the fact that the period of human formation consummated by animation was thus of forty-six days (six-and-a half weeks) duration.

68 *See* Coke's contemporary WILLIAM SHAKESPEARE, LOVE'S LABORS LOST (c. 1593), V.ii.669–70, 673–74: "Fellow Hector, she is gone! She is *two months* on her way!... She's *quick*; the child brags in her belly already. 'Tis yours." (emphasis added). CRYSTAL & CRYSTAL, SHAKESPEARE'S WORDS: A GLOSSARY & LANGUAGE COMPANION 358 (2002) (*quick*: pregnant, with child; 490: *on one's way*: pregnant).

69 *See, e.g., Embryo, in* EPHRAIM CHAMBERS, CYCLOPAEDIA (1728) (defining "embryo" as the beginning of an "animal" before it has "received all the Dispositions of Parts necessary to become animated: which is supposed to happen to a Man on the 42nd day"); *see also id., Animation*:

Animation, signifies the informing of an animal Body with a Soul. Thus, the Foetus in the Womb is said to come to its *Animation* when it begins to act as a true Animal; or after the Female that bears it is quick, as the common way of Expression is. See FOETUS. The Common opinion is that this happens about 40 days after conception. But *Jer. Florentinus*, in a Latin treatise, *Homo Dubius, Sive de Baptismo Abortivorum*, shows this to be very precarious.

Since Florentinus's cited treatise argued embryologically that children are fully human persons as from conception, Chambers is warning readers that the "common opinion" presupposed by Bracton and Coke may move, under pressure of evidence, toward recognizing animation/personhood from conception.

Tracking Bartholomaeus Anglicus's treatise, and probably the most available source of *popular* information (and misinformation) about the child's ante-natal formation, in the period 1684 to c. 1840, was the pseudonymous work misleadingly entitled *Aristotle's Masterpiece*, first published in London in 1684 and going into hundreds of editions on both sides of the Atlantic. Early American editions usually resemble ARISTOTLE'S COMPLETE MASTERPIECE...DISPLAYING THE SECRETS OF NATURE IN THE GENERATION OF MAN, 44–46 (Worcester [Mass.] 1795), near-identical to pp. 43–44 of the same title printed in London in 1702:

How the Child...groweth up in the Womb of the Mother, after Conception.... As to the formation of the child, it is to be noted, that after coition the seed lies warm in the womb for SIX DAYS without any visible alteration.... In THREE DAYS after it is altered from the quality of thick milk or butter, and it becomes blood, or at least resembles it in colour, nature having now begun to work upon it. In the NEXT SIX DAYS following, that blood begins to be united into one body, grows hard, and becomes a little quantity, and to appear a round lump. And as the first creation of the earth was void, and without form, so in this creating work of divine power in the womb, THIS SHAPELESS EMBRIO lies like the first mass [*scil.* of the universe]. But IN TWO DAYS AFTER, the principal members are formed by the plastic power of nature.... THREE DAYS AFTER the other members are formed.... FOUR DAYS AFTER THAT, the several members of the whole body appear, and as nature requires, they conjunctly and separately do receive their perfection. And so in the appointed time, the whole creation hath that essence which it ought to have in the perfection of it, receiving from God A LIVING SOUL, therewith putting into his nostrils THE BREATH OF LIFE. Thus have I shown the whole operations of nature in the formation of the child in the womb.... By some others more briefly, but to the same purpose, the forming of the child in the womb of its mother is thus described; THREE DAYS in the milk, THREE DAYS in the blood, TWELVE DAYS FROM THE FLESH, and EIGHTEEN THE MEMBERS, and FORTY DAYS AFTERWARDS the child is inspired with life, being endued with an immortal living soul.

70 *Roe*, 410 U.S. at 135 n. 26 (citing "Means II," where the passages relied on by *Roe* are at 345–48).

71 (1601) Gouldsb. 176, 75 Eng. Rep. 1075, 1076. Chief Justice Popham and Justice Fenner authoritatively stated the rule that it is [II] murder to strike a woman "great with child" (pregnant) if the child is born living but succumbs from injuries that can "be proved" to have been caused by the battery with a view to causing a miscarriage. The Court of King's Bench went on to emphasize the evidential rationale of the rule, by observing that "when it is born living, and the wounds appear in his body, and then he die, the Batteror may be arraigned of murder, *for now it may be proved whether these wounds were the cause of the death or not*, and for that if it be found, he shall be condemned" [of [II] murder].

72 Mark S. Scott, *Quickening in the Common Law: The Legal Precedent* Roe *Attempted and Failed to Use*, 1 MICH. L. & POL'Y REV. 199 (1996) makes telling criticisms of *Roe* but errs (a) in accepting with little or no nuance that "quick" always referred to "quickening" in the sense deployed in *Roe*; (b) in interpreting [I] murder of the mother by abortion and [II] murder by abortion of the child-born-alive as deploying a "retroactive attribution of humanness" (p. 235) (back to the point of quickening, Scott says; but neither [I] nor [II] treats "quick with child" as a necessary condition of indictability). In truth, Coke and Hale were clear that the unborn child is human all the way through, or at least from completed formation c. day 40; a fiction such as retroactive attribution is foreign to their line of thought, and in no way compelled by Coke's phrase "accounted a reasonable creature, *in rerum natura*, when it is born alive"; that phrase conveys, rather, that from that point on any intentionally death-dealing act will be murder without having to fulfill any condition subsequent (other than the normal year-and-a-day rule)—so from birth the child will be treated (accounted) like everyone else, viz., as being not only a reasonable creature (as it was all along, at least from formation and animation) but also *in rerum natura*, in the ordinary social world.

73 Means II more or less expressly (at 344) and *Roe* by innuendo (at 135 n.26) claim that *Sims* either opposes or does not imply/assume rule [III], and that Coke invented it

(sometime in the thirty-three years between 1601 and his death in 1634) in 3 Inst. 50 (first published 1644). Means and *Roe* ignore all the evidence that [III] abortion was an indictable offense fairly often prosecuted at common law: JOHN KEOWN, ABORTION, DOCTORS AND THE LAW, 6–9 (1988), points to R. v. Lichefeld (1505), R. v. Webb (1602), R. v. Beare (1732); JOSEPH W. DELLAPENNA, DISPELLING THE MYTHS OF ABORTION HISTORY 193 (2006) gives a corrected translation of Webb; at 202 cites further sixteenth-century [III] abortion convictions from 1530/31 and 1581 (twice); and at 194 gives evidence that "English courts prosecuted abortions fairly routinely under the early Stuarts" (before Coke's death), citing abortion [III] convictions in 1615, 1616 (twice), 1617, and 1622, and indictments recorded without indication of outcome in 1615, 1618 and 1629.

74 HALE, H.P.C, *supra* note 33, at 429–30.
75 MATTHEW HALE, PLEAS OF THE CROWN, OR A METHODICAL SUMMARY OF THE PRINCIPAL MATTERS RELATING TO THAT SUBJECT, 53 (1678):
>   If a Woman quick with Child take a potion to kill it, and accordingly [III] it is destroyed without being born alive, a great misprision but no Felony; but [II] if born alive and after dies of that potion, it is Murder.

Both this work and the better known *History* were published posthumously (this work in 1678, the *History* in 1736), and it cannot now be determined which gave Hale's final view of [II] and [III].

76 Hawkins had led the way: WILLIAM HAWKINS, 1 PLEAS OF THE CROWN 80 (1716), where abortion is treated in the chapter on Murder:
>   *Sect.* 15. As to the third Point, *viz.,* Who are SUCH PERSONS BY KILLING OF WHOM A MAN MAY COMMIT MURDER; it is agreed, that the malicious Killing of any Person, whatsoever Nation or Religion he be of, or of whatsoever Crime arainted, is Murder. *Sect.* 16. And it was anciently holden, that [III] the causing of an Abortion by giving a Potion to, or striking, a Woman big with Child, was Murder: but at this Day, it is said to be a great Misprision only, and not Murder, unless [II] the Child be born alive, and die thereof, in which Case it seems clearly to be Murder, notwithstanding some Opinions [*scil.* Hale] to the contrary.

77 Means II at 363.
78 DELLAPENNA, *supra* note 70, at 206 n.184, cites convictions in 1281, 1288, 1589, 1591 and 1600, besides the case Hale himself tried at assize in 1670, and acquittals in 1249, 1292, 1313, 1330 and 1652.
79 As to the shift from the "ancient law" (stated in Bracton) to Blackstone's "present" law (stated by Coke): C'Zar Bernstein, *Fetal Personhood and the Original Meanings of "Person,"* 26 TEX. REV. L. & POL. __ (2022), https://papers.ssrn.com/sol3/papers.cfm?abstract_id=3870441, asserts at 69 that by this shift "the unborn were removed from the category of persons in being, and were therefore outside the protection of the law against homicide." But there is no trace of shift from "the unborn are persons" to "the unborn are not existing persons"; rather, the shift is in legal opinion about the degree of safely cognizable injustice involved in acts lethally impacting on the child *in ventre sa mere*, whether acts of strangers to whom the child was invisible, or of the mother involved intimately with it. Bernstein's claim about the shift is refuted also by

HAWKINS, 1 PLEAS OF THE CROWN 80—a leading work intermediate between Coke and Blackstone—whose treatment of abortion, in the chapter on Murder, is quoted in note 76 supra.

There is in Hawkins (like the other classical common-law authorities) not the slightest suggestion that unborn children were shifted from being—as "anciently holden"—"Persons by killing of whom a Man may commit Murder" to being non-persons. Rather, with the changed liability-rule, they were persons in a new liability-category: persons by killing of whom a man commits murder if—however long after his malicious actions—they succumb from his actions after living outside the womb for however short a time, while if they do not live outside the womb the doer of those same actions is guilty of a lesser but still near-capital "great misprision" (less than capital felony but more than misdemeanor).

In other classic common-law authorities, this sub-category of persons, a sub-category forged in tandem with the newly nuanced liability rule, is marked by saying that they are not persons *in rerum natura* (literally, "in the nature of things," idiomatically more like "in 'reality,'" meaning the visibly shared world, the ordinary world) or *in esse* (same meaning idiomatically; literally, "in being/existence"). Keeping these phrases in the foreign tongue signaled the presence of a fiction deployed in service of the moral and/or pragmatic judgment that justice would be better served by introducing the acknowledgement of appropriate difference in the severity of the crime and its fitting scale of punishment, and the matching sub-category of persons: rational creatures like the rest of us, but not yet sharing our public world, publicly distinct from and partly inter-dependent with their mothers, who are persons whom one can point to and name.

80 *See supra* pp. 134–36.
81 Further compelling evidence that the standard pre-1800 common-legal understanding of "quick with child" was not dependent on a mid-pregnancy, maternally felt "quickening" is Blackstone's treatment of the plea of pregnancy in stay of execution: "the judge must direct a jury of twelve matrons or discreet women to inquire the fact: and if they bring in their verdict *quick with child* (for barely, *with child,* UNLESS IT BE ALIVE IN THE WOMB, is not sufficient) execution shall be stayed generally till the next session…" 4 COMMENTARIES, *supra* note 32, at 395. So she is quick with child if the special jury can detect fetal *life*. (The problem of the dead fetus, not to mention that of the mole or tumor, has a large part in the evidentiary caution that made successful prosecution for elective abortion difficult whatever the stage of gestation at which the unlawful acts charged were done.) *See also* HAWKINS, 2 PLEAS OF THE CROWN 464 (1721), where the final sentence of the discussion of the plea is: "Also it is said both by *Staundforde* and *Coke,* that a Woman can have no Advantage from being found with Child unless she be found quick with Child." The footnote to this sentence cites ten authorities (treatises and abridgements), but the only two quotations are: "it is expressly said, that the Inquiry was whether the Woman were *enseint* [pregnant] with A LIVE CHILD or not" and "'tis said only, That the Woman was found *enseint* or pregnant." Likewise, American criminal-law treatises: see for example, CONDUCTOR GENERALIS, 214 (New York, 1749) ("Jury of Matrons. You the Fore-woman of this jury shall swear, That you shall search the Prisoner at the Bar, whether she be quick with Child OF A LIVING CHILD…"); 371 ("You as Fore-

Matron of this Jury, shall swear, that you shall search and try the Prisoner at the Bar, whether she be quick with Child of a QUICK CHILD...."); 372 ("[B]ut if they find that she is not quick with Child of a quick Child, she shall be hanged presently, for it will not avail her to be young with Child.") (emphases added).

82 Roe v. Wade, 410 U.S. 113, 132 (1973).
83 The absurdity of the argument *Roe* is developing here is only compounded by the fact that its footnote 23 quotes, besides Thorne, the Twiss translation, "if... formed and animated, and particularly if it be animated."
84 22 N.J.L. (2 Zab.) 52, 54 (1849) (cited in *Roe*, 410 U.S. at 135 n.27).
85 *Id.* at 53–54.
86 *Cooper*, 22 N.J.L. at 54. The court, quoting Bracton's line, rightly admitted that it "at first view might seem to favor a different conclusion." *Id.* at 55. Then, assuming precisely what is here in dispute (the sense of "quick with child"), the court appealed to "the unanimous concurrence of all authorities, that that offence could not be committed unless the child had quickened." *Id.* The court relies on Commonwealth v. Parker while failing to note that on the very point for which the New Jersey court is arguing, the Massachusetts court declined to state an opinion. *See id.* at 57. Thus throughout its argumentation the New Jersey court begs the very question left open by *Parker* and *assumed* precisely what needed to be demonstrated, *viz.* that "quick with child" at common law meant "with sense (3) quickened child" rather than "with live child" or perhaps even "with child."
87 *See id.* at 54 ("It is not material whether, speaking with physiological accuracy, life may be said to commence at the moment of quickening, or at the moment of conception.... *In contemplation of law* life commences at the moment of quickening.").
88 *See id.* at 56–57. But it entirely fails to acknowledge the authoritative statements of principle, collected in Hall v. Hancock, undergirding those protections. The handling of authorities is uncertain throughout; for example, Blackstone, 4 COMMENTARIES 395 is cited at 57 to support the claims that "quick with child" and "with quick child" are synonymous, that both phrases "import that the child had quickened in the womb," and that that was when "the life of the infant, in contemplation of law, had commenced." In fact, though Blackstone there treats "quick with child" and "the child was quick" as equivalent, he does use "quickened" or "quickening," and seems most concerned with the question whether the child is or alive ("quick") rather than dead: see *supra* notes 66, 81.
89 *Id.* at 58 (finding "legislative enactments" "far better" on "this... debatable" matter, when courts must give "the accused" the benefit of "reasonable doubt").
90 Act for the Punishment of Crimes (1846, s. 103 Supp., enacted March 1st 1849 (Session Laws 1849, po.199)); State v. Murphy, 27 N.J.L. 112, 114 (1858) ("The statute... was cotemporaneous [*sic*] with that decision [*Cooper*]. An examination of its provisions will show clearly that the mischief designed to be remedied by the statute was the supposed defect in the common law developed in the case of The State v. Cooper."). Against *Roe*'s faulty history, *Cooper* itself clearly confirmed that common law protected the child's right long before "viability," *no later* than the perception of movement four or five months before birth, during which time any "act tending to its destruction" was an indictable offense, a homicide. *See Cooper*, 22 N.J.L. at 56, 58, 55. Note that the Chief Justice, stating the opinion of the court in

Murphy, says—with some roughness of phrasing—that the common law was defective in that it was concerned entirely with the life of the unborn child, *not the health of the mother*; so the statute, by contrast, treats the acts of the abortionist as having the same degree of culpability whether or not they harm or kill the child, whether or not "it has quickened," and so also whether or not the mother had actually ingested the abortifacient supplied by the appellant defendant abortionist, the degree of culpability and applicable scale of punishment under the statute is affected only if the mother dies. See *Murphy*, 27 N.J.L. at 114. (In fact, of course, the 1849 legislation was very much concerned with the life of the child, too: as noted in the text above, offenses under it were committed only if the woman was in fact "then pregnant with child.")

91 PHILIP A. RAFFERTY, *ROE V WADE*: THE BIRTH OF A CONSTITUTIONAL RIGHT 179–180 (1992) argues that it is at best unproven that the common law ever made proof of quickening a criterion of criminal liability, and that the thesis that it did "originally was articulated in the nineteenth century in certain American appellate opinions...." Be that as it may, it was understandable, though not logically ineluctable, that the fact that the introduction—beginning with Lord Ellenborough's Act, 43 Geo. 3 c. 58 (1803)—of statutory type-[III] prohibitions of abortion from conception was accompanied in some jurisdictions (such as England under that Act) of different punishments depending on whether or not the woman was "quick with child" or "with quick child" had the side effect that in the abortion context the word "quick" came quite generally to be assimilated to "quickened," "quickening," and cognates. For the American jurisdictions with such differentiation of penalties, see James S. Witherspoon, *Reexamining* Roe: *Nineteenth-Century Abortion Statutes and the Fourteenth Amendment*, 17 ST. MARY'S L.J. 29, 34–36 (1985).

92 *See, e.g.*, THEODRIC ROMEYN BECK & JOHN B. BECK, 1 ELEMENTS OF MEDICAL JURISPRUDENCE 464–66, 468 (12th ed. Philadelphia, 1863) ("[N]o other doctrine appears to be consonant with reason or physiology, but that which admits the embryo to possess vitality from the very moment of conception.... [W]e must consider those laws which exempt from punishment the crime of producing abortion at an early period of gestation, as immoral and unjust."); WILLIAM GUY, PRINCIPLES OF MEDICAL JURISPRUDENCE 133–34 (1st Am. ed. 1845) ("[T]he absurd distinction formerly made between women quick and *not* quick is done away with...").

93 BECK & BECK, *supra* note 92, at 466–68 (calling the six-week criterion "absurd," "injurious," and "wholly unsupported either by argument or evidence," and going on to denounce as "no less absurd" the "popular belief" and laws, including English and, implicitly, American law, "denying to the foetus any vitality until after the time of quickening" by "consider[ing] life not to commence before the infant is able to stir in its mother's womb," and declaring (against *both* understandings of "quick/quickening") that non-perception of "motions" is "no proof whatever that such motions do not exist.").

94 *Cf.* FINNIS, *supra* note 62, at 186 (explaining why, had Aquinas "known of the extremely elaborate and specifically organized structure of the sperm and the ovum ... and the [embryo's] typical, wholly continuous self-directed growth and development ... from the moment of insemination of the ovum," he would have located "personhood {*personalitas*: ScG IV c. 44 n.3}" at conception).

95 THOMAS PERCIVAL, MEDICAL ETHICS 135–36 (Chauncey D. Leake ed., 1975) (1803), *quoted in* Ohio's 1867 S. Comm., *infra* note 115.
96 *See* BECK & BECK, *supra* note 92; JOHN KEOWN, ABORTION, DOCTORS, AND THE LAW 23–24, 38–39, 179–80 (1988) (citing treatises).
97 *Roe*, 410 U.S. at 141 (citing 12 TRANSACTIONS OF THE AMERICAN MEDICAL ASSOCIATION 73–78 (1859)).
98 WHARTON, *supra* note 66, at 308 (1846); 2 WHARTON at 653 (6th ed. 1868) ("It has been said that [abortion] is not an indictable offence…unless the mother is *quick* with child, though such a distinction, it is submitted, is neither in accordance with medical experience, nor with the principles of the common law. The civil rights of an infant in *ventre sa mere* are equally respected at every period of gestation."); *see also* J.P. BISHOP, COMMENTARIES ON THE CRIMINAL LAW § 386 (2d ed. 1858) (reviewing cases and preferring the view that abortion is indictable at common law without allegation that the mother was quick with child).
99 5 TRANSACTIONS OF THE MAINE MEDICAL ASSOCIATION 38 (1869).
100 *See infra* section I.B.1.
101 *See* DELLAPENNA, *supra* note 73, at 213–28 (2006) (concluding "that English law regarding abortion was fully received in the [American] colonies, and that the purported 'common law liberty to abort' is a myth"); *see also id.* at 263–451 (for all aspects from Independence down to c. 1900).
102 Limitation to post-"quickening" attempts and abortions was rejected by the courts in Pennsylvania and Iowa. *See* Mills v. Commonwealth, 13 Pa. 631, 632–33 (1850); State v. Moore, 25 Iowa 128, 135 (1868).
103 *Parker*, 50 Mass. (9 Met.) at 265. Hale puts it more straightforwardly: the abortifacient is given "*unlawfully to destroy her child within her*, and therefore he that gives a potion to this end, must take the hazard, and if it kill the mother, it is murder." *R. v. Anonymous* (1670), *reported and endorsed in* HALE, H.P.C., *supra* note 33, at 429–30 (emphasis added); the passage is cited by Blackstone to verify his own statement, in which abortion is his third example of felony-murder: "And if one intends to do another felony, and undesignedly kills a man, this is murder.…And so, if one gives A WOMAN WITH CHILD a medicine to procure abortion, and it operates so violently as to kill the woman, this is murder in the person who gave it." 4 COMMENTARIES, *supra* note 32, at *200–01.
104 That is clearly stated by Blackstone: See the previous footnote.
105 That too is clearly stated by Blackstone. *See* 4 COMMENTARIES 198, quoted *supra* text at note 32. Like [I] (the abortion quasi-felony murder of the mother), [II] was not questioned by any American authority.
106 HAWKINS, 1 PLEAS OF THE CROWN 262 (6th ed. 1788).
107 *See* Witherspoon, *supra* note 91, at 33.
108 *See id.* at 48.
109 *See id.* at 34 (finding, however, that in Nebraska, and possibly Louisiana, the statutory prohibition did not at that time extend to abortion by use of instruments). The various shifting arguments made by Aaron Tang, *The Originalist Case for an Abortion Middle Ground*, https://papers.ssrn.com/sol3/papers.cfm?abstract_id=3921358, to the effect that "28" [or 27] here should read "16" [or 15] are refuted in all their strongly different versions from September 13 to September 30, 2021, by the authors of this

chapter in *Indictability of Early Abortion c. 1868*, https://papers.ssrn.com/sol3/papers.cfm?abstract_id=3940378. The latter identifies over fifty serious historical errors in the relevant forty pages of Tang's many-times-revised article; the replies he incorporated in his latest revisions, on October 11 and December 15, 2021, contest none of the fifty-plus identified errors directly, accept many of our charges silently, indefensibly ignore many, confess to a couple, and replace some abandoned errors with new ones the answers to which will easily be supplied by readers of the debate. (These counts of states do not include the territories of Washington (1854), Colorado (1861), Montana (1864), Idaho (1864), and Wyoming (probably 1864, alternatively 1869), which from the dates just mentioned had statutes criminalizing abortion at all stages of gestation.)

110 Act of Jan. 19, 1872, 1872 D.C. ACTS 26–29; Act of Mar. 3, 1899, ch. 429, tit. 1, ch. 2, § 8, 30 STAT. 1253–54 (1899).

111 *See* Act of Apr. 28, 1868, ch. 430, 1868 N.Y. LAWS 856–68; Act of May 6, 1869, ch. 631 1869 N.Y. LAWS 1502–03.

112 *See* Act of Feb. 23, 1866, 1866 ALA. PEN. CODE, tit. 1, ch. 5, § 64, at 31 (*codified* ALA. CODE § 3605 (1867)).

113 *See* Act of Nov. 21, 1867, no 57, 1867 VT. ACTS 64–66.

114 *See* Act of Aug. 6, 1868, ch. 1637, no. 13, ch. 3 §§ 10–11, ch. 8, §§ 9–11, 1868 FLA. LAWS 64, 97; Act of Feb. 28, 1867, 1867 ILL. LAWS 89; Act of Apr. 13, 1867, 1867 OHIO LAWS 135–36.

115 1867 OHIO SEN. J. APP'X 233. Yet the law proposed by the committee and enacted by the legislature aligned with none of the three elements in *Roe*'s notion (at 157 n.54) that acknowledging and acting on the personhood of the unborn requires that the woman be treated as a principal or accomplice, that abortion be punished as murder, and that it be prohibited even when medically necessary to save the life of the mother.

116 *See supra* note 109.

117 See John Keown, *Back to the Future of Abortion Law: Roe's Rejection of America's History and Traditions*, 22 ISSUES L. & MED. 3 (2006).

118 Santa Clara County v. S. Pac. R.R. Co., 18 F. 385, 397 (C.C.D. Cal. 1883) (opinion of Field, J.), *aff'd*, 118 U.S. 394 (1886).

119 *Id.* (quoting Trs. of Dartmouth Coll. v. Woodward, 17 U.S. (4 Wheat.) 518, 644–45 (1819) (opinion of Marshall, C.J.)). In applying this by assessing what falls "within the words of the rule" (the Equal Protection Clause), recall that the ratification in 1868 was not by "the American people" but by legislatures, that these included many lawyers whose basic instruction in legal language was through studying Blackstone, and that legislative reforms to remove common-law criminal law's reference to "quick with child" or "quickening" were in full swing, had prevailed in more than two-thirds of the states and all the territories, and would within fifteen years be virtually universal.

120 *Dartmouth College*, 17 U.S. (4 Wheat.) at 644.

121 *See id.* at 645.

122 *Id.*

123 *See, e.g.*, McDonald v. City of Chicago, 561 U.S. 742, 787 (2010) (rejecting argument that "the scope of the Second Amendment right is defined by the immediate threat that led to the inclusion of that right in the Bill of Rights").

124 *See* Michael Stokes Paulsen, *The Plausibility of Personhood*, 74 OHIO ST. L.J. 13, 23 n.34 (2013) (explaining the argument that the unborn should be held to enjoy

constitutional protection "for the same interpretive methodological reason that corporations properly can be understood as legal persons—that that was conventional term-of-art legal usage, and thus bears heavily on what the legal meaning of the term 'person' was at the time") (emphases omitted).

125 *See supra* section I.A.

126 That reasoning synthesizes the judicial rationale of several restrictive assumptions about the Equal Protection Clause between 1871 and 1888. *See, e.g.*, Insurance Co. v. New Orleans, 13 F. Cas. 67, 68 (C.C.D. La. 1870) (holding that corporations are not Fourteenth Amendment persons); Bradwell v. State, 83 U.S. 130, 139 (1872) (females and the practice of law); Bartemeyer v. Iowa, 85 U.S. 129, 133 (1873); The Slaughter-House Cases, 83 U.S. 36, 81 (1872) ("We doubt very much whether any action of a State not directed by way of discrimination against the negroes as a class, or on account of their race, will ever be held to come within the purview of [the Equal Protection Clause]."); Strauder v. West Virginia, 100 U.S. 303, 304 (1879); The Civil Rights Cases, 109 U.S. 3 (1883); Pembina Consol. Silver Mining & Milling Co. v. Pennsylvania, 125 U.S. 181, 188–89 (1888) (finding that Fourteenth Amendment equal protection is concerned with protecting any class "singled out as a special subject for discriminating and hostile legislation"). For example, the litigants in *Bradwell*, fighting discrimination against women practicing law, appealed to the Amendment's first sentence but never its Equal Protection Clause. That is inexplicable except on the basis of early assumptions about that Clause's application that would also have blocked early appeals to the Clause by those seeking to bolster fetal protections. These blocking assumptions, when articulated by courts, proved to concern not the meaning of "any person" but the import of "deny...the equal protection of the laws." Some of these restrictions were soon rejected; others lingered more or less unchallenged for over a century. *See* John Finnis, *Unborn Persons: Why Equal Protection Slept 102 Years*, FIRST THINGS (Mar. 30, 2021), www.firstthings.com/web-exclusives/2021/03/unborn-persons-why-equal-protection-slept-102-years [https://perma.cc/YLJ9-WYKG]. Under the corrected understanding of "equal protection," plus the public meaning that the Clause's "any person" phrase always had, the Clause protects the unborn against state laws permissive of elective abortion.

127 On guardians of the unborn, *see* 1 BLACKSTONE, quoted in text *supra* at note 17; *see also* WHARTON, quoted *supra* note 98. Ratifiers, in this counterfactual 1870 scenario, would find their willingness to understand the Equal Protection Clause as protecting the unborn against novel and lethal discrimination enhanced by the robust feminists of the day, whose near unanimous condemnation of elective abortion as murder is painstakingly documented in DELLAPENNA, *supra* note 73, at 267–68 ("[T]he leading feminists of the time were virtually unanimous in *demanding* the criminalization of abortion."); *id.* at 324 ("The leading feminists of the time were, if anything, more emphatic [than the medical men] in demanding harsh punishment for abortion, and on precisely the same grounds as the male dominated organized medical profession"); *id.* at 345 ("Women—particularly the founding mothers of feminism—also took the lead in these nineteenth century legislative battles. [footnote omitted]. And women physicians in the nineteenth century took a particularly strong leading role in the 'crusade' against abortion." [footnote omitted]); *id.* at 372, 374 ("[P]erhaps the most impressive demonstration of the new consensus on the nature of human

generation [footnote omitted] was its emphatic embrace by all leading feminists of the period when the abortion statutes were being enacted. Feminist leaders, as a result, were explicit and uncompromising, and virtually unanimous, in condemning abortion as 'ante-natal murder,' 'child-murder,' or 'ante-natal infanticide.'"). *See also id.* at 375, 380, 381–82, 384–85, 387, 392, 404.

128 The Civil Rights Cases of 1883 had stressed that the amendment bears only on "State legislation" or "State action" that impairs privileges or immunities or injures persons in life, liberty, or property or denies to any one of them the equal protection of the law. The implicit baseline for identifying a singling-out, an impairment, an injury, or a denial was the common law and the long-established legal institutions accepted in 1866 in the states that had been loyal to the Union. That baseline, and the strong limitation it imposed on the equal protection clause, was not definitively left behind (repudiated) until *Brown v. Board of Education*, 347 U.S. 483, 494–95 (1954).

129 Such as prevailed from 1871 until 1886: *see supra* note 126.

130 Planned Parenthood of Se. Pa. v. Casey, 505 U.S. 833, 912–13 (1992) (Stevens, J., concurring in part and dissenting in part).

131 Too narrowly, because the *vesting* of rights often counts at least as much as their "perfecting." The present procedural rights of unborn children to have guardians ad litem, like their substantive right to receive income or other property by inheritance or intestate succession or to get an injunction against waste, or to *parens patriae* or other protection against their mothers (or the mother's representatives) (*see infra* note 132), are rights each sufficiently vested ("perfected") to serve the child's interests appropriately and in seamless continuity with the substantive rights as he or she enjoys them after birth and eventually after infancy.

132 Also unavailing is *Roe*'s reliance on a defunct tort doctrine rejecting liability for prenatal injuries. Justice Holmes invented that doctrine well after the Fourteenth Amendment's ratification, in Dietrich v. Inhabitants of Northampton, 138 Mass. 14, 16–17 (1884), based on the fictions that the unborn child is "not yet in being" and so is merely "part of the mother." (State and federal courts gradually exposed those fictions until 1953, when New York's appellate court followed the "clear[]" "biological" reality "that separability begins at conception." Kelly v. Gregory, 125 N.Y.S.2d 696, 697 (App. Div. 1953). By 1971 Prosser could write that almost all jurisdictions had allowed recovery for pre-viability injuries. WILLIAM L. PROSSER, HANDBOOK OF THE LAW OF TORTS 337 (4th ed. 1971). He had approvingly called rejection of Holmes's fictions "the most spectacular abrupt reversal of a well-settled rule in the whole history of the law of torts." *Id.* § 56, at 354 (3d ed. 1964). A. A. White, *The Right of Recovery for Prenatal Injuries*, 12 LA. L.REV. 383, 394–400 (1952) (written just before the Holmes doctrine sank beneath the waves), surveys various insufficient policy and precedential reasons for the doctrine's denial of liability (denial that the unborn infant was a person in the eyes of the law), and shows (399) that "the courts denying recovery for prenatal injuries have not effectively escaped the implications for tort law of the recognition by the criminal law and other fields of the civil law of the infant's prenatal existence." This recognition was induced by physical/physiological facts.

133 Hall v. Hancock, 32 Mass. (15 Pick.) 255, 258 (1834).

134 *See id.*, where Chief Justice Shaw adopts "the principal reason" of Lord Hardwicke's opinion in Wallis v. Hodson, 2 Atk. 117 (Ch. 1740), a reason that Lord Hardwicke promptly exemplified: "on Behalf of such an Infant [*en ventre sa mere*], a Bill might be brought, and an Injunction granted to stay Waste."

135 *See* Raleigh Fitkin-Paul Morgan Mem'l Hosp. v. Anderson, 201 A.2d 537, 538 (N.J. 1964), *cert. denied* 377 U.S. 985 (1964); *see also* Robert M. Byrn, *An American Tragedy: The Supreme Court on Abortion*, 41 FORDHAM L. REV. 807, 844–48 (1973) (collecting cases); Ex parte Phillips, 287 So.3d 1179, 1251-1253 (Ala. 2018) (Parker, J., concurring specifically) (collecting cases).

136 "Thus, as a matter of federal constitutional law, a developing organism that is not yet a 'person' does not have what is sometimes described as a 'right to life.'" Planned Parenthood of Se. Pa. v. Casey, 505 U.S. 833, 913 (1992) (Stevens, J., concurring in part and dissenting in part) (footnote omitted).

137 *See generally* Gerard V. Bradley, *The Future of Abortion Law in the United States*, 16 NAT'L CATH. BIOETHICS Q. 633 (2016).

138 Doe v. Scott, 321 F. Supp. 1385, 1387 (N.D. Ill. 1971); *see also* John D. Gorby, *The "Right" to an Abortion, the Scope of Fourteenth Amendment "Personhood," and the Supreme Court's Birth Requirement*, 4 S. ILL. U. L.J. 1, 8–9 (1979).

139 Roe v. Wade, 410 U.S. 113, 157 (1973). For none of the Constitution's uses of "person" gives any indication of *when* one becomes a person, or entails that one becomes a person only at birth. *See* Joshua J. Craddock, *Protecting Prenatal Persons: Does the Fourteenth Amendment Prohibit Abortion?*, 40 HARV. J.L. & PUB. POL'Y 539, 550–52 (2017). And any reading that excludes the unborn from the Equal Protection Clause's "any person" because most uses of "person" elsewhere in the Constitution cannot apply to them (voting, becoming president, and so forth) applies *a fortiori* to corporations, yet the Court from 1886 has unflinchingly included them within equal protection and due process guarantees for "any person."

140 It asked how to square unborn personhood with (i) not penalizing the mother who consents to elective abortion, (ii) not penalizing operations that save the life of the mother but terminate her pregnancy, or (iii) penalizing abortion less severely "than the maximum penalty for murder." *Roe*, 410 U.S. at 157 n.54. *But see* Craddock, *supra* note 139, at 562–66.

141 DELLAPENNA, *supra* note 73, at 1056; *see also id.* at 336, 351–54, 374–75, 409–10 n.175.

142 *Roe*, 410 U.S. at 136.

143 *See id.* at 134–36.

144 DELLAPENNA, *supra* note 73, at 146–50; *see also id.* at 134–43.

145 Cyril C. Means, Jr., *The Law of New York Concerning Abortion and the Status of the Foetus, 1664–1968: A Case of Cessation of Constitutionality*, 14 N.Y. L. F. 411, 418–28 (1968) [hereinafter Means I]. Pages 418–28 were cited by *Roe* at 132 n.21 (quickening, etc.), and pages 411–12 were cited by *Roe* at 134 n.22 (canon law). The whole was cited by *Roe* at 151 n.47 (purpose of state statutes).

146 Cyril C. Means, Jr., *The Phoenix of Abortional Freedom: Is a Penumbral or Ninth-Amendment Right About to Arise from the Nineteenth-Century Legislative Ashes of a Fourteenth-Century Common-Law Liberty*, 17 N.Y. L. F. 335 (1971) [hereinafter Means II]. The whole was cited by *Roe* at 135 n.26 (no established common-law

prohibition) and 151 n.47 (statutory purpose(s)). Pages 375–76 were cited by *Roe* at 139 n. 33 (state statutes) and pages 381–82 at 148 n.42 (purpose of state statutes).
147   27 N.J.L. 112 (Sup. Ct. 1858).
148   Means I, *supra* note 145, at 418–28 (cited in *Roe*, 410 at 132 n.21).
149   *Id.* at 420.
150   *See id.*
151   *See supra* text accompanying note 55, text after note 79, and text after note 83; for the Bracton sentence, *see supra* text after note 69. *See also* notes 62, 67, and 69.
152   *See supra* notes 67–69.
153   Means I, *supra* note 145, at 418 (cited by *Roe* at 132 n.21).
154   *See id.* at 452, 453, 462; *cf. id.* at 438 ("[T]he common law *tolerated* abortion on request *before* quickening." (emphasis in the original)).
155   "So fond was [the common law] of liberty, that it allowed the pregnant woman to run the risk of death on the operating table, at a time when this risk was real and substantial, if she chose to rid herself of the foetus before quickening; yet so fond was it also of life that, if she did not survive the operation or its aftermath, he who performed it was hanged." (*Id.* at 437 (emphasis added)).

The same page explains that if the purpose of the operation was to save the life of the woman, then the operation would be *with* lawful purpose, in which case, even if the patient died, the physician would not be guilty of any offense, let alone murder. The therapeutic exception was thus already present in the common law, not in the domain of pre-quickening abortion—for all such abortions were noncriminal, provided the patient consented, *and survived*[!]—but rather in the domain of murder as imputed to the abortionist whose patient died.

In this confused passage, Means I admits *at least* that the lawfulness of the pre-quickening elective abortion cannot be determined until the patient has "survived" the abortion and its aftermath. Incidentally, we have not observed in Means I and II anything as mistaken as Professor Aaron Tang's notion that rule [I] merely penalized "botched abortion." *See* John M. Finnis & Robert George, *Indictability of Early Abortion c. 1868*, at 23–24 (2021), https://papers.ssrn.com/sol3/papers.cfm?abstract_id=3940378.
156   Means I, *supra* note 145, at 440 n.64.
157   *See id.*
158   Means I, *supra note* 145, at 446; Means II, *supra* note 146, at 362, quoting the passage from Hale.
159   *Id.*
160   *See* Means I, *supra* note 145, at 435.
161   *Id.* at 435 n.56.
162   Means II, *supra* note 146, at 335–36, 375.
163   *Id.* at 336 (emphasis added) (capitalization adapted).
164   *Id.* at 373.
165   *Id.*
166   *Id.* at 372 (emphasis added).
167   Commonwealth v. Parker, 50 Mass. (9 Met.) 263, 265 (1845).
168   Means II, *supra* note 146, at 363–72. East is discussed *supra* pp. 945–47; *infra* pp. 986–89.

169 *Parker*, 50 Mass. (9 Met.) at 265.
170 *See* 2 JAMES FITZJAMES STEPHEN, HISTORY OF THE CRIMINAL LAW OF ENGLAND 222–23 (London, MacMillan & Co. 1883).
171 *Id.*
172 *Id.*
173 Means II, *supra* note 146, at 367–71.
174 *Id.* at 364.
175 *Id.* at 366–67.
176 Means II even claims that the marginal note citing 1 Hale 429 expresses East's preference for Hale over Coke and for Hale's denial of Coke's rule [II] and non-affirmation of rule [III]. Means II, *supra* note 146, at 367. But neither of those rules was relevant to 1 East 230, which concerns only rule [I], never expounded by Coke—and places the citation to 1 Hale 429 not alongside the skewers case but at the very beginning of the paragraph expounding the transferred malice principle's application to abortion as illustrated by two cases. Presumably that is why Means II, when using East's marginal note to 1 Hale 429 as its first ground for inferring that East disapproved of Coke, takes care to cite not the marginal citation of "1 Hale 429" at 1 East 230—where East is actually discussing rules—but only the marginal note "(1 Hale, 429)" in the quasi-report of *Tinckler* at 1 East 353, at the point where the trial judge's ruling is given: "[Nares J.] was clearly of opinion it was murder [of the mother], on the authority of Lord Hale." Rule (i) in action in 1781. (The divided opinions of "all the judges" concerned only the question of admitting dying declarations of an accessory without corroboration. *See* 1 East 356.)
177 Means II, *supra* note 146, at 368.
178 EAST, 1 PLEAS OF THE CROWN 227 (London 1803, Philadelphia 1806) (citing in the margin Coke (3 *Inst.* 50) and his supporters Hawkins and Blackstone).
179 *Id.* at 277–81 ("But to kill a child in its mother's womb is no murder, *but a great misprision*: and Staundford and Lord Hale are of the same opinion, even where the child is born alive and afterwards dies by reason of the potion or bruises it received in the womb: which opinion they seem to ground on the difficulty of ascertaining the fact: certainly not a satisfactory reason, where the fact is clearly established: and according to all other opinions the latter is murder."). "[T]he latter" is the case of the [II] aborted child born alive and dying from the abortifacient measures; the implicit "former" is the [III] aborted child who dies in the womb. Note in passing the absence of any reference to quickening; the governing phrase "kill a child" necessarily implied that the child was quick in the sense of formed, ensouled, and alive (which is long before "quickening").
180 Means II, *supra* note 146, at 371.
181 *Id.* at 372.
182 *Id.*
183 *See id.*
184 *See supra* text accompanying note 147.
185 State v. Murphy, 27 N.J.L. 112, 114 (Sup. Ct. 1858).
186 Means I, *supra* note 145, at 452 (emphasis in original)
187 *Id.* at 507 (emphasis in original).

188 *See* Means II, *supra* note 146, at 391. "Lister" is shorthand for the use of antiseptics in surgery.
189 Means II, *supra* note 146, at 389–90. Means adds a couple of sentences emphasizing how distinguished and well-informed the *Murphy* court was.
190 Roe v. Wade, 410 U.S. 113, 151 (1973).
191 *Id.*
192 *Id.*
193 See Commonwealth v. Wood, 77 Mass. (11 Gray) 85 (1858), which upheld the trial judge's direction

> that *although at the common law*, as held in this commonwealth, it was no offence to procure an abortion, unless it was alleged and proved that the mother was "quick with child"—that being the stage of pregnancy which, by the common law, was considered to be the commencement of the child's life—yet that under the statute of 1845, c. 27, it was not necessary to allege in the indictment or to offer affirmative proof that the child had life. (Emphasis added).

The appellate court added:

> The [trial] court was also requested to instruct the jury that a lawful justification "would exist if the child with which Sarah Chaffee was pregnant was not a live child." If by this was meant that the mother had not reached the stage of pregnancy in which she would be "quick with child," and when to procure an abortion would be an offence at common law, the prayer in our opinion misconceives the purpose of *the statute*, which *was intended to supply the defects of the common law, and to apply to all cases of pregnancy.*

Id. at 93 (emphasis added).

194 See State v. Howard, 32 Vt. 380 (1859), where the primary question was whether the prosecution need prove that the child was alive in the womb at the time of the unlawful inducing of miscarriage. After comparing the state's 1846 statute with the English criminal abortion statutes of 1803, 1837 and 1851, the State Supreme Court held:

> [U]nder our statute it is expressly required, to constitute the offence, that the attempt be to procure the miscarriage of a woman "then pregnant with child."
>
> ....
>
> .... So that the only new question arising under our statute is, whether it is essential to the pregnancy or "being pregnant with child," that the child should be still alive. IT IS NOT CLAIMED THAT IT IS NECESSARY THE EMBRYO SHOULD HAVE QUICKENED. THE GENERAL FORM OF EXPRESSION "PREGNANT WITH CHILD," SEEMS TO HAVE BEEN USED TO ESCAPE ALL QUESTION OF THIS KIND AND HAVE IT CLEARLY APPLY TO EVERY STAGE OF PREGNANCY, FROM THE EARLIEST CONCEPTION; and if so, we see no reason why it should not extend through its entire term, until the expulsion of the *foetus*.

Id. at 400 (emphasis added).

If the legislative purpose in Vermont or Massachusetts had been protection of women's health *rather than* the child's life, the statutes would have abolished the requirement of proving pregnancy, and would have penalized abortifacient measures on women only believed or feared to be pregnant. For all that is said by the New Jersey supreme court in *Murphy*, the same should be said about the New Jersey statute in that case (see *infra* pp. 166–70).

195 State v. Murphy, 27 N.J.L. 112, 114 (Sup. Ct. 1858) (emphases added).
196 This is not contradicted by the court's remark that—where the common law does recognize a crime of attempt—"[m]ere words do, at the common law, constitute such overt act as amounts to an attempt to commit a crime." *Id.* at 115.
197 *Id.* at 114 (emphasis added).
198 But, *nota bene*, only if there is an unborn child in existence! The statute said:
If any person or persons, maliciously or without lawful justification, with intent to cause and procure the miscarriage of a woman *then pregnant with child,* shall administer to her, prescribe for her, or advise or direct her to take or swallow any poison, drug, medicine or noxious thing; and if any person or persons maliciously, and without lawful justification, shall use any instrument, or means whatever, with the like intent; and every person, with the like intent, knowingly aiding and assisting such offender or offenders, shall, on conviction thereof, be adjudged guilty of a high misdemeanor; and if the woman die in consequence thereof, shall be punished by fine, not exceeding one thousand dollars, or imprisonment at hard labour for any term not exceeding fifteen years, or both; and if the woman doth not die in consequence thereof, such offender shall, on conviction thereof, be adjudged guilty of a misdemeanor, and be punished by fine, not exceeding five hundred dollars, or imprisonment at hard labour, for any term not exceeding seven years, or both.
A further supplement to an act entitled "An act for the punishment of crimes": Penalty for causing or procuring miscarriage (approved Mar. 1, 1849), *in* ACTS OF THE SEVENTY-THIRD LEGISLATURE OF THE STATE OF NEW JERSEY (Phillips & Boswell, 1849).
199 *Murphy*, 27 N.J.L. at 114–15 (emphasis added).
200 It is certain that in states that retained common-law criminal law at all, abortion statutes could be, and were, regarded as supplementing the common law. *See, e.g.,* Smith v. State, 33 Me. 48, 51 (1851).
201 The New Jersey Supreme Court revisited the 1849 statute and *Murphy* in 1881, in State v. Gedicke, 43 N.J.L. 86, 89–90 (Sup. Ct. 1881):
[T]he act of March 1st, 1849…was passed to remedy an adjudged defect in our law, that to cause or procure abortion before the child is quick was not a criminal offence at common law or by any statute of our state. *State v. Cooper, 2 Zab. 52.* As soon as the question was raised and the doubt suggested, this act was passed to punish the offence. The design of the statute was not so much to prevent the procuring of abortions, however offensive these may be to morals and decency, as to guard the health and life of the female against the consequences of such attempts. The guilt of the defendant is not determined by the success or failure of the attempt;

but the measure of his punishment is graduated by the fact whether the woman lives or dies. *State v. Murphy, 3 Dutcher 112.* This law was further extended March 26th, 1872...to *protect the life of the child also*, and inflict the *same* punishment, in case of its death, as if the mother should die. (Emphasis added).

This final sentence (though still inexplicably minimizing the 1849 statute's in fact gapless protection of the life of the unborn child) shows—even without going further afield than New Jersey—how erroneous was *Roe*'s claim, in the opinion's above-quoted sentence citing (only) *Murphy*, that "[t]he few state courts called upon to interpret their laws *in the late 19th and early 20th centuries* did focus on the State's interest in protecting the woman's health *rather than* in preserving the embryo and fetus." Roe v. Wade, 410 U.S. 113, 151 (1973). Means II had quoted and celebrated *Gedicke's* sentence repeating *Murphy* (in decontextualized and over-simplified form) but had—shamelessly—withheld the following sentence, about the 1872 statute's putting the child's death on a par with the mother's. *See* Means II, *supra* note 146, at 381–82. Relying on Means rather than reading the cases on which he purported to rely, *Roe* fell headlong into this advocate-activist's snare.

202   Witherspoon, *supra* note 91, at 61–69 (1985).
203   *Id.* at 70.
204   *See* MATTHEW HALE, ANALYSIS OF THE LAW 1–4 (1st ed. 1713). Hale died in 1676: "*The Analysis of the Law*. Sect. 1. Of the Civil Part of the Law (in general). The Civil Part of the Law concerns, 1. Civil Rights or Interests.... Now all Civil Rights or Interests are of Two Sorts: 1. *Jura Personarum,* or Rights of Persons.... The Civil Rights of Persons are such as do either, 1. Immediately concern the Persons themselves:... As to the Persons themselves, they are either, 1. Persons Natural; Or 2. Persons Civil or Politick, *i.e.*, Bodies Corporate. Persons Natural are consider'd Two Ways: 1. Absolutely and simply in themselves.... In Persons Natural, simply and absolutely considered, we have these several Considerations, *viz.* 1. The Interest which every Person has in himself... 1st, The Interest which every Person has in himself, principally consists in three Things, *viz.* 1. The Interest he has in the Safety of his own Person. And the Wrongs that reflect upon that, are, 1. Assaults.... And all Persons are (presum'd) able in either.... Taking or Disposing... which [persons] by Law are not disabled: and those that are so disabled come under the Title of *Non-ability*, though that Non-ability is various in its Extent, *viz.*, To some more, to some less (as in the several instances following):... 4. Infants: here of the Non-ability of Infants....." The *Oxford Dictionary of National Biography entry for Hale (2004)* says: "[Hale's] *Analysis...* was borrowed by William Blackstone with minimal modification and therefore provides the structure of Blackstone's Commentaries." On Blackstone's own *Analysis* as derivative from Hale's and forerunner of the *Commentaries*, see *J. M. Finnis, Blackstone's Theoretical Intentions, 12 NATURAL L. F. 63, 64–67 (1967).*
205   ROSCOE POUND, 4 JURISPRUDENCE ch. 25 (1959).
206   For the text of 3 INST. 50, *see supra* note 32. Pound's footnote cites seven other English precedents on related points of detail and further cases illustrative of a dispute or difference between Kentucky and older and newer English views.
207   *Id.* at 193–94.
208   Bernstein, *supra* note 79.

209 On Bernstein's understanding of the "common-law meaning" of "person, and the related common-law rules," the following six indented and enumerated propositions (the whole set of relevant propositions) in Shaw's judgment (*supra* at nn. 24–28; where not quoted in the text there, the propositions are stated on pp. 257–58 of the report there cited) should all have been phrased differently:

> [1] We are also of opinion, that...generally, a child will be considered in being, from conception to the time of its birth, in all cases where it will be for the benefit of such child to be so considered....

On Bernstein's fictionalist view, Shaw should have said "a child, if born alive, will be treated as if it had been in being from conception...."

> [2]...the Court are of the opinion, that a child *en ventre sa mere* is to be considered a child living, so as to take a beneficial interest in a bequest, where the description is "children living."

Shaw should, on Bernstein's view, have said "a child born alive is to be considered as if it had been living when the testator died while it was *en ventre sa mere*."

> [3] A child *en ventre sa mere* is *taken to be a person in being, for many purposes*. He may take by descent; by devise...or under the statute of distributions...and generally for all purposes where it is for his benefit.

Shaw should on this view have said "a child born alive is for many purposes taken, by fiction, to have been in being while *en ventre sa mere*."

> [4] Lord *Hardwicke* says, in *Wallis v. Hodson,* the principal reason I go upon is, that [4] *a child en ventre sa mere is a person in rerum naturâ,* so that, both by the rules of the civil and common law, he is to all intents and purposes a child, as much as if born in the father's lifetime.

The correct common-law way of speaking would, on Bernstein's view, have been "a child *en ventre sa mere* is NOT a person *in rerum natura*, but if born alive is treated as if he had been, and is NOT a person for any purposes at all, unless he is born alive."

> [5] And Buller J., in delivering his opinion, in Thellusson v. Woodford, 4 Ves.324, after citing various cases, says, the effect is, that [5] *there is no difference between a child actually born and a child en ventre sa mere.*

Buller and Shaw should have said "there is all the difference in the world between a child actually born and a child *en ventre sa mere* unless the child is actually born, in which event it will by fiction of law be treated, for some purposes (but not others), as having had some existence before birth."

> [6] [I]t was stated [in Doe v. Clarke, 2 H. Bl. 399] as [6] *a fixed principle*, that wherever such consideration would be for his benefit, *a child en ventre sa mere shall be considered as absolutely born.*

No, Hardwicke and Shaw should have said that "the fixed principle is that a child *en ventre sa mere* is not a person and has no being or existence unless born alive, in which case it will then be treated as if it had been born at the time of its conception, if so treating it will be for the benefit of the born child."

> These inversions are, each and all, absurdly unnecessary, and out of line with the common law's willingness to acknowledge human beings in their reality and be ready to adjust the degree, forms, and limits of the protection it affords the life and property interests of the unborn, for the sake not least of avoiding needless complexity and uncertainty in complex family and other property interrelationships.

210 2 Paige Ch. 35, 40 (N.Y. 1830).
211 The ruling in *Marsellis* is that a still-born child does not count as having been born alive for the purposes of the rule that *if a child is born of a marriage*, the surviving spouse has a life estate ("in curtesy") in property in respect of which the deceased spouse was seised of an inheritable estate (whether or not the child had predeceased the deceased spouse). That was a conventional and proper application of doctrine, even though the doctrine of estates in curtesy would not have been subverted had the ruling gone the other way; the ruling in the case is the neater solution, avoiding difficult potential problems of defining whether and when, for the purposes of the curtesy rule, a child miscarried or born dead had indeed been present and living in the womb as a fruit of the marriage.
212 59 Ala. 441, 442–44 (1877).
213 The first of these citations is the above-discussed passage in *Marsellis*, with the sentences following that: "The rule has been derived from the civil law..... although by the civil law of successions, a posthumous child was entitled to the same rights as those born in the life-time of the decedent, it was only on the condition that they were born alive, and under such circumstances that the law presumed they would survive.
…Children in the mother's womb are considered, in whatever relates to themselves, as if already born; but children born dead, or in such an early stage of pregnancy as to be incapable of living, although they be not actually dead at the time of birth, are considered as if they had never been born or conceived." *Marsellis*, 2 Paige Ch. at 40–41 (cited at *Gillespie*, 59 Ala. at 443–44). Notice that the latter fiction is deployed only *after* the death of the unborn, when all need for protecting *that child's* interests (benefit) has ceased.
214 *Gillespie*, 59 Ala. at 444–45.
215 Knotts v. Stearns, 91 U.S. 638, 640 (1875) (cited in Bernstein, *supra* note 76, at 65 n.323).
216 *Id.* at 640–41.
217 Bernstein, *supra* note 76, at 39 (emphases added and omitted).
218 Lord Hardwicke uses this phrase deliberately differently, to mean simply in reality. *See supra* notes 28, 209. Aquinas, writing in the era of Bracton but still read in the age of Coke, uses the phrase 185 times. Reading through these sequentially, in context, with the aid of an electronic contextualized concordance, it is clear that though the phrase can often be safely translated "actually" or "in actuality" or "really", it is rarely if ever used to contrast with "potentially" (as distinct from "actually"), and its central sense is something very like our rather informal phrase "in reality" in the sense of "in the real world." In the context of Coke and his antecedents such as Staundford and his successors like *Russell on Crimes*, the phrase has a narrower but related sense, for none of these writers thought that the unborn child (say a week or a month or six months before birth) was not real or part of the real world, so what they (as distinct from, later, Lord Hardwicke) meant by "not yet *in rerum natura*" was "not yet part of that human, 'social' world of interpersonal communication that everyone enters by birth and (whether or not we are immortal and headed for heaven or hell) leaves by death."

To illustrate Aquinas' usage with one example: in his *Commentary on the Sentences of Peter Lombard* lib. 3 d. 20 q. 1 a. 5 qc. 2c, speaking about judgments in the ordinary sense of historical or scientific or commonsense ["This email is a genuine email from

my boss"] affirmations or denials, Aquinas says:
> [A] judgment about something is unconditional [*absolutum*] when that something is considered precisely as actually [*actu*] existing [*existens*] in the real world [*in rerum natura*]; and it is considered in that way when it is considered with all the circumstances pertaining to it [*cum omnibus circumstantiis quae sunt in ipsa*].
>> [Super Sent., lib. 3 d. 20 q. 1 a. 5 qc. 2 co. Ad secundam quaestionem dicendum, quod judicium absolutum est de re, quando consideratur ipsa secundum quod est actu in rerum natura existens; et hoc est quando consideratur cum omnibus circumstantiis quae sunt in ipsa. Sed quando consideratur res secundum aliquid quod in re est sine consideratione aliorum, illud judicium non est de re simpliciter, sed secundum quid.]

219 HALE, H.P.C., *supra* note 33, at 433 (some emphases added).
220 *See supra* notes 74–76.
221 *See* DELLAPENNA, *supra* note 73, at 143–50, 189, giving full translations of the court documents underlying (and changing the sense of) the brief YB reports.
222 Similarly framed evidential concerns, similarly crystallized into a rule of law, underlie the year-and-a-day rule for murder: "for if he die after that time, it cannot be discerned, as the law presumes, whether he died of the stroke or poison, etc., or if a natural death; and in case of life the rule of law ought to be certain." 1 *Inst.* 53.
223 Bernstein not rarely abbreviates sentences with the result that their meaning is substantially or even radically changed (as here). Another incidental example occurs when he quotes the second of Blackstone's paragraphs on *129 quoted and discussed above at note 17—the one beginning "An infant...in the mother's womb, is supposed in law to be born for many purposes...", and says: "Professor Finnis says of this passage that it establishes that 'the law treats [unborn children], even at [conception], *as equal to a born child.*'[fn. omitted] This is mistaken." Bernstein, *supra* note 79, at 55. But what Finnis in fact says at the place cited is quite different: "For some purposes (guardianship, for example) the law treats such an individual, even at that beginning stage, as equal to a born child." John Finnis, *Abortion is Unconstitutional*, FIRST THINGS (Apr. 2021), https://www.firstthings.com/article/2021/04/abortion-is-unconstitutional [https://perma.cc/VN2Z-GYWZ].
224 *See also supra* note 33.
225 Brief of the United States as Amicus Curiae, *supra* note 11, at 24.
226 Notably *Dietrich v. Inhabitants of Northampton*, 138 Mass. 14, 17 (1884), a case now discredited and abandoned, *see supra* note 132, and cases following it such as *Allaire v. St. Luke's Hospital*, 184 Ill. 359, 367 (1900).
227 *See supra* note 49; Commonwealth v. Wood, 77 Mass. (11 Gray) 85, 86 (Mass. 1858).
228 At 27 n.4, the Brief of the United States again cites *Parker* at 267 mistakenly for the proposition that abortion was "often legal at least before a fetus could be considered legally separate from the pregnant woman." *See* Brief of the United States as Amicus Curiae, *supra* note 11, at 27 n.4. What is said at 267 subtracts nothing from what *Parker* said at 235 to remind readers that even when it is not indictable, elective abortion early or late is always "done without lawful purpose"—was never "legal"—and is murder whenever, however skillfully performed, it happens to result in the death of the woman who while pregnant had consented to it.

229 Brief of Joseph W. Dellapenna as Amicus Curiae in Support of Petitioners, Dobbs v. Jackson Women's Health Org., 142 S. Ct. 2228 (2022) (No. 19-1392).
230 The Historians' Brief, misspelling misprision, erroneously equates it to misdemeanor. *See* Amicus Brief of the American Historical Association and the Organization of American Historians, *supra* note 11, at 5–6.
231 FRANCIS WHARTON, 2 A TREATISE OF THE CRIMINAL LAW OF THE UNITED STATES sec. 1230 (7th ed. 1874). The footnote to the sentence quoted cross-refers to section 90 *b*, actually 90 *c*, a short section on killing "by necessity" as acknowledged by natural law, canon law, and French and German jurists, and promising a fuller discussion in sections 1013 and 1028. Section 1013 is irrelevant, and the reference is evidently to section 1019, the first of several sections on "Homicide from necessity in defence of a man's own person or property, or of the persons or property of others." Section 1028 discusses self-defence in situations of necessity where both parties are innocent, such as two persons on a plank in the shipwreck. Section 1029 discusses "Sacrifice of life in childbed [*scil.* in obstetric emergency], where either the mother or the child must die, because (he writes) 19 out of 20 Caesarean operations to save the child result in the death of the mother. "The dictates of humanity, and, in consequence, those of the law, call for the sacrifice of the child." (Cross-citation to secs. 942 and 1230). Section 942 is the general treatment of the born-alive rule for murder under the doctrine articulated in *Sims*, *supra* note 71, and by Coke, 3 *Inst.* 50, *supra* note 32.
232 *See* Barr v. Am. Ass'n of Pol. Consultants, 140 S. Ct. 2335, 2351 n.8 (2020).
233 874 F.3d 735, 736 (D.C. Cir. 2017) (en banc), *cert. granted, judgment vacated sub nom.* Azar v. Garza, 138 S. Ct. 1790 (2018).
234 *See, e.g.*, David W. Louisell & John T. Noonan, Jr., *Constitutional Balance*, *in* THE MORALITY OF ABORTION 220–260 at 244–45, 255 (John T. Noonan ed., 1970); and *supra* note 135.
235 *Cf.* People v. Liberta, 474 N.E.2d 567, 573 (N.Y. 1984) (reinstating rape charges against a husband despite a statutory marital-rape exception after holding that the exception violated equal protection and failed rational basis review).
236 *See* Bradley, *supra* note 137.
237 *See* John Finnis, *Born and Unborn: Answering Objections to Constitutional Personhood*, FIRST THINGS (Apr. 9, 2021), https://www.firstthings.com/web-exclusives/2021/04/born-and-unborn-answering-objections-to-constitutional-personhood [https://perma.cc/ZE2K-ZLS8]. For example (sec. III) (emphasis added below):

> NY Penal Law, as amended in 2018 to strip out remaining references in section 125.00 to "abortion" and to the "unborn child," says in that section: "Homicide means conduct which causes the death of a person under circumstances constituting murder or...." Section 125.05 says that "'person,' when referring to the victim of a homicide, means a human being who has been born and is alive." Then section 125.25 defines second-degree murder as causing the "death of a person" with "intent to cause the death of" that person or "another person." Abortion is now dealt with exclusively in the state's Public Health Law [which is fully compliant with *Roe* and *Casey*].

Equal protection entails (as *Roe* conceded) that these NY Public Health Law provisions would fall, just like California's, and therefore that Penal Law section 125.05—since it operates quite bluntly to deny to unborn persons the protections they would have as born persons, say ten seconds later—would expressly or by implication be declared inoperative. *Thus the default position would be that most abortions would be murder.* New York, if dissatisfied with the applicability here of the defenses of excuse and justification available to anyone charged with murder, would thus be strongly incentivized to enact new legislation making a fair accommodation between the rights of mother and child, recognizing both their basic and constitutional recognized equality as persons and their significantly differing situations and legitimate interests.

238 Unlike suicide and consensual euthanasia, elective abortion is a zero-sum affair, in which one person's choice extinguishes another person's life without the latter's consent. The courts cannot stand idly by when either state law or state or local prosecutorial policy systematically neglects to protect one class of persons against denial of the right to life at the hands of other persons. The courts are reluctant to interfere with prosecutorial discretion, and their rule against improper selective prosecution is usually invoked as (or for purposes of) a defense against prosecution, rather than to require prosecution. But the general rules articulated by the Supreme Court since *Yick Wo v. Hopkins*, 118 U.S. 356 (1886), certainly extend in principle to judicial action against nonprosecution. Thus *United States v. Armstrong*, 517 U.S. 456, 464–65 (1996):

> [A] prosecutor's discretion is "subject to constitutional constraints." *United States v. Batchelder*, 442 U.S. 114, 125 (1979). One of these constraints, imposed by the equal protection component of the Due Process Clause of the Fifth Amendment, *Bolling v. Sharpe*, 347 U.S. 497, 500 (1954), is that the decision whether to prosecute may not be based on "an unjustifiable standard such as race, religion, or other arbitrary classification," *Oyler v. Boles*, 368 U.S. 448, 456 (1962). A defendant may demonstrate that the administration of a criminal law is "directed so exclusively against a particular class of persons ... with a mind so unequal and oppressive" that the system of prosecution amounts to "a practical denial" of equal protection of the law. *Yick Wo v. Hopkins*, 118 U.S. 356, 373 (1886).

239 *See* Vacco v. Quill, 521 U.S. 793, 799 (1997).
240 *See Roe*, 410 U.S. at 173 (Rehnquist, J., dissenting).
241 *See* City of Boerne v. Flores, 521 U.S. 507, 530 (1997).
242 Transcript of Oral Argument at 43, Dobbs v. Jackson Women's Health Org., 142 S. Ct. 2228 (2022) (No. 19-1392):

> JUSTICE KAVANAUGH: And to be clear, you're not arguing that the Court somehow has the authority to itself prohibit abortion or that this Court has the authority to order the states to prohibit abortion as I understand it, correct?
> MR. STEWART [Solicitor General of Mississippi]: Correct, Your Honor.
> JUSTICE KAVANAUGH: And as I understand it, you're arguing that

the Constitution is silent and, therefore, neutral on the question of abortion? In other words, that the Constitution is neither pro-life nor pro-choice on the question of abortion but leaves the issue for the people of the states or perhaps Congress to resolve in the democratic process? Is that accurate?

MR. STEWART: Right. We're—we're saying it's left to the people, Your Honor.

243 Dobbs v. Jackson Women's Health Organization, 142 S. Ct. 2228, 2261 (2022). That statement is affirmed in the Opinion twice, *verbatim,* and represents the settled position of the Opinion, counter-balancing two incautious declarations. The first is the approving quotation of Justice Scalia's phrase "permissibility of abortion":

It is time to heed the Constitution and return the issue of abortion to the people's elected representatives. "The permissibility of abortion, and the limitations, upon it, are to be resolved like most important questions in our democracy: by citizens trying to persuade one another and then voting." That is what the Constitution and the rule of law demand.

Id. at 2243 (quoting *Planned Parenthood v. Casey,* 505 U.S. 833, 979 (1992) (Scalia, J., concurring in judgment in part and dissenting in part)). The second is the equally sweeping declaration that "the Court usurped the power to address a question of profound moral and social importance that the Constitution unequivocally leaves for the people." *Id.* At 2265.

244 Note, incidentally, that in articulating this qualification, the Court heads up its non-exhaustive list of "legitimate interests" with: "respect for and preservation of prenatal life at all stages of development [and] the protection of maternal health and safety...." *Id.* at 2284 (citing *Gonzales v. Carhart,* 550 U.S. 124, 157–58 (2007)).

CHAPTER TEN: CONSTITUTIONAL STRUCTURES AND CIVIC VIRTUES

1 I explore the meaning and moral significance of the Rule of Law in "Reason, Freedom, and the Rule of Law," *American Journal of Jurisprudence,* 46 (2001): 249–56.

2 I offer some thoughts on moral disagreement between reasonable people of goodwill in "Law, Democracy, and Moral Disagreement," *Harvard Law Review* 110, no. 7 (May 1997): 1388–1406.

3 On the rational (and moral) basis of political authority, see generally John Finnis, *Natural Law and Natural Rights,* 2nd edition (Clarendon Press, 2011), chapter 9.

4 See John Finnis, "Law as Co-ordination," *Ratio Juris* 2, no. 1 (March 1989), 97–104.

5 Finnis, *Natural Law and Natural Rights,* 155.

6 Isaiah Berlin, *The Crooked Timber of Humanity: Chapters in the History of Ideas* (Alfred A. Knopf, 1991), 208.

7 John Finnis, "Is Natural Law Theory Compatible with Limited Government?," in Robert P. George, ed., *Natural Law, Liberalism, and Morality* (Clarendon Press, 1996), 1–26 (esp. at 5–9).

8 Robert P. George, "The Concept of Public Morality," *American Journal of Jurisprudence,* 45, no. 1 (January 2000): 17–31.

9 Patrick Suppes, commenting on Aristotle, explains that "flourishing or happiness is not a state of feeling but an activity. Patrick Suppes, "The Aims of Education," in Alven Neiman, ed., *The Philosophy of Education 1995* (Philosophy Education Society,

1996), 110–26. See also Douglas B. Rasmussen, "Human Flourishing and the Appeal to Human Nature," in E. F. Paul, F. T. Miller, and J. Paul, eds., *Human Flourishing* (Cambridge University Press, 1999), 1–43; and John Finnis, *Fundamentals of Ethics* (Oxford University Press, 1983), 38 ("Aristotle gives heavy emphasis to the fact that the life of *eudaimonia* is a lifetime of activity. . . .")

10 See Peter L. Berger and Richard John Neuhaus, *To Empower People* (American Enterprise Institute, 1977).
11 See Alexander Hamilton, *Federalist Papers*, Number 84.
12 See, e.g., Jeremy Waldron, "The Core of the Case Against Judicial Review," *Yale Law Journal*, 115, no. 6 (April 2006), pp. 1345–1406.
13 See, for example, United States v. Lopez, 514 U.S. 549 (1995).
14 *National Federation of Independent Business v. Sebelius*, 567 U.S. 519 (2012)
15 John Adams, *Message to the Officers of the First Brigade of the Third Division of the Militia of Massachusetts* (1798).

CHAPTER ELEVEN: CATHOLICISM AND THE AMERICAN CIVIC ORDER

1 Some portions of the preceding paragraphs were adapted from "Dignitatis Humanae: The Freedom of the Church and the Responsibility of the State," a chapter that William L. Saunders co-authored with me in the book entitled *Catholicism and Religious Freedom*, edited by Kenneth L. Grasso and Robert P. Hunt and published by Rowman and Littlefield in 2006.

CHAPTER TWELVE: THE BABY AND THE BATHWATER

1 *Dignitatis Humanae*, December 7, 1965, https://www.vatican.va/archive/hist_councils/ii_vatican_council/documents/vat-ii_decl_19651207_dignitatis-humanae_en.html.
2 John Finnis, "Religion and State" in John Finnis, *Religion & Public Reasons: Collected Essays: Volume V* (Oxford University Press, 2011), 94–95.
3 Ibid., 102.

CHAPTER SIXTEEN: CHRISTIANITY AND PAGANISM: THEN AND NOW

1 Steven D. Smith, *Pagans and Christians in the City: Culture Wars from the Tiber to the Potomac* (Eerdmans 2018).
2 Ibid.
3 Ibid.

CHAPTER SEVENTEEN: CATHOLIC TEACHING ON JEWS AND JUDAISM

1 *Nostra Aetate*, October 28, 1965, https://www.vatican.va/archive/hist_councils/ii_vatican_council/documents/vat-ii_decl_19651028_nostra-aetate_en.html.
2 John Paul II, Address to the Representatives of the Jewish Community, Sydney, Australia, November 2, 1986, https://www.vatican.va/content/john-paul-ii/en/speeches/1986/november/documents/hf_jp-ii_spe_19861126_com-ebraica-sidney-australia.html.
3 UPI, "Text of Pope's Speech at Rome Synagogue: 'You Are Our Elder Brothers,'" *New*

York Times, April 14, 1986, https://www.nytimes.com/1986/04/14/world/text-of-pope-s-speech-at-rome-synagogue-you-are-our-elder-brothers.html.
4 William D. Mantalbano, "Hungarian Rabbi Confronts Pope: Religion: John Paul Is Assailed over His Church's Silence During World War II. He Delivers a Ringing Denunciation of Anti-Semitism, Urges Reconciliation," *Los Angeles Times*, August 19, 1991, https://www.latimes.com/archives/la-xpm-1991-08-19-mn-630-story.html.
5 John Paul II, interview by Tad Szulc, *Parade*, April 3, 1994.

CHAPTER EIGHTEEN: GNOSTIC LIBERALISM

1 Francis, *Laudato Si'*, May 24, 2015, https://www.vatican.va/content/francesco/en/encyclicals/documents/papa-francesco_20150524_enciclica-laudato-si.html.

CHAPTER NINETEEN: ALEKSANDR SOLZHENITSYN'S PLEA TO THE WEST

1 Alexander Solzhenitsyn. "A World Split Apart," Commencement Address, Harvard University, June 8, 1978, The Aleksandr Solzhenitsyn Center, https://www.solzhenitsyncenter.org/a-world-split-apart.
2 Abraham Lincoln, "Proclamation 97—Appointing a Day of National Humiliation, Fasting, and Prayer," March 30, 1863, The American Presidency Project, https://www.presidency.ucsb.edu/documents/proclamation-97-appointing-day-national-humiliation-fasting-and-prayer.

CHAPTER TWENTY: HEINRICH HEINE'S PROPHECY OF NAZISM

1 Heinrich Heine, *On the History of Religion and Philosophy in Germany and Other Writings*, trans. Howard Pollack-Milgate and ed. Terry Pinkard, (Cambridge University Press, 2007), 116.

CHAPTER TWENTY-TWO: RABBI JONATHAN SACKS: A MORAL VOICE

1 Jonathan Sacks, *Morality: Restoring the Common Good in Divided Times* (Basic Books, 2022).
2 Ibid.
3 Ibid.
4 Ibid.

INDEX

abortion: advocates of (assumption of), 32; dehumanizing of fetus before, 88; issue (human nature and), 31; natural-law thought approach to, 65–69
Adams, John, 213
"Age of Faith," medieval period as, x
"Age of Feeling," our age as, x–xi, xii
"Age of Reason," Enlightenment period as, ix, x
Akeman, David, 343
Alito, Samuel, 120
American Association of University Professors, 278
American civic order. *See* Catholicism, American civic order and
Amish communities, 255
Analysis of the Law, 185
Anderson, Ryan T. (liberalism), 231–46
Anscombe, Elizabeth, 330, 333
Anselm of Canterbury, ix
Aquinas, Thomas: analytic tradition and, 329; as Aristotle's greatest interpreter and expositor, 202; *determinatio* of, 48, 235; distinctions of common good developed by, 242–43; Hart's misunderstanding of, 54; law defined by, 47; legal theory of, 53; movement defined by, 148, 188; as person of faith, ix; positive law and, 48, 52; prevention of conceptual thought recognized by, 33; relativism and, 233; slogan echoed by, 51; teachings on immorality by, 236
Aristotle, 12, 14, 33, 45, 202, 300, 337
Arneson, Richard, 9
attributed dignity, 96, 97
Augustine (saint), 51, 54

Balkin, Jack, 115
Bellah, Robert, 306
Benedict XVI (pope), 296
Bentham, Jeremy, 7
Benthamism, legal philosophy vs., 55
Berlin, Isaiah, 202, 331

Bernstein, C'Zar, 173
Bird, Colin, 108
Bishop, Joel, 193
Bleich, J. David, 92
Blessed Pius IX (pope), 220, 221, 228
Bloom, Paul, 31, 32
body-self dualism, 32, 104, 307; Catholic Church's rejection of, 37; Christianity's rejection of, 299; marriage and, 302; questions presupposing, 106. *See also* dualistic delusions
Body-Self Dualism in Contemporary Ethics and Politics, 104
Brown, Jeffrey, 345, 346
Brown, Louise, 89
Brown v. Board of Education, 209
Buck v. Bell, 274

campus illiberalism, 261–72; core of the problem, 262; critical thinking skills, refining of, 272; definition of, 261; dissenting speakers, "disinvited," 262; groupthink, 262–65, 271; intellectual diversity, 265, 267–68; intellectual humility, need for, 263; manifestations, 262; motivation to think more critically, 267; plea, 270; politicization of the academy, 261; pre-indoctrinated students, 271; university leaders, groupthink problem acknowledged by, 267; viewpoint diversity, value of, 265; what really matters, 268
capitalism, 249, 250. *See also* markets, morality, and civil society
Catholic Church: freedom of, 226; great stain on the history of, 293; nineteenth-century, attack on, 221; rejection of body-self dualism by, 37; relations with State of Israel established by, 297; as world's largest religious body, 37
Catholicism, American civic order and, 217–30; communion, 224–25; Constitution, 228, 229; Cult of Reason, 222; Cult of the

399

Supreme Being, 222; *Dignitatis Humanae*, 220, 222–28; First Amendment, "five freedoms" protected by, 227; French Revolution, 221–22; human flourishing, religious freedom and, 223; ideal state, Catholics believing in, 218; Jacobinism, 222; North Star principle, 230; preconciliar popes, 220–21, 226; question faced by America Catholics, 217, 219; religious indifferentism, 219; Second Vatical Council, 219, 220, 228; "sectarian Liberalism," 222; separation of church and state, 217–18; "Syllabus of Errors," 221. See also Jews and Judaism, Catholic teaching on

Chauncey, George, 126

Cherlin, Andrew, 123

Christ, Carol, 267

Christianity, paganism and, 281–91; "Benedict Option," 289; challenge, 291; common good, human person and, 283; "comprehensive doctrines," 283–84; era of "woke" ideology, the fight in, 290; God, man fashioned in likeness of, 281, 283; *imago Dei*, 283; Judaism, definition of, 281; "LGBT" movement, 287; marriage, previously embodied ideas about, 284, 286; modernized paganism, 284; moral truths, 282; neo-pagan orthodoxy, 289; non-marital sexual conduct, 286–87; paganism, as internal challenge to Jewish and Christian faith, 282–83; pagan "matrix of assumptions," 286; secular progressives, things sacred to, 285; Sexual Revolution, reversal of, 288; sexual satisfaction, as human need, 287; some religious folk, capitulation of, 289

civic virtues. See constitutional structure, civic virtues and

Civil Rights Act of 1866, 130, 132, 134, 137

Clinton, Hillary, 288

Cold War, 314, 315

Commentaries 134, 137, 154, 170

common good: community and 337; of community of faith, 201; definition of, 49; distinctions of (developed by Aquinas), 242–43; for doctors and patients, 63; "free speech" destructive of, 227; government and, 46, 204, 206, 236, 244; human person and, 283, 339; imperiling act, 225; importance of, 338; law and, 47, 50, 53, 254; means to, 40; political, 45, 80, 243; politics and, 245; private ownership and, 79; promotion of, 226, 232; requirement of, 199–200; ruling for, 199–206; as set of conditions, 203; "temporal" 242; undermining of, 40, 237, 240; violations of, 53

Commonwealth v. Parker, 141

"comprehensive doctrines," 283–84

Concept of Law, The, 327

constitutional structure, civic virtues and, 197–215; "American greatness," 214–15; bad behavior of public officials, 212; civil society, significance of basic institutions of, 214; common good, government and, 204, 206; common good, ruling for, 199–206; constitutional restraints, 206–10; freedom, people worthy of, 211–15; Madison's defense of the Constitution, 213; political culture, 212; public debate, 211; rulers as servants, 198; social mobility, conditions of, 205; subsidiarity, doctrine of, 202; "system of checks and balances," 207

Constitution of the United States, Bill of Rights attached to, 208; Catholic doctrine and, 228; common ground of (*Dobbs*), 195; First Amendment to, 218, 227; interpretation of, much-debated question in, 50; John Paul II's endorsement of principles of, 219; "Madisonian system" of structural constraints of, 207; Madison's defense of (in Federalist Paper Number 51), 213; national government not empowered by (to impose mandate to purchase products), 210; natural-law basis eliminated from, 172; original meaning of "person" in, 173; phrase not appearing in, 217; restriction of religious freedom allowed by, 225; rights-theory of, 174; silence of, on normative and policy decisions on marriage, 121; unborn children as persons under, 131; *Roe v. Wade* lacking any basis in original understanding of, 274. See also *Dobbs v. Jackson Women's Health Organization*, Brief filed on

Cott, Nancy F., 126

Daniels, Ronald, 267

Dartmouth College v. Woodward, 153

death with dignity, dangerous euphemism of, 95–111; attributed, euthanasia and dignity as, 100–104; attributed dignity, 96, 97; autonomy, euthanasia and dignity as, 106–10; body-self dualism, 104, 106; dignity, kinds of, 96–99; discriminatory claim, 109–10; endowment dignity, 98; flourishing, dignity as, 96, 97; flourishing, euthanasia and dignity as, 99–100; intrinsic dignity, 96, 97–98; intrinsic worth, euthanasia and dignity as, 105–6; mercy killing, 109
Declaration of Independence: John Paul II's endorsement of principles of, 219; "self-evident truth" proclaimed by, 228
democratic capitalism, 249
Deneen, Patrick, 245
Devlin, Patrick, 327
Dignitatis Humanae, 219, 220, 222–28
dignity, kinds of, 96–99; attributed, 96, 97; as autonomy, 96, 98; flourishing, 96, 97; intrinsic, 96, 97–98. *See also* death with dignity, dangerous euphemism of; human dignity, nature and basis of
Dobbs v. Jackson Women's Health Organization, 273
Dobbs v. Jackson Women's Health Organization, Brief filed on, 129–96; argument, 131–44; argument, status of children *in utero* in American civil law, 137; argument, three main criminal-law protections of the unborn child, 138–42; argument, unborn children are constitutional persons, 131–36; argument, unimportance of quickening, 143–44; common-law criminal law, 179–85; common-law rules, 175; dismissal of main thesis, 195; doctrine of common-law criminal law, 135; errors made by predecessors, 191–93; failure of Amicus Briefs and associations of Historians, 185–93; "fixed principle," 137; Founding and Ratification Era legal thought, constitutional status as a person in, 170–85; future decision of the Supreme Court, 196; meanings shared by drafters/ratifiers of the Constitution, 173–85; Means, extremist escape of, 160–69; Means falsified by Hale, 157–60; mistaken claims, 188–91; Pound, Roscoe, 170–72; "proto-felony-murder rule," 194–95; recognizing unborn personhood, 193–94; summary of argument, 130–31; three senses of "quick[en]," 144–57
Doe v. Clarke, 137
dogmatism, xiii
Dred Scott v. Sandford, 209, 274
Dreher, Rod, 245, 289
dualistic delusions, 31–37; abortion issue, 31; Catholic Church, rejection of body-self dualism by, 37; consciousness-body dualism, 35; fertilization, 35; materialism, Bloom's acceptance of, 36; materialism, defenders of abortion embracing, 32; pro-lifers, 32; rational animal, human being as, 37; religion, no "great conflict" between science and, 34
Dummett, Michael, 330
Dworkin, Ronald, 50, 107, 327, 331, 332
dynamism, 255

Edwards, Robert, 89
Einstein, Albert, 91
Eisgruber, Christopher, 267, 275
embryos. *See* human embryos, humanity of
endowment dignity, 98
Enforcement of Morals, The, 327
Enlightenment period, ix
Essays on Bentham, 54
ethics, natural law and, 72
euthanasia, 69–72. *See also* death with dignity, dangerous euphemism of
"expressive individualism," 306

family: attacks on, 256; as pillar of decent society, 253; supporters of, 259; weakening of, 257
Finnis, John, 327, 330, 333; commissioning of book by, 54; common good, as set of conditions (defined by), 201, 203; common goods explained by, 243; conclusions of (state's relation to religion), 243–44; decision-making process argued by, 76; definition of common good proposed by, 201; *Dobbs* brief, 129–96; questions on value of person's life asked by, 109–10
Foot, Philippa, 333
Francis (pope), 241–42, 296, 306
freedom, philosopher of. *See* Raz, Joseph (as philosopher of freedom)
"free exchange" of ideas, attainment of truth not guaranteed by, xiii
Fried, Charles, 327

Fuller, Lon L., 327

Garza v. Hargan, 193
Geach, Peter, 330
gender stereotypes, 119–20
Georgia Supreme Court, 137
Gewirth, Alan, 108
Gillespie v. Nabors, 177
Ginsburg, Ruth Bader, 119
Girgis, Sherif (*Obergefell v. Hodges*, dissenting of), 115–28
Gnostic liberalism, 299–309; body-self dualism, 299, 302; dynamic unity, view of human person as, 300; "expressive individualism," 306; gender identity, observations about, 305–6; Gnosticism, description of, 299; "hylomorphism," 300; marriage, companionship as essence of, 303; marriage, as socially constructed institution, 302; neo-Gnostic, 305; person-as-conscious-subject, 301; pre-operative "male-to-female" transgender individual, 305; same-sex marriage, 303; sensing, 307, 308; some human beings, as non-persons, 301; transsexualism and transgenderism, 304
God: being courageous owed to, 317; human beings called by (vocation), 64–65; man fashioned in likeness of, 281; people having forgotten, 319–20; voice of (Adam and Eve hearing), 341
Golden Rule, 21, 62–63, 74
government: common good and, 46, 204, 206, 244; limits of, liberalism and, 236; regulation, undermining of common good with, 240
Gregory XVI (pope), 220, 221, 222, 228, 229
Grounding for the Metaphysics of Morals, 105
groupthink, xiii, 239, 262–65, 271, 277

Hale, Matthew, 170, 183–84
Hall v. Hancock, 137, 150, 175–77
Hand, Learned, 263
Harper, Kyle, 287
Hart, Herbert, 330; "content-independent peremptory reasons" described by, 54; "descriptive" social theory of, 52; "legal positivism" of, 327
hedonism, 11, 12
Hefner, Hugh, 287
Heine, Heinrich (prophecy of Nazism by), 323–26; Christian worldview, abolition of, 325; conspiracy-theorizing, 323; French Revolution, 325; ideologically polarized nation, 323; mission, 326; quote, 324–25; transformations in intellect (good consequences of), 326
Himmelfarb, Milton, 281
Holmes, Oliver Wendell, Jr., 121
Holocaust, 293–94
human dignity, nature and basis of, 3–23; animal welfarist position, 7–9; capacity for enjoyment or suffering, 7–14; degrees of dignity, 4; difference in kind between human beings and other animals, 14–19; full moral worth, rational nature and, 19–21; Golden Rule, 21; hedonism, 11, 12; interests, 10; marginal cases, 5, 21–23; moral status, problem of, 5–7; processing of dignity, 5; sense of dignity, 4; undignified treatment, 5
human embryos, humanity of, 87–93; debate, 88; dehumanizing before killing, 87, 88; deliberate killing of human beings, 87–88; denial of, 88, 90; elective abortion, 88; embryos differing in kind, 91; first "test-tube baby," 89; "imposing religion," sideshow of imposing, 92; moral worth, 92–93; pro-life view, 93; rhetorical stratagems of abortion advocates, 92
"hylomorphism," 300

Ibn Sina, ix
identity politics, trap of, 338
intellectual diversity, 265, 267–68
intellectual humility, 263
intrinsic dignity, 96, 97–98
Iraq War, 331

Jacobinism, 222
James Madison Program in American Ideals and Institutions (Princeton University), 267, 273–74
Jehovah's Witnesses, 75
Jews and Judaism, Catholic teaching on, 293–98; Catholic Church, great stain on the history of, 293; Holocaust, 293–94; important difference between Judaism and Christianity, 296; Jews as "the people of the original Covenant," 295; John Paul II, 294–95, 297; *Nostra Aetate*, 294, 296; Second Vatical Council, 294; spiritual bond, 296

Jim Crow laws, 125
  laws, no-fault divorce, 124
John XXIII (pope), 219
John Paul II (pope), 219, 228–29, 230, 294–98, 321
Johnson, Lyndon, 257
Judaism, definition of, 281. *See also* Jews and Judaism, Catholic teaching on
Judeo-Christian worldview, defense of, 337, 339
judicial review: criticism of, 208–9; "Madisonian system" and, 207; problem with, 210

Kaczor, Christopher (death with dignity, dangerous euphemism of), 95–111
Kalven, Harry, 275
Kant, Immanuel, 45, 105, 106, 282
Kantian liberalism, 232
Kavanaugh, Brett, 195
Kelsen, Hans, 51
Keown, John, 109
Kinsey, Alfred, 287
Knotts v. Stearns, 177
Korematsu v. U.S., 274
Ku Klux Klan, 151

law: Aquinas's definition of, 47; cultural object, 50; justifying point of, 47; moral validity of, 51; unjust, as act of violence (Aquinas), 53. *See also* natural law
laws: forgotten God reflected in, 320; Jim Crow, 125
Lee, Patrick, 104; on dualistic delusions, 31–37; on human dignity, 3–23; on the soul, 25–30
legal positivism, 327, 331–32
Legutko, Ryszard, 245
Leninism, 256
Leo XIII (pope), 241–42
Leonard, Thomas, 277
LGBT couples, 124
"LGBT" movement, 287
liberal arts education. *See* campus illiberalism
liberalism, critique of, 231–46; Aristotelian-Thomistic moral tradition, 232; civil liberties as political rights, 237; common good, undermining of, 237, 240; debate, 233–35; groupthink, 239; human flourishing, property ownership and, 240; Kantian liberalism, 232; limits of government, 236; Lockean liberalism, 232; "neutralist" liberalism, 231; political common good, 243; politics, practicality of, 235–38; "pre-liberal" limit on government power (Aquinas), 236; proper understanding of liberalism, 245–46; prudence, 235; Rawlsian liberalism, 232; religion, flourishing of, 241; religion, liberal society and, 241–45; speech and property, 238–41; systems ruled out, 240; "temporal common good," 242; today's political discourse, flaw in, 234
liberalism, Gnostic. *See* Gnostic liberalism
Lincoln, Abraham, proclamation issued by, 319, 320
Lochner v. New York, 209
Locke, John, 232
Lockean liberalism, 232
logical laws, 27
Lord Ellenborough's Act, 192
Loving v. Virginia, 118, 122

MacIntyre, Alasdair, 330
Macklin, Ruth, 98
Madison, James, as author of Federalist Paper Number 51, 213
Maimonides, ix
Maine Supreme Court, 150
Marcus, Ruth, 88, 89
"marketplace of ideas," attainment of truth not guaranteed by, xiii
markets, morality, and civil society, 249–60; Amish communities, 255; attacks on business, 256; capitalism, democratic, 249; capitalism, as moral system, 250; civilizing institution, market as, 251; common good, law and, 254; dynamism, 255; family, 253, 256, 257, 259; Great Society initiatives (Johnson), 257; intelligible value, human good as, 250; law and government, system of, 254; Leninism, 256; liberty, Smith's idea of, 250–51; market economy, fundamental goodness of, 260; market system, maintenance of, 252; pillars of healthy society, 252; religious fanaticism, 253; respect for the human person, 252, 253; social mobility, economic dynamism and, 258; totalitarian regimes, 252
marriage: -based families, 215; conjugal understanding of, 316; fundamental goodness of, 260; Gnostic

anthropology's rejection of vision of, 301; goal of weakening the institution of, 124; normative and policy decisions on (Constitution and), 121; one-flesh-union conception of, 302; previously embodied ideas about, 284, 286; same-sex, 117, 303; States' normative vision of marriage, 122; supporters of, 259
Marsellis v. Thalhimer, 176
Marshall, John, 131, 153
Massachusetts Supreme Court, 137, 166
materialism: Bloom's acceptance of, 36; defenders of abortion embracing, 32
McHugh, Paul, 304
Means, Cyril, 141, 145, 156, 157–69
"medical assistance in dying," 69
medical law, natural-law foundations of, 57–86; abortion, 65–69; autonomous acts, 78; basic human goods, 59; bioethicists, 75; common good, for doctors and patients, 63; conscience, 82–86; decision-making process, 76; developed nations, political authority in, 80; disputed areas, 65–78; double effect, 72–75; euthanasia, natural law's assessment of, 69–72; foundations of natural law, 58–60; Golden Rule, 62–63, 74; health care, authority in, 75–78; health-care resources, 78–82; indeterminacy, 82; Jehovah's Witnesses, 75; law, medical practice and (killing), 65–78; "medical assistance in dying," 69; "moral absolutes," 72; morality, immediate principles of, 60–65; perceived social contract, 83; physician-assisted suicide, natural law's assessment of, 69–72; political authority, 80; political common good, 80; Principle of Double Effect, 58, 74; private ownership, 79; religion, good of, 85; "right to health care," 81; unreasonable damage or destruction of basic human goods (norm of), 61–62; vocation (norm of), 64–65; welfare rights, 80
mercy killing, 109. *See also* death with dignity, dangerous euphemism of
Merricks, Trenton, 26
Middle Ages, importance of faith to people of, ix
Mill, John Stuart, 263, 333
Mirari Vos, 220
Monroe, Bill, 343
morality: biblical standard of, 337; Judeo-Christian, 318; Kantian rejection of aggregative accounts of, 44; political, 202, 332; as principle of right action, 39; sexual, Judeo-Christian norms of, 287. *See also* markets, morality, and civil society
Morality of Law, The, 327
Morality: Restoring the Common Good in Divided Times, 337, 340
moral subjectivism, xii, 219
Moynihan, Daniel Patrick, 257
Murray, John Courtney, 222

National Review, 323
natural law, 39–55; approaches to ethics distinguishing, 72; Benthamism, legal philosophy vs., 55; common good, governments and, 46; common good, law and, 47, 50, 53; communities, common good of, 45; critical-moral viewpoint, 53; erroneous judgment, 43; foundations of, 58–60; human nature, basic goods of, 42; human rights, 41; judge, role of, 50; law, justifying point of, 47; law, moral validity of, 51; legislator, task of, 49; moral failings, cultures infected with, 44; political common good, 45; practical reasoning, 44–45; Rule of Law, 50; slavery, 41, 42, 44; theories of, 39; unjust laws (per Aquinas), 53. *See also* medical law, natural-law foundations of
Natural Law and Natural Rights, 54, 201, 327
Nazism, prophecy of. *See* Heine, Heinrich (prophecy of Nazism by)
Neuhaus, Richard John, 245
"neutralist" liberalism, 231
New Jersey Supreme Court, 164
New York Times, 25, 31, 207, 271, 345
Nicomachean Ethics, 337
Nietzsche, Friedrich, 316
North Star principle, 230
Nostra Aetate, 223, 294, 296
Novak, David, 92

Obama, Barack, 209, 210
Obergefell v. Hodges, dissenting of, 115–28; affirmative action policies, 120; caste, 125–26; "comprehensive doctrine," 121; due process clause, 127–28; equal protection challenge, 116–27; equal protection challenge, appropriate level of scrutiny, 116–20; equal protection

challenge, rational basis, 120–27; gender stereotypes, 119–20; "identity formation," 124; LGBT couples, 124; marriage long enshrined, 128; motives, 126–27; policy judgments, 116; same-sex marriage, no argument for constitutional right to, 117; sentences disposing of case, 115; sex-discrimination cases, 119; sexes as necessarily interdefined, 118; States' empirical judgments, 122–25; States' normative vision of marriage, 122
Objects and Persons, 26
obscurantism, xiii
O'Rourke, Beto, 290, 291

paganism. *See* Christianity, paganism and
Patient Protection and Affordable Care Act, 209, 210
Paul VI (pope), 226, 294
PBS NewsHour, 345, 346
Perry, Louise, 284, 288
physical laws, 27
physician-assisted suicide. *See* death with dignity, dangerous euphemism of
Pius XI (pope), 203, 204
Plato, 12, 264, 300
Plessy v. Ferguson, 274
political common good, 45, 80, 243
political morality, 202
politics: common good and, 245; desire to separate economics from morality rampant in, 249; identity, trap of, 338; practicality of, 235–38
"polyamorous" lifestyles, xi
popes: Benedict XVI, 296; Blessed Pius IX, 220, 221, 228; Francis, 241–42, 296, 306; Gregory XVI, 220, 221, 222, 228, 229; John XXIII, 219; John Paul II, 219, 228, 230, 294–98, 321; Leo XIII, 241–42; Paul VI, 226, 294; Pius XI, 203, 204
pornography, 227, 239, 287
Posner, Richard, 241
Pound, Roscoe, 170–72
practical reasonableness, value of, 333
Practical Reason and Norms, 327, 329
Principle of Double Effect, 58, 74

Quadragesimo Anno, 203
Quanta Cura, 221

Rawls, John, 64, 332
Rawlsian liberalism, 232

Raz, Joseph (as philosopher of freedom), 327–34; analytic tradition, 329–31; autonomy, centrality of, 332–34; birth of Raz, 334; "central tradition" of thought, 331; death of Raz, 334; deployment of the concept of "law" by, 52; legal positivism, 331–32; paper criticized by, 328; "perfectionist" liberalism, 332; practical reasonableness, value of, 333; as Socratic philosopher, 333
Rehnquist, William, 74
religion: abortion and, 92; flourishing of, 241; good of (medical law and), 85; liberal society and, 241–45; no "great conflict" between science and, 34; state's relation to (Finnis), 243–44
Reno, Don, 344
Rescher, Nicholas, 330
Roberts, John, 210
Rodriguez v. United States, 124
Roe v. Wade, 155, 209, 274
Roth, Michael, 267
Rowling, J. K., 323
R. v. Sims, 145

Sacks, Rabbi Jonathan (moral voice of), 335–41; Adam and Eve, 340–41; biblical message, 341; common good, community and, 337; common good, human person and, 339; common good, importance of, 338; connectedness to others, 339; dignity, bearers of, 336; fixation on the individual, 338; God's voice, 341; Hobbes, 335; identity politics, trap of, 338; *imago Dei*, 336; intelligible value, 335–36; Judeo-Christian worldview, defense of, 337, 339; morality, biblical standard of, 337; reasons for action, Genesis and, 336
same-sex marriage, 117, 303
Sandel, Michael, 91, 339
Santa Clara County v. Southern Pacific Railroad Co., 153
Scruggs, Earl, 343
Scruton, Roger, 25
Second Vatican Council (Vatican II): claiming of discontinuities of the Church in aftermath of, 220; Declaration on Religious Freedom of, 219; differences of Judaism and Christianity not denied by, 296; papal endorsements of principles of American civic life (since conclusion of), 228; recognition of other religious

traditions, by, 223; "sectarian Liberalism" and, 222; teaching authority of, 220; teachings on political common good by, 242; time of deep reflection for the Church before, 294
"sectarian Liberalism," 222
Sexual Revolution, xi, 288
Shrier, Abigail, 323
Singer, Peter, 7–8, 90, 266
Smith, Adam, 250–51, 255, 258
Smith, Steven, 284, 285, 287
Solzhenitsyn, Aleksandr, plea to the West by, 313–21; anti-Americanism, 314; background, 313; Bolshevik Revolution of 1917, 313; Cold War, 314, 315; compassion, as essential virtue, 315–16; eugenics, 316; God, being courageous owed to, 317; God, men having forgotten, 319, 320; Lincoln's proclamation, 319–20; loss of courage, 314, 315; mission, 321; "moral equivalency" between American democracy and Soviet communism, 314; quote, 315; rationalization, 318; Templeton Prize in Religion, 318, 319; West's weakness in standing up to Soviet aggression, 314; what is good, redefining of, 316; worst selves, 317
the soul, 25–30; brain processes, 27; "composite substances," animals as, 26; genetics and, 25–26; irreducible types of reality, 29; logical laws, 27; neuroscience, 27; physical laws, 27; principle of unity, 28; substantial form, 28, 30; traditional philosophical and theological concept of, 25; unitary objects, 26
Stanley, Carter, 344, 347
Stanley, Lucy, 344
Stanley, Ralph (traditionalism of), 343–47; bluegrass, founding fathers of, 343, 344; as Christian believer, 345; "clawhammer" banjo style, 343; Clinch Mountain Boys, 344; as Doctor, 344; Grammy Award won by, 345, 347; honorary doctorate awarded to, 344; as man of constant sorrow, 347; songs of, 346–47
State v. Cooper, 149, 167
State v. Murphy, 156, 164, 165
Stevens, John Paul, 155, 170
subsidiarity, doctrine of, 202
Sulmasy, Daniel, 96–98
Supreme Court, cases of: *Brown v. Board of Education*, 209; *Buck v. Bell*, 274;

Dartmouth College v. Woodward, 153; *Dobbs v. Jackson Women's Health Organization*, 129–96, 273; *Dred Scott v. Sandford*, 209, 274; *Knotts v. Stearns*, 177; *Korematsu v. U.S.*, 274; *Lochner v. New York*, 209; *Loving v. Virginia*, 118, 122; *Obergefell v. Hodges*, 115–28; *Plessy v. Ferguson*, 274; *Rodriguez v. United States*, 124; *Roe v. Wade*, 155, 209, 274; *Santa Clara County v. Southern Pacific Railroad Co.*, 153; *Turner v. Safley*, 127; *United States v. Virginia*, 119; *United States v. Windsor*, 120, 127; *Vacco v. Quill*, 74, 75; *Zablocki v. Redhail*, 128
Supreme Court, chief justices of: Marshall, John, 131; Rehnquist, William, 74; Roberts, John, 210; Warren, Earl, 227
Supreme Court, justices of: Alito, Samuel, 120; Ginsburg, Ruth Bader, 119, 120; Holmes, Oliver Wendell, Jr., 121; Kavanaugh, Brett, 195; Stevens, John Paul, 155, 170; White, Byron, 274
Szulc, Tad, 297

Taking Rights Seriously, 327
Tang, Aaron, 152
Taylor, Charles, 330
Taylor, Paul, 10
Thomson, Judith Jarvis, 74
Thorpe, Jim, 91
Thunberg, Greta, 285
Tollefsen, Christopher O. (medical law, natural-law foundations of), 57–86
tribalism, xiii
Turner v. Safley, 127
Tushnet, Mark, 288, 290–91

United States v. Virginia, 119
United States v. Windsor, 120, 127
universities, need for institutional neutrality of, 273–79; consensus on normative matters, questioning of, 277; groupthink, 277; institutional neutrality, commitment to, 275; Kalven Report, 275; nonsectarian universities, 275, 276, 279; Program in Gender and Sexuality Studies (Princeton University), statement issued by, 273; university statements, rules regarding, 275; Vietnam War controversy, 275
ur-principle, 230

Vacco v. Quill, 74, 75

van Fraassen, Bastiaan, 330
Vatican II. *See* Second Vatican Council
Vermont Supreme Court, 166

Waldron, Jeremy, 208, 211
Wallis v. Hodson, 137
Warren, Earl, 227
Washington Post, 88
Wealth of Nations, The, 250
West, Cornel, 268–70
Wharton's Criminal Law, 150
What Obergefell v. Hodges *Should Have Said*, 115
White, Byron, 274

Williams, Bernard, 340
Wilson, James F., 134
Wilson, Woodrow, 258
wisdom: achievement of, xiii; acquisition of, 235, 240; conclusions requiring, 241; in-between position decided through, 244; religious traditions as sources of, 245; seeking, dialectical process of, 268; source of, forgotten God and, 319, 320
Wojtyła, Karol, 294. *See also* John Paul II (pope)

Zablocki v. Redhail, 128
Zimmer, Robert, 267